D1476949

Agricultural Trade

Agricultural Trade
Principles and Policies

Luther Tweeten
THE OHIO STATE UNIVERSITY

Westview Press
BOULDER AND SAN FRANCISCO

IT Publications
LONDON

Copyright © 1992 by Westview Press, Inc.

Published in 1992 in the United States of America by Westview Press, Inc., 5500 Central Avenue, Boulder, Colorado 80301-2847

Published in 1992 in the United Kingdom by Intermediate Technology Publications, 103/105 Southampton Row, London WC1B 4HH, England

Library of Congress Cataloging-in-Publication Data
Tweeten, Luther G.
  Agricultural trade : principles and policies / by Luther Tweeten.
    p. cm.
  Includes bibliographical references and index.
  ISBN 0-8133-8578-4 — ISBN 0-8133-8579-2 (pbk.)
  1. Produce trade. 2. Agriculture—Economic aspects I. Title.
HD9000.5.T84 1992
382′.41—dc20   92-15629
                                                                                                      CIP

British Library Cataloguing in Publication Data
A CIP catalogue record of this book is available from the British Library.
  ISBN 1-85339-158-1

Printed and bound in the United States of America

The paper used in this publication meets the requirements
of the American National Standard for Permanence of Paper
for Printed Library Materials Z39.48-1984.

10   9   8   7   6   5   4   3   2   1

Contents

Tables and Figures

Preface

Agricultural Trade: Principles and Policies responds to needs and voids that I have observed over thirty years of professional experience in agricultural trade, policy, and development. The effort assumes that we all need to be students of trade, whether as consumers, producers, taxpayers, or policymakers, or as members or teachers of a formal class of instruction.

The book was written because much of the developed world economy is moribund. A more open world economy is the best hope for a new frontier to unleash the creative potential of international resources and technology in the twenty-first century. The effort recognizes that agricultural interests constitute the greatest impediment to unleashing this potential for a world that can offer a better life and cleaner environment for developed and developing nations alike.

The effort recognizes that an uninformed public by default is a friend to special-interest protectionists and an enemy of trade liberalization. It recognizes that justice and development for the Third World depend on more open markets in the first world. The effort contends that open international trade offers a rich source of positive sum gains -- where parties at both ends of trade are made better off.

Agricultural Trade is a compilation of class notes from a course I instruct on international agricultural trade at The Ohio State University. The course and the book are intended to provide students quick access to the fundamentals of agricultural trade.

The book is an introduction to trade principles and policies for upper-division undergraduate students and for graduate students who have a background in intermediate microeconomic and macroeconomic theory. It can be a terminal course for those who desire only the fundamentals and an introduction to trade for those who will make agricultural trade their major field. For the latter, additional courses will need to be taken in both the microeconomics and macroeconomics of trade.

Journal articles and entire books have been written on subjects contained in this work. Students are strongly encouraged to use such supplements and to read widely about currently emerging trade theories, practices, and policies.

The book is also intended to be a convenient reference or source of selected readings. Chapters 1, 9, 10, and 11 are quite readable for persons with little, if any, background in economics.

Agricultural Trade goes beyond existing agricultural trade books. First, it is the first such text to include the so-called "new" strategic trade theory, recognizing both the strengths and weaknesses of that way of thinking. Second, the book provides a richer menu of theoretical background than previous international agricultural trade books. And third, the institutional foundations of trade are examined in some detail.

This book is possible only because I have received much help. The Department of Agricultural Economics and Rural Sociology, the Anderson Endowment, and administrators of The Ohio State University were highly supportive. Cynthia Dishon was the most able assistant with whom I have worked. Critiques by James Gleckler, Shiva Makki, Ian Sheldon, and many others, including classroom students, were invaluable. Shortcomings of the book are solely my responsibility.

Luther Tweeten
The Ohio State University

CHAPTER 1

Introduction

Economic fortunes of agriculture depend on exports. The relationship between exports and farm prices depicted in Figure 1.1 would be even closer if the government had not intervened to support farm prices when exports fell in the mid-1980s. The economy of agriculture is closely tied to international trade because domestic demand is quite stable. Domestic supply shifts somewhat predictably over time from technology and is randomly influenced by weather, which quickly averages out. Hence trade, characterized by extended periods of expansion and contraction, is left to determine periods of high or low farm prices and incomes.

Domestic demand for farm products grows predictably by just under 1 percent each year. Aggregate productivity shifts supply forward about 1.5 percent per year. Hence, the farming plant would have to be scaled back about 0.5 percent per year to maintain economic equilibrium without export markets. Export growth of just over 3 percent annually expands overall demand to nearly the rate of growth in supply of farm output, allowing aggregate farm resources to remain nearly stable.[1] In short, farm export growth avoids the trauma of downsizing the agricultural plant each year.

The benefits of expanding trade noted in Figure 1.1 help to explain why farmers and agribusiness firms relentlessly pursue export growth. However, agricultural export markets will not solve chronic farm economic problems. Agriculture adjusts to chronic low exports or to chronic high exports by resource movements until reasonably well-managed, adequate-size firms are making a return on resources comparable to those in other sectors (Tweeten, 1989, ch. 4). The principal problem of commercial agriculture is instability -- and more trade does not dampen that problem. Nonetheless, overall national and international gains from trade are huge. The challenge is to devise an appropriate trade strategy to obtain the gains from trade while minimizing unfortunate side effects. That is one purpose of this book.

Farmers and agribusiness firms have a love-hate relationship with trade. The tendency is to seek to control trade when outcomes are undesirable and inscrutable. Foreign markets have been manipulated by US policymakers with impunity. As often as not, these manipulations have been counterproductive. A major purpose of this book is to help to understand trade and to supply tools for estimating gains and losses from trade. Another purpose, based on this understanding, is to outline a trade policy strategy serving the interests of the US and its trading partners.

---

[1]The shifting mix of resources has caused productivity gains as capital has replaced labor. The result has been considerable adjustment problems for displaced farmers although aggregate input volume is not much changed.

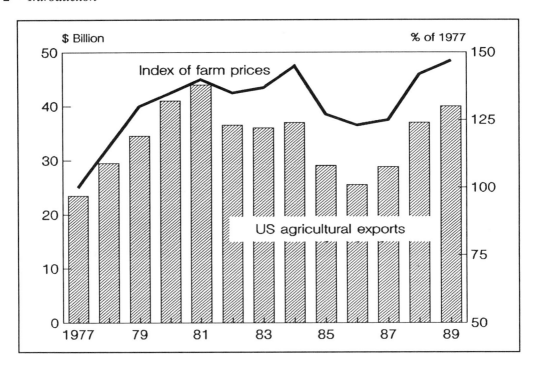

Figure 1.1. US Agricultural Exports and Farm Prices.
Source: USDA.

OTHER INDICATORS OF THE
IMPORTANCE OF AGRICULTURAL TRADE

Evidence of the importance of farm exports is apparent in other data:

1. On average, farm exports have been an outlet for one-fifth of farm output since 1970. Without exports, farm prices and incomes would have been low indeed. However, exports were fickle (Figure 1.2). They were nearly one-third of cash receipts in 1921-22, then dropped sharply to World War II, but even by the mid-1980s did not reach the share of 1921. The volatility of farm exports in part accounts for six decades of government commodity programs to cushion economic shocks.
2. In several years of the 1980s (Figure 1.3) as well as in 1990, exports added $40 billion or more to farm receipts and foreign exchange earnings. Those earnings helped pay for oil and other imports highly valued by Americans.
3. Americans import nearly $20 billion of farm and food products each year. These imports include coffee, cocoa, bananas, and other items that do not compete with temperate zone farm products we export. Arbitrarily combining all supplementary and competitive agricultural imports and subtracting them from total agricultural exports, the net trade balance surplus averaged approximately $20 billion per year in the early and late 1980s. American agriculture historically has been a consistent source of trade surpluses. This contrasts sharply with nonfarm products. The latter registered annual trade deficits of up to $150 billion in the mid-1980s.

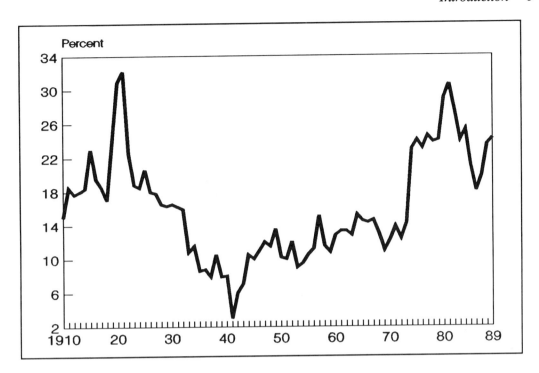

Figure 1.2. Agricultural Exports as a Percent of Farm Cash Receipts.
Source: USDA.

4. Although US agriculture (including related industries supporting farm exports) accounted for just over 2 percent of national income, it accounted for over 10 percent of the nation's exports in the late 1980s and early 1990s. The nation's balance of payments problems would be far less if other industries performed as well.

5. American agriculture accounted for 10 percent of world agricultural output but for 15 percent of world agricultural trade in the 1980s. This and previously cited data point to a strong competitive position for American agriculture in the world.

6. In the 1980s, American national income accounted for 23 percent of world income while overall American merchandise trade accounted for 11 percent of world trade. The US exported 11 percent of its output while the world exported 20 percent of its output in the 1980s. A major reason is because a large country tends to trade more internally and less externally. American agriculture had a higher-than-average propensity to export while the economy as a whole had a lower propensity to export than did other nations on average in the 1980s. American agriculture was more trade intensive than was the American economy in total.

7. World trade in all goods and services increased faster than world gross output (GDP) from 1961 to 1988. Trade trends differed sharply among agricultural commodities and years. Feed grain trade, for example, increased on average by 5 percent per year while real international gross domestic product increased on average 4 percent per year.

8. Patterns of agricultural trade are shifting. In contrast with previous decades, more than half of US agricultural trade in the future is likely to be with third-world countries, with Asia, and in high-value commodities.

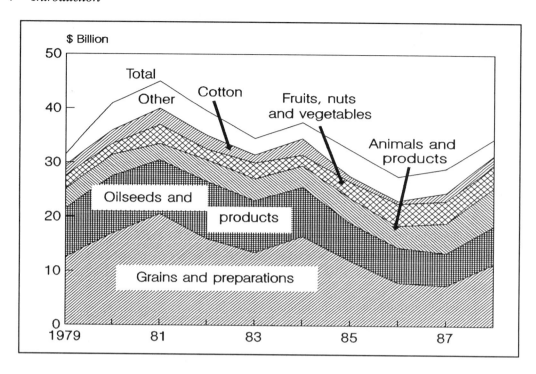

Figure 1.3. Value of US Agricultural Exports by Commodity.
Source: USDA.

- *Third-world countries* (Figure 1.4). Less developed countries accounted for only 38 percent of US agricultural exports and 51 percent of US agricultural imports in fiscal 1991 (US Department of Agriculture, pp. 6, 18). Less developed countries are likely to overtake developed countries as a market for our farm and food products in the 1990s. Reclassification to first-world status of Taiwan, South Korea, Singapore, and other newly industrialized developing countries could hide that change, however.
- *Asia.* Nearly half of US farm exports went to Asia in 1990 and 1991. The proportion will exceed half in the 1990s. Japan alone is a larger market than the combined European Community 12-country market. Japan, Taiwan, and South Korea together account for one-third of total US farm exports. If India and China, other countries with high man-land ratios, took as much US farm exports per capita, American farm exports would triple. Horace Greeley's advice to "Go West, young man" might well apply to American agricultural exporters. The "Tigers" of Asia save and invest at home; they also invest heavily elsewhere on the continent. Partly because of that investment stimulating economic growth, mainland China, Thailand, Malaysia, Indonesia, and India will be better customers for American farm exports in the future.
- *High-value products.* High-value or high-value-added products include horticultural products, animal products, and processed food products. Traditionally, farm exports have been dominated by bulk commodities such as grains and oilseeds (see Figure 1.3). High-value products have constituted over three-fourths of world agricultural trade but only approximately 45 percent of American agricultural trade since 1965. The trend share of all agricultural exports has been mixed but generally upward. In the 1990s, high-

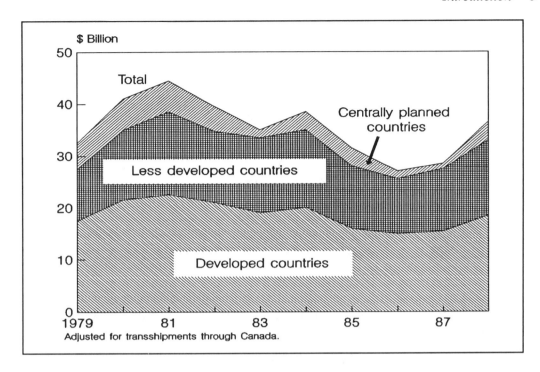

Figure 1.4. US Agricultural Exports to Major Areas.
Source: USDA.

value products are expected to rise to over half of US agricultural exports. In 1988, the percentage of agricultural product exports that were shipped unprocessed for selected countries are shown in Table 1.1.

Only Canada, with 55 percent, shipped more of its agricultural products in bulk form than did the United States. Americans can promote rural jobs and development and can more fully utilize technological superiority of its food processing sector by exporting high-value products, the argument runs.

Table 1.1. Unprocessed Agricultural Product Exports.

	Percent Exported Unprocessed
Netherlands	2
Germany	3
Italy	7
U.K.	8
Australia	20
France	25
US	51
Canada	55

Source: Van Dyne, p. 24.

A long debate has raged over the government's proper role in promoting export of high-value products. Proponents of more government promotion contend that adding value to exports creates jobs, income, and an enlarged tax base. *Multipliers* measuring income generated per additional dollar of agricultural export sales have been estimated as shown in Table 1.2.

An additional dollar of high-value product exports is estimated to add 31 cents to input supply industries, 78 cents to farmers, and $1.79 cents to processors and distributors for a total of $2.88. Bulk commodities add less to income.

The counter-argument is that multipliers are engineering impact coefficients with little economic meaning. What counts is the return to resources, a measure of economic efficiency in producing and selling commodities. (Producing ice in the Sahara Desert for world use would provide high multipliers indeed but would be economic folly.) It makes sense to expand exports of high-value products only if justified by profits. The argument continues that, if the Europeans choose to reduce their national income by heavily subsidizing high-value product exports, we should not feel obligated to waste our resources by competing with equally ill-advised product subsidies. This book provides an analytical framework for studying such issues.

SOME HISTORICAL DEVELOPMENTS

The development of civilization has closely paralleled the growth in agriculture and agricultural trade. Agricultural trade has played no less a part in American development than in world development. For example, the search for improved trade routes was influential in the discovery of America by the Europeans.

Governments of that time prized gold because it gave them prestige and resources to explore new lands and fight wars to protect claims and colonial settlements. *Mercantilism* emphasized policies that encouraged exports of domestic products and discouraged imports. The resulting trade surplus was accumulated in the medium of exchange of that day, *gold*.

World trade and economic growth would have been inhibited if one country would have accumulated all the world's gold. Classical economists contended not only that singular focus on gold accumulation was unwise but that in fact a well-functioning market with gold as the medium of exchange would work against concentration of gold ownership. Regarding the first point, Adam Smith noted that the wealth of a nation rested on how well its people lived rather than on how high the nation piled gold. David Hume reasoned that a trade

Table 1.2 Income Generated from Agricultural Export Sales.

	Input Industries	Farms	Processing & Distribution	Total
	($ income / $ exports)			
All Food & Agricultural Products	$0.59	$0.83	$0.81	$2.23
High-Value Products	0.31	0.78	1.79	2.88
Bulk Commodities	0.72	0.85	0.29	1.86

Source: Henderson and Frank, p. 11.

surplus bringing gold accumulation would increase a nation's prices relative to those of its trade partners, encouraging imports of cheaper foreign merchandize and discouraging export of expensive domestic goods and services. A trade deficit would result, moving out gold. This so called *specie flow mechanism* would move toward equilibrium in exchange reserves (gold) and trade. Up to World War I the gold standard served as a self-regulating instrument to help stabilize domestic economies and trade.

Colonial Period to the Revolutionary War

Mercantilism in part explained European colonization policies. Colonies provided raw materials to the mother country. The mother country provided manufactured or finished products and protection to the colonies. Following the settlement of Jamestown in 1607, Virginia was exporting tobacco to England by 1613 (Duncan *et al.*, p. 7). For many years, tobacco was America's chief export and principal means to pay for finished goods from England. The tobacco surplus over domestic use could be traded by England to other countries for gold reserves.

Several events radically changed trading patterns. The industrial revolution began in Britain about 1750, creating efficient methods to manufacture textiles and building a heavy demand for cotton. The cotton gin invented by an American, Eli Whitney in 1793, sharply reduced labor requirements to produce cotton lint. The resulting strong demand and high profitability of cotton in the South brought a heavy influx of slaves and ultimately the Civil War.

American Revolution to the Civil War

After the Revolutionary War, the Northeast gradually replaced England as the center for textile and other manufactured goods production for the American market. The Midwest opened, creating surpluses of grain shipped to the industrial Northeast and fiber producing South. Surpluses of grain from the Midwest and cotton and tobacco from the South were exported but the exports were erratic because of European wars, the British Embargo Act of 1807, and the Corn Laws placing duties and quotas on grain imports.

Despite impediments, trade expanded markedly before the Civil War. From 1820 to 1860, tobacco exports doubled, wheat exports quadrupled, and cotton exports expanded nine-fold (Duncan *et al.*, p. 9). Agricultural products dominated the nation's exports and cotton remained king. A world capital market emerged with London its center. Americans borrowed especially from the British to finance railroads, which commercialized agriculture by allowing farmers to sell output to purchase manufactured consumption goods and production inputs.

Tariffs were a significant means to raise federal revenue since the country's beginning. Rates were low and the aim was to raise revenue, not to protect domestic industry. As an exporter of raw materials and importer of finished goods, the South opposed tariffs. The Northeast, which favored protection for local industry, was instrumental in enacting the Tariff Act of 1816, which was the first American act to protect industry. Europe generally retained low tariffs while the US remained protectionist.

Civil War to World War I

As the world's most competitive and powerful industrial nation, Britain moved toward trade liberalization and the gold standard. British sterling (convertible into gold at a fixed exchange rate) became the de facto world currency.

The industrial revolution began in America about 1850, a century behind England. Eventually, Britain was replaced as the world's industrial giant by a United States promoted by investment and technology from abroad, rapid work force and labor growth augmented by immigration, an abundance of natural resources, and the westward scramble opening new resources and markets. Americans increasingly concentrated in cities and made their living in relatively well-paying industrial jobs. This created a big domestic market for farm products, raised the opportunity wage of farm labor, and reduced pressures to export.

Agricultural exports were a sizable 75 to 80 percent of total exports from 1869 to the early 1890s but then dropped gradually until they fell below half of all the nation's exports before World War I (Strauss, p. 12). The share of farm income accounted for by export revenue varied considerably from year to year but showed no major trend at about 17 percent for the Civil War - WWI era. (This percentage is close to that of recent years.) With westward expansion (until the frontier was closed about 1890), the western Cornbelt and Great Plains brought grains and livestock (and products) export volumes to rival those of cotton and tobacco.

In part because America was a debtor nation with large debt-service obligations, and because international demand for farm output was strong, the world allowed the US to run trade surpluses aided by high protection from imports. Import duties under the Dingley Tariff of 1897 rivaled the high rates of the Smoot-Hawley Tariff that came later. Markets grew even better for our food and fiber as Europe first prepared for (1910-14) and then fought (1914-1918) World War I. The former were called "golden years" for American agriculture -- hence it is not surprising that the ratios of prices received to prices paid by farmers in 1910-1914 were later to be designated the standard of "fairness" or parity against which all future prices were to be judged.

World War I to World War II

The interwar period between the Napoleonic Wars and World War I had been one of remarkable growth for world trade and prosperity. Britain was the driving force for financial innovations, open markets, currency exchange, and capital investment. Again, events intervened to change the system in ways too little predicted and hence too little prepared for. First, American agriculture had overextended itself as Europe regained its farm production capacity following the destruction wrought by World War I. Second, Britain was losing its economic supremacy and was no longer in a position to maintain its benevolent leadership in world trade. Third, industrialization prone to business cycles coupled with underdeveloped macroeconomic theory and practice combined to create a situation ripe for economic depression.

Collapse of the farm export market brought US farm recession in the 1920s. Farmers thought protection in the form of higher tariffs would bring relief and Congress rewarded them with ever higher rates, culminating in the notorious Smoot-Hawley Tariff of 1930. Other nations retaliated. Combined with wrong-headed monetary-fiscal policies, slower demand and population growth in industrial nations, and overcapacity built to alleviate shortages after World War I, the result was the greatest depression the world had ever known. In the 1920s only agriculture had been depressed; now agriculture and business seemed hopelessly mired in economic depression and psychological despair.

The depression of the 1930s was apparent in farm trade. The contribution of US farm exports to the nation's total exports fell from 50 percent in 1910 to under 30 percent by 1937 (Strauss, p. 12). Farm exports comprising 17 percent of gross farm income from 1910 to 1923 declined to less than half that percentage from 1934 to 1937.

World War II (1941-1945)

Exports, at low levels before World War II, increased sharply during the war. Programs such as Lend-Lease to assist allies during the war, the Marshall Plan after the war, and other such relief efforts abetted rising commercial demand after the war. Again exports brought farm prosperity and many farmers thought it would last. We return in detail to post-World War II trade institutions and policies in later chapters.

Some Lessons

Some lessons from history are useful in understanding later chapters.

1. The leadership of world trade had moved from Britain to the United States. The US belatedly recognized that role: bilateral reciprocal trade arrangements initiated by the United States gradually began to open trade channels in the 1930s but serious efforts at building an International Trade Organization did not begin until after World War II and with much reluctance by Congress.
2. The United States initiated farm commodity programs in the 1930s that became a model for other countries. These programs aided farmers but took a cynical view of world trade as something to be exploited to serve domestic ends. Such *beggar thy neighbor* policies of attempting to gain national advantage at the expense of the international community were not new but set a poor example. As discussed in later chapters, the European Community carried the practice to new heights of irresponsibility in the 1960s and beyond. To this day, the effort to exempt farm programs from liberal trade discipline remains the major stumbling block to success in multilateral negotiations covering all trade.
3. History illustrates that agriculture is highly sensitive to monetary, fiscal, and military policies. Agricultural output indeed is responsive to price expectations but large price reductions are necessary to scale down the farm plant. American agriculture has overexpanded to meet transitory demand numerous times: due to war, world food crises, excessive macroeconomic stimulation, or other reasons. Sometimes years of adjustment painful to farmers and taxpayers were required to properly scale-back the agricultural plant.
4. Unpredictable and uncontrollable weather and policies noted above make trade the residual claimant on excess supply or demand for food. Commodity stock policies cannot be separated from sound trade policies reducing adjustment trauma to producers and consumers at home and abroad. A world free of trade distortions dampens worldwide impacts of weather vagaries but countries have rarely been able to resist exporting their domestic shocks to others. Unfortunately, a more affluent world is not necessarily less committed to beggar thy neighbor trade policies.

A country can hardly be faulted for carrying on domestic policies (e.g., redistributing gains from farm production or trade among consumers, taxpayers, and producers) whose effects are confined to the country itself. When these policy interventions damage the economies of other countries, they become an externality that the world wants to do something about. This book addresses this issue of trade policy in an imperfect world.

NEW DEVELOPMENTS IN WORLD TRADE

Comparatively recent institutional and other developments of worldwide scope change the way we view the American agricultural economy and trade.

1. The seminal economic event of recent decades is the collapse of Marxist communism. Whether democratic-capitalism or communism could better serve the needs of society was once an abstract argument; now reality has solidly sided with the market. A New Economic Order or NEO world has formed that continues to be highly flawed but recognizes some realities of importance to trade (Tweeten *et al.*):

   - World influence and prestige in this techno-scientific age derive more from economic than from military prowess. Economic competitiveness is more important than military might.
   - Democratic capitalism has triumphed over totalitarian socialism featuring central planning and public ownership of the means of production. The newly industrialized countries with spectacular rates of economic growth have kept macroeconomic "prices" right on real exchange rates and real interests rates. Most importantly, they have maintained open economies. This raises questions regarding the wisdom of "industrial policies," managed trade, and protectionism.
   - *Regionalism* through trading blocs has replaced *multilateralism* through international negotiations as a principal means to freer trade (Tweeten, forthcoming). Common markets in North America (US-Canada) and Europe (EC-12) are expected to expand. Three major trading blocs are forming around currencies and the economies of three countries -- the United States, Germany, and Japan. Common markets appear to be contagious, inducing geographic expansion. The US-Canada market could expand to encompass first North America and perhaps eventually all of the Western Hemisphere. The EC could expand to include first the Nordic countries, Austria, and Switzerland and eventually Poland, Czechoslovakia, Hungary, and other countries of eastern Europe. If Europe and the Western Hemisphere form blocs, Asia may feel compelled to form a countervailing bloc with Japan the nucleus. Such blocs have vast potential for good or evil. They could become "fortress Europe" or "fortress America," leading to trade wars and eventually to hot wars. Or free trade zones could merge to form a world of liberalized trade unattainable by multilateral negotiations.

     The third alternative is *unilateralism*, such as use of "super 301" trade sanctions by the US to break down barriers to trade country by country. As discussed later, such strong-arm jungle tactics could predominate if multilateralism and regionalism fail. With the poor performance of the Uruguay Round, multilateralism no longer stands as a bulwark against or ready alternative to unilateralism (or bilateralism) and regionalism.

2. A notable institutional change is the shift from fixed to flexible exchange rates (Schuh). The rules that governed trade relations among nations in the post-

World War II period were largely established by the Bretton-Woods Conference of 1944. That remarkable effort established the World Bank, International Monetary Fund, and, ultimately, the General Agreement on Tariffs and Trade. Central features of the system initially included reliance on fixed exchange rates and a number of reserve currencies, the most important being the US dollar. With the dollar the major reserve currency, the world tolerated a persistent deficit in the US balance of payments to provide trade liquidity.

With inflation accelerating in the US economy during the late 1960s and early 1970s, the US dollar became increasingly overvalued in relation to currencies of its major trading partners. The deficit in the balance of payments grew. In August 1971, the dollar was devalued in relation to gold by 8 percent and again in February 1973 by another 10 percent. The United States closed its gold window.

Flexible exchange rates determine terms of trade by market forces of supply and demand. A nation that accumulates excess foreign exchange sees the value of its currency rise relative to that of other nations, decreasing the price of its imports from other countries and increasing the price of exports. The opposite occurs when a nation sustains an extended deficit in its international accounts. The exchange rate adjustments help to correct trade imbalances and free domestic macroeconomic policies for pursuing other objectives. Thus, flexible exchange rates make domestic policies less dependent on balance-of-payments considerations. Flexible exchange rates reduce discipline on the part of public officials to pursue sound monetary-fiscal policies. Thus institutions and trade (exchange rate) policies can influence monetary-fiscal policies, which all mightily influence the farming economy.

3. The growth and strengthening of worldwide liquid financial markets, the shift to flexible exchange rates, and growth in world trade now integrate world trade markets. It is often said that agriculture is part of a global market, that it is interdependent and internationalized. Food and other consumer items are made up of components from over the world. Food processing activities too are heavily integrated among world markets. Information required to coordinate such markets has taken on relatively greater value.

4. The conventional wisdom that developing countries tax agriculture and rich countries subsidize agriculture holds but with exceptions. Nigeria and Argentina tax agriculture but South Korea, a borderline developing country, heavily subsidizes its agriculture. New Zealand and Australia support their farm economies less than does Taiwan. Rigid stereotypes of what is a developed country and what is a developing country are breaking down, but trading policies and institutions are just beginning to catch up.

5. Many of the trade problems attributed to international trade policies in fact stem from commodity program and macroeconomic (monetary and fiscal) policies. In the 1970s, excessive monetary expansion brought low real interest rates, excessive borrowing, and overexpansion of the world's agricultural capacity. US full-employment federal budget deficits played a major role in creating high real interest rates in the 1980s. This caused financial crises in several heavily indebted developing countries and motivated the push for a more favorable trade balance (higher exports to and lower imports from the US and elsewhere) to service debt. High real interest rates in the US raised real interest rates worldwide, siphoning off world savings to service US debt rather than to be invested in productive capital at home. High US real interest rates created high

interest rates worldwide, mobilizing foreign savings to finance US consumption that otherwise would have provided capital to raise income and living standards abroad. The higher foreign income growth would have raised US farm exports. Macroeconomic excesses of the 1980s dampened ability to use stimulative fiscal policy when needed, extending the 1990-1992 recession.

6. Economic growth is characterized by an accumulation of human, material, and technological capital relative to labor. This cheapens capital relative to labor, and is attended by growth of human capital-intensive industry such as services relative to raw labor-intensive industries such as manufacturing. As economic growth progresses it is quite normal for relatively labor-intensive manufacturing of shoes, textiles, clothing, steel, and automobiles in developed countries to give way to imports of these products from newly industrialized countries. Developed countries shift to high-tech manufacturing using robots and to service industries such as entertainment, finance, insurance, higher education, health care, and science. Capital will flow from where it is abundant (in developed countries) to where it is scarce (in developing countries). The balance of merchandise trade normally will be negative for developed countries but the trade deficit will be offset from export of services and from earnings on capital. Thus developed and developing countries have incentive to remove impediments to trade in services. Respect for patents, trademarks, and copyright laws, and for open financial markets are examples. The best development policy is open world markets.

7. Persons who competently build, operate, and manage the highly complex machines and institutions of an advanced developed economy have substantial human resources and command high economic rewards. We will learn in later chapters how trade raises the returns to the abundant factors used to turn out products with comparative advantage. In the United States open trade improves the income of Michael Jackson relative to a Detroit auto worker. Thus trade can widen the distribution of income even as it raises mean income in a country. Those left behind by inadequate investment in human resources in developed countries tend to have high reservation wages and are often left unemployed or underemployed. Measures to preserve jobs tend to interfere with trade.

8. From time to time, agricultural groups in the United States have viewed trade as a threat and have attempted to cut foreign aid improving agricultural productivity in developing countries. Such aid, it is charged, reduces US farm exports. Empirical data indicate that countries expanding their agricultural production at the most rapid rate also expanded imports of US farm products at the most rapid rate (Paarlberg). That increased farm production abroad would increase farm imports from the US may seem implausible.

On average, agricultural production accounts for only 36 percent of gross domestic product in the poorest countries and 10 percent in the upper-middle-income countries where import demand for US farm products has increased. Still, demand for grains and soybean meal from the US may increase faster than farm output because the income elasticity of demand for US wheat and meat exceeds 1.0.[2] Another explanation is that countries that are good at increasing

---

[2]The arithmetic is compelling. If the overall income elasticity of demand for food is 0.6, if real income per capital is growing 4.0 percent per year, and if population is growing 2.6 percent per year, the growth in total demand for farm output is 2.6 + 0.6(4) = 5.0 percent annually. If food production is increasing at an unusually brisk 4.0 percent per year, imports as a percent of output grow 1 percent per year. If only 10 percent of consumption is from imports, imports grow at a hefty 10 percent per year.

farm output are equally good at increasing nonagricultural output and overall income.

Recognition that investments in technology and infrastructure to improve agricultural and industrial sectors also improve the well-being of people in developing countries may be motivation enough for the US and multinational agencies to help such countries. That the process might increase US farm exports is a side benefit. Neither farmers nor other sectors of the US economy benefit from the poverty that pervades Haiti, Nepal, Mozambique, or Ethiopia. The US benefits much more from growing nations such as South Korea, Kenya, Singapore, and Taiwan.

Growth of exports follows a pattern of stages. The poorest countries exhibit little increase in agricultural output or imports. Middle-income countries increase agricultural and industrial output fastest; agricultural output though increasing rapidly cannot keep up with the rapid increase in demand from population and income growth. As countries approach developed status, birth rates decline, population growth slows, and indigenous institutionalized agricultural research expands productivity to meet food demand with only modest increases in conventional resources. Demand for US farm imports slacks off as nations mature economically.

In conclusion, recognition of the role played by domestic commodity programs, macroeconomic policies, economic growth, and by other forces in trade helps to divert attention from counter-productive trade sanctions to the root causes of shifting trade patterns. For example, to correct a trade deficit, a more nearly balanced federal budget with attendant lower real interest and exchange rates sustained over a period of years is likely to be more constructive than a 25 percent surtax on imports from other nations. Just as it is a myth that unfair trade and commercial policies are the principal cause of US trade deficits, so it is also a myth that removal of such barriers alone will correct trade deficits. An attack on unbalanced trade relationships worldwide must address domestic commodity program, macroeconomic, and structural growth policies as well as the traditional border interventions. This book takes that position.

OUTLINE

Many of the topics introduced above are treated in greater detail in later chapters. The remainder of this book is organized as follows:

- Chapters 2 and 3 detail concepts and measurement of comparative advantage and gains from trade.
- Chapter 4 shows the impacts of border interventions such as taxes, subsidies, and quotas on trade.
- Chapter 5 analyzes how farm commodity programs influence world trade.
- Chapter 6 outlines the interrelationship between macroeconomic (monetary and fiscal) policy and trade. The chapter completes the trilogy of major trade distortions: border measures, commodity programs, and macroeconomic policies.
- Chapter 7 is the first of four chapters addressing trade policy. The chapter introduces strategic trade theory. This frontier in trade thinking views a nation's

trade policy in terms of how best to use trade instruments to its advantage. Conjectural variations, game theory, and duopoly theory provide background.

- Chapter 8 examines market power and political economy in strategic trade theory. It continues the pattern established in Chapter 7 of viewing trade in a world of imperfect competition.
- Chapter 9 outlines institutions influencing trade. Special attention is given to the so called "Bretton Woods" creations: The World Bank, International Monetary Fund, and the General Agreement on Tariffs and Trade.
- Chapter 10 analyzes major players in world trade and some of their policies. These players including trading blocs, major trading nations, and less developed countries as a group of nations facing common trading problems.
- Chapter 11 applies strategic trade theory to formulate a coherent trade policy for the United States. The nation's trade institutions and negotiating position are detailed not only in their current form but, more importantly, in more nearly ideal form.
- Chapter 12 discusses some of the trade models used to quantify for practical use the trade concepts discussed in previous chapters.

More than most books, this book emphasizes economic welfare measured by the impact of trade policies and practices on real income of consumers, producers, taxpayers, and the nation. It measures welfare for the country in question, for the rest of the world, and for the world as a whole. The purpose is to demonstrate how the world as a whole as well as any one country can benefit from trade. Current policies fall far short of realizing possible gains from trade. Multilateral trade institutions often are ineffective. But current policies are not immutable. Trade can benefit all nations and in greater depth than currently. To do so, a vision of the possible is useful -- in principle, practice, and policy.

REFERENCES

Duncan, Marvin, Blaine Bickel, and Glenn Miller, Jr. 1976. *International Trade and American Agriculture*. Kansas City: Federal Reserve Bank.

Henderson, Dennis and Stuart Frank. Fall 1990. Export performance of US food manufacturers. Pp. 11-14 in *Ohio's Challenge*. Columbus: Department of Agricultural Economics and Rural Sociology, The Ohio State University.

Paarlberg, Robert. 1987. Agriculture and the developing world: Partners or competitors? Chapter 8 in Randall Purcell and Elizabeth Morrison, eds., *US Agriculture and Third-World Development*. Boulder, CO: Lynne Rienner.

Ryan, Mary and Robert Tontz. 1978. A historical review of world trade policies and institutions. Chapter 1 in *Speaking of Trade*. Special Report No. 72. St. Paul: Agricultural Extension Service, University of Minnesota.

Schuh, G. Edward. 1976. The new macroeconomics of agriculture. *American Journal of Agricultural Economics* 58(5):802-811.

Strauss, Frederick. 1940. The composition of gross farm income since the Civil War. Bulletin No. 78. New York: National Bureau of Economic Research.

Tweeten, Luther. 1989. *Farm Policy Analysis*. Boulder, CO: Westview Press.

Tweeten, Luther. Forthcoming. Agricultural trade policy in the post-Uruguay-round era: Multilateralism, regionalism, or unilateralism? In Ray Goldberg, ed., *Research in*

Domestic and International Agribusiness Management. Vol. 11. Greenwich, CN: JAI Press.

Tweeten, Luther, Carl Zulauf, and Norman Rask. Third Quarter 1990. US agriculture in the new international order. *Choices* 5:26-29.

US Department of Agriculture. May 29, 1991. Outlook for US agricultural exports. Washington, DC: Economic Research Service, USDA.

Van Dyne, Donald. 1990. The economic development perspective of new crops/products. Pp. 24-30 in *Economic Development via New Crops/Products from Agriculture*. Special Report No. 422. Columbia: Agricultural Experiment Station, University of Missouri.

CHAPTER 2

Conceptualizing
Comparative Advantage
and the Gains from Trade

Adam Smith and many other of our economist forbearers noted that free trade offers advantages of specialization and economies of size, which in turn lower costs and raise living standards. Life as a Robinson Crusoe trading with no one would be primitive and short. The human race could not survive without trade. Even subsistence farmers trade goods and services extensively among family members. What is desirable for the family can scarcely be folly for countries -- to paraphrase Adam Smith. The United States would most certainly have a lower standard of living if trade among states were as restricted as trade among nations.

It will appear intuitively obvious to many that a country will be better off importing a commodity other countries can supply at a lower cost than the commodity can be produced at home. Less obvious is that it can pay to import commodities that can be produced more cheaply at home than abroad.

Economists at times seem to be alone in calling for more open trade and for less market intervention. What are the advantages of free trade and of managed trade? Why isn't free trade more widely advocated and found if it has merit? This chapter provides background to answer these and related questions. The chapter provides a conceptual framework used in subsequent chapters.

ABSOLUTE ADVANTAGE

We first illustrate benefits of trade when the US possesses an absolute advantage in production of wheat. Employing classical assumptions, labor is presumed to be the only variable input. Variable costs and productivity are presumed to be linear functions of output in the United States (US) and the rest of the world (ROW).

The coefficients for production of wheat and sugar are presumed to be

	US	*ROW*
Wheat (W)	$a_{LW} = 1$	$a'_{LW} = 4$
Sugar (S)	$a_{LS} = 3$	$a'_{LS} = 2.$

The US is said to have an *absolute advantage* in wheat production because only 1 hour of labor is required to produce a ton of wheat ($a_{LW} = 1$), whereas in the rest of the world (ROW) 4 hours of labor are required to produce a ton of wheat ($a'_{LW} = 4$). ROW is said to have an absolute advantage in sugar production because only 2 hours are required to produce a ton of sugar ($a'_{LS} = 2$) versus 3 hours in the US ($a_{LS} = 3$).

The inverse of these cost coefficients measures *productivity*. Productivity of labor for wheat in the US is 1 ton produced per hour of labor compared to 0.25 tons per hour of labor in ROW. And only 0.33 tons of sugar are produced per hour of labor in the US versus 0.50 tons per hour of labor in ROW.

Because labor supply is limited and is presumed to be transferable between commodities but not between countries, wheat output is foregone to produce sugar. The three hours of labor used to produce one ton of sugar in the US could have been used to produce three tons of wheat, hence the *opportunity cost* or *marginal cost* of producing one ton of sugar is said to be three tons of wheat. And the opportunity cost or marginal cost of producing one ton of sugar in ROW is 0.5 tons of wheat because the two hours utilized to produce a ton of sugar could have been used to produce 0.5 tons of wheat.

In summary, the marginal cost per ton of sugar (MC_S) is the ratio of labor coefficients or

$$MC_S = \frac{a_{LS}}{a_{LW}} = \frac{3}{1} = 3 \qquad (US)$$

$$MC_S' = \frac{a_{LS}'}{a_{LW}'} = \frac{2}{4} = 0.5 \qquad (ROW).$$

In the absence of trade, the cost of an additional ton of sugar is 3 tons of wheat foregone in the US but only 0.5 tons of wheat foregone in ROW. Thus, measured by labor coefficients or marginal cost, sugar production is cheaper abroad than in the US, i.e.

$$a_{LS}' = 2 < a_{LS} = 3$$

$$MC_S' = 0.5 < MC_S = 3.$$

Suppose one person's labor of 2,000 hours per year is available in the US and a similar amount in ROW. That 2,000 hours would produce in the US:

$$\frac{2000}{a_{LW} = 1} \qquad or \qquad 2{,}000 \text{ tons of wheat}$$

$$\frac{2000}{a_{LS} = 3} \qquad or \qquad 667 \text{ tons of sugar}$$

and in ROW would produce

$$\frac{2000}{a_{LW}' = 4} \qquad or \qquad 500 \text{ tons of wheat}$$

$$\frac{2000}{a_{LS}' = 2} \qquad or \qquad 1{,}000 \text{ tons of sugar.}$$

By specializing in wheat production, the US could consume 2,000 tons of wheat or ship it all to ROW to purchase up to 1,000 tons of sugar. The US could have various combinations of wheat and sugar between these extremes. By specializing in sugar production, ROW could consume 1,000 tons of sugar or export it to the US in return for up to 2,000 tons of wheat. The student can determine that the trade-adjusted "production" possibility curve axis for wheat in the US and for sugar in ROW remains unchanged but the sugar axis in the US is extended from 667 tons to 1,000 tons and in ROW the wheat axis is increased from 500 tons to 2,000 tons. Clearly, trade shifts outward the "production" possibility curves both in the US and ROW.

COMPARATIVE ADVANTAGE

The above may belabor the obvious benefits of trade under absolute advantage. Less obvious is the gain from trade when one country possesses an absolute advantage in production of both wheat and sugar. There is no basis for trade only in the unlikely case that the ratio of costs for two commodities is the same between two countries. The country requiring *relatively* the least resources to produce a commodity unit is said to have a *comparative advantage* even if it does not have an absolute advantage.

David Ricardo is recognized for first presenting the comparative advantage basis for trade using examples of wine and cloth trade between England and Portugal. We use an example of wheat and sugar trade. Raising the labor coefficient a'_{LS} to 6 hours per ton of sugar in ROW gives the US an absolute advantage in production of wheat and sugar. Critical coefficients are summarized as follows:

	US	ROW
Wheat (W)	$a_{LW} = 1$	$a'_{LW} = 4$
Sugar (S)	$a_{LS} = 3$	$a'_{LS} = 6$
MC_S (or MC'_S)	$\dfrac{a_{LS}}{a_{LW}} = 3$	$\dfrac{a'_{LS}}{a'_{LW}} = \dfrac{6}{4} = 1.5$
MC_W (or MC'_W)	$\dfrac{a_{LW}}{a_{LS}} = \dfrac{1}{3} = 0.33$	$\dfrac{a'_{LW}}{a'_{LS}} = \dfrac{4}{6} = 0.67.$

The opportunity cost or marginal cost of producing another unit of sugar in terms of foregone wheat is 3 tons in the US and 1.5 tons in ROW. ROW is said to have a comparative advantage in production of sugar because $MC'_S < MC_S$. MC_W is $a_{LW}/a_{LS} = 0.33$ tons of sugar for US wheat and is $a'_{LW}/a'_{LS} = 0.67$ tons of sugar for ROW wheat, hence the US has a comparative advantage in production of wheat.

Assume 2,000 hours of labor are available in the US and 8,000 hours in ROW. Production possibilities are as follows:

	US (2,000 hours)	ROW (8,000 hours)
Wheat	$\dfrac{2,000}{a_{LW}}$ = 2,000 tons	$\dfrac{8,000}{a_{LW}'}$ = 2,000 tons
Sugar	$\dfrac{2,000}{a_{LS}}$ = 667 tons	$\dfrac{8,000}{a_{LS}'}$ = 1,333 tons.

The US could produce and consume 2,000 tons of wheat or 667 tons of sugar in isolation. By exporting all of its wheat to ROW and trading at the marginal cost of production in ROW, the 2,000 tons of US wheat will purchase 1,333 tons of sugar, paying ROW its marginal cost of production. Hence trade can double sugar available to the US.

ROW can produce and consume 2,000 tons of wheat or 1,333 tons of sugar in isolation. With trade, ROW can send 1,333 tons of sugar to the US where it can purchase 4,000 tons of wheat at the US terms of trade as measured by the marginal cost $MC_S = 3$.

Figure 2.1 graphically illustrates that trade expands the production possibility frontier outward to permit greater consumption in both countries than with *autarky* (no trade). Trade reduces the marginal cost of acquiring sugar in the US from 3 under autarky to the lower level of 1.5 of ROW. Trade reduces the marginal cost of acquiring wheat in ROW from 2/3 to 1/3 units of sugar.

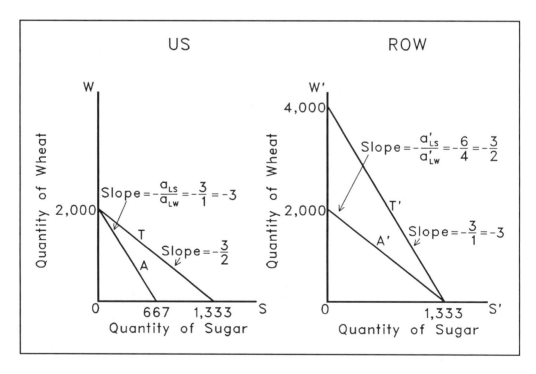

Figure 2.1. Production Possibilities Curves Without Trade (A) and With Trade (T) in the United States (US) and the Rest of the World (ROW).

Trade raises the effective production possibility curve from A to T in the US and from A´ to T´ in ROW (Figure 2.1, and *assuming the US can find labor to supply additional wheat to ROW*). In essence, trade superimposes the other country's production possibility curve on top of the initial curve with convergence at the point of maximum production of the commodity with comparative advantage.

Trade provides no gain only in the unlikely case that consumers in the US strongly prefer wheat so the highest attainable indifference curve touches T at 2,000 tons of wheat, or that consumers in ROW strongly prefer sugar so that the highest attainable indifference curve touches T´ at 1,333 tons of sugar. Trade provides the greatest benefit if US consumers strongly prefer sugar and ROW consumers strongly prefer wheat. The law of one price precludes such simultaneous opposite-extreme-point solutions, however, in the absence of transport costs and market distortions.

Figure 2.2 demonstrates that the equilibrium price of wheat relative to sugar must fall between the marginal costs of home production shown in Figure 2.1. The US will not pay more than sw wheat for 0s of sugar (sw/0s = 3) from ROW because it can produce sugar at home for that price. ROW will not accept less than st wheat for 0s sugar from the US because it can produce that quantity of wheat with its own resources without sacrificing more than 0s of sugar. Thus with trade the world price of sugar P_S will fall between the US

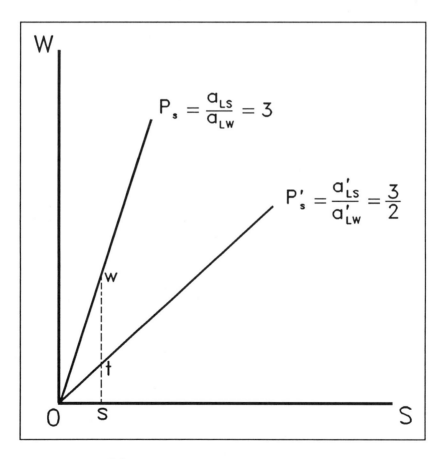

Figure 2.2. Equilibrium Price Range for the US and ROW.

and ROW marginal costs of production or $dw'ds' = a'_{LS}/a'_{LW} = 1.5 < P_S < dw/ds = a_{LS}/a_{LW} = 3.$[1] If preferences are so strong for either wheat in both countries or for sugar in both countries that prices lie outside of these extremes, production is specialized and trade does not take place.

Productivity, defined earlier as the inverse of the production coefficients, is also the wage rate. The wage rate shows why a country can export when it has no absolute advantage and also illustrates the gains from trade. The wages in tons per hour of labor are as follows:

	US	*ROW*
Wheat	*1*	*0.25 (after trade 0.50)*
Sugar	*0.33 (after trade 0.67)*	*0.17*

Despite lower productivity in ROW, lower wage rates allow exports to the US. It is notable that trade doubles buying power of wages in the US and ROW in the commodities lacking comparative advantage.

Figure 2.3 further clarifies benefits from trade with constant marginal rates of product transformation. Resources available to the rest of the world, ROW, and the US provide production possibility surfaces ABD and DEF respectively. Because aggregate resources underlying the transformation surfaces need not be specified but may be large or small for each of the surfaces, nothing need be said of absolute production costs. Note that relative costs designated by the slopes AD and DE differ, indicating comparative advantage for US in wheat and ROW in sugar as shown earlier in Figure 2.1.

The *global* production possibility surface OADE is formed from the ROW surface at the top and the US surface at the right. If the terms of trade (price) line is flatter than segment AD, it is tangent to the production possibility curve ADE at point A, the countries specialize in wheat, and no trade occurs. If the terms of trade line is steeper than segment DE, it is tangent to the production possibility curve at E, both countries specialize in sugar, and no trade occurs. If the price is between 3/2 and 3, as Figure 2.2 illustrated, the basis for trade exists. Production is at D with BD of sugar produced by ROW and DF of wheat produced by the US.

If consumers strongly prefer wheat so price is less than 3/2 for sugar, both countries will produce wheat and trade is zero. If consumers strongly prefer sugar so its price exceeds 3, both countries produce only sugar and no trade occurs.

Another world production possibility surface OACE can be formed providing specialization by each country in the commodity in which it has a *comparative disadvantage*. The US production surface is moved to A$\bar{B}$C at the top of the world surface and the ROW production surface is moved to C$\bar{F}$E on the world surface. With US specializing in sugar and ROW specializing in wheat, production is at point C -- clearly an inferior, production minimizing position. The gains from utilizing comparative advantage are product space ACED measured by additional sugar or wheat available.

---

[1]The d's refer to very small changes and are often designated as deltas (Δ's).

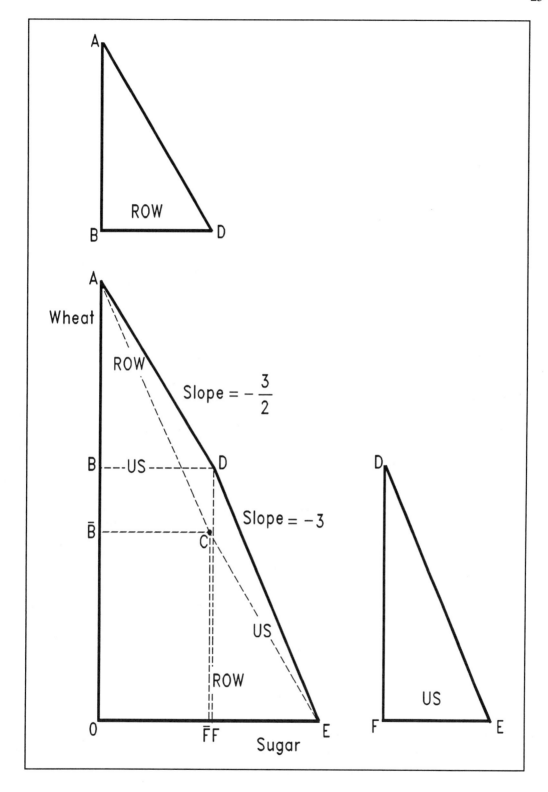

Figure 2.3. Illustration of Gains from Trade.

MODERN THEORY OF COMPARATIVE ADVANTAGE
AND GAINS FROM TRADE

Classical theory presented thus far has numerous shortcomings in explaining trade flows. Two major flaws are:

1.   Assuming constant marginal productivity and marginal cost.
2.   Ignoring consumer choice and demand among countries.

Differences in preferences can bring benefits from trade among countries possessing exactly the same factor endowments and production possibility curves. Diminishing returns cause increasing quantities of output of other commodities to be foregone as output of any one commodity is expanded another unit. The modern theory of comparative advantage accommodates these conditions and more fully explains trade in the real world.

Terms of Trade

Figure 2.4 illustrates how demand and supply curves can be used to derive the terms of trade T between two countries, say the US and Brazil. The production possibility curve for wheat and sugar in Brazil is utilized to derive supply curves for the two commodities. For example, the supply quantity of sugar s_2 in the lower middle graph of Figure 2.4 is derived directly from the production possibility curve for wheat shown in the upper panel of the figure. Including the demand curves for wheat and sugar in Brazil allows the excess supply (supply quantity in excess of the demand quantity) to be determined at various prices. These excess supplies trace the offer curve G_b for sugar and wheat in Brazil. It is apparent that the demand curve can strongly influence the offer curve and hence the level and terms of trade.

A similar procedure would trace out the offer curve G_u for wheat versus sugar in the US. At lower quantities, Brazil is willing to offer considerable sugar to obtain more wheat. The US in turn is willing to supply considerably more wheat for a given amount of sugar. For example, Brazil can offer only z level of wheat for b-a sugar but by trading with the US it can get x (vertical distance in right panel) of wheat, hence the potential trade dividend is x-z. At f-e of wheat, the US offers only y units of sugar but by trading it can obtain z units, hence the dividend from trade is z-y measured in sugar. These gains are positive until the equilibrium is reached at point v with terms of trade T. (Although T appears to be a 45 degree angle in Figure 2.4, representing one ton of sugar trading for one ton of wheat, that outcome is coincidental -- sugar could be in tons and wheat in bushels.)

Introducing Indifference Curves

Figure 2.5 further illustrates the modern concept of comparative advantage and the benefits of trade. The farm resources of the United States and Brazil will produce wheat and sugar in the combinations indicated by the respective production possibility curves P. In isolation, the highest societal indifference curve that can be reached with the given resources is I_0 in each country. The terms-of-trade line (not shown) in isolation, indicating the ratio of the price of sugar to the price of wheat, is tangent to the production transform-

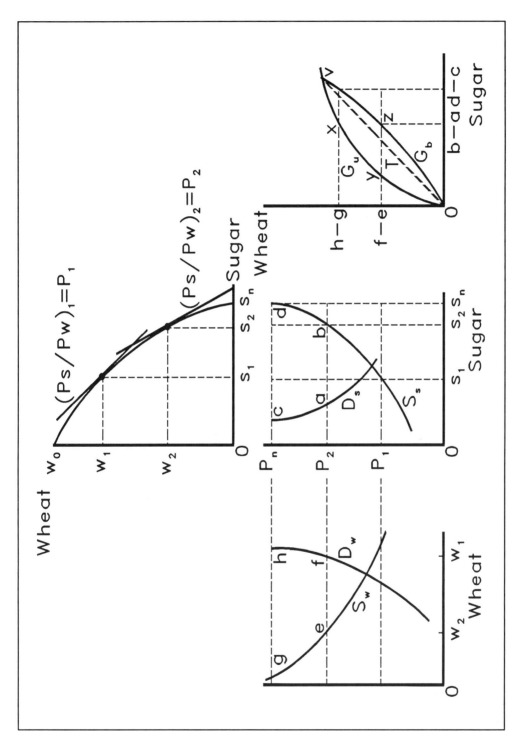

Figure 2.4. Terms of Trade T Derived from Production Possibility and Demand Curves.

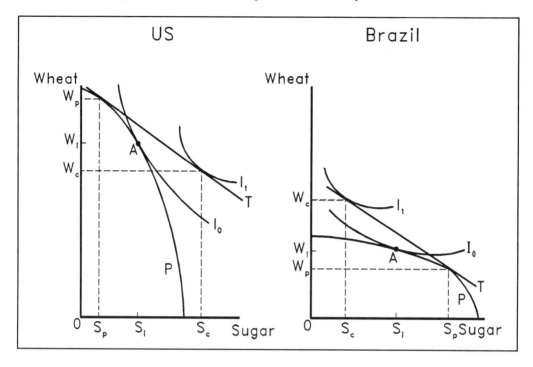

Figure 2.5. Production Possibility Curves and Indifference Curves for Wheat and Sugar in the United States and Brazil.

ation curves and the societal indifference curves I_0 at A. The slope of this price line is considerably steeper for the United States than for Brazil. The relative high price for sugar in the United States and wheat in Brazil in Figure 2.5 reflects differences in production capabilities more than the modest differences in consumer preferences.

In isolation, quantities of wheat and sugar produced and consumed in the countries are W_i and S_i. The resources of the United States are relatively better suited to produce wheat than sugar, and those of Brazil are relatively better suited to produce sugar than wheat. Hence, even in isolation, with similar preferences reflected in similar indifference curves in each country, the United States consumes relatively much more wheat than sugar. The reverse is true for Brazil.

The United States is said to have a *comparative advantage* in production of wheat, Brazil in sugar. That is, with resources available to each country, the US produces a higher ratio of wheat to sugar than does Brazil. The US may also have an *absolute advantage*. That is, it can produce a commodity at a lower cost (measured in hours of labor, or, more properly, in a weighted value-sum of inputs) per unit than Brazil.

Assume the production possibility curve P in Figure 2.5 for Brazil is rotated 180 degrees and placed on top of the curve for the United States. By making the two curves tangent at various points, different combinations of total sugar and wheat will be produced efficiently by the two countries. It is apparent that, because of the shape of the curves, the United States will tend to specialize in wheat and Brazil in sugar. However, theory must also take into account the nature of consumer preferences and demand.

Trade results in greater specialization in production of wheat (W_p) in the United States and sugar (S_p) in Brazil. However, more wheat (W_c) is consumed in Brazil and more sugar (S_c) in the United States after trading than in isolation. The quantity $W_p - W_c$ is a net wheat export from the United States and a net import into Brazil. The quantity S_p - S_c is the net sugar export from Brazil and a net import to the United States. This trade enables each country to move from a lower indifference curve (I_0) in the absence of trade to a higher indifference curve (I_1) through greater specialization in production of what it does best. The new terms of trade line T represents the same price ratio for both countries in the absence of trade barriers. It follows that tangency of the same price line to the product transformation curves and indifference curves in each country indicates equal marginal rates of substitution in consumption and production. This outcome is economically efficient. The price line in reality does not have the same slope for each country because of transport costs and institutional impediments to trade such as duties, quotas, export subsidies, and domestic price supports.

Comparative Profits

Recognition that T in Figure 2.5 may differ among nations because of demand, transport, and institutional circumstances leads to rejection of comparative advantage based only on relative production costs as a basis for trade. The inadequacy of the concept of comparative advantage in *production* to explain or predict trade is apparent because trade will occur among countries to reach a higher indifference curve even if each country has exactly the same production possibility curve. Comparative advantage also must account for differences in demand to explain trade.

According to modern trade theory, a country is said to have a *comparative advantage* in the commodity that it can produce and export at the highest return per unit of fixed factors of production (nontraded inputs such as land and labor) in a well-functioning world economy. A country without market distortions is said to have a *competitive advantage* in a commodity it can produce and export at highest return per unit of fixed factors of production in the *actual* world economy with all its imperfections.[2] Because of taxes, subsidies, quotas, and other market interventions in the actual world economy, competitive advantage is a more widely applicable concept than comparative advantage. *Competitiveness* is defined as a nation's ability to maintain or gain market share by exploiting competitive advantage in world markets through increasing productivity from technological advances or other sources.

Country A may have higher profits in all potentially exportable commodities than does country B. But if the return to fixed resources is highest in wheat among all commodities produced in A and is highest in sugar among all commodities produced in B when exposed to the world market, then A will export wheat and B will export sugar. Return above variable costs are maximized. Hence, in the short or intermediate run, a country may rationally export at a loss because variable but not necessarily fixed costs are covered.

Supply, Demand, and Trade

Gains from trade also can be shown with Marshallian supply and demand curves. Figure 2.6 shows trade between the United States and foreign countries, given the domestic demand and supply curves in the United States (US) and in foreign countries (ROW) taken as an aggregate entity. The supply of US exports is the amount by which domestic supply

---

[2]Competitive advantage ideally is analyzed by assuming the home country retains only those programs without deadweight losses. Thus public programs to preserve the environment and promote productivity growth can be continued while most commodity programs are assumed to be ended.

28

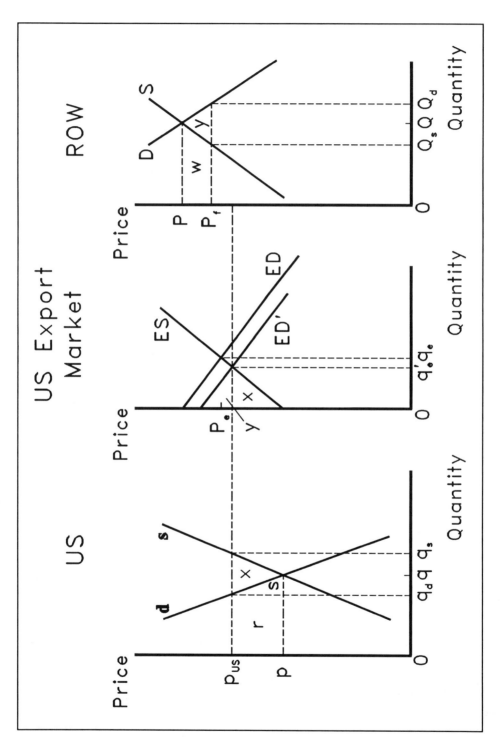

Figure 2.6. Domestic US Demand and Supply Curves (d and s), US Export Excess Demand ED and Supply ES Curves, and Foreign Demand and Supply Curves (D and S).

exceeds domestic demand **s-d** at all possible prices, hence is the excess supply curve ES. The demand for US exports is the amount by which foreign demand exceeds foreign supply D-S at all possible prices, and hence is the excess demand curve ED. Export supply and demand intersect at an equilibrium price P_e where q_e is the quantity exported by the United States and imported by ROW. This does not allow for transport costs $P_f - p_{us}$. Transport costs lower the United States' export demand by the amount of the cost -- from ED to ED´. The equilibrium price is then p_{us} in the United States and P_f in the foreign market. Other barriers to trade such as foreign tariffs have an effect similar to transport costs in reducing the demand for United States' exports. The exports from the United States are $q_s - q_d$, the same quantity as q'_e, and foreign imports $Q_d - Q_s$.

Export markets raise the domestic price of the commodity in the United States to p_{us} from the equilibrium price p in market isolation. The price P_f in the foreign market is lower than the market-isolated price P. With trade, the gain in producer surplus r+s+x exceeds the loss in consumer surplus r+s in the United States by the net social gain represented by the triangle x in Figure 2.6. (For definitions of consumer and producer surplus and for concepts of classical welfare analysis, see Tweeten (1989, ch. 6)). In the foreign market, the gain in consumer surplus w+y exceeds the loss in producer surplus w by the net social gain represented by the area y.

Thus the public (made up of consumers and producers) in each trading area realizes a positive net gain from trade, but US consumers are disadvantaged and foreign producers are disadvantaged in the example in Figure 2.6. These groups may resist freer trade. The losses focused on a few well-organized foreign producers may motivate such producers to press for barriers to curtail trade and cut off the widely dispersed consumer gains, though the consumers' gains in total outweigh producers' losses. Each consumer receives such a small gain that he or she does not consider it worthwhile to lobby for free trade. A consumer group attempting to organize for free trade will be hampered by holdouts who are *free riders*, expecting to gain the benefits from lobbying by others. In contrast, the large potential gain per producer from retaining trade barriers makes it worthwhile individually and collectively to lobby for interventions. A tariff equal to the price difference in isolation, P(ROW) - p(US), stops trade even in the absence of transport costs.

Figure 2.7 further illustrates the impact on consumers, producers, taxpayers, and society of free trade and trade distortions. The hypothetical demand and supply curves in the United States (US) are **d** and **s** and in the rest of the world (ROW) are D and S respectively. In isolation, price is 0 in US and P in ROW; quantity is q in US and Q in ROW.

The world demand curve for US exports is the excess demand curve ED formed by subtracting the supply quantity from the demand quantity at each price along D and S. The supply curve for US exports is the excess supply curve ES, found by subtracting the demand quantity from the supply quantity at all prices along **d** and **s**. Assuming no transportation costs or trade barriers, the equilibrium world price is $p_e = P_e$ and quantity is $q_e = q_s - q_d$ (US exports) = $Q_d - Q_s$ (ROW imports). Compared to isolation, the gains from free trade are as follows:

	US	ROW
Gain to consumers	-1-2	a+b+c+d+e+f
Gain to producers	1+2+3+4+5+6	-a-b
Gain to society	3+4+5+6	c+d+e+f

US producers gain and consumers lose; the opposite holds in the rest of the world. In net, both US and ROW benefit from free trade.

30

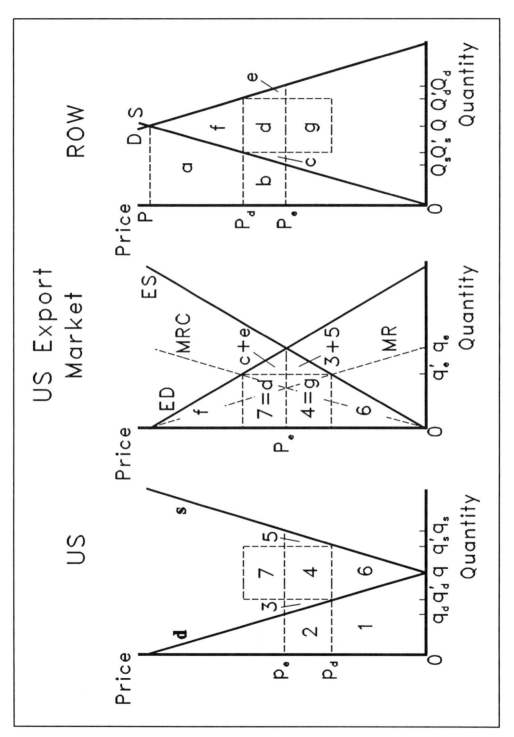

Figure 2.7. Illustration of Benefits from Free Trade.

We now introduce trade imperfections. A quota limiting imports or exports to zero or a tariff equal to P-0 would erase the gains from trade and make the world worse off. However, one country may gain by taxing exports or imports.

Suppose the US wishes to impose an optimal tax on exports. The marginal revenue in the foreign market is MR. Because MR is negative in the inelastic portion of the demand curve, the optimal strategy would be for the US to export no more than the free trade quantity q_e. The optimal export is quantity $q'_e = q'_s - q'_d = Q'_d - Q'_s$ where MR intersects ES. Price is p_d in the US market and P_d in the ROW market with a tax of $P_d - p_d$ per unit bringing revenue of 4+7 in Figure 2.7. The summary of gains to the US and ROW from American state monopoly selling compared to free trade is as follows:

	US		ROW
Gain to consumers	2		-b-c-d-e
Gain to producers	-2-3-4-5		b
Gain to taxpayers (govt.)	4+7		---
Gain to society (nation)	7-3-5		-c-d-e
Gain to world (7=d)		-3-5-c-e	

US consumers gain and producers lose from the export tax. Producer losses exceed consumer gains but tax revenues of 4+7 more than offset net loss, so in theory producers could be compensated. ROW is a net loser; national income falls by c+d+e and the big loss is borne by ROW consumers. Part of the loss, d, is a transfer 7 to the US leaving c+e as the deadweight loss. ROW loses more than the US gains; the world deadweight (real income) loss from the US export tax is 3+5+c+e.

An alternative trade distortion is for ROW to impose a tariff on imports from the US. The optimal tariff to maximize net revenue is where the marginal resource cost MRC intersects ED at price P_d in ROW, p_d in the US, and with import quantity $q'_e = Q'_d - Q'_s$ (Figure 2.7). Results are as follows:

	US		ROW
Gain to consumers	2		-b-c-d-e
Gain to producers	-2-3-4-5		b
Gain to taxpayers (govt.)	---		d+g
Gain to society (nation)	-3-4-5		-c-e+g
Gain to world (4=g)		-3-5-c-e	

The tariff of $P_d - p_d$ per unit brings revenue d+g to government or taxpayers of ROW. Producers in ROW gain b while consumers lose b+c+d+e. Consumers and producers experience the same redistribution as with the export tax imposed by the US. However, the import tariff brings sufficient revenue to compensate consumers in ROW for losses. Deadweight loss to the world from the case of monopsony buying by ROW equals that from monopoly selling by the US. (This outcome arose from the special way the curves in Figure 2.7 were constructed; deadweight losses would occur with other constructions although not necessarily of the magnitudes shown in Figure 2.7.)

A situation as in Figure 2.7 where the seller operates as a monopolist and the buyer as a monopsonist is called *bilateral monopoly*. It is a prelude to strategic trade theory discussed in Chapters 7 and 8. Bilateral monopoly has no unique price (it depends on bargaining power) but output and welfare losses are predictable.

Any number of combinations of US export taxes and ROW import tariffs could produce similar outcomes for prices and quantities. Suppose the US export tax were p_e -

p_d and the ROW tariff were P_d - P_e. The outcomes would be the same as with distortions shown above except tax revenue would be only area 4 in the US and d in ROW. Neither the US nor ROW would be able to compensate losers from tax revenues, and deadweight or national income losses would be 3+5 in the US and c+e in ROW.

US producers controlling production and exports could obtain the gains (area 7) accruing to taxpayers in Figure 2.7. However, if ROW retaliates to remove 7, producers will be worse off than with free trade. Whether gains from an export cartel are feasible depends not just on retaliation but also on the elasticity of demand for exports. The elasticity of receipts with respect to export price is $1+E_x$ where E_x is the price elasticity of export demand. If export demand is elastic, $1+E_x$ is negative and raising price and reducing quantity reduces export receipts.

Elasticity of Export Demand

It is apparent that whether it would pay the US to restrict exports and raise export price to increase export receipts and farm income depends heavily on the elasticity of export demand. The following analysis indicates that for major US export commodities export revenues may be raised by restricting exports in the short run but are lowered by restricting exports in the longer run. The high absolute magnitudes of elasticity of demand for exports may come as a surprise because *domestic* demand and supply are frequently inelastic.

To analyze the responsiveness of US exports to price it is well to digress to estimate the elasticity of export demand in any one country as a function of variables in all other countries i = 1 to n. We begin with the *food balance equation*, which specifies that supply comprised of beginning carry-in stocks BC plus imports M plus production Q_s equals utilization comprised of exports X plus consumption Q_d plus end-of-year carry-out stocks EC for country i:

$$BC_i + M_i + Q_{si} = X_i + Q_{di} + EC_i \qquad (i=1,2,...n).$$

Assuming the US is a net exporter of the commodity in question and the rest of the world is a net importer, then US exports X are imports of the rest of the world so the food balance equation can be rearranged to state

$$X = \sum_{i \neq US} [M_i - X_i] = \Sigma[Q_{di} - Q_{si} + EC_i - BC_i].$$

Designating addition to stocks EC_i - BC_i as C_i and summing over all nations except the US, it is apparent that exports of a commodity X from the US are

$$X = \sum_{i=1}^{n} [Q_{di} - Q_{si} + C_i].$$

It can be shown (Tweeten, 1967) that

$$E_x = \sum_{i=1}^{n} \left[E_{di} E_{pdi} \left(\frac{Q_{di}}{X} \right) - E_{si} E_{psi} \left(\frac{Q_{si}}{X} \right) + E_{ci} E_{pci} \left(\frac{C_i}{X} \right) \right]$$

where E_x is the price elasticity of demand for US exports, the percentage change in American exports associated with a 1 percent change in world price. For computational purposes, the US price is assumed to be the world price. Other variables are defined below.

The formula ordinarily utilizes data for each country involved in exports and imports of a commodity. However, average but reasonably realistic values over all countries for wheat are assumed for illustrative purposes in this example where

E_{di} = price elasticity of domestic demand in country i with respect to domestic price in i, assumed to average -0.15 in both the short and long run over all countries for wheat.

E_{pdi} = demand price transmission elasticity, defined as the percentage change in domestic price to consumers in country i associated with a 1 percent change in world price. The value would be 1.0 in a perfect market. In the example, the US price is assumed to be the world price, and the transmission elasticity is only 0.17 in both the long and short run for wheat, implying major impediments to free trade.

Q_{di}/X = ratio of consumption in country i (a total of 484 million metric tons of wheat in 1987/88) to US exports (33 million metric tons of wheat in 1987/88), or a ratio of 14.7.

E_{si} = price elasticity of domestic supply in country i with respect to domestic supply price in country i, assumed to average 0.11 in the short run and 0.66 in the long run for wheat over all countries.

E_{psi} = supply price transmission elasticity, defined as the percentage change in price to producers in country i associated with a 1 percent change in world price. In a perfect market, the value would be 1.0. In the example, the US price is assumed to be the world price and the transmission elasticity is assumed to be only 0.15 in both the short run and the long run for wheat, implying major market distortions impeding the flow of price signals to producers.

Q_{si}/X = ratio of production in country i (a total of 451 million metric tons of wheat in 1987/88) to US exports (33 million metric tons in 1987/88), or an average ratio of 13.7.

E_{ci} = price elasticity of stock change in country i with respect to domestic price. Stock accumulation is inversely related to price and the negative elasticity exceeds unity (absolute value) in many instances. Foreign stock demand can add much to the short-run elasticity E_x but is inconsequential in long-run elasticities because long-term stock levels do not change much. Also, stock elasticity estimates are even more subject than other elasticities to error. Hence, stock demand is omitted here in estimating long-term demand for exports.

Because stock demand tends to be elastic, omission of it
biases short-run E_x toward zero.

E_{pci} =   stock price transmission elasticity in country i.

C_i/X =   ratio of stock change in country i to US exports.

A simple illustration to calculate E_x, ignoring stock demand and using the foregoing judgment consensus estimates for ROW from previous studies, is instructive.   With reasonably realistic but modest estimates of domestic demand and supply elasticities and with extremely low but again reasonably realistic price transmission elasticities from previous estimates, the calculated US elasticity of wheat export demand E_x is a sizable -0.60 in the short run and -1.73 in the long run.

The low price transmission elasticity indicates that on average only one-fifth of the price change in world markets is passed to domestic markets.   Worldwide open markets could raise the transmission elasticities to near 1.0 and quintuple the elasticity of US export demand for wheat.   Disaggregate data from Tyers and Anderson (see World Bank, p. 131) support the conclusion that world price variation also would be sharply dampened by free trade.

Gardiner and Dixit reviewed a large number of US export demand elasticity estimates from diverse sources that used various methods of parameter estimation.   Their results are summarized in Table 2.1.   These average estimates from many previous studies (dropping the highest and lowest estimates to avoid distorted outliers in cases such as wheat and cotton, which had a large number of estimates) indicated that export restrictions or a price hike would lose revenue for major US exports except in the short run.   The averages tend to underestimate elasticities for rising prices and overestimate elasticities for falling prices.   Thus imposition of an export tax (even if legal) would not benefit US gross except perhaps in the short run.   Net impacts not calculated here would need to consider the behavior of costs as well as receipts.

Table 2.1. US Export Elasticity of Demand.

	Short Run	**Long Run**
Wheat	-0.60	-1.71
Coarse Grains	-0.73	-2.00
Corn	-0.35	-0.63
Sorghum	-1.57	-2.36
Soybeans	-0.76	-1.13
Soybean Meal	-0.47	NA
Soybean Oil	-0.59	NA
Rice	-0.57	-7.00
Cotton	-0.40	-4.60

Source: Gardiner and Dixit. See Carter and Gardiner for other trade elasticities and Henneberry and Tweeten for supply elasticities.

An alternative is export subsidies to raise revenue and sales. However, extensive use of such measures brings charges by American consumers that they are unfairly paying more than foreigners for US farm products if a two-price plan is used, charges by American taxpayers that they should not have to subsidize domestic farmers or foreign consumers, and charges by foreign producers of unfair competition if either a two-price plan or subsidies are used to dump produce abroad. Retaliation may be swift. The United States could contend that it is not subsidizing exports but only retaliating against subsidized foreign exports. Again, however, export subsidies are a dubious long-term strategy because retaliation by competing exporters erodes benefits to exporters and merely transfers income to importers. This issue is revisited in the later chapter on strategic trade theory.

RESOURCE ENDOWMENT AND TRADE

The *Heckscher-Ohlin synthesis* (sometimes called the *Heckscher-Ohlin-Samuelson synthesis* because of Paul Samuelson's significant theoretical contributions) provides theorems giving important insights into the relationship between commodity trade and factor endowments. Key simplifying assumptions of the neoclassical synthesis are:

1. Consumer preferences are the same in all countries.
2. Technology is the same in all countries.
3. Factor intensity or endowments apparent in ratios of capital and labor differ among countries.
4. Factor intensity reversals do not occur. That is, a country with a higher capital-labor ratio than other countries does not change its relative position as production changes. A good that is capital intensive does not become labor intensive as output changes.

For illustration, assume two countries and goods.

> US is capital abundant.
> Brazil is labor abundant.
> Wheat is capital intensive.
> Sugar is labor intensive.

Comparative production advantage for the United States is in wheat and comparative advantage for Brazil is in sugar, as is apparent from their respective production possibility curves in Figure 2.8. Comparative advantage arises from relatively greater factor intensity of capital utilized well by wheat in the US and of labor utilized well by sugar in Brazil. Production and consumption patterns arise solely from factor endowments because technology and indifference curves for consumers are presumed to be the same in each country.

In isolation, the US produces and consumes W_{ui} of wheat and S_{ui} of sugar while Brazil produces and consumes W_{bi} of wheat and S_{bi} of sugar. With trade, the US produces W_{up}, consumes W_{uc}, and exports $W_{up} - W_{uc}$ of wheat to Brazil. With trade, Brazil produces W_{bp} of wheat, consumes W_{bc}, and imports $W_{bc} - W_{bp} = W_{up} - W_{uc}$.

In isolation, Brazil and the US produce and consume respectively S_{bi} and S_{ui} of sugar. With trade, Brazil produces S_{bp} of sugar, consumes S_{bc}, and exports $S_{bp} - S_{bc}$. The US produces S_{up} of sugar, consumes S_{uc}, and imports $S_{uc} - S_{up} = S_{bp} - S_{bc}$. Trade enables each

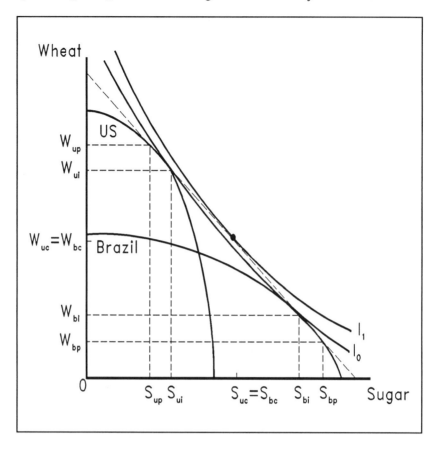

Figure 2.8. Illustration of Relationship Between Factor Intensity and Trade.

country to move from a lower level of utility represented by indifference curve I_0 to a higher level of utility represented by indifference curve I_1 in both countries. Dissimilar indifference curves for the two countries would give different results.

Several conclusions can be drawn:

1. With autarky, a country consumes proportionately more of a commodity in which its relative factor endowment is greatest compared to other commodities, other things equal.

2. With trade, production of the commodity favored by factor endowment increases. Capital abundance favored expansion of capital-intensive wheat for export in the US, and labor abundance favored expansion of labor-intensive sugar in Brazil.

3. With trade, consumption of the commodity favored by factor endowment decreases. However, trade moves consumers in both countries to higher indifference curves.

4. Trade increases use of the abundant factor relative to the scarce factor of production. Increasing output of wheat expands capital use relative to labor in the US and of labor relative to capital in Brazil.

5. Trade raises the return to the abundant factor and reduces the return to the scarce factor. Given diminishing factor returns and rising supply prices for inputs, increasing output of capital-intensive wheat and decreasing output of

labor-intensive sugar increase the price of capital and diminish the price of labor in the United States. In Brazil with trade, increasing output of labor-intensive sugar and diminishing output of capital-intensive wheat raise the price of labor relative to capital.

6. A corollary of conclusion 5 is that trade tends to equalize rates of return to resources among countries and uses. Arbitrage in the form of market participants buying in markets where prices are low to sell in markets where prices are high results in the *law of one price* in the absence of impediments to trade. A significant contribution of the Heckscher-Ohlin synthesis, however, is to conclude that resource returns or prices also tend to equalize over time for nontraded immobile inputs (see Annex). Thus resource returns will tend to equalize among countries if either (a) commodity trade is unrestricted and factors are fixed, (b) factors are mobile and open to trade while commodity trade is restricted, or (c) both commodities and factors are traded.

In the real world, this conclusion must be heavily qualified. Except for financial capital, factors are not highly mobile among countries even in the absence of trade restrictions. The frictions of space such as transport costs as well as trade barriers, uncertainty, culture, and inertia heavily impede both product and resource mobility. Thus, even under the best conditions likely to prevail in the world, factor returns will not be equalized in the foreseeable future and nations will continue to experience individual, regional, and national low income and returns to labor.

In the long term, the assumptions of the Heckscher-Ohlin (H-O) synthesis are especially violated. Technology, knowledge, and capital resources flow among countries to cloud the relationship between production possibilities and original factor endowments. Mundell amended H-O by assuming trade is in inputs rather than outputs, hence recognizing that trade in inputs substitutes for trade in outputs.

Markusen allowed factor abundance to be determined by conditions rather than be taken as a given endowment. He showed that two countries with equal factor endowment and trade in inputs and outputs could have a basis for trade because of different technologies. The resulting relatively high price for the factor used intensively in production of the export good would attract imports of that factor, causing further product export.

Schooling and training in knowledge imported by country B from country A can make a once labor-poor country B rich in human capital. Technology and material capital (machinery, irrigation pumps, etc.) imported by country A from country B may make a once land-poor country A rich in improved land per capita. It would appear that opportunities for technology, knowledge, and financial capital inputs to flow freely among countries will equalize factor endowments and remove the gains from commodity trade in the long run. That has not happened; commodity trade could be expected to slow but it has not. International trade has grown faster than international real income since the decade of the 1950s.

The Leontief Paradox

In a celebrated and controversial study, Leontief found that export intensities did not conform with factor endowment intensities as predicted by the Heckscher-Ohlin theorem. Leontief found that countries with high capital-labor ratios were exporting labor-intensive commodities.

Excessive criticism has already been made of a fundamentally flawed study but it is useful to repeat the major weaknesses. Capital was incompletely measured. Human capital and technological capital were ignored; only conventional capital was included. Massive investments in research and extension to improve productivity were omitted in the study. So were investments in vocational and general education, which made farmers and others better decision makers and permitted fewer of them to supply the nation's food and fiber. Studies accounting for all forms of capital would reach results supporting the Heckscher-Ohlin theorem that market economies with high capital-labor ratios export capital-intensive commodities.

Some have erroneously interpreted the Heckscher-Ohlin synthesis to mean that the US would export high-value or high-value-added farm commodities. The US exports proportionately less high-value commodities than the European Community in part because the EC heavily subsidizes processed commodity exports. Many high-value commodities such as fruits, vegetables, and floral products are labor intensive. Hence, as predicted, third-world countries are prominent exporters.

Stolper-Samuelson Theorem

The *Stolper-Samuelson Theorem* states that imposition of a tariff on an import benefits the factor used most intensively in domestic production of the imported commodity. The Theorem is closely related to the Heckscher-Ohlin synthesis.

Suppose that the capital-abundant US exports capital-intensive wheat and imports labor-intensive sugar from labor abundant Brazil. Suppose Brazil imposes a tariff on wheat imports. This increases the domestic price of wheat relative to sugar and the price of capital relative to labor in Brazil. With equilibrium under the tariff, the capital-labor ratio is increased in production of both sugar and wheat.

The so-called *Metzler case* demonstrates that a reduced domestic commodity price (lowered by a tariff or related measure) diminishes the price of the factor used intensively to produce the commodity. A tariff imposed on sugar imports into the US or a tax imposed by Brazil on its sugar exports reduces the price of sugar and the labor wage in Brazil.

Rybczynski's Theorem

Rybczynski's Theorem holds that an increase in the quantity of a factor will cause an increase in output of the commodity that is intensive in the factor and a decrease in output of the other commodity -- given unchanged commodity and factor prices and technology. The theorem is another in the class from the Heckscher-Ohlin synthesis.

An expansion of capital in Brazil will increase production of wheat and decrease production of sugar. This outcome strictly applies only in a two-commodity, two-factor, two-country world.

Figure 2.9 shows isoquants to produce capital-intensive wheat and labor-intensive sugar in Brazil. The curved line from the origin for wheat 0_w to the origin for sugar 0_s is the locus of equal marginal rates of substitution between labor and capital used in production of the two commodities. Given factor and product prices, the equilibrium is at E with capital used in wheat production AB and in sugar production $B0_s$. Labor used in wheat production is CD and in sugar production $C0_s'$.

Now assume capital availability expands from $A0_s$ to $A0_s'$. With fixed factor and product prices and constant returns to scale, new equilibrium output and factor use lie on a straight line ray 0_wE extended to $0_wE'$. The rays 0_sE and $0_s'E'$ are parallel given fixed factor prices and equal marginal rates of substitution before and after expansion of capital

39

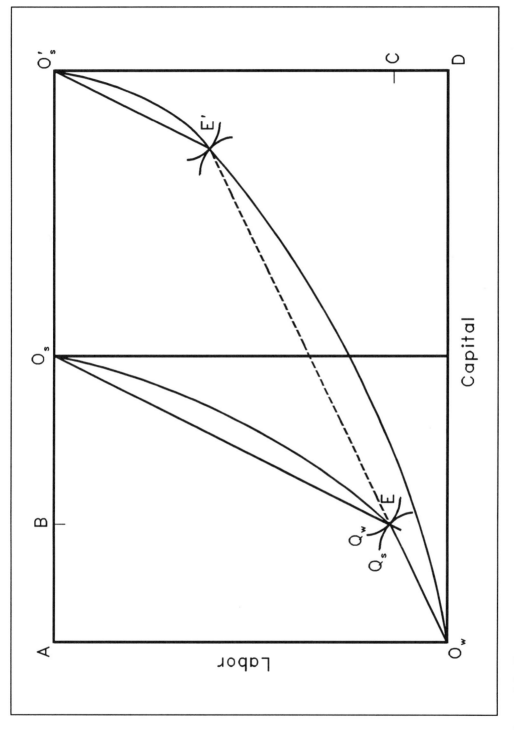

Figure 2.9. Isoquants to Produce Wheat Q_w and Sugar Q_s with Labor and Capital.

and output. Given fixed technology and other assumptions, $0_wE'$ must be longer than 0_wE and 0_sE is longer than $0_s'E'$. Hence output of capital-intensive wheat is increased and output of labor-intensive sugar is decreased by expansion of capital.

ARGUMENTS FOR TRADE BARRIERS

Classical welfare analysis thus far has made a case for free trade. On the other hand, several reasons can be given to justify trade barriers. These include efforts to protect or promote national security, infant industry, balance of payments, countervailing power, and employment. These issues are discussed in later chapters but a few comments are in order here.

Seldom is the macro-micro inconsistency more apparent than in negotiations over trade barriers. Economists have repeatedly demonstrated -- and history has supported -- the contention that free trade generates greater economic progress than protection with but few exceptions. A major impediment to movement toward freer trade is that in reality it is not a Pareto optimum or Pareto better situation because someone is made worse off. Removal of trade barriers is consistent with the *new welfare economics*, which stresses greater efficiency irrespective of the distribution of the efficiency gains. Given resources are able to produce more output -- greater efficiency means that gainers can compensate the losers and make them no worse off than before the change. The problem is that compensation is seldom made. The gains are often widely dispersed over millions of consumers. The losses, on the other hand, are often narrowly focused on a few producers.

In the arena of pressure groups and power politics, millions of indifferent gainers are no match for the intense opposition generated by a few determined big losers. A few big losers can individually or collectively have so much influence over outcomes that it is worth their while to lobby for trade barriers. Unorganized consumers are ineffective.

A small *total* dollar loss to a few producers with high marginal utility of money, coupled with a large dollar gain to a large group of consumers with low marginal utility of money, may mean a net welfare loss from liberalized trade arrangements. The value judgment of most economists is that this is not usually the case, and they continue to press for freer trade. Protection of US jobs in the textile and agricultural industries from foreign competition is often pursued in the name of economic justice -- maintaining jobs of low-income textile and cane field workers. But foreign textile and sugar workers displaced have even lower incomes and opportunities. Commitment is almost universal among economists to the proposition that the United States and the world have far more to gain than to lose from a reduction of trade barriers. Worldwide trade distortions testify to the triumph of self-interest politics over sound economics.

Proponents of trade barriers have reasoned that unilateral reduction of trade barriers may not be in the interests of the United States and that countervailing trade barriers may be necessary. Out of such thinking has grown a theory of the second best, i.e., what kind and level of trade barriers are optimal for country A facing a world of existing and mounting institutional barriers to free trade?

A NOTE ON THE THEORY OF THE SECOND BEST

The *theory of the second best* holds that in a world where one or more conditions for an efficient market are being violated all other conditions for an efficient market need not necessarily be fulfilled for global efficiency. A corollary is that eliminating one distortion does not necessarily bring a more efficient outcome if other distortions remain. The theory has been used to justify trade barriers because other countries have trade barriers.

Suppose in Figure 2.10 that total labor available for serving farm and nonfarm export markets is S. Although laborers are perfect substitutes in either market, suppose the labor market is segmented so that farm and nonfarm workers respectively face demand curves D_F = D_N. Total demand is $D_F + D_N$, the wage is W_{cc}, and employment is E_{cc} in each sector operating competitively.

Now suppose that a strong labor union forms among laborers serving the nonfarm export market. The union faces marginal revenue MR. The wage rate in the competitive farm sector is W_{mc} where $MR + D_F$ intersect S. The wage is M in the nonfarm sector. Employment of E_c in the farm sector and E_m in the nonfarm sector equals labor supply S.

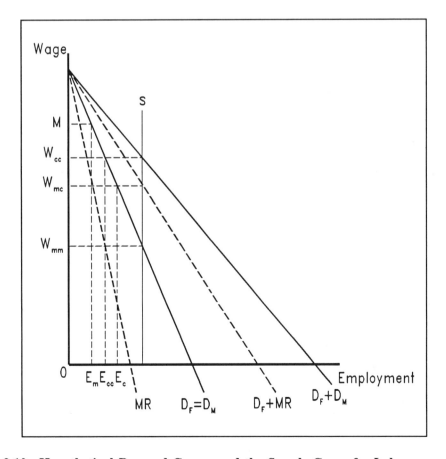

Figure 2.10. Hypothetical Demand Curves and the Supply Curve for Labor.

Next suppose farm sector labor also organizes and faces marginal revenue curve MR. Total marginal revenue is curve $D_F = D_N$ intersecting S at marginal revenue W_{mm} but bringing wage W_{cc} and employment E_{cc} in both sectors. Thus the efficient competitive outcome is achieved if both sectors are organized or if no sectors are organized. However, the outcome is a low wage for farm labor if only nonfarm labor is organized.

The outcome in Figure 2.10 favoring market intervention for both sectors or for neither sector but not for just one sector is probably a rare situation in the real world. Figure 2.7, shown earlier, represents a more typical second-best outcome. That graph and estimates of export demand elasticities prompt the following conclusions regarding second best theory.

1. As a general rule, open worldwide trade minimizes social costs (deadweight losses).
2. Trade interventions and counter interventions can improve well-being of any one country but will reduce full income of the world.
3. Whether the US can increase income from export market interventions depends heavily on the elasticity of export demand, which is near unity in the intermediate run or longer for many farm commodities. Hence neither restricting nor subsidizing sales has much impact on revenues.

   Even if revenue is unchanged, restricting output can raise profit by reducing cost. However, that conclusion raises other issues such as the administrative costs and complexities of supply control.
4. A multiple-price plan differentiating domestic and foreign markets frequently requires controls on domestic production or marketing. Such controls are difficult and expensive to administer, reduce producers' freedom, waste resources, and are inequitable among producers.

In short, second-best theory is often just that. The theory is blindly invoked to justify trade barriers just because other nations practice trade interventions. The issue of whether and to what degree the US is better off economically by erecting or maintaining trade interventions in a world of trade interventions is an empirical question addressed later.

REFERENCES

Abbott, P. and S. Haley. 1988. International trade theory and natural resource concepts. Chapter 2. *Agricultural Trade and Natural Resources.* Boulder, CO: Lynne Rienner.

Carter, Colin and Walter Gardiner, eds. 1988. *Elasticities in International Agricultural Trade.* Boulder, CO: Westview Press.

Heckscher, Eli. 1919. The effect of foreign trade on the distribution of income. *Economisk Tidskrift* 21:497-512. Reprinted in Howard Ellis and Lloyd Metzler, eds., *Readings in the Theory of International Trade.* Homewood, IL: Richard D. Irwin, 1949.

Henneberry, Shida and Luther Tweeten. December 1990. A review of international agricultural supply response. *Journal of International Food and Agribusiness Marketing* 2(3):49-68.

Houck, James. 1986. *Elements of Agricultural Trade Policies.* New York: Macmillan.

Gandolfo, Giancarlo. 1987. *International Economics I.* New York: Springer-Verlag.

Gardiner, Walter and Praveen Dixit. 1986. Price elasticity of export demand. ERS Staff Report No. AGES860408. Washington, DC: ERS, USDA.

Grennes, Thomas. 1984. *International Economics*. Englewood Cliffs, NY: Prentice-Hall.

Leontief, Wassily. September 1953. Domestic production and foreign trade: The American position re-examined. Proceedings of the American Philosophical Society. Reprinted in Richard E. Caves and Harry G. Johnson, eds., *Readings in International Economics*. Homewood, IL: Richard D. Irwin, 1968.

Markusen, J. May 1983. Factor movements and commodity trade as complements. *Journal of International Economics*, pp. 341-356.

McCalla, Alex and Timothy Josling. 1985. *Agricultural Policies and World Markets*. New York: Macmillan.

Mundell, R. June 1957. International trade and factor mobility. *American Economic Review* 48:321-335.

Ohlin, Bertil. 1933. *Interregional and International Trade*. Cambridge, MA: Harvard University Press.

Tweeten, Luther. 1967. The demand for United States farm output. *Food Research Institute Studies* 7:343-69.

Tweeten, Luther. 1989. Classical welfare analysis. Ch. 6 in *Agricultural Policy Analysis Tools for Economic Development*, Luther Tweeten, ed. Boulder, CO: Westview Press.

World Bank. 1986. *World Development Report 1986*. New York: Oxford University Press.

ANNEX TO CHAPTER 2

PROOF OF HECKSCHER-OHLIN THEOREM

Proof that prices for a given input will equalize under unrestricted commodity trade without factor shifts among countries requires the assumption that trade equalizes product prices and that production functions are homogeneous of degree one. Other assumptions are that consumers' tastes are identical and the income elasticity of demand is 1.0 for each good in each country. Demand structure and technology are identical between countries. Commodities are traded without transportation costs but inputs are not traded.

The conclusion that input prices are equalized among countries flows from rigid assumptions giving rise to three not-so-obvious propositions to be proven:

1. Equalization of product price ratios between countries also equalizes input price ratios.
2. Equal input price ratios cause input quantity ratios to be equal between countries although overall input levels and input-output ratios may differ widely.
3. Equal input quantity ratios imply equal marginal products for a given input among countries.

Annex Figure 2.1 shows initial terms of trade lines T_1 for wheat and T_2 for sugar produced from capital K and labor L in the US and Brazil respectively in isolation. The level of the isoquant for wheat production is W_o and for sugar production is S_o. With trade, the ratio of W_o to S_o in equilibrium is determined by the world price ratio between the two commodities. For example, the ratio may be 4.0 with 4 units of sugar S_o equal in value to 1 unit of wheat W_o. It is important to note that this product price ratio uniquely specifies the input price ratio. Each country faces the same input price ratio T with trade.

Before trade, the price of capital was low in the US relative to labor as indicated by the terms of trade line T_1. Before trade, the price of labor was low relative to capital in Brazil as indicated by terms of trade line T_2. Note that with trade and terms of trade T between capital and labor in both countries, the capital-labor ratio declines in the US and rises in Brazil. Without trade, as overall production expands with a given price ratio, input use expands along rays F_u and F_b respectively in the US for wheat and in Brazil for sugar. With trade, respective expansion is along F_{uT} and F_{bT} with terms of trade line T in the two countries.

The marginal rate of substitution between capital and labor as well as the marginal products of the two inputs will be equal in wheat (or sugar) for each country even if the isoquants are at very different levels in Annex Figure 2.1. To demonstrate, assume a production function for wheat W where K is capital and L is labor:

$$W = W(K,L).$$

Given first degree homogeneity, a proportional change λ in each factor results in the same proportional change in output or

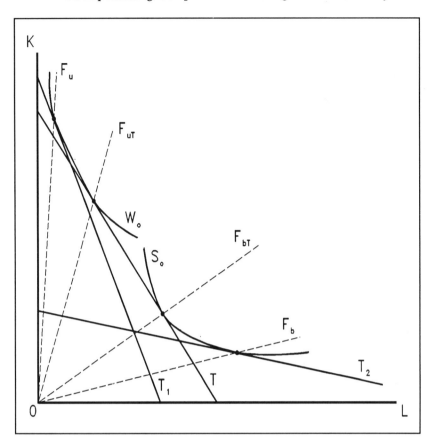

Annex Figure 2.1. Illustration of Terms of Trade Lines for Capital and Labor in the US and Brazil.

$$W(\lambda K, \lambda L) = \lambda W(K, L).$$

Such a function has the property that

$$W = LW(K/L, 1) = Lw(K/L) \tag{1}$$

and

$$W = KW(1, L/K) = Kv(L/K). \tag{2}$$

This can be illustrated for a Cobb-Douglas function:

$$W = K^\alpha L^{1-\alpha}. \tag{3}$$

Dividing by L, the result is

$$W/L = (K/L)^\alpha$$

or

$$W = L(K/L)^\alpha.$$

From (3), the marginal product of labor is

$$\frac{\partial W}{\partial L} = (1-\alpha)K^\alpha L^{-\alpha} = (1-\alpha)(K/L)^\alpha.$$

The marginal products of labor and capital are functions of the capital-labor *ratios* rather than the absolute magnitudes of L and K in the ratios.

A scale line or ray is defined as a locus of combinations of K and L for different levels of W such that

$$L/K = R$$

where R is a constant. From (1)

$$\frac{\partial W}{\partial L} = w(K/L) - w'(K/L)(K/L)$$

and from (2)

$$\frac{\partial W}{\partial K} = v(L/K) - v'(L/K)(L/K).$$

Thus the marginal products are a function of input ratios only and do not change with the absolute level of inputs used in constant proportions. The marginal product is constant along a ray.

Proof of the factor price equilibrium theorem requires the assumption that each country continues to produce both goods -- trade does not bring complete specialization. Extending the isoquants in Annex Figure 2.1, we note that with trade two countries will face the same *relative* input prices and the same relative output prices. It follows that two countries producing the same product will have the same capital-labor ratio and hence the same marginal product for L (or K) used to produce a commodity sugar S or wheat W.

Subscripts refer to the US (u) and Brazil (b). Thus the marginal products must be equal between countries producing the same product:

$$\frac{\partial W_u}{\partial L_u} = \frac{\partial W_b}{\partial L_b} \qquad\qquad \frac{\partial S_u}{\partial L_u} = \frac{\partial S_b}{\partial L_b}$$

$$\frac{\partial W_u}{\partial K_u} = \frac{\partial W_b}{\partial K_b} \qquad\qquad \frac{\partial S_u}{\partial K_u} = \frac{\partial S_b}{\partial K_b}.$$

Given that the price of wheat P_w must be equal in the US and Brazil and the price of sugar P_s must be equal in each country and that the marginal value product equals the factor price in equilibrium, it follows that

$$\frac{\partial W_u}{\partial L_u} P_w = P_{Lu} = \frac{\partial W_b}{\partial L_b} P_w = P_{Lb}$$

$$\frac{\partial S_u}{\partial L_u} P_s = P_{Lu} = \frac{\partial S_b}{\partial L_b} P_s = P_{Lb}$$

$$\frac{\partial W_u}{\partial K_u} P_w = P_{Ku} = \frac{\partial W_b}{\partial K_b} P_w = P_{Kb}$$

and

$$\frac{\partial S_u}{\partial K_u} P_s = P_{Ku} = \frac{\partial S_b}{\partial K_b} P_s = P_{Kb}.$$

Thus with trade in commodities but not in inputs the price of labor P_L is the same in the US and Brazil whether used to produce wheat or sugar. The price of capital P_K also is the same in the US and Brazil whether used to produce wheat or sugar.

CHAPTER 3

Measuring Comparative Advantage, Protection, and the Gains from Trade Liberalization

Economists have devised numerous measures of comparative (or competitive) advantage, gains from freer trade, and losses from market distortions. The purpose of this chapter is to review some of these measures. Four widely used measures from least to most comprehensive are (1) nominal protection coefficient, (2) effective protection coefficient, (3) producer (and consumer) subsidy equivalent, and (4) classical welfare analysis. Domestic resource cost coefficients, often used to measure comparative advantage, are closely related to effective protection coefficients and hence also are presented in this chapter.

POLICY INTERVENTIONS

All governments intervene in agricultural markets. Reasons include raising tax revenue, supporting producers' income, reducing consumers' food costs, attaining self-sufficiency, or countering interventions of other governments. Policy instruments for interventions are numerous; several are listed in Table 3.1. Some policies such as provision of agricultural research, extension, infrastructure, environmental protection, grades, and sanitation standards have favorable benefit-cost ratios and are considered acceptable in world trade policy forums. (Exceptions include some types of sanitation standards which in fact are disguised trade barriers.) Other policies such as export subsidies are condemned. Commodity programs designed to reduce food costs or raise farm income often inadvertently influence trade.

The wide variety of interventions makes measuring their magnitude, impact, and the gains from trade liberalization a formidable task. That will be apparent in the following sections. The long list of policies in Table 3.1 highlights that liberalization to obtain the full gains from trade cannot stop with export subsidies, taxes, and quotas, but also must extend to domestic commodity and macroeconomic policies.

NOMINAL PROTECTION COEFFICIENT

The *nominal protection coefficient* (NPC) of a commodity i is defined as the ratio of its domestic producer price P_d to its border price P_b

$$NPC_i = \frac{P_{di}}{P_{bi}}$$

where

NPC_i = nominal protection coefficient for the ith commodity in a given country

Table 3.1. Examples of Policies Influencing Competitiveness and Trade.

Direct Trade Intervention
- Tariffs and taxes
- Import and export quotas
- Export subsidies

Controlled Exchange Rates
- Fixed rates
- Differential rates
- Crawling-peg rates
- Exchange controls, licenses

Other Macroeconomic Variable Distortions
- Interest rates
- Wage rates
- Inflation rates

Market Price Support
- Domestic price supports linked with border measures (quotas, permits, tariffs, variable levies, and export restitutions)
- Two-price systems and home consumption schemes
- Price premiums (often used for fluid milk)
- Domestic price supports linked with production quotas
- Government inventory and commodity loan activities
- Marketing board price stabilization policies
- State trading operations

Commodity Programs
- Direct payments -- deficiency, disaster, payment-in-kind (PIK) entitlements, stabilization payments
- Producer co-responsibility levies (taxes on commodity to pay for surplus disposal)
- Supply control -- marketing quota, acreage diversion, land retirement
- Storage programs

Programs Affecting Marketing of Commodities
- Transportation subsidies
- Marketing and promotion programs
- Inspection services

Programs Affecting Variable Costs of Production
- Fertilizer subsidies
- Fuel tax exemptions
- Concessional domestic credit for production loans
- Irrigation subsidies
- Crop insurance

Programs Affecting Long-Term Agricultural Production
- Research and extension services
- Conservation, environmental, and natural resource programs
- Structural programs to adjust farm size and numbers
- Infrastructure -- roads, ports, etc.

P_{di} = *domestic price* of the ith commodity at the producer or wholesale level

P_{bi} = *border price* of the ith commodity at the same market location as the domestic price, with the border price being its international trade or world price times the rate of exchange. The border price is the world price less all resource costs such as transportation, insurance, and spoilage to the local market in question and corrected for distortions in exchange rates, taxes, subsidies, etc. The border price would be exactly the same as the local price in the absence of market distortions.

In general, the higher the NPC the greater the degree of protection provided to domestic industry and the greater the market distortion.

The NPC can be illustrated with an example of an import tax or export subsidy. International trade prices are often measured in dollars. Suppose the exchange rate is 20 shillings (sh) per dollar, the small-country assumption applies, and the cif (cost, insurance, freight) import border price of coffee is $1 per unit or sh 20 per unit. A 10 percent ad valorem import tax (tariff) raises the domestic price to sh 22 per pound. The nominal protection coefficient is then

$$NPC = \frac{P_d}{P_b} = \frac{22}{20} = 1.10.$$

The *nominal protection rate* (NPR), a form of the NPC, is the percentage by which the domestic price exceeds the border price. It can be expressed as

$$NPR = 100(NPC-1)$$

and in the above example is

$$NPR = 100(1.10-1) = 10 \ percent.$$

Quotas, subsidies, and other measures in addition to tariffs can drive a wedge between border and domestic prices. NPR is a means to convert such measures to a tariff-equivalent rate.

Where policy brings a major change in production, consumption, or trade, the macroeconomic impacts need to be considered. With the *small-country assumption*, changes within the country are so small in relation to world markets that impacts on *border* (world) price can be ignored. With the *large-country assumption*, changes within a given country can change border price. Under the large-country assumption, the appropriate border price for an import is the marginal import price (MIP) equal to the cif (cost plus insurance and freight) import price P_m times $(1 + 1/E_m)$ or

$$MIP = \left(1+\frac{1}{E_m}\right)P_m$$

where E_m is the import supply elasticity. For a small country, the term in parentheses will be 1.0 because import supply is infinitely elastic.

Under the large-country assumption, the appropriate border price for an export is the marginal export revenue (MER) equal to the fob (free on board) export price P_x times $(1 + 1/E_x)$ or

$$MER = \left(1 + \frac{1}{E_x}\right) P_x$$

where E_x is the export elasticity of demand. If import supply and export demand are perfectly elastic, $MIP = P_m$ and $MER = P_x$, the border prices.

Border prices are taken to be efficient prices because they are opportunity costs. In a well functioning market, fewer national resources will be required to import a commodity than to produce it at home if its border price is below the domestic price. Real national income will be higher by importing. If its border price exceeds the domestic price, a commodity can be exported and the proceeds used to purchase desired imports -- all at a savings in national resources. The border price is an efficient price because forcing a higher commodity price costs consumers more than producers gain. And a market intervention to force a commodity price below the border price costs producers more than consumers gain, hence full national income is reduced.

Similar reasoning applies to inputs. The border price is the opportunity cost of the input. Distortions causing domestic input prices to deviate from border prices reduce national income.

Empirical estimates of NPCs for several countries (or groupings) show that the United States had less distorted domestic agricultural prices relative to border prices than did other industrial countries on average for the 1980-82 period and 1988 (Table 3.2). The ratio of domestic to border prices of agricultural commodities in 1988 averaged 1.5 or 150 percent for the United States (50 percent protection rate) and 2.0 or 200 percent for all industrial countries. NPCs increased from 1980-82 to 1986 because world prices fell while supports changed little.

Tyers and Anderson, who compiled the estimates in Table 3.2, counted the target price, which is used to set a direct deficiency payment to producers, as part of the domestic price. However, the actual domestic *market* price that farmers receive does not include the target price. The border price in the United States is very close to the domestic market price but differs slightly because of modest export subsidies on several farm commodities.

The issue is whether Tyers and Anderson were correct to include direct payments (the target price) in domestic price. If direct payments are *decoupled* from incentives so that they do not influence production, consumption, and trade, then to include them in NPCs is incorrect because they do not distort trade and do not protect domestic farmers from international competition. The truth is that the target price is neither a fully decoupled nor a fully coupled (production incentive) supply price. The purpose here is not to resolve whether the US target price is decoupled but to note the importance of concepts and assumptions in measuring NPC -- some of which are noted below.

Border Price

The relevance of the border price as an efficiency standard and opportunity cost in calculating the NPC and other measures may not be obvious. As noted above, the border price is the international trade price converted into a country's currency -- usually at the official exchange rate. Sometimes an open-market equilibrium exchange rate which is variously called the *parallel* or *shadow* exchange rate, is employed.

Table 3.2. Nominal Protection Coefficients Measuring the Effect of Agricultural Programs on Domestic Farm Prices, 1980-82 Average and 1988.

	United States		EC		Japan		All Industrial Economies	
	1980-82	1988	1980-82	1988	1980-82	1988	1980-82	1988
Wheat	1.15	2.20	1.40	3.40	3.90	8.00	1.25	2.45
Coarse Grains	1.00	1.60	1.40	2.40	4.30	11.65	1.15	1.75
Rice	1.30	1.85	1.35	2.40	3.35	8.20	2.50	5.65
Beef and Veal	1.10	1.30	1.95	2.75	2.80	5.40	1.50	2.05
Pork and Poultry	1.00	1.00	1.25	1.60	1.50	1.90	1.20	1.40
Dairy	2.00	2.20	1.75	2.50	2.90	5.55	1.90	2.55
Sugar	1.40	2.05	1.50	2.80	3.00	7.10	1.50	2.60
Weighted Avg., All Commodities	1.20	1.50	1.55	2.25	2.35	3.80	1.40	2.00

Source: Tyers and Anderson, p. 204.

The border price relevant to a particular producers' market A in the case of an import is the cif minimum delivery price at the nearest port plus additional transport and other costs to market A. This is the price to be paid by locals for the imported good at market A in the absence of market distortions by the importing country.

In the case of an export, the border price is the fob maximum price available at the nearest port less transport and other marketing costs of getting the commodity to the port from point A. That price can be received by locals selling in the world market in the absence of market distortions by the exporting country.

Producer groups in a country strongly object to border prices as indicators of efficient prices when other countries "distort" border prices by subsidies or other "dumping" devices. *Dumping* is selling a product abroad at a lower price than it is sold at home.[1] Sometimes dumping is defined as selling abroad at less than the domestic cost of producing the product. But from the standpoint of the United States, for example, it does not matter for efficiency whether a low import price of cheese arises from foreign export subsidies or from foreign comparative advantage in cheese production. The border price remains the opportunity cost to the US -- any intervention to distort that price will lose real national income. National income is maximized by importing at prices subsidized by other countries and then adjusting displaced domestic workers to higher-payoff industries. Some of the savings from importing "dumped" merchandise can be used to compensate displaced workers so no one is worse off.

A legitimate efficiency and equity concern is whether the border price is transitory. It is inefficient (and some would say cruel to workers) to shut down and then gear up a

---

[1]So called "weak form" dumping is selling abroad at below average production cost, a practice that can raise profit. So called "strong form" dumping is selling abroad below marginal cost of production. The latter dumping is not justified by profit seeking. It is not possible for trade officials to determine exactly what costs are marginal and what constitutes profit in the short and long run.

domestic cheese or soybean industry in response to transitory world price shifts. Hence border prices used to measure protection or to plan future production ordinarily should be based on a moving average or trend that ignores short-term price aberrations.

In judging *global* economic costs from trade distortions, the approach is different. In measuring global losses from distortions, dumping or other deviations from efficient pricing and output need to be considered jointly and set at zero for all countries. Modern international trade models accommodate such simultaneous, interdependent systems.

Welfare Impact of Dumping on World Markets

Figure 3.1 employs classical welfare analysis to demonstrate gains to the rest of the world when one country decides to dump exports in world markets. Assume a country reduces prices from an original equilibrium at P_b to price P_b' because it adopts improved technology, enhancing comparative advantage, or because it subsidizes exports. First assume "country A" is the rest of the world (ROW) in Figure 3.1 -- it must be an importer because the dumping country C (not shown) is an exporter. Domestic production in ROW falls from Q_p to Q_p', consumption increases from Q_c to Q_c', and imports increase from $Q_c - Q_p$ to $Q_c' - Q_p'$ when price falls given supply S and demand D in ROW.

Welfare impacts on ROW are as follows:

Gain to consumers	$a+b+c+d$
Gain to producers	$-a$
Net social gain	$b+c+d$

Because consumers gain more than producers lose, ROW gains national income when C dumps. If producers protest and receive tariff protection to maintain price P_b with a tariff $P_b - P_b'$, welfare impacts compared to price at P_b' are as follows:

Gain to consumers	$-a-b-c-d$
Gain to producers	a
Gain to government (tariff revenue)	c
Net social gain	$-b-d$

In short, ROW gains $b+c+d$ from dumping by country C. An attempt to restore producers' income with a tariff reduces overall gain by $b+d$ to ROW from being dumped on. It would appear that a wise choice would be to provide a purer transfer than by tariff to compensate producers in ROW for losses. An alternative is a special program of mobility assistance helping producers adjust their resources to uses more valued by society.

Now assume ROW is divided into two categories -- country A a net importer and country B a net exporter of the commodity dumped by C. In country A, impacts are as described for ROW above. In country B, a net exporter competing with C, the fall in world prices increases consumer surplus by area $1+2$ and decreases producer surplus by $1+2+3$ for a net social loss of area 3. Thus exporting country B loses from dumping by country C. An example is the US incurring losses from wheat exports subsidized by the European Community.

Suppose exporting country B retaliates by subsidizing exports to restore the former level $q_p - q_c$ compared to $q_p' - q_c'$ after border prices fall from P_b to P_b'. Welfare results from domestic intervention are as follows compared to a domestic open market:

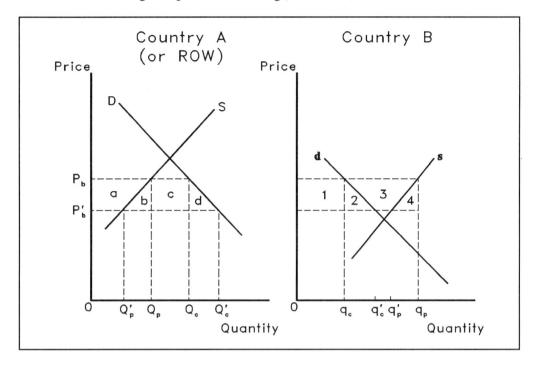

Figure 3.1. Impact of Reducing the Border Price from P_b to P_b'.

Gain to producers	$1+2+3$
Gain to consumers	$-1-2$
Cost to taxpayers (export subsidy)	$-2-3-4$
Net social gain	$-2-4$

The net social cost in foregone full income of country B is $2+4$ because it intervenes to shield its producers from losses imposed by C's dumping. Thus country B worsens an already unfortunate situation by retaliation. Of course, country B just might force country C to rescind its price decrease. And it is possible that marginal utility of income of producers is sufficiently high compared to that of taxpayers and consumers so that national well-being is increased by market interventions expanding deadweight losses while transferring income to producers.

Excluding country C from the calculation because it presumably judged that dumping made it better off, success of country B in rescinding C's price decrease likely would reduce welfare in country A by more than the gain in B so the world would be worse off by an end to dumping. The conclusion follows because A's imports must exceed B's exports and because deadweight loss $2+4$ in Figure 3.1 is difficult to avoid. The implication is that country A could afford to compensate country B for avoiding a confrontation with C to stop the dumping.

EXCHANGE RATE DISTORTION

The official exchange rate may not be a realistic measure of the real domestic value of foreign currency in measuring NPCs. Overvalued exchange rates are found frequently among developing countries because they delay adjusting nominal exchange rates in the face of inflation in excess of that of trading partners.

An overvalued currency is an implicit tax on exports and a subsidy to imports (see Chapter 6). Because agriculture is often a net exporter, the industry is disadvantaged by an overvalued currency. The *nominal protection coefficient* for commodity i is

$$NPC_i = \frac{P_{di}}{P_{bi}^{\$} OER}$$

where OER is the *official exchange rate*, P_{di} is domestic price in local currency, and $P_{bi}^{\$}$ is border price in dollars. Adjusted to the *shadow, parallel*, or *accounting exchange rate* (SER) as is necessary where currency value is distorted, the formula is

$$NPC_i = \frac{P_{di}}{P_{bi}^{\$} SER}.$$

In local currency (shillings) for the border price, the nominal protection coefficient is

$$NPC_i' = \frac{P_{di}}{P_{bi}^{sh}(SER/OER)}$$

or

$$NPC_i' = \left(\frac{P_{di}}{P_{bi}^{sh}}\right)\left(\frac{OER}{SER}\right)$$

where P_{bi}^{sh} is the border price expressed in shillings and is equal to $P_{bi}^{\$}$ x OER.

Suppose the official exchange rate is sh 40 per dollar but the shadow exchange rate is sh 50 per dollar. The shilling is said to be overvalued at the OER because a dollar will purchase too few domestic goods (resources) for foreign buyers to purchase enough domestic goods and services to supply dollars equal to the demand quantity of foreign exchange at a market clearing rate.

Using the earlier example of a 10 percent ad valorem import tax on an item costing sh 20, the NPC was 1.10. The nominal protection coefficient adjusted for the SER is

$$NPC'_i = \left(\frac{22}{20}\right)\left(\frac{40}{50}\right) = .88.$$

The overvalued currency more than offsets the 10 percent import tax so that the nominal protection coefficient for the domestic coffee producing industry is lowered to 0.88 and the nominal protection rate is -12 percent, an implicit tax on the exports of the industry.

Most developed countries use floating or moving peg exchange rates to keep OER and SER closely aligned. Developing countries are far less successful in avoiding overvalued currency. Thus measures of trade distortions in developing countries must consider SER. Estimating SER can be illusive; various ad hoc approaches have been proposed.

The most common procedure is to observe the parallel market exchange rate. Most developing countries will have private merchants who serve as middlepersons finding an exchange rate equating supply (from foreign tourists, local exporters, and domestic laborers working abroad bringing hard foreign currency to the market) and demand (from importers and from locals intending to travel abroad or seeking to protect savings from domestic inflation). Shadow exchange rate estimates are published or observed in the market. A problem is that the observed measure is the disequilibrium rate SER′ rather than the desired equilibrium exchange rate SER as shown in Figure 3.2.

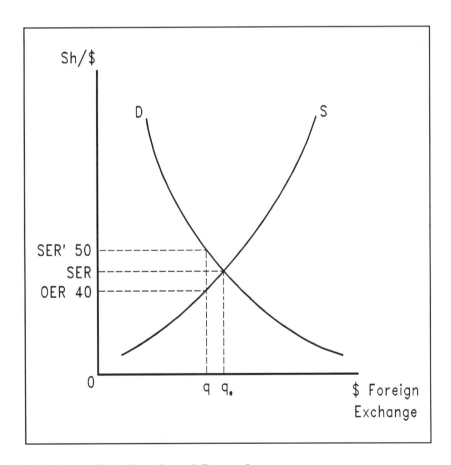

Figure 3.2. Exchange Rate Supply and Demand.

Assume that at the official exchange rate of sh 40/$ the demand quantity falls short of supply. Price in the parallel market is sh 50/$ but it is not an equilibrium because many transactions must be at the official rate and because numerous other factors impede trade in currency including illegality of such activities in many countries.

A second general approach is to compute the equilibrium exchange rate SER in Figure 3.2 from observable data on SER´ and exchange quantity q. Alternatives for doing so include calculation from a general equilibrium macroeconomic model available for some countries. Such calculation is not often possible so an option is to estimate SER from a partial equilibrium model which requires knowledge of the slopes or elasticities of S and D in Figure 3.2. Bela Balassa (see Appleyard, pp. 76, 77) has suggested the formula

$$SER = OER \times \frac{\sum_i E_{mi}(M_i + T_{mi}) + \sum_j E_{xj}(X_j - T_{xj})}{\sum_i M_i + \sum_j X_j}$$

where
M_i = value of imports of good i
T_{mi} = net value of taxes on imports of i
E_{mi} = elasticity of import demand for i
X_j = value of exports of good j
T_{xj} = net value of taxes on exports of good j
E_{xj} = elasticity of export supply of j.

This approach corrects for the impact of border tax and subsidy distortions on the exchange rate. The approach does not account for existing disequilibrium between SER´ and OER as apparent in parallel markets. Also, reliable estimates of exchange market supply and demand elasticities are rarely available.

Sometimes unitary elasticities heroically are assumed so the formula with aggregated sums resolves to

$$SER = OER \frac{[(M + T_m) + (X - T_x)]}{M + X}.$$

This adjustment (or better, with the previous formula for SER) for terminating taxes and subsidies may be combined with the parallel market rate to estimate SER with full adjustment to equilibrium.

In many instances, for lack of an alternative, the parallel market rate will be the best estimate of an equilibrium exchange rate. Inflation is likely to be prominent with devaluation because import prices rise directly and domestic prices rise indirectly from greater foreign demand for exports. The result of greater inflation at home than abroad is to raise the parallel market exchange rate from sh 50/$ to (say) sh 60/$. Corrected by the ratio of the increases in general price level gains in the home country to that of trading partners, the real exchange rate may not change much with nominal devaluation.

EFFECTIVE PROTECTION COEFFICIENT

The *effective protection coefficient* (EPC) is the ratio of actual value added by domestic resources (land, labor, management, durable capital) to value added in a well functioning market free of distortions. Compared to NPC as a measure of trade distortions, an advantage is that EPC includes taxes and subsidies on *inputs* as well as on outputs. The formula is

$$EPC_i = \frac{P_{di} - \sum\limits_{j=1}^{k} a_{ij} P_{dj}}{P_{bi} - \sum\limits_{j=1}^{k} a_{ij} P_{bj}}$$

where
a_{ij} = quantity of the jth traded input (j = 1,2...k)
   used to produce one unit of output i
$P_{di(j)}$ = domestic price of output i (or input j)
$P_{bi(j)}$ = border price of output i (or input j).

An important issue in calculating EPC is which inputs to include in j = 1,2,...k and which to exclude. The value added is the return to excluded inputs.

The distinction is between traded and nontraded inputs, a classification that pervades much of international trade literature. *Traded inputs* in the EPC formula refer to inputs or goods that are potentially traded across the border whether or not they are actually traded. *Nontraded (fixed) inputs* usually include land, fixed capital such as drainage and irrigation systems, and labor -- inputs immobile across borders. Although labor generally is treated as nontraded, in some small countries (such as in the Middle East) a major share of labor is temporarily imported or exported and hence is tradable.

Whether a good is traded or nontraded depends partly on location. *A good is classified as nontraded in a particular location if it pays to produce it but it doesn't pay to import or export the good.* The *accounting price* of the nontraded good is the quantity of inputs required to produce it times *accounting* input prices established by their value in producing traded goods. This commodity price will lie between the export and import price.

Sometimes a distinction is made between financial and economic prices. *Financial prices* are actual market prices and are also called domestic prices. *Economic prices* are border prices of traded inputs or outputs and accounting prices of nontraded inputs or outputs. Economic prices are those that would prevail in a well-functioning market.

The EPC can be illustrated with an example. Suppose the border price of coffee is sh 100 per kilo. Each kilo of coffee production requires tradable input 1 of a_{c1} = 2 units at border price P_{b1} = sh 20 per unit and input 2 of a_{c2} = 5 units at border price P_{b2} = sh 4 per unit. Thus the border price value added is

$$sh\ 100 - 2\,(sh\ 20) - 5\,(sh\ 4) = sh\ 40,$$

the denominator in computing EPC.

Suppose to protect the local industry the import tariff is 20 percent on coffee (t_c) and 10 percent on inputs (t_j). The numerator in computing EPC is

$$sh\ 100(1 + t_c) - 2(sh\ 20)(1 + t_1) - 5(sh\ 4)(1 + t_2)$$
$$= sh\ 100(1.20) - 2(sh\ 20)(1.10) - 5(sh\ 4)(1.10)$$
$$= sh\ 120 - sh\ 66 = sh\ 54$$

so that

$$EPC = \frac{54}{40} = 1.35.$$

The *effective protection rate* (EPR) is 100(EPC - 1) = 35 percent. Tariffs on imports of commodities and inputs increased returns to domestic factors of production by 35 percent. This contrasts with a NPC of 1.20 and an NPR of 20 percent.

In local currency, each price in the denominator of EPC is multiplied by SER/OER. If the currency is overvalued 25 percent so the ratio of the shadow exchange rate SER (sh/$) to the official exchange rate is 1.25, then the denominator or valued added at domestic prices is sh 40 (1.25) = sh 50. The effective protection coefficient adjusted for overvalued currency is

$$EPC' = \frac{54}{40(1.25)} = \frac{54}{50} = 1.08 = EPC\ \frac{OER}{SER}.$$

The effective protection coefficient is reduced to 1.08 by an overvalued currency and the effective protection rate is reduced to 8 percent. Cheap imports of inputs and outputs competing with domestic production reduce economic protection of domestic resources.

The presumption in the above calculation is that the commodity is produced domestically or imported. On the average, third-world countries are net exporters of farm products. An overvalued currency as a tax on exports and subsidy on imports makes them worse off in net because product exports exceed input imports. The problem is intensified because producers often do not gain from presumably cheap imports under an overvalued currency. The reason is that overvalued currency means foreign exchange shortage and hence imported input shortage. The importer, who is usually not the producer, collects the economic rent made possible by importing cheaply and selling dearly to input-short farmers.

Table 3.3 shows nominal and effective protection coefficients for selected commodities in seven relatively low-income countries. Most coefficients are less than 1.0, indicating agricultural commodities are being taxed. The same pattern was found in a more recent World Bank study (p. 64). Out of 90 observations of NPCs for 12 commodities in low-income countries, 66 percent were less than unity indicating a tax on agriculture, 24 percent exceeded unity indicating a subsidy to agriculture, and only 10 percent were unity indicating no net market intervention. On the other hand, studies of developed countries indicate a consistent pattern of NPCs (and EPCs) exceeding 1.0 as noted earlier, indicating subsidies to agriculture.

Several concluding observations are noted:

1. Input or output subsidies and taxes can be included in calculating the EPC.
2. The numerator -- value added at domestic prices -- of EPC can be computed (a) directly from domestic prices or (b) from border prices adjusted for tariffs, subsidies, and other interventions. The two procedures ordinarily will not give the same result because market forces work to offset the observed impact of interventions on prices.
3. The effective protection coefficient is highly sensitive to error or arbitrary assumptions used to classify inputs into tradables and nontradables. Enterprise budgets used to calculate the EPC are inexact, especially in developing countries. NPCs and EPCs are often more reliable indicators of *rankings* among commodities than of absolute levels of protection.

Table 3.3. Nominal and Effective Protection Coefficients for Selected Countries and Commodities.

Country/Commodity	NPC	EPC
Argentina		
Wheat	.54	.51
Maize	.58	.57
Beef	.69	.64
Egypt		
Rice	.37	.38
Cotton	.43	.43
Wheat	.57	.68
Kenya		
Maize	.96	.92
Coffee	.94	.88
Beef	.76	.64
Pakistan		
Wheat	.84	.80
Cotton	.68	.67
Rice	.75	.74
Sugarcane	.68	.67
Portugal		
Wheat	.84	.75
Olive Oil	.78	.64
Maize	1.20	1.27
Beef	1.75	.45
Rice	.70	.64
Thailand		
Sugarcane	1.19	1.24
Rubber	.77	1.03
Yugoslavia		
Wheat	.69	.59
Maize	.78	.63
Beef	1.21	.41
Pork	.93	1.71

Source: Scandizzo and Bruce, p. 36.

DOMESTIC RESOURCE COSTS:
MEASURING COMPARATIVE ADVANTAGE

We digress briefly from measuring policy interventions in agriculture to measuring comparative advantage of a commodity in an economy characterized by policy interventions. The procedure is to estimate the *domestic resource cost coefficient* (DRC), a concept originated by Bruno and closely related to the EPC, the ratio of value added in domestic prices to value added in border prices. In fact, in a well-functioning market in the absence of interventions, the two concepts are the same and EPC = DRC = 1.0.

The DRC measures the real domestic resource cost required to save (import substitution) or earn (export) a unit of foreign exchange. The denominator is the same for EPC and DRC. In simplified notation, the numerator of EPC is value added V per unit of output; that is, price P less costs of traded inputs C_T so $V = P - C_T$. V is the cost of nontraded (fixed) inputs in equilibrium at accounting prices -- the numerator in DRC.

In short, the denominators of EPC and DRC are the same but the numerator of EPC is computed as the residual return to nontraded inputs while the numerator of DRC is computed as the actual cost of nontraded inputs. Nontraded input cost and residual return are equal only in a well-functioning market.

The formula for DRC is

$$DRC_i = \frac{\displaystyle\sum_{j=k+1}^{n} a_{ij}P_{dj}}{P_{bi} - \displaystyle\sum_{j=1}^{k} a_{ij}P_{bj}}$$

where the denominator and its variables were defined earlier for EPC and P_{dj} is the domestic accounting price or opportunity cost of domestic resource j.

Data on nontraded inputs a_{ij} used to produce a unit of a commodity i can be obtained from enterprise budgets. The numerator and denominator must be of the same units. DRC's are usually calculated from enterprise budgets expressed per hectare, per ton, or per kilogram, but the DRC is invariant to choice of unit as long as it is used consistently.

A major challenge is to determine the appropriate accounting price P_{dj} to charge for nontraded land, labor, and capital inputs $k+1, k+2, ... n$. The opportunity cost per unit of domestic labor, land, and other nontradable inputs is sought. It is the return to the respective resources in their best alternative use. This may be the rent per unit for land and the wage for similar type labor in nonfarm employment -- with appropriate adjustments to remove effects of economic distortions such as taxes, quotas, or subsidies. Irrigation structure overhead can be charged based on amortized cost of construction and operation and prorated (along with costs of operation and maintenance) to crops. In many countries water is one of the most limiting resources but irrigation water is unpriced or underpriced. The numerator in DRC may be calculated with a charge for irrigation water derived from a linear programming shadow price or other source.

Suppose the denominator for DRC_i , product price less traded input cost at border prices, is found to be $1 per kilo of the commodity. Suppose also that the domestic resource cost of producing that kilo is sh 30. The DRC is then 30/1 = sh 30. If the shadow exchange rate is sh 40, that means that only sh 30 are required to generate (or save) sh 40 of foreign exchange, so the commodity enjoys a comparative advantage. If sh 50 had been required to produce a kilo, the DRC would have exceeded the exchange rate and the commodity would be cheaper to import than produce with domestic resources.

Ordinarily, both the numerator and denominator are expressed in local currency, preferably in SER terms. Then a DRC less than 1.0 indicates comparative advantage; a ratio greater than 1.0 indicates comparative disadvantage. Because a country will optimally export those commodities for which its DRCs are lowest, it follows that the value added or return to nontradable fixed resources is being maximized -- the inverse of the DRC.

In fact, the value added per unit of nontraded (fixed) resources, called the *competitiveness coefficient* (CC), is conceptually equivalent but is operationally preferred to the DRC for two main reasons:

1. It is intuitively appealing. It makes sense to emphasize enterprises with the highest return to fixed resources to maximize full national income. Of course, CC = 1/DRC, so the two concepts are equivalent.

2. It is easily interpreted. The CC is consistently higher for commodities with higher comparative advantage. In contrast, the DRC is discontinuous, going from a small negative value to minus infinity and then from positive infinity to a small positive value for commodities with ever greater comparative advantage.

      The domestic resource cost coefficients and competitiveness indices for American farm commodities were computed by Tweeten and Pai based on assumptions that (1) only the US liberalized and (2) the world including the US removed all trade distorting measures, including farm commodity programs. If just the US liberalized, the nation's comparative advantage is estimated to be strong in soybeans and cattle -- the latter helped by lower grain prices. If the whole world liberalized trade, the US comparative advantage is in soybeans, grains, hogs, and cattle.

      Bucyanayandi *et al.* provide an example of CC applied to Uganda. Excellent examples of the DRC calculation are found in Appleyard (see also Bucyanayandi *et al.*; Jiron *et al.*; Scandizzo and Bruce; Tsukok; and Tweeten *et al.*). Table 3.4 provides an example of DRC calculation by Appleyard for rice in Pakistan. The table contains several

Table 3.4. Example of DRC Calculations, Basmati Rice, Punjab, All Farms, 1982-83, SER Basis, per Acre.

Item	Rs
1. Bullock capital	32.07
2. Labor for bullocks	27.12
3. Tractor labor	19.09
4. Seed (valued at international farmgate price)	31.83
5. Labor for nursery preparation	20.27
6. Additional nursery expenses	9.07
7. Labor for transplanting	92.18
8. Labor for irrigation	86.04
9. Labor for cleaning of water courses, etc.	11.59
10. Canal irrigation labor equivalent	26.32
11. Canal irrigation capital equivalent	75.70
12. Labor component associated with tubewell operations	71.27
13. Capital component associated with tubewell operations	205.00
14. Labor for weeding	16.01
15. Farmyard management cost	8.67
16. Harvesting costs (valued at international farmgate price)	547.94
17. Land rent	293.80
18. Management	54.00
19. International value of tradable inputs	748.44
20. Domestic resource cost per acre (sum of 1-18)	1,627.97
21. Domestic resource cost per 40 kg (20 ÷ yield)	76.11
22. Value added at border prices (SER)	198.42
23. DRC coefficient (21 ÷ 22)	0.38

Source: Appleyard, p. 100.

categories of nontradable labor, fixed capital, and land. Capital inputs used in the production process are adjusted to the shadow exchange rate SER. The DRC of 0.38 indicates comparative advantage; only Rs 0.38 are required to generate or save Rs 1 of foreign exchange by producing Basmati rice.

Domestic resource costs coefficients can be computed for numerous commodities and resource situations in a country. However, it is very difficult, for example, to account for opportunity costs and availability of operator and family labor and of irrigation water by season. Thus *linear programming* of representative resource situations utilizing appropriate resource constraints and accounting prices for nontradables and border prices for tradables is recommended as a superior methodology. Epplin and Stoecker, Hazel and Norton, and Epplin and Li provide examples of methods and results. Epplin and Li found for Liberia that with typical farm resources 27 cents of tree crop exports were sacrificed to produce a pound of rice, the staple, which could be imported for 9 cents per pound. Comparative advantage was in tree crops and the government was subsidizing rice production at a substantial cost in lost national income. The rice subsidization program was scaled back as the real cost became obvious.

PRODUCER AND CONSUMER SUBSIDY EQUIVALENTS

Where the focus is on measuring protection from world markets provided to local producers by tariffs and other border policies that only directly influence commodity price, the nominal protection coefficient is a convenient and adequate measure. The effective protection coefficient goes farther to record also the impact of protection policies that directly influence input prices of the commodity in question.

However, neither the NPC nor EPC is adequate for including the wide range of policies such as those listed in Table 3.1 that influence agriculture. The *producer subsidy equivalent* (PSE) and the *consumer subsidy equivalent* (CSE) are flexible and easily computed measures of all domestic policy transfers to producers and consumers. The PSE, unlike the EPC, can readily accommodate the cross effects such as the influence on the beef PSE of policy interventions in corn production. Producer subsidy equivalent often is expressed as a percent of gross value of farm production; consumer subsidy equivalent often is expressed as a percent of food cost.

Although the PSE/CSE can be used to express in a single number the aggregate effects of numerous government subsidies and restrictions, a unique feature is detailed listings of the contribution of individual policies. The PSE shows the subsidy equivalent needed to compensate producers for termination of commodity programs, tariffs, quotas, and other supports. The subsidy equivalent is calculated by (1) the sum of direct payments to farmers and (2) the policy intervention price wedge (caused by a tariff, tax, or quota) equal to the difference between the domestic price and the international price.

Policies reflected in the PSE obviously have the potential to influence trade volume, but it is not possible to interpret a PSE solely as a measure of protection. For example, two countries with the same PSE and size of agriculture will have a very different impact on trade if one country's instrument to raise farm income is to subsidize exports while another country's instrument is payments to cut production. PSE estimates provide rich detail on sources of domestic subsidies measured in policy transfers and could be converted crudely to tariff equivalents to measure trade effects similar to the EPC. PSE includes decoupled domestic direct payments that are not included in EPCs because they presumably do not influence trade. However, because PSEs and EPCs are not strictly comparable and serve different purposes, it is not fruitful to contend that one measure is uniquely superior to the other.

The EPC and PSE are variants of what is more generally called *aggregate measures of support* (AMS) in international trade discourse. Clearly, the need is great for an improved AMS that will more accurately measure trade distortion from policy interventions (for a more complete discussion see Bredahl). An improved AMS would exclude efficient policies such as research to raise productivity. By excluding programs with favorable social benefit-cost ratios, the remaining AMS is designed to be a single target to reduce through trade negotiations.

Timothy Josling first proposed the PSE/CSE concept as part of a Food and Agriculture Organization of the United Nations (FAO) study on international agricultural adjustments. For lack of a better AMS, the concept has been especially useful in multilateral trade negotiations where dealing with dozens of policies individually is impossible. It is easier to negotiate a reduction in one aggregate measure such as PSE. One proposal is that countries reduce the rate of income support provided by government policies to agriculture (as measured by the PSE) at a prescribed rate of (say) 5 percent per year for 10 years. The proposal would also specify that less trade distorting policies (such as a payment decoupled from output) could be substituted for a more trade distorting policy such as an export subsidy. Another option is for countries first to convert a given PSE to decoupled payments and tariffs (*tariffication*), then reduce these over time through multilateral trade negotiations.

The FAO, the Organization for Economic Cooperation and Development (OECD), and Economic Research Service of the US Department of Agriculture (USDA) have estimated PSEs and CSEs for a number of commodities. The arbitrary nature of policy coverage in PSEs is apparent from Table 3.5. The PSE/CSE OECD and USDA coverage is more comprehensive than FAO coverage, and results from the former two agencies are somewhat comparable.

Table 3.5. Comparison of Policy Coverage, PSE Studies.

FAO	OECD	USDA
Policies Included		
Market price support	Market price support	Market price support
Deficiency payments	Direct income support	Direct income support
Input subsidies	Indirect income support	Input policies
Storage subsidies	Extension and research	Extension and research
Transport subsidies	Structural policies	Structural policies
	Taxation concessions	Marketing subsidies
	Sub-national measures	Controlled exchange rates
Policies Excluded		
Administrative costs	Administrative costs	Administrative costs
Income subsidies	Social security benefits	Social security benefits
Acreage control		
Extension and research		
Structural policies		
Social security benefits		

Source: Josling and Tangerman, p. 7.

Table 3.6 shows transfers to US farm producers by policy source from 1982 to 1986. Total value of transfers ranged from $19.2 billion in 1982 to $36.9 billion in 1986, for a total PSE averaging 25 percent of the value of farm commodities to producers from 1982 to 1986. PSEs increased in the 1980s as excess production capacity increased and world prices fell.

Producer subsidy equivalents have been larger in Japan and the European Community than in the United States (Figure 3.3). In Japan, a payment equal to 79 percent of farm income in 1986 would have been needed to compensate for termination of actual supports. Of the major industrial nations, New Zealand and Australia rank lowest in income support of agriculture.

The source of subsidies to producers vary by country. The proportion of PSE contributed by consumers ranges from a high of 85 percent in the EC-10 and 75 percent in Japan to 43 percent in Canada and 37 percent in the US. The remainder comes from taxpayers.

Table 3.6. Producer Subsidy Equivalents by Policy, United States, 1982-86.

Item	1982	1983	1984	1985	1986	1982-86 Average
	($ Million of Policy Transfers)					
Direct Payments/Levies	2,039.8	11,673.7	4,201.2	7,083.2	14,161.8	7,831.9
Disaster	16.3	0.6	0.0	0.0	0.0	3.4
Deficiency	1,158.8	1,050.5	3,285.3	4,781.8	11,262.8	4,307.8
Diversion	0.0	1,364.2	505.5	741.1	368.4	595.8
Storage	970.5	506.8	349.2	397.7	584.2	561.7
PIK entitlements	0.0	9,397.3	329.3	0.0	0.0	1,945.3
Dairy diversion payments	0.0	0.0	335.5	631.1	0.0	193.3
Dairy assessments	0.0	-656.6	-662.5	-164.6	-511.2	-399.0
Marketing loans	0.0	0.0	0.0	271.6	374.5	129.2
Loan forfeit benefits	-105.7	10.7	58.9	424.4	2,083.2	494.3
Market Price Support	9,665.9	9,606.4	12,201.2	10,764.7	13,436.4	11,134.9
Price enhancing policies	0.0	0.0	0.0	220.6	1,868.4	417.8
Fluid milk premium	268.9	266.4	257.1	289.8	297.2	275.9
Price support/quotas	8,937.1	8,867.9	11,463.3	9,607.6	10,549.7	9,885.1
Tariffs	460.0	472.2	480.8	484.9	487.4	477.0
Beef purchases	0.0	0.0	0.0	161.8	233.7	79.1
Input Subsidies	2,445.4	2,591.1	2,401.0	3,516.5	4,370.6	3,064.9
Commodity loans	1,333.3	1,452.2	990.0	1,259.9	1,633.1	1,333.9
Farm storage facility	4.2	4.3	0.0	0.0	0.0	1.7
Farmers Home Administration	741.4	830.8	1,169.5	1,849.3	2,546.2	1,427.4
Crop insurance	222.3	219.4	178.7	349.2	135.1	220.9
Fuel excise tax	75.5	23.1	0.0	0.0	0.0	19.7
Emergency feed	19.2	0.0	0.0	0.2	0.9	4.0
Grazing fees	49.5	61.3	61.9	58.0	55.3	57.2
Long-term	1,449.8	1,381.0	1,472.1	1,548.7	1,411.6	1,452.6
Research	554.4	566.9	581.9	609.1	605.5	583.5
Advisory	222.3	231.0	231.3	248.1	234.1	233.3
Pest and disease control	225.9	163.3	205.4	211.2	190.8	199.3
Land improvements	447.2	419.8	453.5	480.5	381.2	436.4
Other	2,623.4	2,429.3	2,441.4	2,567.4	2,875.6	2,587.4
Taxation	1,210.6	960.7	941.5	923.9	1,072.0	1,021.7
State Programs	1,412.8	1,468.6	1,499.9	1,643.6	1,803.6	1,565.7
Total Policy Transfers	19,202.3	28,282.6	23,301.0	26,063.0	36,863.7	26,742.5
Value to Producers	111,298.1	110,436.0	107,735.1	109,177.1	103,073.6	108,510.0
12-Commodity PSE (Percent)	17.3	25.6	21.6	23.9	35.8	24.6

Source: US Department of Agriculture, pp. 162, 163.

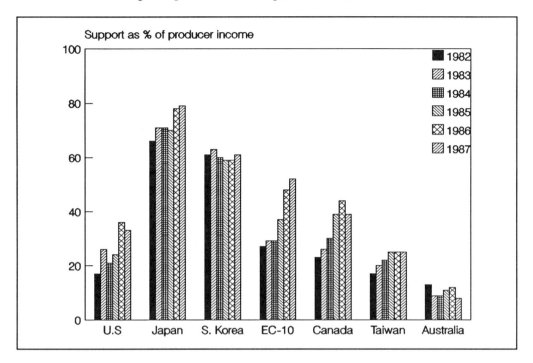

Figure 3.3. Average Producer Subsidy Equivalents for Grains, Livestock, Dairy, Oilseeds, and Sugar.
Source: US Department of Agriculture.

Like NPCs and EPCs, PSEs are low for developing countries. In a comprehensive analysis (useful for viewing the methodology of PSE calculation), Emara *et al.* calculated a PSE of -24 percent for five major farm commodities in Egypt for 1987. The high net implicit tax imposed by an overvalued currency more than offset input subsidies so that Egyptian agriculture experienced net taxation.

Table 3.7 summarizes consumer subsidy equivalents (CSEs) for the United States by policy and commodity. Although protection from imports is sizable for sugar and dairy products, tariffs constitute a modest source of income transfers to producers and costs to consumers. Food cost to consumers of the nine commodities covered in the analysis averaged $80 billion over the 1982-86 period; policy transfers in various forms raised the cost by 12 percent -- the consumer subsidy equivalent. The negative coefficients indicate implicit taxes.

CLASSICAL WELFARE ANALYSIS

A final measure of costs of market interventions and benefits from trade liberalization is classical welfare analysis (see Tweeten, ch. 6). The coefficients presented earlier did not show *economic costs* measured in lost national or world income from trade distortions. PSE/CSE estimates show gross policy transfers among producers and consumers. Those transfers may be decoupled direct payments, which do not affect production, consumption, stocks, or trade. A given policy transfer to producers may not raise their income by an equivalent amount because resource use (and cost) may rise,

Table 3.7. Consumer Subsidy Equivalents by Policy and Commodity, United States, 1982-86.

Item	1982	1983	1984	1985	1986	1982-86 Average
			($ Million of Policy Transfers)			
Policy Transfers by Policy						
Price support/quota	-7,879	-7,885	-10,281	-8,687	-9,546	-8,855
Tariff	-367	-377	-381	-387	-388	-380
Fluid milk	-269	-257	-264	-290	-297	-275
Price enhancing policies	0	0	0	-87	-1,373	-292
Policy Transfers by Commodity						
Beef	-367	-377	-381	-387	-388	-380
Sugar	-2,510	-2,606	-2,829	-2,687	-2,798	-1,567
Cheese	0	0	0	0	0	0
Butter	-448	-436	-691	-699	-796	-641
Non-fat dry milk	-204	-197	-270	-190	-243	-123
Fluid milk	-3,167	-3,049	-4,086	-3,328	-3,624	-3,451
Wheat	0	0	0	-87	-292	-76
Barley	0	0	0	0	-342	-68
Poultry	0	0	0	0	-739	-148
Total Transfers to Consumers	-8,515	-8,519	-10,926	-9,451	-11,604	-9,803
Food Cost to Consumers	76,705	79,090	81,249	79,941	81,025	79,602
			(Percent)			
CSE by Commodity						
Beef	-0.8	-0.8	-0.8	-0.9	-0.9	-0.8
Sugar	-50.6	-54.2	-65.7	-61.0	-66.1	-59.1
Cheese	-15.4	-15.3	-20.1	-14.7	-16.4	-16.4
Butter	-24.4	-23.6	-35.9	-35.8	-40.2	-32.2
Non-fat dry milk	-50.5	-48.7	-62.0	-53.7	-50.4	-53.2
Fluid milk	-26.2	-24.9	-32.9	-26.5	-28.8	-27.9
Wheat	0.0	0.0	0.0	-2.5	-9.0	-2.0
Barley	0.0	0.0	0.0	0.0	-47.6	-7.9
Poultry	0.0	0.0	0.0	0.0	-5.0	-1.2
9-Commodity CSE	-11.1	-10.8	-13.4	-11.8	-14.3	-12.3

Source: US Department of Agriculture, p. 166.

commodity prices may fall, or consumers may reduce commodity purchases. Classical welfare analysis, which shows the level and distribution of program benefits and costs among producers, consumers, taxpayers, and society as a whole, attempts to correct some of these shortcomings by including supply and demand responses. NPC, EPC, and PSE/CSE estimates can be important inputs into classical welfare analysis.

Welfare Analysis Contrasted with Other Measures of Policy Interventions

Figure 3.4 helps to illustrate the difference between classical welfare analysis and other measures of trade distortions. Suppose domestic demand is D, domestic supply is S, and import supply is horizontal line M in Figure 3.4. Total supply, SaM, intersects demand in open market equilibrium at price P_b with domestic quantity produced q_p, quantity consumed q_c, and imports $q_c - q_p$.

Now assume a tariff is imposed that raises domestic price to P_d. Domestic production increases to q_p', consumption falls to q_c' and imports fall to $q_c' - q_p'$. Consumer

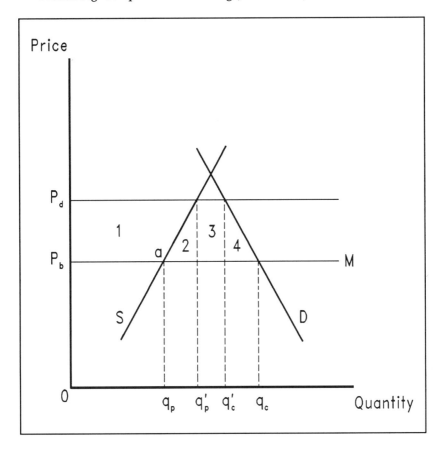

Figure 3.4. Effect of a Tariff on Producers, Consumers, Taxpayers, and Society.

	Area in Figure 3.4
Loss to consumers	1+2+3+4
Gain to producers	1
Gain to government	3
Loss to society	2+4

The deadweight or welfare loss, defined as full national income lost by society, is the value shown by areas 2+4. Gains to producers and the government fall short of the loss to consumers from the tariff.

The effect of the tariff in Figure 3.4 as measured by the NPC is P_d/P_b. PSE/CSE estimates are observed in the presence of the tariff and hence imprecisely measure changes in welfare. The PSE or policy transfer is measured as the product of the tariff ($P_d - P_b$) times quantity q_p' -- area 1+2. However, net income of producers increases only by area 1. The CSE is measured by the negative of the tariff, $P_d - P_b$, times consumption quantity q_c' -- area 1+2+3 -- when in fact the actual increase in real cost to consumers is 1+2+3+4. In short, the PSE/CSE framework omits deadweight losses and thus overestimates gains and underestimates losses of policy transfers.

Blandford *et al.* estimated that American producers received only 41 percent of the cost of agricultural policies to taxpayers and consumers in the mid-1980s. Over half of the leakage of benefits to producers was to offset price support policies of other countries.

Omitting this dubiously classified leakage, deadweight losses alone were approximately 25 percent of policy transfers to producers. If administrative costs and other leakages properly attributed to policy transfers are included, producers received about 65 percent of the outlay for policies by taxpayers and consumers. A decoupled direct payment program could reduce welfare losses to approximately 10 percent of transfers. Much of this loss is administrative cost.

Welfare (deadweight) gains from trade and agricultural policy liberalization are shown for several countries in Figure 3.5. Multilateral agricultural trade and commodity program policy liberalization would have added $12 billion to EC full national income, $9 billion to US income, and $6 billion to income in Japan. Other estimates indicate lower deadweight loss to the US and higher loss to Japan and the EC.

Tyers and Anderson provide estimates of gains from free trade in 1995 in Table 3.8. The large negative numbers for producers in the EC and Japan indicate they would experience large losses of buying power from trade and commodity program liberalization. Consumer gains more than offset producer losses so that net welfare (full national income) gains would be $18 billion in the EC-12, $20 billion in Japan, and $3 billion in the US from liberalization. The gain shown above for US producers under free trade contrasts with other studies showing losses to US producers from free markets. The seeming inconsistency is explained by the fact that most US studies allow for only US liberalization while Tyers and Anderson allow for global liberalization, which would raise prices to US producers. American producers would benefit from foreign trade and commodity program liberalization. Although gross US program costs (not shown) are high, most of the outlay

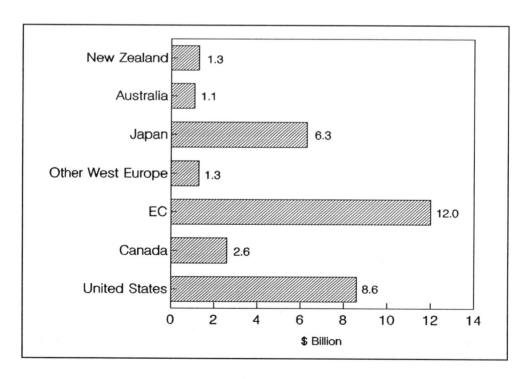

Figure 3.5. Change in Economic Welfare from Trade Liberalization in Industrial Countries, 1986.
Source: Blandford *et al.*

is a transfer cost from taxpayers to producers so that national income loss is low compared to the loss in Japan and the EC.

Developing countries benefit from export subsidies of the US and European Community, hence would be worse off with worldwide free trade. (Some other studies including more commodities and policies show gains to developing countries from free trade.) *World* gains from free trade are estimated to be $39 billion by Tyers and Anderson. These gains would accrue each year. If gains persist, the present value of all future losses is $800 billion discounted at 5 percent. The world can invest much indeed in successful negotiations to open trade. Adding deadweight costs of *directly unproductive profit seeking activities* (DUPs as defined by Bhagwati) such as lobbying would enlarge the numbers. This deadweight cost is high compared to that shown later for 1989 in Chapter 11, yet probably underestimates actual losses in real international income from agricultural trade distortions. One reason is that many trade distortions are not recorded and hence not included. Totals would be much higher if deadweight costs of lobbying, administration, evasion, saving and investment disincentives, technology restraint, and environmental degradation were included.

Price and Volume Changes

Other benefits accrue from trade liberalization. Average prices of farm commodities in the EC and Japan would be sharply lower with free trade, but prices of most commodities in international trade and hence border prices would be higher. Estimates of price changes are shown in Table 3.9. Taking only estimates for years after 1981, predictions are for world prices to be up for all commodities shown but especially for sugar, dairy products, and beef.

Tyers and Anderson estimate that trade liberalization would reduce the *coefficient of price variation* for dairy products to 7 percent from 16 percent and for wheat to 30 percent from 45 percent (Figure 3.6). The reduction in variability for these and other products would especially benefit developing country food importers with fragile balance of payments situations highly sensitive to world food prices.

Benefits from more open trade would also be apparent in export volume (Table 3.10). Analysts estimate for 1986 conditions that trade liberalization in all market economies would raise pork and poultry trade 295 percent, beef and lamb 235 percent, and dairy products 190 percent. Gains when only one country liberalizes policies would be much less, emphasizing the advantages of multilateral liberalization.

Table 3.8. Estimated Gains from Free Trade, 1995.

	Farm	Consumer	Net
	($ Billion)		
US	3.1	0	3.1
EC-12	-73.7	91.3	17.6
Japan	-38.7	58.2	19.5
All industrial countries	-122.9	173.8	50.9
All developing countries	50.4	-63.9	-13.5
World	-59.0	98.2	39.2

Table 3.9. The Predicted Effects of Industrial Country Trade Liberalization on World Agricultural Prices.

Study	Period	Wheat	Coarse Grains	Rice	Beef[b]	Dairy Products	Sugar
			(percent change in world price)				
OECD[a]	1979-81	-1	-3	1	15	44	10
Tyers and Anderson	1980-82	10	3	11	27	61	11
Roningen and Dixit	1984	7	11	18	22	30	48
Tyers and Anderson	1985	2	1	5	16	27	5
Roningen and Dixit	1986	30	23	24	18	50	39
Parikh *et al.*	2000	18	11	21	17	31	NA

Source: Summarized by Blandford *et al.*
[a]Organization for Economic Cooperation and Development.
[b]All ruminant meat.

A NOTE ON COMPETITIVE ADVANTAGE

Comparative advantage was defined earlier as those commodities that could be exported at the highest return per unit of nontraded (fixed) resources when exposed to well-

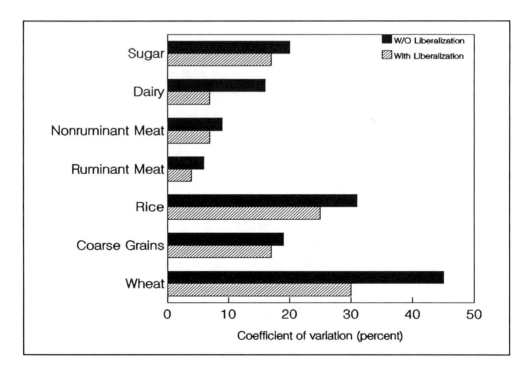

Figure 3.6. Effect on World Price Stability of Trade Liberalization in Industrial Countries.
Source: Tyers and Anderson.

functioning world markets. The exchange rate will adjust until sufficient commodities are exported to equate foreign exchange supply with foreign exchange demand to purchase imports.

In contrast, a nation has a *competitive advantage* in those commodities that can be exported at greatest return per unit of nontraded resources without domestic market distortions but in the world of existing trade distortions. *Competitiveness* is defined as the ability to compete for world markets in the world as it exists. Static measures of competitive advantage include enterprise budget costs of production plus transportation costs to foreign export markets -- compared to like estimates for competitors (see Barkema *et al.* for example). Variants of such estimates can include trade barriers, commodity programs, and short- and long-run cost estimates. The latter include land cost to recognize that (say) soybeans may be profitable to export considering only nonland costs but may be unprofitable when high land costs inflated by corn subsidies are included.

Dynamic trends in farm competitiveness can be judged from domestic trends in productivity of agriculture versus other industries, and of trends in crop and livestock yields at home versus in competing countries (see Barkema *et al.*). Export shares over time also are used widely to measure dynamic competitiveness. These measures supplement domestic resource cost coefficients often used to measure comparative advantage (Tweeten and Pai, 1990).

Table 3.10. International Price and Trade Effects of Liberalization of Selected Commodity Markets, 1985.

Country or Country Group in which Liberalization Takes Place	Wheat	Coarse Grains	Rice	Beef & Lamb	Pork & Poultry	Dairy Products	Sugar
Percentage Change in International Price Level Following Liberalization							
European Community	1	3	1	10	2	12	3
Japan	0	0	4	4	1	3	1
United States	1	-3	0	0	-1	5	1
OECD	2	1	5	16	2	27	5
Developing Countries	7	3	-12	0	-4	36	3
All Market Economies	9	4	-8	16	-2	67	8
Percentage Change in World Trade Volume Following Liberalization							
European Community	0	4	0	107	3	34	-5
Japan	0	3	30	57	-8	28	1
United States	0	14	-2	14	7	50	3
OECD	-1	19	32	195	18	95	2
Developing Countries	7	12	75	68	260	330	60
All Market Economies	6	30	97	235	295	190	60

Source: World Bank, p. 129

CONCLUSIONS

Various means have been devised by economists to measure gains from trade and commodity policy liberalization and the cost of protectionism. Based on mid-1980s conditions and prices, worldwide liberalization would raise world real income at least $40 billion annually and $800 billion in perpetuity. Worldwide gross gains of farm producers from market interventions totalled $250 billion but about $200 billion of that was merely transfers from consumers and taxpayers. The gains to farmers were in developed countries; on average farmers in developing countries were "taxed" by consumers and governments. Agricultural commodity prices in international trade would be on average higher and more stable, and quantity traded would be greater with liberalization. The export elasticity of demand could at least double, reducing the shock of drought or glut to world prices.

Clearly, the world has a major stake in reducing trade interventions. Transition programs would be necessary to cushion adjustments, especially for producers in Japan and the EC who have been supported at high levels. Direct payments and other human resource mobility adjustment programs could help producers while domestic support prices are being reduced to world levels.

REFERENCES

Appleyard, D. 1987. *Comparative Advantage of Agricultural Production Systems and Its Policy Implications in Pakistan.* FAO Economic and Social Development Paper 68. Rome: Food and Agriculture Organization of the United Nations.

Barkema, Alan, Mark Drabenstott, and Luther Tweeten. 1989. The competitiveness of US agriculture in the 1990s. Pp. 253-284 in Kristen Allen, ed., *Agricultural Policies in a New Decade.* Washington, DC: Resources for the Future and National Planning Association.

Bhagwati, Jagdish N. October 1982. Directly unproductive, profit seeking (DUP) activities. *Journal of Political Economy* 90(5).

Blandford, David, Harry deGorter, Praveen Dixit, and Stephen Magiera. 1989. Agricultural trade liberalization: The multilateral stake in policy reform. (Mimeo). Ithaca, NY: Department of Agricultural Economics, Cornell University.

Bredahl, Maury, ed. 1990. Potential use of an aggregate measure of support. International Agricultural Trade Research Consortium Paper No. 5. Columbia: Department of Agricultural Economics, University of Missouri.

Bruno, M. 1972. Domestic resource costs and effective protection: Clarification and synthesis. *Journal of Political Economy* 80:16-33.

Bucyanayandi, Tress, Luther Tweeten, Cesar Amorin, Sam Zziwa, and Edward Nsubuga. 1990. *Uganda Accelerated Foodcrop Production Strategy.* Kampala: USAID.

Corden, W.M. 1971. *The Theory of Protection.* Oxford: Clarendon Press.

Emara, Azza, Hoda Abass, Adnan Nassar, and George R. Gardner. 1989. *Egypt's Producer Subsidy Equivalents: Measures of Government Intervention in Agriculture.* APC Project Tranche III. Benchmark 3, Sector Analysis Paper. Cairo: USAID.

Epplin, Francis and Elton Li. 1986. *An Introduction to MUSAH86*. Working Paper A-13 of the Agricultural Policy Analysis Project. Stillwater: Department of Agricultural Economics, Oklahoma State University.

Epplin, Francis and Arthur Stoecker. 1989. Mathematical programming. Chapter 9 in Luther Tweeten, ed., *Agricultural Policy Analysis Tools for Economic Development*. Boulder, CO: Westview Press.

FAO. November 1973. *Agricultural Protection: Domestic Policy in International Trade*. 73/LIM/9. Rome: Food and Agriculture Organization of the United Nations.

Hazell, Peter and Roger Norton. 1986. *Mathematical Program for Economic Analysis in Agriculture*. New York: Macmillan.

Jiron, Rolando, Luther Tweeten, Beshir Rassas, and Robert Enochian. 1988. *Agricultural Policies Affecting Production and Marketing of Fruits and Vegetables in Jordan*. Agricultural Policy Analysis Project Report. Washington, DC: Abt Associates.

Josling, Tim and Stefen Tangerman. 1988. Measuring levels of protection in agriculture: A survey of approaches and results. (Paper presented to *Twentieth Conference of the International Association of Agricultural Economists*, Buenos Aires, Argentina, August 24-31, 1988.) (Mimeo.) Stanford, CA: Food Research Institute, Stanford University.

Scandizzo, Pasquale and Colin Bruce. 1980. *Methodologies for Measuring Agricultural Price Intervention Effects*. World Bank Staff Working Paper No. 394. Washington, DC: World Bank.

Tsukok, Isabelle. 1991. *Agricultural Price Policy*. Ithaca, NY: Cornell University Press.

Tweeten, Luther. 1989. Classical welfare analysis. Chapter 6 in Luther Tweeten, ed., *Agricultural Policy Analysis Tools for Economic Development*. Boulder, CO: Westview Press.

Tweeten, Luther, Beshir Rassas, and Thomas Earley. June 1989. *Prices and Incentives in the Yemen Arab Republic*. Technical Report 104. Washington, DC: Abt Associates.

Tweeten, Luther and Dee-Yu Pai. March 1990. Public policy and the competitive position of US agriculture in world markets. Pp. 383-401 in *Proceedings of Third Annual Symposium of the Institute for International Economic Competitiveness*. Radford, VA: Radford University.

Tyers, Rodney and Kym Anderson. May 1988. Liberalizing OECD agricultural policies in the Uruguay round: Effects on trade and welfare. *Journal of Agricultural Economics* 30:197-215.

US Department of Agriculture. April 1988. *Estimates of Producer and Consumer Subsidy Equivalents*. ERS Staff Report No. AGES880127. Washington, DC: Economic Research Service, USDA.

World Bank. 1986. *World Development Report 1986*. New York: Oxford University Press.

CHAPTER 4

Border Interventions:
Taxes, Subsidies,
and Quotas

Three major types of public measures altering trade patterns are border interventions, macroeconomic policies, and commodity programs. Chapters 5 and 6 treat the latter two. This chapter analyzes impacts on the level and distribution of costs and benefits from border interventions in the form of taxes (tariffs), subsidies, and quotas. These policies can be applied to exports or imports.

Border measures have different impacts for very large, large, and small countries where size refers not to geographic area or aggregate output but rather whether the actions of a nation affect world prices:

- A nation is a *small-country case* if the demand for its exports or supply of its imports is perfectly elastic (horizontal).
- A nation is a *large-country case* if the demand for its exports or supply of its imports is neither perfectly elastic nor perfectly inelastic.
- A nation is a *very-large-country case* if the demand for its exports or supply of its imports is perfectly inelastic (vertical).

Negotiations under the General Agreement on Tariffs and Trade (GATT) have focused mainly on reducing tariff barriers. The negotiations have been highly successful in reducing tariff barriers (Table 4.1). US tariffs as a percent of all import value fell from 57 percent in 1830 to 3.1 percent in 1980. For the world as a whole, tariffs average approximately 5 percent of trade value.

Border interventions are now dominated by nontariff measures. The nontariff border measures take numerous forms but many resolve to forms of subsidies or quotas. For example, unofficial and unauthorized delays in processing import or export permits behave like quotas. The monopoly-like guild of wholesale merchants in Japan who frequently reject foreign merchandise also constitutes de facto quota behavior. Excessive packing requirements or shipping costs behave like taxes. Credit concessions provided by the United States and other exporters to foreign buyers of wheat are agricultural export subsidies. The European Community imposes a variable levy on imports equal to the difference between the domestic support price and the world price -- a hybrid between a tariff and a nontariff barrier but generally classified as the latter. A host of nontariff distortions were listed in Table 3.1 of the previous chapter.

The purpose of this chapter is to illustrate conceptually who gains and who loses from border interventions. The three types of interventions, three country size cases, and the exporter-importer dichotomy represent 18 cases. The organization of this chapter is to present first the situations for importers, then for exporters.

Table 4.1. US Tariff Rates Through 1984.

| Year | Imports | Duty-Free | Calculated Duties | Ratio of Calculated Duties to: | | |
				Total Imports	Dutiable Imports	Federal Revenue
	($ Mil.)	(Percent)	($ Mil.)		(Percent)	
1791	NA	NA	4	NA	NA	99.5
1800	91	NA	9	9.9	NA	83.7
1810	85	NA	9	10.6	NA	91.5
1820	74	NA	15	20.3	NA	83.9
1830	50	8.0	28	57.3	61.7	88.2
1840	86	48.0	15	17.6	34.4	69.3
1850	164	9.8	40	24.5	27.1	91.0
1860	336	20.2	53	15.7	19.7	94.9
1870	426	4.7	192	44.9	47.1	47.3
1880	628	33.1	183	29.1	43.5	55.9
1890	766	33.7	227	29.6	44.6	57.0
1900	831	44.2	229	27.6	49.5	41.1
1910	1,547	49.2	327	21.1	41.6	49.4
1915	1,648	49.2	206	12.5	33.5	30.1
1920	5,102	61.1	326	6.4	16.4	4.8
1925	4,176	64.9	552	13.2	37.6	14.5
1930	3,114	66.8	462	14.8	44.7	14.1
1932	1,325	66.9	260	19.6	59.1	16.3
1935	2,039	59.1	357	17.5	42.9	9.0
1940	2,541	64.9	318	12.5	35.6	5.9
1945	4,098	67.1	381	9.3	28.2	0.7
1950	8,743	54.5	522	6.0	13.1	1.0
1955	11,337	53.3	633	5.6	12.0	0.9
1960	14,650	39.5	1,084	7.4	12.2	1.2
1965	21,283	34.9	1,643	7.7	11.9	1.2
1970	39,756	34.9	2,584	6.5	9.9	1.2
1975	96,516	32.2	3,780	3.9	5.8	1.3
1980	224,007	43.8	7,535	3.1	5.7	1.4
1984	322,990	31.9	12,042	3.7	5.5	1.4

Source: Lande and Van Grasstek.

INTERVENTIONS BY IMPORTERS

This section considers impacts on producers, consumers, governments, nations, and the world of taxes, subsidies, and quotas imposed by importers on commodities.

Import Tax (Tariff)

Assumptions

Conditions underlying Figure 4.1 are defined as follows:

t = import tariff applied by importer per unit imported
P_w = world price before the tariff
P_w' = world price after the tariff
$P_w'+t$ = domestic price in A with the tariff
s = domestic supply in country A
d = domestic demand in country A
S = supply in ROW
D = demand in ROW
ES = excess supply for importer A, S-D
ED = excess demand for importer A, **d-s**
q_c = consumption in country A before the tariff
q_c' = consumption in country A after the tariff
q_p = production in country A before the tariff
q_p' = production in country A after the tariff
Q_c = consumption in ROW before the tariff
Q_c' = consumption in ROW after the tariff
Q_p = production in ROW before the tariff
Q_p' = production in ROW after the tariff
q_c-q_p (imports of A) = Q_p-Q_c (exports of ROW) = q_e before the tariff
$q_c'-q_p'$ (imports of A) = $Q_p'-Q_c'$ (exports of ROW) = q_e' after the tariff.

The tariff (import tax or duty) lowers the excess demand curve for imports of A to ED - t. The *specific* tariff makes ED and ED - t parallel, differing vertically by distance t. (An *ad valorem* tariff proportional to price would make the lower curve proportional to ED; that is, the lower curve would be ED(1-t) where t is the tax rate so that ED and ED(1-t) would have the same vertical axis intercept.)

In the large-country case, ES slopes upward to the right so that less excess demand ED - t lowers world price to P_w'. In the extreme large-country case where ES is vertical (perfectly inelastic), the world price is reduced by the full amount of the tariff t. Then producers and consumers in A face the same price $P_w' + t = P_w$ with or without the tariff. ROW price falls by the amount of the tariff. Quantities are the same with and without the tariff.

Taking the other extreme, the small-country case, ES is perfectly elastic. It is a horizontal line at P_w. Hence the equilibrium indicated by intersection of ES and ED-t is at zero trade. The impact of the tariff shows up only in ROW price in the very-large-country case and only in quantity and in A's price in the small-country case.

Welfare Analysis

Changes in welfare compared to an open market with imposition of an import tax are shown by areas in Figure 4.1:

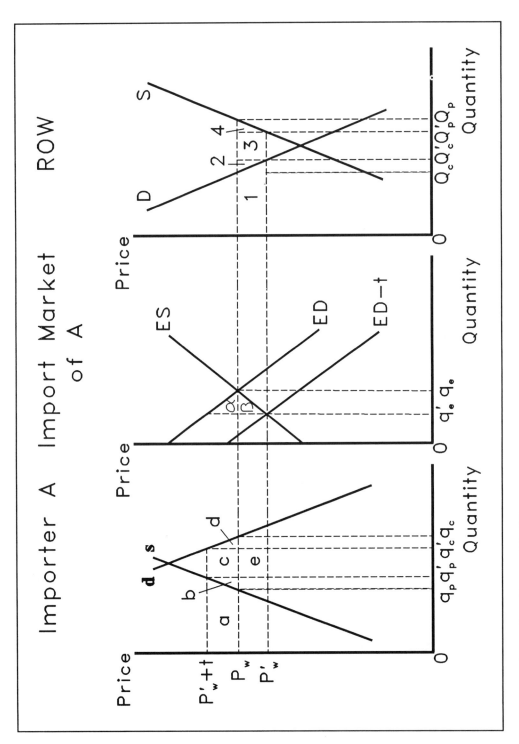

Figure 4.1. Effects of an Import Tariff.

	Importer A	**ROW**
Consumer surplus gain	-a-b-c-d	1
Producer surplus gain	a	-1-2-3-4
Government revenue change	c+e	---
Net national welfare	-b-d+e	-2-3-4
Net world welfare (because e=3)	-b-d-2-4	

Because area b+d is equal to area α and area 2+4 is equal to β, it follows that world deadweight loss can be taken directly from the middle panel in Figure 4.1.

Summarizing welfare effects by "size" of country, results are as follows:

Very large country. If ES is vertical, the entire impact of the tariff shows up as a low world price $P_w' = P_w - t$. Areas 2 and 4 would not exist if D and S were vertical. Domestic price would be $P_w = P_w' + t$. Hence producers and consumers in A would face the same prices as with no tariff, removing b+d. Net social cost would be zero and the tariff would provide a pure transfer from ROW to A. If the purpose of the tariff is to raise government revenue or to raise producers' income, transfer efficiency is high -- assuming in the latter case that the tariff revenue would be transferred to producers at no deadweight loss. In this and later cases, the "government" might be a quasi-public organization such as a marketing board or state trading company.

Large country. Given that ES is neither perfectly elastic nor perfectly inelastic and assuming that the purpose of the tariff is to raise full national income, it follows that the *optimal tariff* for the nation maximizes the area e-b-d. If ES is elastic, b+d is likely to exceed e in value so that A is worse off from the import tax.

Small country. Where ES is perfectly elastic, the tariff on imports will show up solely as a change in domestic price in A. With the tariff, the price in A will be P_w+t and in ROW will be P_w. In this case, areas 2 and 4 for ROW will vanish but full national income loss b+d in A will be larger than in the large-country case. Because e will no longer exist, small-country importer A will be irrational to impose a tariff if its goal is to maximize full national income. Gains to producers or government will be more than offset by losses to consumers.

If its goal is to raise government revenue, a tariff will do so but at a deadweight loss of (b+d)/c per unit of revenue raised. Producers in A will be better off; the gain to producers, deadweight loss, and gain to government come at the expense of consumers in A.

In the small-country case, consumers in A may spend more or less on the commodity after imposition of the tariff depending on the price elasticity of domestic demand. If demand is elastic, the tariff proportionately will increase domestic price less than decrease quantity so consumers will spend less. If demand is inelastic, the tariff will decrease domestic quantity relatively less than it will increase domestic price so consumers will spend more.

Figure 4.1 can be used to illustrate an *optimal import tariff*. The tariff on each unit is the difference between ED and ES curves to the left of q_e in the middle panel of Figure 4.1. The marginal tariff is highest at 0 but quantity is zero so revenue is zero. Similarly, revenue is zero at q_e because the tariff rate (difference between ES and ED) is zero. A perfectly discriminating tariff collector could reap the entire area between ED and ES from 0 to q_e. If only one tariff rate can be charged on all units, maximum tariff revenue is at quantity $q_e/2$ if ES and ED are straight lines.[1] The exact maximum position will depend on the elasticity of excess supply E_m for imports by A. In the general case, the *optimal import tariff* is where the ratio of domestic price p to the tariff t is E_m, i.e. $E_m = p/t$.[2] Because $t = p/E_m$, it is apparent that the optimal tariff is zero in the small-country case (E_m is very large) and approaches infinity in the very-large-country case where E_m is very small.

Maximizing revenue from a tariff does not necessarily maximize revenue to domestic producers, the nation, or the world. In the small-country case, the revenue comes from domestic consumers, thus the maximum revenue tariff merely maximizes transfers from domestic consumers to government as noted from Figure 4.1. An optimal tariff maximizes net revenue from the import market but not necessarily from the import plus the domestic market as noted in Chapter 8.

The host of individual tariff and nontariff measures to support farm income defy individual attention in international trade negotiations. Consequently, the United States in the Uruguay Round of GATT proposed in November 1988 that all nations over time convert all income supports to tariffs. This process is called *tariffication* (see Bredahl *et al.*). The intent after tariffication would be to gradually reduce all agricultural product tariffs to zero or low levels as had been done so successfully for industrial products. The US recommendation in part reflected a lack of confidence that an earlier proposal for *decoupling* (lump-sum direct government payments unrelated to production replacing other supports) would be acceptable and in part satisfaction with an agreement with the Japanese to replace their beef and citrus quotas with tariffs that in turn will gradually be phased out.

Import Subsidy

We now turn to the import subsidy. The subsidy is assumed to be a flat amount paid by the government on each unit of import of a good.

Assumptions

Conditions in Figure 4.2 are defined as follows:

su = specific fixed-rate import subsidy by importer A per unit of imports
P_w = world price before the subsidy
P_w' = world price after the subsidy
P_w'-su = price faced by producers and consumers in importing country A with the subsidy
s = domestic supply in country A
d = domestic demand in country A
S = supply in ROW
D = demand in ROW
ES = excess supply for importer A, S-D
ED = excess demand for importer A, d-s
q_c = consumption in country A before the subsidy

---

[1]Given demand curve $p_d = a + bq_d$ and supply curve $p_s = c + dq_s$, the unit tariff is $t = p_d - p_s = (a-c) + (b-d)q$ with equilibrium at $q_s = q_d = q$. The total tariff is $(p_d-p_s)q$ or $T = (a-c)q + (b-d)q^2$. The tariff T is maximized where $dT/dq = (a-c) + 2(b-d)q = 0$. Given that market equilibrium quantity is where $p_d = p_s$ or $q_e = (c-a)/(b-d)$, it follows that the optimal tariff quantity is $q = (c-a)/2(b-d) = q_e/2$. This optimal tariff quantity $q_e/2$ applies where ES and ED are linear and only one price can be charged.

[2]Marginal cost of imports is $p + p/E_m$. Marginal revenue is $p + t$. Equating marginal cost with marginal revenue gives optimal import tariff $t = p/E_m$. Issues of retaliation are ignored.

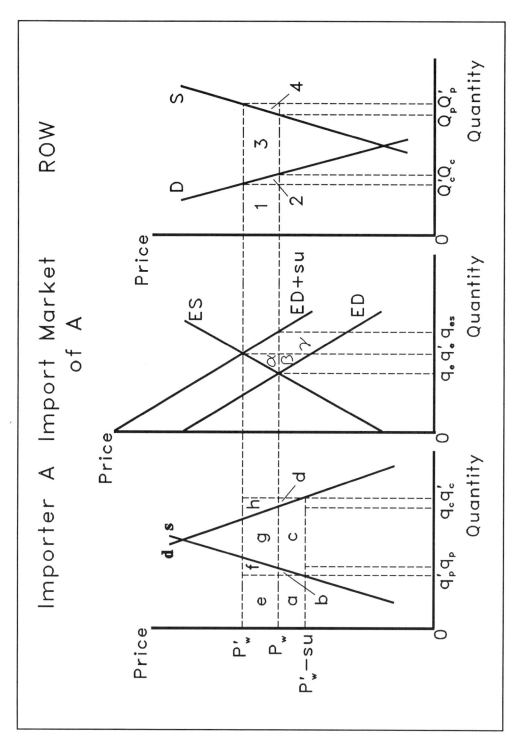

Figure 4.2. Effects of an Import Subsidy.

83

q_c' = consumption in country A after the subsidy
q_p = production in country A before the subsidy
q_p' = production in country A after the subsidy
Q_c = consumption in ROW before the subsidy
Q_c' = consumption in ROW after the subsidy
Q_p = production in ROW before the subsidy
Q_p' = production in ROW after the subsidy
$q_c - q_p$ (imports by A) = $Q_p - Q_c$ (exports of ROW) = q_e before the subsidy
$q_c' - q_p'$ (imports by A) = $Q_p' - Q_c'$ (exports of ROW) = q_e' after the subsidy.

When importing country A subsidizes each unit of its imports by su, the excess demand ED for imports is raised vertically by su to ED + su. In the large-country case, ES slopes upward to the right so the additional excess demand raises world price from P_w to P_w'. In the extreme large-country case where ES is vertical (perfectly inelastic), P_w' rises by the amount of the subsidy so that $P_w = P_w'$ - su and producers and consumers in A face the same price for q with or without the import subsidy. At the other extreme of a small-country case, ES is horizontal (perfectly elastic) so that $P_w' = P_w$ and the entire subsidy is passed to producers and consumers in A.

Welfare Analysis
Changes in welfare compared to an open market with imposition of an import subsidy as shown by areas in Figure 4.2 are as follows:

	Importer A	ROW
Consumer surplus gain	a+b+c	-1-2
Producer surplus gain	-a-b	1+2+3
Government revenue change	-b-c-d-f-g-h	---
Net national welfare	-b-d-f-g-h	3
Net world welfare		
(because f+g+h=2+3+4)	-b-d-2-4	

Welfare effects differ by country "size."
Very large country. If ES is perfectly inelastic because S and D are perfectly inelastic, areas 2 and 4 vanish. And because the subsidy is entirely above P_w for A, areas a+b+c+d do not exist, hence area b+d+2+4, the world social cost, is zero. The import subsidy does not result in a lower price to producers and consumers in country A but instead is passed as a higher price to ROW. ROW producers rather than the intended beneficiary, consumers in A, receive the entire subsidy. The transfer efficiency to consumers, a+b+c divided by the subsidy, is zero.
Large country. Where ES is neither perfectly elastic nor perfectly inelastic, the transfer inefficiency to consumers, defined as (b+d+f+g+h)/(a+b+c), is greater than zero. Although consumers gain, the country imposing an import subsidy loses national income. ROW gains, however.
Small country. Where ES is perfectly elastic, there is no import subsidy price slippage to ROW. That is, the subsidy goes solely "below P_w." Imports are q_{es}' rather than q_e'. Area e+f+g+h does not exist but a+b+c+d becomes larger because P_w - su, the new domestic price, is below P_w' - su, the former price with large-country slippage. The net social cost is α(i.e. 2+4) + β(i.e. b+d) in the large-country case and β + γ in the small-country case. Whether social cost is greater or smaller than in the large-country case depends on whether α is greater or smaller than γ.

In conclusion, an import subsidy by A results in a net welfare loss to the importer because of (1) deadweight domestic loss and (2) leakage of the subsidy to the rest of the world.

Import Quota

Assumptions

Conditions in Figure 4.3 are defined as follows:

$P_d = P_w$ = domestic price equal to world price before the quota
P_d' = domestic price after the quota
P_w' = world price after the quota
q_e' = quota y-x, the horizontal distance between s and s´
s = domestic supply in country A
s´ = domestic supply in country A including quota imports
d = domestic demand in country A
S = supply in ROW
D = demand in ROW
ES = excess supply for importer A, S-D
ED = excess demand for importer A, **d-s**
ED´ = excess demand for imports with the quota
q_c = consumption in country A before the quota
q_c' = consumption in country A after the quota
q_p = production in country A before the quota
q_p' = production in country A after the quota
Q_c = consumption in ROW before the quota
Q_c' = consumption in ROW after the quota
Q_p = production in ROW before the quota
Q_p' = production in ROW after the quota
$q_c - q_p$ (imports of A) = $Q_p - Q_c$ (exports of ROW) = q_e before quota
$q_c' - q_p'$ (imports of A) = $Q_p' - Q_c'$ (exports of ROW) = q_e' after quota.

Markets are initially assumed to be in equilibrium at world price P_w and imports q_e to A. A quota q_e' is imposed on imports to A, which shifts the excess demand curve from ED to a new position ED´. The latter follows ED to the quota, then becomes perfectly inelastic.

If the excess supply curve ES would have intersected ED´ along its segment common with ED, the *inoperative quota* would have left world market prices and quantities unchanged. In fact, we have an operative quota that changes the equilibrium price and quantity.

Welfare Analysis

Welfare effects of the operative quota compared to competitive world market equilibrium are illustrated with areas shown in Figure 4.3:

86

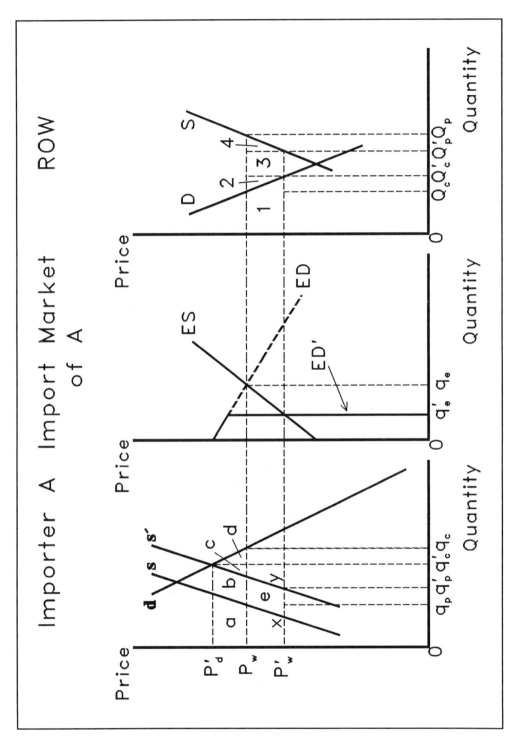

Figure 4.3. Effects of an Import Quota.

	Importer A	ROW
Consumer surplus gain	-a-b-c-d	1
Producer surplus gain	a	-1-2-3-4
Quota revenue change	b+e	---
Net national welfare	-c-d+e	-2-3-4
Net world welfare (because e=3)		-c-d-2-4

Results are summarized below by "size" of country.

Very large country. With ES assumed to be perfectly inelastic in the very-large-country case, only two outcomes are possible with a quota. One is for ES to intersect ED´ in its ED segment, giving the same outcome as with no quota. The other outcome is for ES to lie to the right of ED´ in which case the outcome is indeterminate.

Large country. In the large-country case where the ES elasticity is between zero and infinity and the quota is operative, imports of A fall to the quota level, driving a tariff-like wedge between world and domestic price P_w' - P_d'. The quota is like an import tariff in benefitting producers and hurting consumers. The Japanese food agency uses a variable quota on grains to maintain stable domestic prices -- a policy giving outcomes similar to the EC variable levy. Either policy exports instability to ROW.

An economic rent of b+e in excess of necessary costs to import accrues to the government if it imports q_e' at the world price and sells domestically at the market clearing price or if it auctions quotas to foreign exporters. In contrast, the benefit accrues to ROW if foreigners are allowed to administer the quota established by a mandatory or voluntary export agreement. Quotas have been widely used to control US imports of beef, sugar, autos, steel, footwear, and textiles. Foreigners prefer quotas for which they receive the economic rent as compared to a tariff accruing to the home country.

Importer A will gain from a quota if it retains quota rent e exceeding c+d in Figure 4.3. In the large-country case, where quotas are operative, foreign producers are big losers. However, if ROW is allowed to obtain rents it can be a gainer from quotas if b+e exceeds 2+3+4. At any rate, the world loses from quotas.

Small country. In the small-country case, an operative quota for importer A does not export social costs to ROW. Economic rent e from ROW does not accrue even if A controls the quota so that any economic rent b accruing to the government or agency of A must come from A's consumers. Cost of the quota to consumers is a+b+c+d, gain to producers is a and to the quota administrator is b, leaving a net national and world deadweight loss of c+d.

In short, import quotas are designed to help producers of an importing country. Whether the transfer inefficiency measured by the ratio (c+d)/a is large or small depends on elasticities of supply and demand of A in the small-country case. In the large-country case, it is also necessary to include the social cost 2+4 in Figure 4.3 borne by ROW. Importer A or ROW may be a net gainer depending on who retains quota rents, but the world is a net loser.

INTERVENTIONS BY EXPORTERS

Interventions by exporters have analytical parallels with interventions by importers examined in the previous section. Again we examine taxes, subsidies, and quotas by country "size." The very large- and small-country cases are instructive but in the real world are never found in the precise forms shown here.

Export Tax

The export tax is widely used by developing countries to provide hard currency to the government. An overvalued currency to be analyzed in the next chapter is an implicit export tax. Export taxes are often on agricultural exports. They constitute a "cheap food policy" and can cause large deadweight losses in developing countries fitting the "small-country" assumption.

Assumptions

The following apply to Figure 4.4:

t = specific export tax (tariff) applied by exporter A
P_w = world price before the tax
P_w' = world price after the tax
P_w-t = domestic price in country A after the tax
s = domestic supply in country A
d = domestic demand in country A
S = supply in ROW
D = demand in ROW
ES = excess supply for exporter A, **s-d**
ES_t = excess supply for exporter A after tax
ED = excess demand for exporter A, D-S
q_c = consumption in country A before the tax
q_c' = consumption in country A after the tax
q_p = production in country A before the tax
q_p' = production in country A after the tax
Q_c = consumption in ROW before the tax
Q_c' = consumption in ROW after the tax
Q_p = production in ROW before the tax
Q_p' = production in ROW after the tax
q_p - q_c (exports of A) = Q_c - Q_p (imports of ROW) = q_e before export tax
q_p' - q_c' (exports of A) = Q_c' - Q_p' (imports of ROW) = q_e' after export tax.

Imposition of the specific fixed-rate export tariff or tax shifts upward the excess supply curve ES by the vertical distance t to ES_t. In the large-country case, the excess demand curve ED slopes upward to the left so that the lower export supply quantity at a given price raises the world price to P_w'.

Welfare Analysis

Changes in welfare with imposition of the export tax compared to unrestricted market equilibrium are shown by areas from Figure 4.4.

89

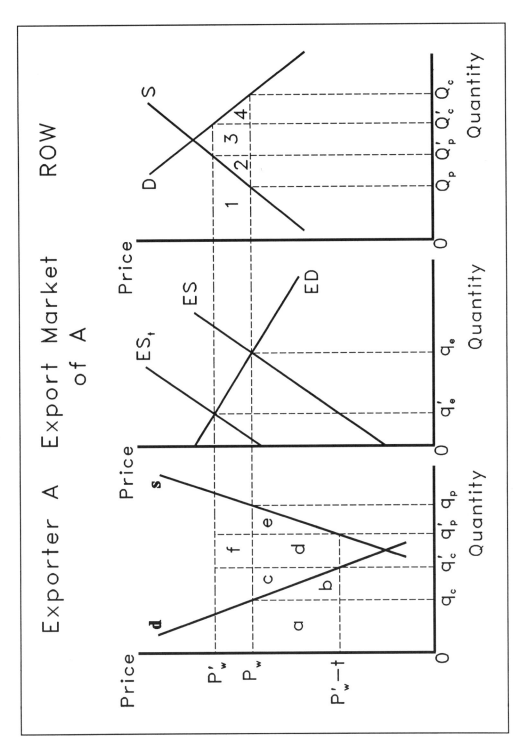

Figure 4.4. Effects of an Export Tax.

	Exporter A	**ROW**
Consumer surplus gain	a+b	-1-2-3-4
Producer surplus gain	-a-b-c-d-e	1
Government revenue change	d+f	---
Net national welfare	-c-e+f	-2-3-4
Net world welfare (because f=3)	-c-e-2-4.	

Welfare effects are summarized by "size" of country.

Very large country. If D, S, and ED are perfectly inelastic (vertical), $P_w' = P_w + t$. The world price rises by the amount of the export tax imposed by A. In that case, social cost 2+4 is small as D and S approach perfect inelasticity. Domestic price in A is $P_w = P_w' - t$ so social costs are zero and national welfare gain is f in country A. The magnitude of transfer f from ROW to A depends on the amount of exports and the export tax rate t.

Large country. The elasticity of ED is between zero and infinity in the large-country case. The optimal tariff would be where f-c-e is a maximum. Of course, for any arbitrary value of t the net benefit to A is negative if c+e exceeds f. A could be better or worse off from the tariff, depending on elasticities of supply and demand.

Small country. With ED perfectly elastic in the small-country case, P_w equals P_w' and f is zero. The entire cost of the tariff is borne by producers in A. Exporter A loses c+e, hence imposing the tariff is irrational. Welfare in ROW does not change.

Whether the case is for a very large, large, or small country, the world loses from export tariffs as indicated by the negative value c+e+2+4 in the welfare analysis. Tariffs are prohibited by law on American exports.

An *optimal export tariff* maximizes area f+d in Figure 4.4. A perfectly discriminating monopolist exporter could reap revenue equal to the entire triangle bounded by the price axis and ES and ED in the middle panel of Figure 4.4. If only one price can be charged and the demand ED and supply ES are linear, the optimal export tariff is at quantity $q_e/2$ (see footnote 1). In the general case, the optimal export tariff is $t = -p/E_x$ where E_x is the export elasticity of the demand curve ED.[3] In the small-country case where $E_x = -\infty$, t is zero. In the very-large-country case where E_x approaches zero, the optimal export tariff approaches infinity.

The analysis ignores issues of retaliation. It assumes that tariff revenue is all important. In fact, extraction of economic rent from monopoly pricing in the domestic market can be a larger source of additional revenue to producers. As Figure 4.4 showed, a tax that maximizes export revenue can make domestic producers, the nation, and the world worse off.

Export Subsidy

Assumptions

Conditions are defined as follows for Figure 4.5:

su = fixed-rate export subsidy applied by exporter A
P_w = world price before the subsidy
P_w' = world price after the subsidy
$P_w' + su$ = domestic price in country A with the subsidy
s = domestic supply in country A

---

[3]Marginal revenue from exports is $p + p/E_x$. Marginal cost is p - t. Equating marginal cost and marginal revenue gives optimal export tariff $t = -p/E_x$.

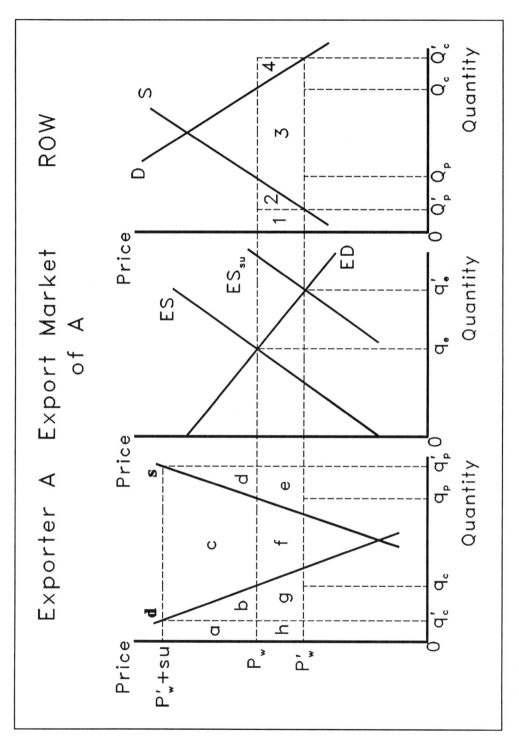

Figure 4.5. Effects of an Export Subsidy.

d = domestic demand in country A
S = supply in ROW
D = demand in ROW
ES = excess supply for exporter A, **s-d**
ES_{su} = excess supply for exporter A with the subsidy
ED = excess demand for exporter A, D-S
q_c = consumption in country A before the subsidy
q_c' = consumption in country A after the subsidy
q_p = production in country A before the subsidy
q_p' = production in country A after the subsidy
Q_c = consumption in ROW before the subsidy
Q_c' = consumption in ROW after the subsidy
Q_p = production in ROW before the subsidy
Q_p' = production in ROW after the subsidy
q_p - q_c (exports of A) = Q_c - Q_p (imports of ROW) = q_e before subsidy
q_p' - q_c' (exports of A) = Q_c' - Q_p' (imports of ROW) = q_e' after subsidy.

The export subsidy is widely used by developed countries to enhance income of producers. The subsidy reduces world price, expands exports of A, and expands imports of ROW. The subsidy at a flat amount of su per unit causes the new excess supply curve of A, ES_{su}, to be below the former excess supply, ES, by the vertical distance su.

Welfare Analysis
        Compared to open market equilibrium, imposition of the export subsidy causes changes indicated by areas in Figure 4.5 as follows:

	Exporter A	ROW
Consumer surplus gain	-a-b	1+2+3
Producer surplus gain	a+b+c	-1-2
Government revenue change	-b-c-d-e-f-g	---
Net national welfare	-b-d-e-f-g	3
Net world welfare		
(because 2+3+4=e+f+g)		-b-d-2-4

We now turn to welfare impacts by "size" of country.
        Very large country. With ED perfectly inelastic, the export subsidy drives the world price down to P_w' = P_w - su. As a net importer, ROW gains from this maximum reduction in world price. The entire export subsidy is transferred from A to ROW. The larger the country the less rational the subsidy.
        Large country. With ED neither perfectly elastic nor inelastic, some but not all the export subsidy provided by A is transferred to ROW. Although A's producers gain, the loses to taxpayers and consumers more than offset the gain to producers so the export subsidy makes A worse off. That the European Community provides export subsidies despite overall losses to the community is partly a testimony to the power of producers and partly an indication of the worth of other objectives such as price stability and food security. By varying the export subsidy in the face of shifting domestic supply and demand, the domestic price can be maintained at a constant level P_w' + su for domestic consumers while price variability is exported to ROW.
        Small country. In the small-country case, ED is perfectly elastic. Thus P_w' = P_w and the domestic price is P_w + su. Domestic consumers may object to paying a higher price

than ROW consumers for the commodity and ROW may object to A's dumping in world markets at less than prices charged at home. However, ROW experiences no welfare effects in the small-country case. The entire cost of the transfer $a+b+c$ to producers is borne by domestic consumers and taxpayers. Full national income of A is reduced by $b+d$. However, the export subsidy is more successful for A than in the larger-country case because benefits of the subsidy do not leak to ROW.

Because of the welfare losses to exporters using export subsidies, their widespread use by the US and the European Community seems incongruent. The beneficiaries of export subsidy competition are importing countries.

Export Quota

Assumptions

Definitions and assumptions for Figure 4.6 are as follows:

$P_d = P_w$ = domestic price equal to world price before the export quota
P_d' = domestic price after the quota
P_w' = world price after the quota
q_e' = export quota y-x, the horizontal distance between **d** and **d'** in A
d = domestic demand before the quota in country A
d' = domestic demand plus the quota in country A
s = domestic supply in country A
S = supply in ROW
D = demand in ROW
ES = excess supply for exports of country A, **s-d**
ED = excess demand for exports of country A, D-S
ES' = excess supply for export of country A, given the quota
q_c = consumption in country A before the quota
q_c' = consumption in country A after the quota
q_p = production in country A before the quota
q_p' = production in country A after the quota
Q_c = consumption in ROW before the quota
Q_c' = consumption in ROW after the quota
Q_p = production in ROW before the quota
Q_p' = production in ROW after the quota
$q_p - q_c$ (exports of A) = $Q_c - Q_p$ (imports of ROW) = q_e before the export quota
$q_p' - q_c'$ (exports of A) = $Q_c' - Q_p'$ (imports of ROW) = q_e' = the export quota.

World markets, initially assumed to be in equilibrium at world price P_w equal to domestic price P_d with exports of q_e from A, are subjected to an export quota q_e' imposed by A. If q_e' would have exceeded q_e, the quota would have been inoperative and had no effect.

With q_e', the world market finds a new equilibrium where ES' intersects ED at world price P_w'. However, excess supply remains in country A at that price. The excess is eliminated at the domestic equilibrium price P_d' where **d'** and **s** intersect. Thus domestic price falls, world price rises, and trade falls if the quota is operative.

Welfare Analysis

Welfare impacts of an operative exporter quota compared to an open market solution are summarized below using areas of Figure 4.6:

94

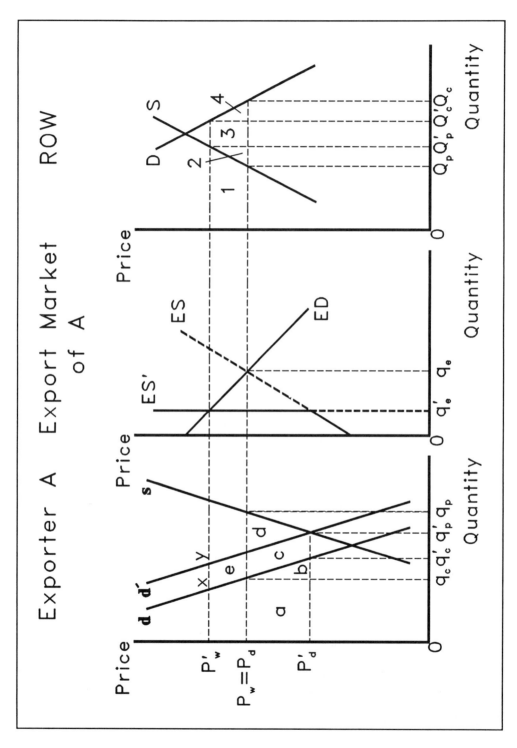

Figure 4.6. Effects of an Export Quota.

	Exporter A	ROW
Consumer surplus gain	a+b	-1-2-3-4
Producer surplus gain	-a-b-c-d	1
Quota revenue change	c+e	---
Net national welfare	-d+e	-2-3-4
Net world welfare (because e=3)	-d-2-4	

Welfare impacts of export quotas vary by "size" of country.

Very large country. With ED perfectly inelastic for the very-large-country case, the outcome of an export quota imposed by exporter A is trivial. Either ED will lie to the right of the quota q'_e represented by ES´ and the outcome is inconclusive, or ED will lie to the left of q'_e and the outcome will be the same as a free market. The quota in that case is inoperative.

Large country. If area e exceeds area d in Figure 4.6, exporter A gains from an export quota. Consumers and quota holders gain. If the government or other quota holder is willing to redistribute revenue, then consumers, producers, and taxpayers can gain if e exceeds d.

ROW loses from an operative quota. With the quota, losses to ROW exceed gains to A so that the world loses d+2+4 of full income.

Small country. With ED perfectly elastic, $P_w = P'_w$. Because A receives no transfers from ROW, e vanishes and rent transfers from the quota are from producers to the government or other quota holders. Net social cost to A is d.

Trade Embargo

A trade *embargo*, which may be a partial or complete withholding of exports to one or more importers by one or more exporters, is a form of quota (see also Chapter 11). From 1970 to 1990, the United States engaged in five farm export embargoes (see US Department of Agriculture for extensive history and analysis).

Export embargoes are effective if they are a concerted effort of all major exporters, if supplies are short and stocks are low, if there are no good substitutes for the commodity, and if compliance can be assured. Most embargoes have not met these conditions and have not been effective. Following the US embargo in 1980, for example, the Soviet Union merely turned to other exporters for grains. The US directly lost few sales in the short run because world grain supplies were sufficiently tight so that the US merely switched sales to markets vacated by competing exporters' sales to the Soviets. The greatest cost, in addition to deadweight losses depicted in Figure 4.6, is the long-term sales foregone because of our lost reputation for being a reliable supplier. Importers work to diversify supply sources as evidenced by Japan's investments in Brazil's soybean industry. Whether costs have outweighed benefits to the US of embargoes is difficult to judge because issues are political as well as economic.

IMPORT AND EXPORT TAX SYMMETRY

Import and export taxes have been addressed separately but in fact they are interconnected (Lerner). Developing countries trying to protect industry and promote import substitution by taxing imports are also retarding industry by implicitly taxing exports.

To see why an explicit tax on imports (exports) is an implicit tax on exports (imports), a distinction between importables, exportables, and nontraded goods is useful. In the small-country case, a tax on imports raises domestic import prices and costs. If importables are inputs into exportables, export good costs are raised. Exporters in the small-country case must absorb the cost -- an implicit tax. Higher input prices also cause prices of import goods to rise relative to nontradables, causing substitution of nontradables for imports. The price of nontradables rises. If nontradables such as labor are inputs for exportable products, again the result is a tax on exportables.

The process applies also to an explicit tax on exports which becomes an implicit tax on imports. This so called *Lerner symmetry* is not 1:1, however. The degree of tax passthrough depends on the degree of substitution among importables, exportables, and nontradables, among inputs in production, among products in consumption, and also on small- and large-country assumptions. Studies for developing countries indicate on average that half or more of import taxes are passed on as implicit export taxes (Thomas and Nash, p. 53; see also Clements and Sjaastad for procedures and estimates).

CONCLUSIONS

Border interventions in some but not all cases enhance welfare of nations imposing them. However, in the absence of externalities or other market failures that are corrected by interventions, policy distortions reduce full income in global perspective. That is one reason why nations seek to reduce trade barriers through international negotiations.

Sometimes combinations of border interventions are employed. The United States uses both quotas and import duties for sugar. The quotas are allocated in part by political considerations. The quotas entitle the holder to receive more than the world price for delivery to the US. Hence, the quota in part transfers the rents from import tariffs to favored less-developed-country quota holders. Following a complaint by Australia to the General Agreement on Tariffs and Trade (GATT) organization, the American sugar quota system was rejected as a violation of trade rules by a panel of GATT in 1989.

This chapter has treated trade distortions in a first-round, partial equilibrium analysis. In fact, an action by country A tends to invite retaliation by country B. Country A, B, or third countries may gain or lose in the swirl of measures and counter-measures. Strategic trade policy for such situations is addressed in Chapters 7 and 8.

REFERENCES

Bredahl, Maury E., Larry Deaton, Tim Josling, Karl Mielke, and Stefan Tangermann. 1989. Tariffication and rebalancing. Commissioned Paper No. 4 of *Bringing Agriculture into the GATT*. St. Paul: International Agricultural Trade Research Consortium, Department of Agricultural and Applied Economics, University of Minnesota.

Chacholiades, Miltiades. 1981. *Principles of International Economics*. New York: McGraw-Hill.

Clements, Kenneth and Larry Sjaastad. 1984. How protection taxes exporters. London: Trade Policy Research Center.

Corden, W.M. 1971. *The Theory of Protection*. Oxford: Clarendon Press.

Henneberry, Shida and David Henneberry. 1989. International trade policies. Chapter 12 in Luther Tweeten, ed., *Agricultural Policy Analysis Tools for Economic Development*. Boulder, CO: Westview Press.

Houck, James. 1986. *Elements of Agricultural Trade Policies*. New York: Macmillan.

Lande, Stephen and Craig Van Grasstek. 1986. *The Trade and Tariff Act of 1984: Trade Policy in the Reagan Administration*. Cambridge, MA: Lexington Books.

Lerner, A.P. August 1936. The symmetry between import and export taxes. *Economica* 3:306-313. (Reprinted in Richard Caves and Harry Johnson, eds. 1968. *Readings in International Economics*. Homewood, IL: Richard D. Irwin.)

McCalla, Alex and Timothy Josling. 1985. *Agricultural Policies and World Markets*. New York: Macmillan.

Thomas, Vinod and John Nash. 1991. *Best Practices in Trade Policy Reform*. Washington, DC: World Bank.

US Department of Agriculture. 1986. *Embargoes, Surplus Disposal, and US Agriculture*. Agricultural Economics Report No. 564. Washington, DC: Economic Research Service, USDA.

CHAPTER 5

Agricultural
Commodity Programs
and World Trade

We noted in Chapter 3 that world agricultural trade market interventions not only are large but also have grown in many countries despite the best efforts of international trade negotiators to move toward free trade. Commodity programs are the major source of agricultural trade distortions and, because trade distortions are larger in agricultural products than in other products, may be the single greatest source of *total* trade distortions.

Agricultural exports have remained largely outside the discipline of the General Agreement on Tariffs and Trade (GATT). Nations, taking their initiative from early exemptions obtained by the United States, have pursued their own separate commodity programs for agriculture. These programs, designed to promote self-sufficiency and farm income and save family farms, often restrict imports or subsidize exports. Governments have found internal political pressures for commodity programs (and the trade distorting policies attending them) more difficult to resist than international pressures for open trade markets.

Each of the numerous public policies listed earlier in Table 3.1 has some impact on trade. Some are more tolerated by the world community than others. Policies of (1) agricultural research, extension, and education and (2) road, port, and irrigation infrastructure development with favorable benefit-cost ratios are accepted in world trade forums. To stop them would be to reduce agricultural productivity -- hardly fitting for world bodies committed to increasing efficiency. Even export competitors of donors do not protest food aid to truly needy countries faced with starving people. GATT also has tolerated policies to promote self-sufficiency in food staples although such policies may be inefficient and damaging to export markets. Sanitary and phytosanitary border regulations are essential. These barriers become another source of protectionism when not scientifically or medically justified.

Strong opposition has been voiced to export subsidy (dumping) policies that persist, in the case of the European Community grains, for example, well beyond self-sufficiency. Food exporters such as the US also resent trade policies that protect domestic production of nonbasic commodities such as beef and citrus in Japan. Many protectionist policies of the US, Japan, the European Community, and of other traders are the result of commodity programs to aid local producers.

This chapter examines commodity programs typical of large numbers of developing countries and of the US, EC, and Japan. Commodity programs of the US, EC, and Japan are examined because these programs entail the largest social costs in foregone world income. Price ceilings, widely used in developing countries, are common commodity program interventions. Border taxes, subsidies, and quotas analyzed in the previous chapter often are the result of domestic farm commodity programs.

FARM AND FOOD COMMODITY PRICE CEILINGS

It was noted in Chapter 3 that developing countries on average discriminate against agriculture by systematically holding domestic prices below border prices. Instruments include food or farm commodity price controls and overvalued currency. Price ceilings are prominent where urban consumers have a strong influence in national policies. The impact of such policy on a representative third-world (TW) country is illustrated in Figure 5.1.

Assumptions

P_w = world price before price ceiling in TW
P_w' = price in ROW after ceiling in TW
P_m = ceiling price in TW
s = domestic supply in TW before ceiling
s' = domestic supply in TW after ceiling, including s up to $P_m q_p'$ intersection
d = domestic demand in TW before ceiling
d' = domestic demand in TW after ceiling
S = supply in ROW
D = demand in ROW
ES = excess supply, s-d, in TW before price ceiling
ES' = excess supply, s'-d', in TW after price ceiling
ED = excess demand, D-S, in ROW
q_c = consumption in TW before ceiling
q_c' = consumption in TW after ceiling
q_p = production in TW before ceiling
q_p' = production in TW after ceiling
Q_c = consumption in ROW before ceiling in TW
Q_c' = consumption in ROW after ceiling in TW
Q_p = production in ROW before ceiling in TW
Q_p' = production in ROW after ceiling in TW
q_p - q_c (exports of TW) = Q_c - Q_p (imports of ROW) = q_e before ceiling
q_p' - q_c' (exports of TW) = Q_c' - Q_p' (import of ROW) = q_e' after ceiling.

The imposition of the price ceiling in TW creates vertical supply and demand curves above P_m because even if world prices rise above P_m producers and consumers in TW have no incentive to respond. Thus the new excess supply curve ES' (including ES to q_e') is vertical above P_m and intersects the excess demand curve ED at q_e', a reduced export compared to an open world market. The price ceiling in TW moves the price in ROW to P_w'.

Government gain is c+e, making the policy attractive to a government short of foreign exchange and tax revenue. An export quota q_e' or export tax P_w-P_m collected by state marketing boards or parastatal corporations in third-world countries operates essentially the same way as price ceilings shown in Figure 5.1. In the frequent instances where third-world nations are small-country cases, e does not exist and c comes at the expense of local producers. If P_m is pushed down to the intersection of d and s, benefits of trade and transfers to government end. A policy of self-sufficiency in ROW -- setting domestic price where D and S intersect -- cuts off trade and removes the gains from trade

101

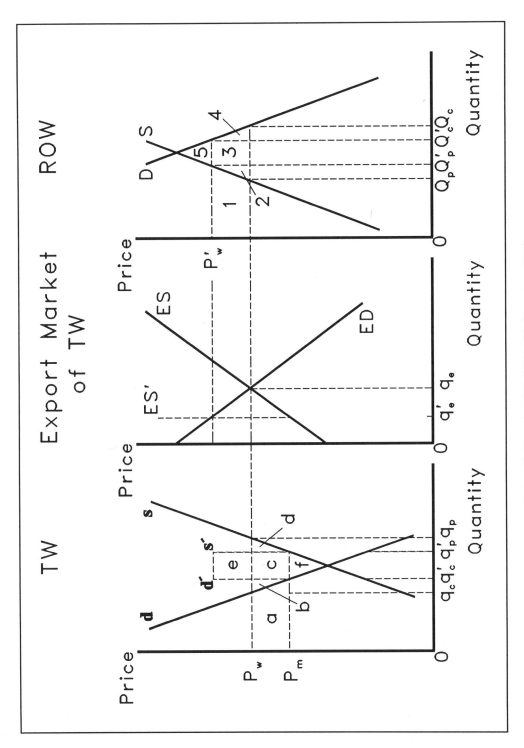

Figure 5.1. Effects of Farm Commodity Price Ceiling in Third-World Country (TW).

in TW (b+c+d+f) as well as in ROW (2+3+4+5). Generalized welfare effects from the price ceiling in TW are summarized below.

Welfare Analysis

	TW	**ROW**
Consumer surplus gain	a	-1-2-3-4
Producer surplus gain	-a-b-c-d	1
Government or taxpayer gain	c+e	---
Net national welfare	-b-d+e	-2-3-4
Net world welfare (because e=3)		-b-d-2-4

Results are summarized for very large-, large-, and small-country cases from Figure 5.1.

Very large country. ED is vertical (perfectly inelastic) in the very-large-country case at q_c. Two results are possible: If ED lies to the right of vertical line ES´, trade price is indeterminate; if ED lies to the left of ES´, then the ceiling price P_m will not affect trade.

Large country. In the large-country case depicted in Figure 5.1, TW will gain national income from the price ceiling if area e exceeds b+d. Under any circumstances, producers in TW lose while consumers gain. Consumers in ROW lose. Producers then gain too little to compensate so that ROW loses overall from the price ceiling in TW. The price ceiling reduces trade.

Small country. Except for countries such as Brazil in the case of coffee or Ivory Coast in the case of cocoa, the small-country case is likely to apply to nation TW. Then ED is horizontal (perfectly elastic), pivoting to lie along P_w in Figure 5.1. Then e does not exist so TW lowers full national income by b+d. Benefits of the ceiling in the form of price stability or desirable income redistribution must compensate for TW to be better off with price control. The redistribution is likely to reduce welfare, however, because income is transferred from farmers to higher-income urban consumers or to government. Stability also may not be well served because foreign exchange may be depleted to the point where TW is unable to enter international markets to purchase imports when local production falls short -- as it will from time to time due to weather and pestilence. In short, a price ceiling is likely to reduce exports and make TW worse off.

PRODUCTIVITY AND TRADE

Rapid productivity gains can generate political support for domestic programs to cushion farm income and sustain employment. Although agricultural research, extension, education, and infrastructure development ordinarily are not classified in commodity programs, they are instructive in demonstrating what happens to economic welfare when domestic supply is shifted -- as it often is, not only by technological progress but by controls or subsidies for pesticides, credit, or fertilizers. Such efforts bring deadweight changes in input markets that can show up as shifts in commodity supply curves.

The analysis demonstrates that if one nation expands productivity and another does not, the laggard can be left behind to face difficult adjustments to lower world prices (terms of trade). It also demonstrates that productivity advances can more than compensate for falling commodity terms of trade (ratio of prices received to prices paid by farmers) so that productivity gains improve factor terms of trade for farmers and reduce food costs to consumers (see Tweeten, ch. 1 for factor terms of trade).

Assumptions

In Figure 5.2, definitions are as follows:

S_0 = supply before productivity advances
S_1 = supply after productivity advances
D = domestic demand
X = perfectly elastic export demand
P_0 = initial equilibrium price
P_1 = equilibrium price after productivity advance, without trade
q_c = domestic production = domestic consumption before productivity advance
q_c' = domestic production = domestic consumption after productivity advance
  without trade
q_p = domestic production after productivity advance with trade
q_p-q_c = exports after productivity advance
C = cost to taxpayers, government, or others to develop technology.

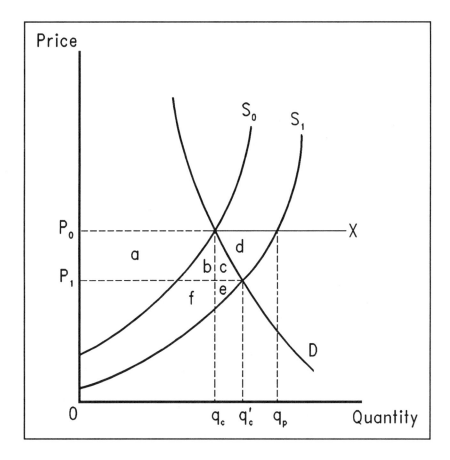

Figure 5.2. Productivity Advances and Trade.

Welfare Analysis

Welfare gains from productivity advances with and without trade:

	Without Trade	With Trade
Consumer surplus gain	a+b+c	---
Producer surplus gain	e+f - a	b+c+d+e+f
Government (taxpayer) gain	-C	-C
Net national welfare gain	b+c+e+f-C	b+c+d+e+f-C

Figure 5.2 and the welfare analysis teach several lessons regarding productivity and trade. Exposure to international markets influences both the magnitude and distribution of gains from productivity.

- Consumers gain directly from productivity advances without trade (area a+b+c in Figure 5.2). Consumers gain indirectly with trade because exports earn foreign exchange to purchase imports.
- Improved technology or other measures to raise productivity are of greater value and hence more likely to be adopted by producers facing demand made more elastic by liberalized trade. Producers obtain *all* the gains from technological advances (b+c+d+e+f) with trade but may lose (if area a exceeds e+f) with autarky in Figure 5.2.
- Investment C in technology to promote productivity growth is more likely to be profitable to the nation if the gain from trade (area d) is added to the net national welfare gain -- all properly discounted or compounded over time. If the decision to invest in research to increase productivity is political, as it is especially likely to be when technology is funded by a public sector in which producers have clout, then research support has a better chance of success with open trade.

Figure 5.2 is a small-country scenario. In a larger-country scenario (not shown), more of the benefits of productivity advances are passed to foreign consumers while losses accrue to foreign producers.

A large number of studies indicate a favorable economic payoff from investments in science and education (see Braha and Tweeten; Ruttan). Figure 5.2 indicates that the impact is to lower real food prices, benefitting consumers and freeing resources from farming to produce other goods and services such as housing and health care more favored by society at the margin. Productivity gains have expanded trade on average.

In a world of steadily improving agricultural productivity, an agricultural exporting country attempting merely to stand still by ignoring opportunities to invest in agricultural research and extension will in fact fall behind and be worse off. Terms of trade will decline for all agricultural product exporters, but welfare will improve in countries increasing productivity while it will decline in countries failing to improve productivity. In some countries, lower producer prices resulting from productivity gains have brought government interventions to maintain income of producers.

In short, Figure 5.2 has illustrated and the United States has demonstrated that a nation's producers can improve their economic welfare even as commodity terms of trade fall. Productivity advances can more than offset falling commodity terms of trade so that factor terms of trade, the better measure of economic welfare, rise.

AMERICAN COMMODITY PROGRAMS

American commodity programs are unique in many ways. Several countries control production (e.g., dairy output in Canada and the EC), but the United States is the only nation that diverts millions of acres to soil-conserving uses to reduce farm output. As noted in Chapter 3, the deadweight losses have been modest in relation to government transfers to producers in the US. One reason for low losses is that excess production incentives provided by price supports are offset by production controls.

US sugar programs are not shown here because they function mainly as import tariffs shown in the previous chapter (see Figure 4.1). Dairy programs also rely partly on import border restrictions to maintain domestic prices above world levels. Welfare impacts on producers, consumers, government, and society of sugar and dairy programs are presented in Tweeten (ch. 12). Tariffs or variable levies operate quite simply and effectively to support income of producers of commodities for which a country is a net importer. Export commodities often employ much more elaborate means to support domestic producers. US grain programs are examples of fairly complex government interventions.

This section illustrates economic impacts of US grain programs. Three principal instruments are used.

1. *Loan rates.* Farmers who participate in programs are eligible for a nonrecourse government loan after harvest with the crop pledged as collateral. If the market price per unit rises above the loan rate advanced to them, producers can repay the loan plus interest and sell their crop for the best price possible. If the market price remains below the loan rate, the producer can deliver the crop to the government as full repayment of the loan. Hence the loan rate tends to set a market price floor.

2. *Target price and deficiency payment.* The government establishes a target price above the loan rate. A *deficiency payment* (direct income transfer) is made to producers equal to the difference between the target price and the loan rate (or market price if higher) on normal (historic) production on allowable acreage. The direct payment may be paid in lump sums said to be *decoupled* -- free of incentives for changing production, consumption, or trade.

3. *Production controls.* To be eligible for nonrecourse loans and deficiency payments, producers are required to cut back production by a prescribed percentage of the historic base under an *acreage reduction program* (ARP). Under the *paid diversion program* (PDP) producers are paid to divert additional land from production of a specific crop. ARP and PDP acres must be placed in soil conserving uses and cannot be cropped, grazed, or hayed under ordinary circumstances. In addition, the *Conservation Reserve Program* (CRP) encourages producers to convert part or whole farms from crops to soil conserving land uses under long-term contracts.

The impacts of grain programs are shown with the help of two diagrams. Figure 5.3 depicts impacts in the short run and a subsequent figure shows impacts in the long run.

106

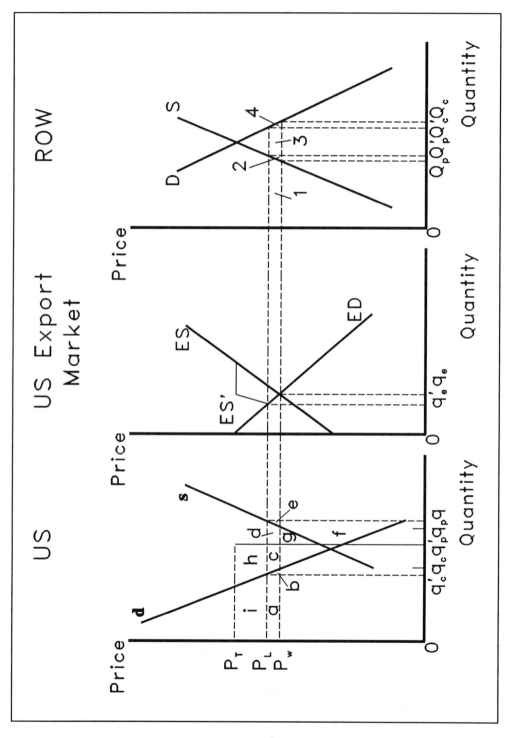

Figure 5.3. Short-Run Effect of US Acreage Diversion, Target Price, and Loan Rate Programs for Grains.

Assumptions

A number of assumptions in addition to those listed above are noted.

P_w = world price without commodity programs
P_L = nonrecourse loan rate
P_T = target price
s = domestic supply in US
d = domestic demand in US
S = supply in ROW
D = demand in ROW
ES = excess supply without programs
ES′ = excess supply with programs
ED = excess demand
q_c = consumption in US before programs
q_c' = consumption in US after programs
q_p = production in US before programs
q_p' = production in US after programs
q = intended production in US without diversion program
q_e = US exports before program
q_e' = US exports after program
Q_p = ROW production before programs
Q_p' = ROW production after programs
Q_c = ROW consumption before programs
Q_c' = ROW consumption after programs
q_p-q_c (exports of US) = Q_c-Q_p (imports of ROW) = q_e before programs
q_p'-q_c' (exports of US) = Q_c'-Q_p' (imports of ROW) = q_e' after programs.

With the loan rate P_L set above P_w, a paid diversion program costing the government d+e+f+g is required to reduce production from q to q_p', which is less than free market output q_p in the short run. (Figure 5.3, no ARP is assumed.) Deficiency payment i+h also is made to producers.

In theory, the government should only have to pay the "rent" d+g above variable cost to induce acreage diversion; in reality the payment must be much higher (see Tweeten, ch. 12). If only d+g were paid to producers for diversion, producer income and taxpayer cost would be down by e+f. This simple transfer is presumed not to influence deadweight loss.

The loan rate fixing price at P_L holds domestic consumption to q_c'. With production fixed at q_p', the excess supply curve shifts to ES′, which slopes slightly to the right between P_L and P_T because consumption decreases along demand curve **d**. At a market price above P_T, producers opt out of the program and produce along ES. It is apparent that the quantity of exports q_e' in relation to q_e depends heavily on the position of ED.

The US is a large-country case. It sets world price at P_L by its loan program. In Figure 5.3 that excess moved in world markets but in the past the supply generated by the loan often exceeded the quantity that could be exported at that price P_L. Given ED and price P_L, if not all excess supply ES′ will move in world markets two options are possible -- subsidize exports or remove supply from the market to accumulate in storage stocks. Although the US has used export subsidies, its main tool has been commodity stock accumulation to maintain world price at P_L. US commodity stocks and acreage diversion programs have buffered world grain market variability. On average, US export subsidies have not increased exports above free market level q_e. We subsequently observe that, while the US policy often has stabilized world markets, EC and Japanese farm policies have destabilized world markets.

Welfare Analysis

The short-run impacts of US grain policies depicted in Figure 5.3 closely parallel their operation under the 1981 farm bill from 1982 to 1986. Loan rates were held above world levels and stocks were accumulated or production controlled. The US provided an "umbrella," protecting competing exporters who sold just under the high loan rates P_L to raise their share of world markets.

Welfare implications of the grain program in the short run are summarized as follows:

	US	ROW
Consumer surplus gain	-a-b	-1-2-3-4
Producer surplus gain	a+b+c+d+e+f+h+i	1
Government gain	-d-e-f-g-h-i	---
Net national gain	c-g	-2-3-4
Net world gain (b+c approximate 3)	-b-g-2-4	

The world net deadweight cost includes four elements included in Figure 5.3 plus at least three excluded elements. Costs shown are:

1. Area b from consumption lost that had greater value to consumers than the cost of production and resulting from price P_L in excess of border price P_w in the US.
2. Area g in the US from foregoing production of grain at less resource cost than the border price value in consumption P_w.
3. Area 2 from production in ROW at a resource cost in excess of that (P_w) attainable with an open market.
4. Area 4 of ROW consumption foregone because price was excessive. ROW sacrificed the opportunity to utilize grain valued more highly by consumers than the resource cost of production.

Other sizable deadweight costs are not shown in Figure 5.3:

5. Program administration. Such costs commonly are 5-10 percent of overall Treasury costs.
6. Resources devoted by interest groups to lobbying the US government for commodity program benefits, including import quotas or export subsidies.
7. An inefficient resource mix that shifted s upward as retired land was replaced with chemicals and other purchased inputs used to increase production on land actually cropped. Intensive pesticide and synthetic fertilizer use raises environmental costs.

In short, the US program reduced consumers' welfare worldwide, raised producers' welfare, raised US government outlays, and reduced world income. We now turn to the welfare impacts of the American grain programs as they operated in the *long run* under the 1985 farm bill (see Figure 5.4):

109

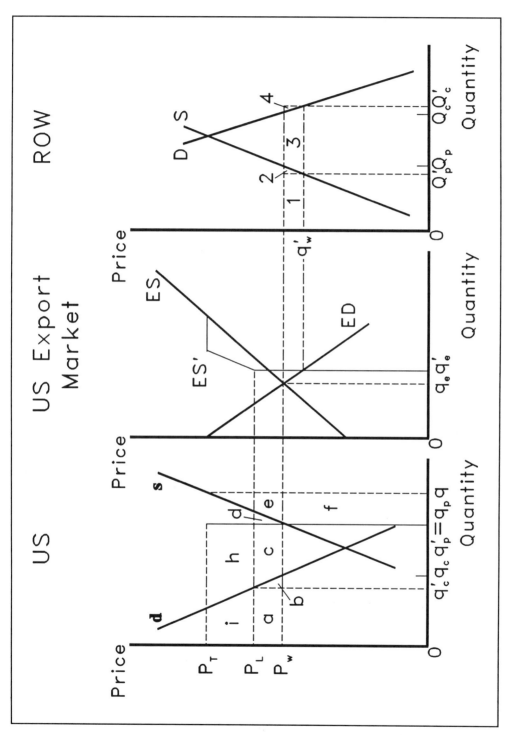

Figure 5.4. Long-Run Effects of US Acreage Diversion, Target Price, and Loan Rate Programs for Grains.

	US	ROW
Consumer surplus gain	-a-b	1+2+3
Producer surplus gain	a+b+c+d+e+f+h+i	-1-2
Government gain	-b-c-d-e-f-h-i-2-3-4	---
Net national gain	-b-2-3-4	3
Net world gain	-b-2-4	

Patterns are broadly similar to those for the short run in Figure 5.3. Several notable changes are apparent, however: (1) The target price has become the supply price so that the acreage diversion program does not reduce net production. So $q_p' = q_p$, the same output as if no program had ever been in place. (2) Exports q_e' exceed those of a free market q_e. (3) The government subsidizes exports by the area $0q_e'(P_L-P_w')$ to bridge the gap between domestic price P_L and the world price P_w', which is *below* the free market price P_w. Some of this subsidy cost (2+3+4) shows up as a gain to ROW. (The area g in Figure 5.3 does not appear in Figure 5.4 because production controls are less effective.)

While ROW gains on the whole, producers abroad and competing net exporter countries lose. The American export share is retained at large Treasury cost and international objection to export subsidies. It is not possible to say with precision whether commodity programs have increased or decreased American exports or the nation's share of world exports.

MANDATORY CONTROLS

The United States once used mandatory controls for a large number of crops including wheat, rice, and cotton. Tobacco remains under mandatory controls. If at least two-thirds of producers approve in national referendum, then all producers are required to produce within established poundage quotas. They are rewarded with a high guaranteed price but receive no diversion payment. Mandatory controls also are used for selected commodities in other countries including dairy in Canada. An advantage is low government cost. Impacts are depicted in Figure 5.5.

Assumptions

P_w = world price before mandatory controls

P_w' = US support price and world price after mandatory controls

s = domestic supply in US before mandatory controls

s´ = domestic supply in US after mandatory controls

d = domestic demand in US

S = supply in ROW

D = demand in ROW

ES = excess supply, **s-d**, in US before mandatory controls

ES´ = excess supply, **s´-d**, in US after mandatory controls

ED = excess demand, D-S, in ROW

q_c = consumption in US before mandatory controls

q_c' = consumption in US after mandatory controls

q_p = production in US before mandatory controls

q_p' = production in US after mandatory controls

111

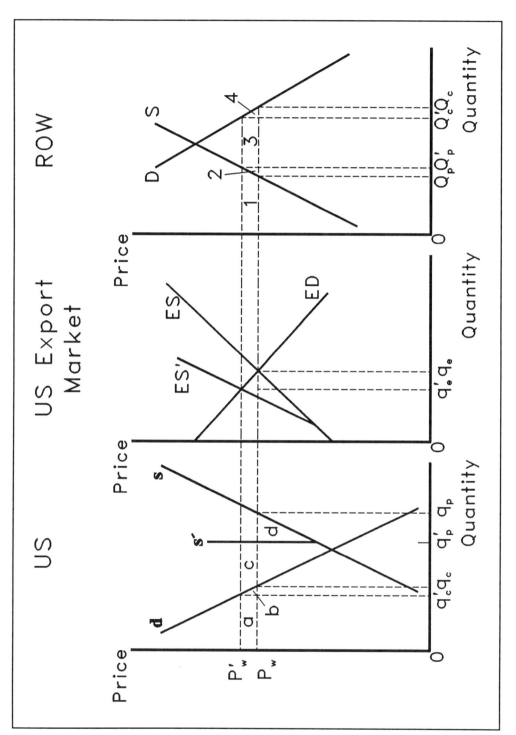

Figure 5.5. Effect of Mandatory Controls.

Q_c = consumption in ROW before US mandatory controls
Q_c' = consumption in ROW after US mandatory controls
Q_p = production in ROW before US mandatory controls
Q_p' = production in ROW after US mandatory controls
q_p-q_c (US exports) = Q_c-Q_p (ROW imports) = q_e before mandatory controls
q_p'-q_c' (US exports) = Q_c'-Q_p' (ROW imports) = q_e' after mandatory controls.

With supply controls, the excess supply curve follows ES up to the price where controls become binding, then follows ES´. Intersection of ES´ with ED gives exports q_e' at world price P_w'. World price rises, US production, consumption, and exports fall; ROW production rises while consumption falls to reduce US imports.

Welfare Analysis

	US	ROW
Consumer surplus gain	-a-b	-1-2-3-4
Producer surplus gain	a+b+c-d	1
Net national welfare	c-d	-2-3-4
Net world welfare (because b+c=3)	-b-d-2-4	

Welfare impacts are measured from the efficient market base, i.e., before mandatory controls. Mandatory controls reduce real money income of consumers at home and abroad and raise income of foreign producers by area 1. Income of US producers rises if area a+b+c exceeds area d. That will be likely if demand is highly inelastic. Net US welfare is positive if c exceeds d. ROW is worse off. World welfare is reduced by b+d+2+4.

Mandatory controls on tobacco represent a unique case because social costs exceed private costs and hence the social supply curve lies above and to the left of the private supply curve to which producers respond. The social supply curve adds medical, morbidity, and mortality costs to private costs. *Welfare areas should always be measured from social supply and demand curves.* If the true social supply curve lies closer to s´ than to s, as seems likely, mandatory controls may move the US closer to a welfare maximum even as it has eroded export markets and encouraged production abroad. In addition, a larger proportion of tobacco program economic rents than benefits of other programs go to low-income farmers. As such, the tobacco program, despite an unfavorable press, may have more merit than many other commodity programs. Less tobacco leaf is exported because of the program, hence foreign producers benefit.

SELF-SUFFICIENCY RICE POLICY IN JAPAN

As noted in Chapter 3, producer subsidy equivalents are higher for Japan than for any other country. The country is self-sufficient in rice. The high costs of the policies are paid mainly by consumers because much cheaper imports are kept out. The policy reduces urban living standards and raises housing costs and congestion because land is kept in farming that has much higher real value in urban uses.

Japan has taken steps to rationalize its policies. Under the 1988 Beef and Citrus Agreement with the United States, it consented to eliminate quotas on beef and oranges over the next three years and on orange juice concentrate over the next four years (U.S. Department of Agriculture, p. 122). Japan also has reduced support prices on rice and instituted modest production controls. It has introduced incentives for producers to shift from rice to production of wheat, which it imports in large volume. The injury to world wheat exporters is compounded by Japan's high wheat support price -- four times the border price in 1988. The Food Agency of the Ministry of Agriculture, Forestry, and Fisheries (MAFF), which controls much of the grain trade in Japan, uses a variable quota to maintain high domestic prices paid by consumers. The earnings from what is effectively a variable levy on imports are used to subsidize domestic producers of crops that compete with imports.

Japan justifies agricultural protectionism on food security and religious grounds. Decision makers presumably compare subjective benefits of the above to conventional costs, which are shown below and can be quantified. Figure 5.6 illustrates the social cost of the rice self-sufficiency policy and a suggested alternative, partial decoupling. A rice price of P_J maintains self-sufficiency in rice using trade barriers to protect from cheaper imports. The social cost is $e+f$ if the border price of P_w remains firm.

Full decoupling requires an end to subsidies, controls, and other policies that interfere with market-oriented production, consumption, and trade. Full decoupling could include an untied direct payment to rice producers that would continue whether operators produce rice or other commodities. The decoupled payment would remain with them whether they farmed or left farming. Such policy would save full national income of area $e+f$ in Figure 5.6 but would sacrifice the self-sufficiency goal.

A suggested alternative, *semi-decoupling*, would continue to provide a tied payment of P_J per unit of rice to producers to a limit of q_p' units (self-sufficiency in isolation) of production. Japanese consumers, however, would be able to purchase at the world price. Consumers but not producers would be decoupled. Effects are summarized after listing of assumptions.

Assumptions

P_w = world price without self-sufficiency policy
P_w' = world price with semi-decoupling
P_J = self-sufficiency price
P_R = autarky price in ROW
s = domestic rice supply in Japan
d = domestic rice demand in Japan
D = ROW rice demand
S = ROW rice supply
ES = excess supply, S-D, for rice in Japan
ED = excess demand, **d-s**, for rice in Japan
ED' = excess demand, **d**-q_p', for rice in Japan with semi-decoupling
q_c = consumption in Japan with open market
q_c' = consumption in Japan with semi-decoupling
q_p = production in Japan with open market
q_p' = production in Japan with semi-decoupling
Q_c = consumption in ROW with open market
Q_c' = consumption in ROW with semi-decoupling in Japan
Q_p = production in ROW with open market
Q_p' = production in ROW with semi-decoupling in Japan
q_c-q_p (Japan imports) = Q_p-Q_c (ROW exports) = q_e with open market
q_c'-q_p' (Japan imports) = Q_p'-Q_c' (ROW exports) = q_e' with semi-decoupling.

114

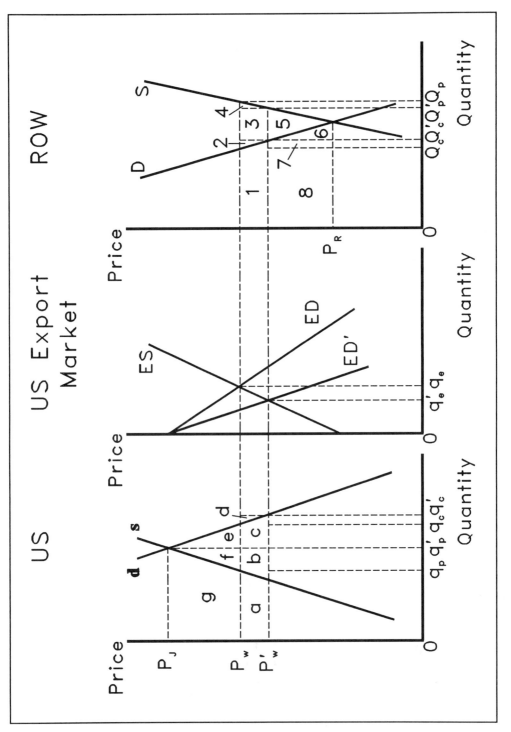

Figure 5.6. Effect of Self-Sufficiency and Semi-Decoupling of Japanese Rice Program.

Welfare Analysis

The following analysis shows impacts of current policies and semi-decoupling compared to an open market. Under semi-decoupling, producers would not change output, costs, or income compared to current self-sufficiency at P_J and q_p'. A government payment replaces consumer outlays to maintain production while consumers buy at the world price. We first examine the welfare impact of current self-sufficiency versus open markets. The loss to consumers $e+f+g$ less the gain to producers of g leaves a net social cost to Japan of $e+f$. The deadweight cost of Japanese self-sufficiency to ROW is $2+3+4+5$. The world loses $e+f+2+3+4+5$.

	Current Policy		Semi-decoupling	
	Japan	**ROW**	**Japan**	**ROW**
Consumer surplus gain	-e-f-g	1+6+7+8	a+b+c	1
Producer surplus gain	g	-1 to -8	g	-1-2-3-4
Government gain	---	---	-a-b-f-g	---
Net national welfare	-e-f	-2-3-4-5	c-f	-2-3-4
Net world welfare (because c+d=3)	-e-f-2-3-4-5		-d-f-2-4	

Compared to a free market, consumer surplus rises $a+b+c$ with semi-decoupling. Consumer surplus would rise much more ($e+f+g$) if semi-decoupling were compared with the current policy holding consumer price at P_J. Producer surplus gain at g remains the same with semi-decoupling as with the current self-sufficiency policy. Government cost is up more than consumer cost is down so net national welfare is reduced by c-f compared with a free market and full decoupling. This compares with net national welfare reduced by $e+f$ with current policies.

Compared to open markets in Japan, semi-decoupling adds area 1 to consumers in ROW, subtracts $1+2+3+4$ from producers, and hence reduces net national welfare by area $2+3+4$. Of course, ROW would be better off with a free market than with semi-decoupling. But ROW is better off with semi-decoupling than with current policies giving net national welfare loss of area 5 plus $2+3+4$. With semi-decoupling, the world is better off by e-d+3+5.

Japan's net social cost likely is less with semi-decoupling than with the current self-sufficiency policy. It is notable however, that "self-sufficiency" quantity q_p', though adequate to supply consumption when price is P_J to consumers, falls short by $q_c'-q_p'$ of self-sufficiency when the price to consumers is P_w'. It follows that the first-best Japanese policy for ROW is a free market, the second-best is semi-decoupling, and the third-best or worst is the current self-sufficiency policy.

EUROPEAN COMMUNITY POLICY

The European Community (EC-12) exported $28 billion of agricultural products to nations outside of the Community in 1986. The Community operated under the *Common Agricultural Policy* (CAP), which protected from outside competition (Harris *et al.*). The policy was not "common," however, because differential "green" exchange rates and other devices allowed agricultural supports to differ among countries within the EC.

Under *Europe 1992*, green rates and other differences in protection rates among member countries are, in principle, to terminate by the end of 1992. However, domestic prices in the EC have been and will continue to be well above border prices. In part because of that price policy, the EC has shifted from a major importer to a major exporter of grains. The Community also exports massive quantities of dairy products and other high value foods. These products must be heavily subsidized in world markets. Such trade distortions cannot be rationalized by self-sufficiency -- production far exceeds self-sufficiency in the commodities.

The EC market is sheltered by variable levies that maintain high domestic supports by imposing a tax (adjusted as often as necessary) to bring import prices to domestic support levels. Tax revenues from imports are used to provide export and production subsidies. The EC tax on US corn imports can be used to subsidize EC wheat exports in competition with US wheat exports in third-world countries.

Previous GATT negotiations left the US and the EC with policies each approved for the other and now regrets. The US did not anticipate that high rigid price supports would turn the EC into a large grain exporter, hence did not insist on adequate safeguards to preclude EC dumping through export subsidies. The EC failed to anticipate the deep inroads into their markets and competition with domestic production forthcoming from duty-free access of soybeans and non-grain feeds. So the EC has resorted to subsidies to domestic production of oilseeds that indirectly drive out American soybeans and corn gluten while the US subsidizes wheat and flour exports to combat EC grain export subsidies. The EC employs a host of other market interventions including slaughter and other processing subsidies, government buying of surpluses, storage aid, and border measures.

The EC has introduced several production disincentives including cow slaughter premiums, co-responsibility levies (taxes on producers used to pay for production cuts), a support trigger threshold (support price is cut if production exceeds a prescribed level for grains), and sugar and dairy production quotas. The latter have been somewhat effective but, overall, disincentives have been modest compared to those in the US. The EC is a large exporter of sugar, poultry, beef, dairy products, and wheat and products although the Community would export much less in a well-functioning market without subsidies. Figure 5.7 illustrates the impact of the EC price support and export subsidy policy.

Assumptions: Variable Levy

P_w = world price with free trade
P_d = EC domestic support price
P_r = ROW price with EC export subsidy
P_d-P_r = export subsidy allowed to vary as necessary to hold P_d constant as P_r changes
s = EC domestic supply
d = EC domestic demand
S = ROW supply
D = ROW demand
ED = excess demand, **d-s**, of EC under free trade
ES = excess supply, S-D, of ROW under free trade
ED' = excess demand, D-S, of ROW under EC interventions
ES' = excess supply, q_p'-q_c', of EC with export subsidy
q_c-q_p (EC imports) = Q_p-Q_c (ROW exports) = q_e before export subsidy
q_p'-q_c' (EC exports) = Q_c'-Q_p' (ROW imports) = q_e' after export subsidy.

117

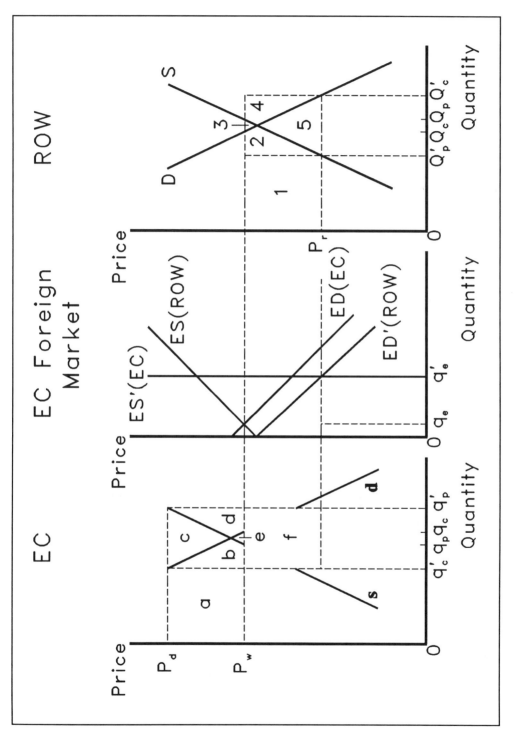

Figure 5.7. Effect of European Community (EC) Export Subsidy.

A notable feature of Figure 5.7 is that high domestic price supports and export subsidies shift the EC from an importer to an exporter.   Consequently, prices and trade determined by intersection of ES and ED before intervention are determined by ES´ and ED´ after intervention. We now turn to the welfare effect.

Welfare Analysis: Variable Levy

	EC	ROW
Consumer gain	-a-b-e	1+2+5
Producer gain	a+b+c	-1-2-3
Government gain	-b-c-d-e-f	---
Net national welfare	-b-d-2e-f	-3+5
Net world welfare (f=2+3+4+5)	-b-d-2e-f-3+5	
	or -b-d-2(e+3)-2-4	

Compared to free trade, EC consumers lose a+b+e while producers gain a+b+c. High government cost, which has threatened survival of the CAP from time to time, leaves an unequivocal welfare loss of b+d+2e+f to the EC. Of the net social cost to the EC, b+e arises from foregoing valued consumption, d+e arises from inducing high-cost production, and f arises from subsidizing ROW.

ROW has net welfare gains only if area 5 is greater than area 3. Area 3 is a welfare loss because *trade reversal* by the EC first drives ROW to autarky, denying gains from trade; then subsidies expand exports. Note that the conventional gains from trade, areas e and 3, become double penalties in the overall world loss from trade reversal.

Competing exporters are especially disadvantaged by EC subsidy policies. The US has responded with countervailing export subsidies to the delight of importing beneficiaries such as Russia. Big losers are competing exporters such as Argentina, which are victimized first by EC export subsidies and again by US counter-subsidies.

Oilseed Subsidy

The final example illustrates how a domestic commodity program price support can distort trade where the use of tariffs or other border measures have been ruled out. The case in point is soybean exports to the EC diminished by an EC subsidy to its oilseed processors. Processors passed the subsidy mostly to sunflower and rapeseed producers. Higher oilseed prices caused these producers to expand output and crowd out soybean imports mostly from the US and South America.

In December 1987, the American Soybean Association (ASA) filed a section 301 Unfair Trade Petition against the European Community. The petition alleged that the EC oilseed subsidies constituted unfair discrimination against imports. The Dispute Settlement Panel of the General Agreement on Tariffs and Trade (GATT) ruled in December 1989 that the European oilseed subsidies violate GATT trading rules and discriminate against oilseed imports. Figure 5.8 illustrates the economic impact on ROW and the European Community of EC oilseed subsidies.

Assumptions: Oilseed Subsidy

P_w = world oilseed price with free trade
P_d = EC domestic support price
P_w' = ROW oilseed price with oilseed subsidy

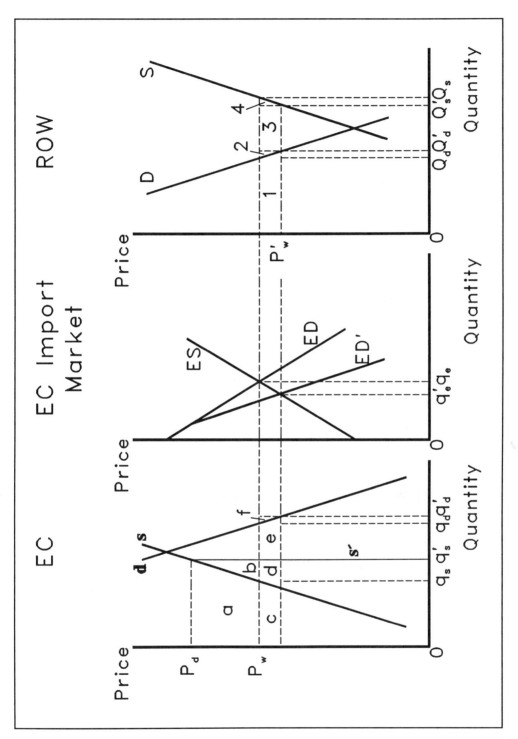

Figure 5.8. Effect of EC Oilseed Subsidy on Oilseed Market.

P_d-P'_w = EC oilseed subsidy per unit
s = EC domestic oilseed supply
s´s = EC domestic oilseed supply with subsidy maintaining domestic price at P_d
d = EC domestic oilseed demand
S = ROW supply of oilseeds
D = ROW demand for oilseeds
ED = excess demand, **d-s**, of EC without oilseed subsidy
ED´ = excess demand, **d-s´s**, of EC with oilseed subsidy
ES = excess supply, S-D, of ROW
q_d-q_s (EC oilseed imports) = Q_s-Q_d (ROW exports) = q_e without subsidy
q'_d-q'_s (EC oilseed imports) = Q'_s-Q'_d (ROW exports) = q'_e with subsidy.

A conceptual model in Figure 5.8 depicts the effect of EC oilseed subsidies P_d-P'_w. With EC oilseed subsidies, supply in the EC is **s´s** and demand is **d**; supply in the rest of the world (ROW) is S and demand is D. With subsidies, the world price of oilseeds is P'_w and the EC domestic price is P_d.

With subsidies, European demand in world markets shifts from ED to ED´. ROW export quantity decreases from q_e to q'_e. Price decreases from P_w to P'_w.

Welfare Analysis: Oilseed Subsidy

Welfare impact of the EC oilseed subsidy compared to a free market is approximated as follows:

	EC	ROW
Producer gain	a	-1-2-3-4
Consumer gain	c+d+e	1
Government or taxpayer gain	-a-b-c-d	---
Net national welfare	e-b	-2-3-4
Net world welfare (e+f=3)	-b-f-2-4	

EC producers gain and the government loses from oilseed subsidies. Because the EC is a large-country case, area e may be sizable so that the Community could gain. The issue of how much consumer benefits are enhanced by allowing unrestricted EC markets in oilseeds is best estimated empirically (see Gleckler and Tweeten).

ROW and world national welfare would be enhanced by termination of the EC oilseed processing subsidy. The end to subsidies raises ROW's oilseed exports, price, revenue, and welfare, the latter by area 2+3+4. Of this gain, 2+4 is a deadweight gain and area 3 is a transfer from the EC.

CONCLUSIONS

Commodity programs frequently drive a nation's trade policies. Such programs are particularly intractable in trade negotiations because they are often defended on emotional grounds of national sovereignty, right to food security (self-sufficiency), and need to preserve family farms and jobs in a basic industry. Programs command support from powerful agricultural lobbies.

The United States' leadership deserves much blame for exempting agriculture from the discipline of international trading rules. That initiative has backfired, however, as other countries have grown wealthy enough to subsidize their agriculture to compete in world markets utilizing GATT commodity program trade exemptions.

While American commodity programs rely heavily on direct payments and offset price supports with production controls to interfere only modestly with international trade, commodity programs of other major trading nations -- particularly Japan and the European Community -- have severely distorted trade. These programs produce large deadweight losses as noted in Chapter 3. US commodity programs have tended to absorb world weather and other shocks through buffer stocks and acreage controls. Countries protecting their agriculture with variable levies or quotas export internal shocks and fail to buffer external shocks.

REFERENCES

Braha, Habtu and Luther Tweeten. 1986. Evaluating past and prospective future payoffs from public investments to increase agricultural productivity. Technical Bulletin T-163. Stillwater: Agricultural Experiment Station, Oklahoma State University.

Gleckler, James and Luther Tweeten. July 1990. Benefits to US agriculture from terminating European oilseed subsidies. OP-14. Columbus: World Food Systems Project: NC-194, The Ohio State University.

Harris, S., A. Swinbank, and G. Wilkinson. 1983. *The Food and Farm Policies of the European Community*. Chichester, UK: Wiley.

Paarlberg, Philip, Alan Webb, Arthur Morey, and Jerry Sharples. 1984. Impacts of policy on US agricultural trade. ERS Staff Report No. AGES840802. Washington, DC: ERS, US Department of Agriculture.

Ruttan, Vernon W. 1982. *Agricultural Research Policy*. Minnesota: University of Minnesota Press.

Tweeten, Luther. 1989. *Farm Policy Analysis*. Boulder, CO: Westview Press.

US Department of Agriculture. February 1989. Trade policies and market opportunities for US farm exports, 1988 annual report. Washington, DC: Foreign Agricultural Service, USDA.

US Department of Agriculture. February 1990. The basic mechanisms of Japanese farm policy. Miscellaneous Publication No. 1478. Washington, DC: Economic Research Service, USDA.

US Department of Agriculture. September 1990. The basic mechanisms of European Community farm policy. Miscellaneous Publication No. 1485. Washington, DC: Economic Research Service, USDA.

US Department of Agriculture. December 1990. The 1990 Farm Act and the 1990 Budget Resolution Act. Miscellaneous Publication No. 1489. Washington, DC: Economic Research Service, USDA.

CHAPTER 6

Macroeconomic Policy, Exchange Rates, and Trade

Agricultural trade is highly unstable from year to year due to weather and other natural sources but also due to changes in border policies and commodity programs discussed previously. Another major source of agricultural trade changes is monetary policy (money supply, interest rates, and credit regulations) and fiscal policy (government expenditures, receipts, and the balance thereof). International trade and capital flows form a critical linkage between macroeconomic policy and the agricultural economy.

Agriculture accounts for 2 percent of gross national product (GNP) but for nearly 15 percent of US exports. It uses about twice as much capital per worker as industry and is a net debtor. Hence it is especially sensitive to macroeconomic policies through interest and exchange rates. The advent of an efficient international financial capital market and flexible exchange rates has created a global macroeconomic environment where an affluent nation is able to live beyond its means for an extended period -- with profound implications for the farming economy and other interest rate and exchange rate sensitive sectors.

Macroeconomic policies were the major source of cyclical variation in US farm exports in the 1970s and 1980s. The influence of macroeconomic policies on agriculture is often indirect and hence inscrutable. For this reason US wheat producers, for example, blamed Ottawa, Tokyo, and Brussels for trade failures in the 1970s and 1980s that in fact traced to Washington.

A major purpose of this chapter is to explicate how macroeconomic policy affects agriculture through international trade and capital flows. Substantial attention is given to foreign exchange supply and demand and to the exchange rate because these are critical linkages between macroeconomic policies and trade.

The close association between macroeconomic policy and trade is introduced with a simple example (see Tweeten, 1989a, pp. 188, 189). Gross national product (GNP) can be defined in terms of income disposed as

$$GNP = C + FT + ST + S \qquad (6.1)$$

where C is consumption expenditures, FT is federal tax payments, ST is state and local tax payments, and S is gross private (individual and corporate) domestic savings.[1] Alternatively, GNP can be defined as expenditures on final product

---

[1]Gross National Product includes income from US factors wherever they are employed, whereas Gross Domestic Product (GDP) includes income from factors within the US. Remittances sent home by US workers employed abroad are part of GNP but not of GDP.

$$GNP = C + FE + SE + I + (X - M) \qquad \text{(6.2)}$$

where FE is federal expenditures, SE is state and local government expenditures, I is gross private domestic investment, X is exports, and M is imports. Subtracting (6.2) from (6.1), the result is

$$(S - I) \quad + \quad (ST - SE) \quad + \quad (FT - FE) \quad = \quad (X - M) \qquad \text{(6.3)}$$

	Private Savings Surplus	State and Local Govt. Surplus	Federal Budget Surplus	International Trade Surplus
		($ billion)		
1980	41.4 +	26.8 +	(-61.3) =	9.5
1982	109.8 +	35.1 +	(-145.9) =	0.3
1986	(-3.9) +	60.8 +	(-204.0) =	(-125.7)

Equation 6.3 is interpreted with the help of specific numbers for 1980 (a somewhat normal employment year with a modest budget deficit), 1982 (a recession year), and 1986 (a full-employment budget deficit year). The federal budget deficit can be financed from net domestic private savings surpluses (individual and corporate savings less investment), from state and local government surpluses (revenue less expenditures), or from foreign savings inflow supplied dollars by our international trade deficit. In 1980, the federal deficit was financed domestically because private savings surplus plus the state-local government surplus exceeded the deficit, hence a trade deficit was unneeded to provide foreigners with dollar "savings" to finance the US budget deficit.

With recession in 1982, individuals and corporations saved for a "rainy day" and cut investment in a pessimistic business climate. Hence, the private savings surplus was large. A federal deficit was appropriate in such circumstances to maintain aggregate demand and stimulate the economy. The budget deficit did not lead to a trade deficit because domestic net private savings ($109.8 billion) plus domestic state-local government surplus ($35.1 billion) approximately equalled the deficit. (The relationship is not exact in equation 6.3 because time lags, foreign currency reserves, and international capital flows are not fully accounted for.)

With full employment in 1986, private investment exceeded private savings so the net domestic funds available to finance the $204 billion deficit totalled only $60.8 billion from state and local government surplus less $3.9 billion from net private savings for a total of only $60.8 - 3.9 = $56.6 billion. Foreign sources filled most of the savings gap. The current account, by definition, always balances: the 1986 deficit in goods and services of $125.7 billion was precisely offset by capital inflow. In other words, the $125.7 billion trade deficit created by high real interest and exchange rates supplied dollars to foreigners whose savings then financed the US budget deficit (aside from a statistical discrepancy of $21.4 billion, perhaps accounted for by drawing on dollar reserves).

A conclusion from the above analysis is that in a full-employment economy where private savings surplus and state and local government surplus sum to near zero, the federal budget deficit and the trade deficit tend to be roughly equal to each other and to net capital inflow and net addition to foreign debt incurred by the US. The domestic private savings surplus is not very responsive to higher interest rates so foreign savings must be attracted. The associated high real interest and exchange rates (dollar value) generating the trade deficit to finance the budget deficit damaged the economy of agriculture and other US net export sectors. Erection of trade barriers to end the trade deficit while continuing the budget deficit would have forced interest rates to levels crowding out private investment. Resulting national stagnation would have damaged the economy of agriculture. Of course, a nation cannot indefinitely consume more than it produces, import more than it exports, invest more than it saves, and borrow more than it lends. Agricultural trade disadvantaged in the first phase of the economic degradation cycle is advantaged in the second phase as imbalances of the first phase are redressed (Tweeten, 1989a). The net result probably is less output and trade on average over the entire cycle and certainly is more instability than under sound macroeconomic policies.

To understand the above process we must understand the workings of markets that determine trade quantities and prices, aggregate income, savings, investment, and international capital flows. Such markets also establish interests rates, wage rates, unemployment rates, exchange rates, and inflation rates.

THE FOREIGN EXCHANGE MARKET

Markets set foreign exchange rates in a flexible exchange rate system. Although not apparent to the typical layperson, such markets play an important role in the life of each of us. The price in that market, the exchange rate, is defined as the price of some foreign currency in terms of domestic currency, or π_D. Using this terminology for the US, the exchange rate for a shilling (sh) of country A is (say) \$.05 or 5 cents. Alternatively the exchange rate of the dollar may be expressed as the price of domestic currency in terms of some foreign currency, or π_F. Using this terminology, the exchange rate of the dollar is 20 shillings. Note that $\pi_D = 1/\pi_F$.

A change in the exchange rate to $\pi_F = 25$ shillings is described as an *appreciation, revaluation*, or rise in the value of the dollar and a *depreciation, devaluation*, or fall in the value of the shilling. Note that a rise in the value of the dollar means an increase in the exchange rate expressed in foreign currency π_F but a decrease in π_D expressed in domestic currency.

The *Wall Street Journal* publishes spot (current market) exchange rates for a large number of currencies. Forward market rates for 30, 90, and 180 days along with futures and put and call option prices are published for the major currencies -- the only currencies in which such markets exist. Futures markets enable participants to hedge against changes in exchange rates for purchase or sale of real goods and services to be delivered abroad at a later date. By that process the risk associated with fluctuating exchange rates is shifted by hedgers to speculators.

For many purposes such as gauging the overall influence of the exchange rate on aggregate exports, imports, and balance of payments, it is desirable to know how the value of the dollar has changed with respect to an aggregate of currencies and not just with respect to any one currency. For this purpose, the exchange rate is weighted by trade volume of individual countries and summed to form a US exchange rate index. It is important to note that a published exchange rate index for *all* US trade is not necessarily applicable to agricultural trade. Even within agriculture, the exchange rate index for wheat, which must be weighted heavily by sales to developing countries, will differ significantly from an exchange rate index for soybeans, which must be weighted heavily by sales to developed countries (Henneberry *et al.*).

It is also important to distinguish between dollar exchange rates for agricultural *export markets* versus *competing exporters*. For example, the dollar may depreciate relative to currencies of soybean buyers, thereby expanding export demand for US soybeans. But if at the same time currencies of competing exporters depreciate even more relative to the real value of currency in countries importing soybeans, our competitors will have an advantage in competing for soybean export markets.

Various means are used to establish the foreign exchange rate magnitude. One is *absolute purchasing power parity*. If a pair of shoes is produced and sold for $100 in the United States and a comparable pair of shoes is produced and sold in country A for 200 francs, the absolute purchasing power parity, defined as the price of the franc in terms of dollars, is

$$\pi_D = \$100/200 \ francs = \$.50$$

and the price of the dollar in terms of francs is

$$\pi_F = 200 \ francs/\$100 = 2 \ francs.$$

A change in the exchange rate from 1 franc = $.50 to 1 franc = $.40 is called appreciation or revaluation of the dollar. And a change from 1 franc = $.50 to 1 franc = $.67 is called depreciation or devaluation of the dollar.

Some prefer to use the π_F form to express the exchange rate. Given $\pi_D = 1/\pi_F$, in the first case, above, the dollar appreciated or rose from 2 francs to 2.5 francs. In the second case the dollar depreciated or declined in value from 2 francs to 1.5 francs.

Dynamic purchasing power parity is constant purchasing power of a currency over time regardless of whether the currency initially or currently represents absolute purchasing power parity. In a hypothetical case, assume the exchange rate initially was $1 = 2 francs and the consumer price index in country A increased from an index of 100 to an index of 120 or 20 percent and in the US increased from an index of 100 to 140 or by 40 percent over a 5-year period from 1985 to 1990. Then dynamic purchasing power parity is

$$\pi_F(1990) = \frac{2.00 \ francs(120/100)}{(140/100)} = 1.71 \ francs.$$

$$\pi_D(1990) = \frac{\$.50(140/100)}{(120/100)} = \$.58.$$

It follows that an exchange rate of 2 francs in 1985 was equal in purchasing power to an exchange rate of 1.71 francs in 1990. Dynamic purchasing power parity adjusts for general price level changes only. Differential productivity gains, capital accumulation, wars, and fiscal policy also cause the real exchange rate to change but were not considered in the foregoing calculation. Expectations of *future* changes in factors that influence terms of trade heavily influence spot exchange rate markets.

Nominal exchange rates are those we observe from day to day and are the result of the market and other forces. The nominal rate may change for a host of reasons including different rates of change in (1) the general price level between countries and (2) technology, resources, supply, and demand between countries. (Expectations of the future course of these variables play a critical role, but we abstain from that issue for now.) A *purely* nominal exchange rate adjustment due to a difference in the general price level between countries merely corrects the market exchange rate for inflation to leave the real exchange rate and trade unchanged. In contrast, a change in the real exchange rate (nominal rate adjusted for inflation) because of forces in (2) above causes trade to change between countries because purchasing power is changed.

The same principle as above is used to calculate changes in real exchange rates over time. If inflation is high in one country versus another, comparisons of market (nominal) exchange rates over time are likely to be meaningless in terms of their effect on trade. For any traded commodity in an open world market, the domestic price of a good in A can be expressed as a function of the price of the good in ROW, or

$$P_A = \pi_D P_R \tag{6.4}$$

where P_A is domestic price in home currency, π_D is the exchange rate expressed in home currency, and P_R is the ROW price. Thus if corn is $3 per bushel in the US and one mark is $.50, and the price of corn is 6 marks in Germany, then the price of corn in Germany expressed in dollars is

$$P_A = \$3 \; per \; bushel = \$.50 \; x \; (6 \; marks \; per \; bushel). \tag{6.5}$$

The law of one price (assumptions of absolute purchasing power parity, no transport cost, and arbitrage if price deviates from this relationship) assures this result.

It follows from (6.4) that

$$\frac{dP_A}{P_A} = \frac{d\pi_D}{\pi_D} + \frac{dP_R}{P_R}. \tag{6.6}$$

The percentage change in domestic price from a change in the exchange rate is equal to the percentage change in the exchange rate plus the percentage change in ROW price of the commodity. In the small-country case, the exchange rate does not influence world price so dP_R/P_R is zero and the percentage change in domestic price is equal to the percentage change in the exchange rate.

An alternative is to express prices in ROW's currency instead of country A's currency; that is

$$P_R = \pi_F P_A \quad or \quad \frac{P_A}{\pi_D}.$$

Using earlier numbers, the price of corn per bushel in Germany is

$$P_R = 6 \; marks \; per \; bushel = 2 \; marks \; x \; (\$3 \; per \; bushel) = \$3/\$.50.$$

where $\pi_F = 2$ marks and $\pi_D = \$.50$. The two expressions are equivalent.

Suppose the consumer price index (CPI) in the US changed from an index of 150 in 1985 to an index of 210 in 1990. Suppose that the consumer price index in country A changed from 160 in 1985 to 192 in 1990. And suppose the value of the dollar appreciated from 2.0 francs per dollar in 1985 to 3.0 francs in 1990 in nominal market terms. The real exchange rate is calculated as the increase in the nominal exchange rate 3.0/2.0 = 1.5 (50 percent gain) times the relative inflation rate in the two countries. US prices increased by a factor of 210/150 = 1.4 or 40 percent and in country A by 192/160 = 1.20 or 20 percent. The nominal US exchange rate increased 50 percent and the US inflation rate exceeded A's inflation rate by 40 - 20 = 20 percentage points so real appreciation was approximately 30 percent.

The formula for the US real exchange rate π_{Foi} in any year i compared to year 0 is

$$\pi_{Foi} = \frac{\text{real exchange rate appreciation}}{\text{from year 0 to year i}}$$

$$= \frac{\begin{array}{c}\textit{nominal exchange rate}\\\textit{francs/dollar in year i}\\\hline\textit{nominal exchange rate}\\\textit{francs/dollar in year 0}\end{array} \times \frac{\begin{array}{c}\textit{Country A CPI year i}\\\textit{Country A CPI year 0}\end{array}}{\begin{array}{c}\textit{US CPI year i}\\\textit{US CPI year 0}\end{array}}$$

or in the above case

$$\pi_{Foi} = \frac{3.0}{2.0} \frac{\dfrac{192}{160}}{\dfrac{210}{150}} = 1.5 \frac{1.2}{1.4} = 1.286.$$

The 28.6 percent appreciation in the real exchange rate contrasts with the 50 percent appreciation in the nominal exchange rate from 1985 to 1990. Rational markets respond to real rather than nominal exchange rates.

When the exchange rate is expressed in domestic currency π_D, the nominal rise in the dollar corresponds to a change in the exchange rate from \$.50 in 1985 to \$.33 per franc in 1990. The formula for the real US exchange rate in π_{Doi} terms is

$$\pi_{Doi} = \frac{\text{real exchange rate appreciation}}{\text{from year 0 to year i}}$$

$$= \frac{\begin{array}{c}\textit{nominal exchange rate}\\\textit{dollars/franc in year i}\\\hline\textit{nominal exchange rate}\\\textit{dollars/franc in year 0}\end{array} \times \frac{\begin{array}{c}\textit{US CPI year i}\\\textit{US CPI year 0}\end{array}}{\begin{array}{c}\textit{Country A CPI year i}\\\textit{Country A CPI year 0}\end{array}}$$

or in the above case

$$\pi_{Doi} = \frac{.33}{.50} \frac{\dfrac{210}{150}}{\dfrac{192}{160}} = .67 \frac{1.4}{1.2} = .778.$$

The formula indicates that the dollar appreciated in real terms from an index of 100 in 1985 to an index of 77.8 in 1990. Because $\pi_F = 1/\pi_D$, this corresponds to a rise in the dollar to 1/.778 = 1.286 or an index of 128.6 in 1990 from 100 in 1985, the same 28.6 percent real appreciation found by the earlier formula.

DETERMINANTS OF DEMAND AND SUPPLY
OF FOREIGN EXCHANGE

The demand for foreign exchange arises from needs to pay for imports of goods and services, to finance capital outflows to purchase foreign assets, and to finance government interventions in financial markets influencing exchange rates. For simplicity, demand here is confined to goods and services. The demand for foreign exchange is taken to be determined initially by the demand for imports of goods and services. Demand for foreign exchange in A is the value of imports of A times the foreign exchange rate at alternative exchange rates. Thus the foreign exchange demand is a schedule of the value of imports expressed in foreign currency. The foreign exchange supply is equal to the value of exports expressed in foreign currency.

Foreign Exchange Supply

We first address the determination of foreign exchange supply. Foreign exchange supply derives from the supply of exports. The steps followed herein are first to show the impact of a change in the exchange rate on exports of country A to ROW, then to show how the elasticity of foreign exchange is a function of elasticities of excess supply and demand for goods and services.

Given initial equilibrium in markets of country A and ROW at world price P_w and exports q_e, an appreciation of the exchange value of A's currency shifts downward the excess demand curve ED to ED´ because ROW will be willing to pay a lower price in A's currency at any quantity (Figure 6.1). Given that

$$P_A = \pi_D P_R$$

then π_D falls as A's currency appreciates, pivoting ED counterclockwise around the intersection on the horizontal axis. That is, at a given export quantity q_e, and P_R, a lower π_D (revaluation of A's currency) lowers the demand price P_A. The result in Figure 6.1 is to reduce the domestic price in A, raise the price in ROW, reduce exports from A, and reduce imports of ROW. The example can be interpreted as a devaluation of ROW's currency.

In the lower middle panel of Figure 6.1, the export market for A is expressed in currency of ROW so the π_F form of the exchange rate is convenient. Excess supply comes from A, which must be converted to ROW's currency by

$$P_R = \pi_F P_A.$$

The impact of appreciation of A's currency is to raise the numerical value of π_F at each quantity q_e and hence to raise P_R. This rotates ES counterclockwise to ES´. The revaluation acts as an implicit export tax, reducing the export quantity supplied at any given price. Real prices and quantities are the same as in the top panel of Figure 6.1. Results illustrate that the analysis differs but the outcome is the same whether the exchange rate is expressed in domestic currency of A (π_D) or in foreign currency (π_F).

It is noted in Figure 6.1 that appreciation of the currency of A is deflationary in A because price falls from P_w to P_a'. This is equivalent to saying that depreciation of currency in ROW is inflationary because price rises from initial equilibrium to P_r'.

130

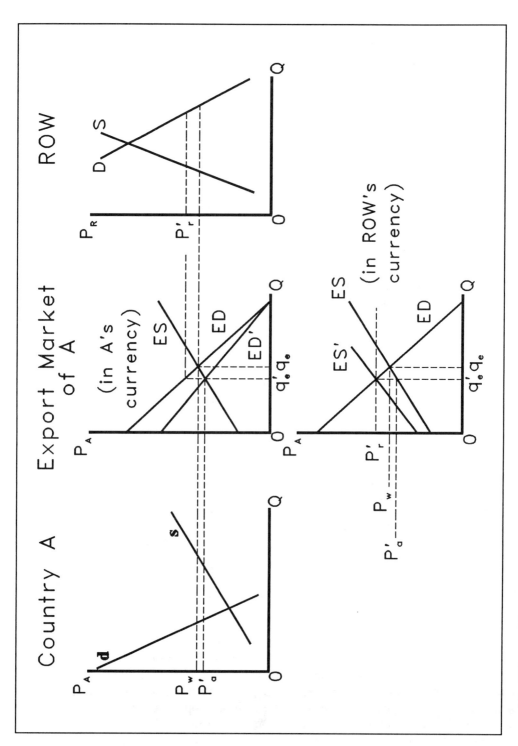

Figure 6.1. Effect of Revaluation of Currency of Exporting Country A.

The supply of foreign currency F_s in A is the value of exports expressed in foreign currency or

$$F_s = \pi_F P_A q_e \quad or \quad P_r q_e$$

where $\pi_F P_A$ is the price of exports in foreign currency. As noted in Figure 6.1, the foreign price P_r and export quantity q_e move in opposite directions with changes in π_F. Whether $P_r q_e$ ($P_r = P_w$) exceeds or falls short of $P'_r q'_e$ in the lower panel of Figure 6.1 depends on elasticities in the market.

The elasticity E_{S_π} of foreign exchange supply with respect to π_F depends on the elasticity of export excess supply ES with respect to price of exports in foreign currency units, or E_{ES}, and the elasticity of export excess demand ED with respect to the price of exports, or E_{ED} (Grennes, 1984, p. 407)

$$E_{S_\pi} = \frac{E_{ES}(1 + E_{ED})}{E_{ED} - E_{ES}}.$$

Because E_{ED} is negative and E_{ES} is positive, the denominator is negative. If export demand is elastic, the numerator also is negative, making E_{S_π} positive so the foreign exchange supply curve slopes upward to the right. A rise in π_D (depreciation of the currency of A) raises the supply of foreign exchange in A.

If ED is perfectly inelastic (the very-large-country case), E_{S_π} is -1. If ED is perfectly elastic (the small-country case), E_{S_π} is equal to the elasticity of excess supply and hence is positive. Thus the supply curve for foreign exchange will slope upward to the right for a small-country case. It follows that devaluation is more effective in correcting a balance of payments shortfall for a small country than for a large country. In a small country dominated by one export, the foreign exchange supply elasticities can be approximated by the excess supply curve elasticity calculated from the weighted domestic supply and demand elasticities for the good.

Because the foreign exchange supply elasticity often is unavailable for a country, an approximation is sometimes useful. If a country's exports do not influence world prices and the exchange rate, an approximation for the foreign exchange elasticity of supply is

$$E_{E_\pi} \approx \frac{E_s - E_d}{Domestic \ share \ exported}.$$

This foreign exchange supply elasticity is likely to exceed the domestic output supply elasticity E_s and the domestic farm level price elasticity of demand E_d.

A typical domestic supply elasticity is 0.2 in the short run and 1.0 in the long run for domestic farm commodities. A typical farm level commodity demand elasticity is -0.2. Thus a typical E_{E_π} value is (0.2+0.2)/share or 0.8 in the short run if half of domestic production is exported. The value of E_{E_π} is (1.0+0.2)/share or 2.4 in the long run if half of domestic production is exported. The elasticity of exchange supply rises as the share exported falls. Of course, the net impact on foreign exchange depends on what happens to imports in addition to what happens to exports. The latter was considered above; what happens to import value will be examined later.

Foreign Exchange Demand

The demand for foreign exchange derives from the demand for imports. Foreign exchange demand is equal to the value of imports expressed in foreign currency. This demand depends on the level of the exchange rate and the behavior of price and quantity. This subsection first illustrates the impact of exchange rates on imports before relating imports of goods and services to foreign exchange demand quantity.

Revaluation (appreciation) of country A's currency can be expressed in the import market for A either in prices of A or prices of ROW. If expressed in A's currency, the price in A is

$$P_A = \pi_D P_R.$$

For a given import quantity q_e and foreign price P_R, appreciation of A's currency (lower π_D) reduces the supply price P_A. The reduced supply price at each quantity offered by ROW to A rotates ES clockwise to ES´ around an imaginary horizontal axis intercept (upper middle panel in Figure 6.2). Appreciation of A's currency is an implicit ad valorem import subsidy, reducing the domestic price in A to P_a' and raising price in ROW from the original P_w to P_r'. Imports of A rise from q_e to q_e'. This outcome is equivalent to a devaluation of ROW's currency, which causes its exports and domestic price to rise.

Alternatively, the revaluation of A's currency may be analyzed in the import market of A with currency of ROW -- the lower middle panel of Figure 6.2. Price in ROW is

$$P_R = \pi_F P_A.$$

With a given q_e and P_A, appreciation of A's currency raises π_F and hence P_R. It follows that in ROW's currency, the imports of A bring a higher price at every quantity, pivoting ED clockwise to ED´ in Figure 6.2. Although the analyses differ, results are precisely the same for prices and quantities in the lower and upper middle panels of Figure 6.2.

The demand for foreign exchange F_d in A is the value of exports expressed in foreign currency or

$$F_d = \pi_F P_A q_e \quad or \quad P_r q_e.$$

It is apparent from the lower panel of Figure 6.2 that appreciation of currency in A raises both price P_r and quantity q_e from the initial equilibrium in Figure 6.2, hence higher values of π_F raise the quantity of foreign exchange F. Thus the exchange demand curve ordinarily slopes downward to the right.

The elasticity of demand for foreign exchange with respect to the foreign exchange rate π_F can be expressed as (Stern, ch. 2 appendix; Grennes, 1984, p. 406):

$$E_{D\pi} = \frac{E_{ED}(1 + E_{ES})}{E_{ES} - E_{ED}}.$$

Normally E_{ED} is negative and E_{ES} positive. Hence $E_{D\pi}$ ordinarily will be negative so the demand for foreign exchange, as expected, will slope downward to the right. In the very-large-country case ES is vertical so $E_{ES} = 0$. Then $E_{D\pi} = -1$. Each 1 percent rise in π_D (devaluation) reduces the demand quantity of foreign exchange by 1 percent. In the small-country case, ES is horizontal, hence $E_{ES} = \infty$. Dividing numerator and denominator by E_{ES}

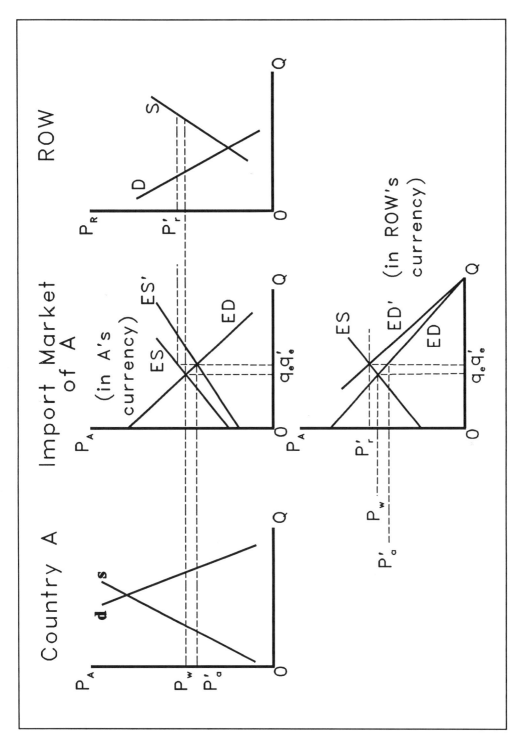

Figure 6.2. Effects of Revaluation of Currency of Importing Country A.

in the formula, it is apparent that $E_{D\pi} = E_{ED}$ and hence is negative. That is, the elasticity of demand for foreign exchange is equal to the elasticity of excess demand for commodities in A. $E_{D\pi}$ is not easily measured empirically but in a small country dominated by one major import can be approximated from the weighted domestic demand and supply elasticities for that good.

If a country's imports leave world price and exchange rate unchanged, an approximation for the foreign exchange demand elasticity is

$$E_{D\pi} \approx \frac{E_d - E_s}{\text{Domestic share imported}}.$$

In absolute value, the exchange demand elasticity is likely to exceed the domestic output demand elasticity E_d and the domestic output supply elasticity E_s.

To illustrate using a typical commodity demand elasticity of -0.2 and supply elasticity of 0.2 in the short run and 1.0 in the long run, the short-run demand elasticity of foreign exchange is (-0.2-0.2)/share or -0.8 if 50 percent of domestic use is from imports. In the long run the elasticity is (-0.2-1.0)/share or -2.4 again assuming that half of domestic use is from imports.

FOREIGN EXCHANGE, SUPPLY-DEMAND EQUILIBRIUM, AND PRICE RESPONSE

The aggregate supply of foreign exchange is found by multiplying price in foreign currency value times quantity of exports from Figure 6.1 and summing over all commodities at various exchange rates. The aggregate demand for foreign exchange is found by multiplying price in foreign currency value times quantity of imports from Figure 6.2 and summing over all commodities at various exchange rates.

Figure 6.3 shows foreign exchange supply curve S derived from demand and supply for exported products as in Figure 6.1 and foreign exchange demand D derived from demand and supply for imported products as in Figure 6.2. Equilibrium is at foreign exchange rate π_0 and foreign exchange quantity (value) F_0. At that point a (say) dollar of imports has the same marginal value to country A as a dollar of exports. If no or too few goods of A can be exported at a profit to earn foreign exchange to meet the demand for foreign exchange, the currency of A will depreciate until sufficient commodities are competitive in international markets so that the values of foreign exchange in supply and demand are equal to the margin. In this way, comparative advantage in production and tastes in consumption are turned into absolute profit in production at home and absolute price advantage for export in some commodities of A in international markets.

In equilibrium, a kilo of wheat produced in A has the same value to consumers in A whether exported (to buy desired imports) or consumed domestically. At the margin, a resource also has the same value whether used to produce for the domestic or foreign market. Hence if soil erosion in wheat production is a problem, it makes as much sense to curtail domestic consumption as to curtail exports for saving soil. However, the preferred approach is to target soil conservation to the minority of wheat produced on erosion-prone soil.

An overvalued currency at π_d resulting from a pegged exchange rate unresponsive to greater inflation in A than ROW results in exchange quantity F_1. At that quantity, the marginal cost in domestic resources of earning another unit of foreign exchange is π_s and

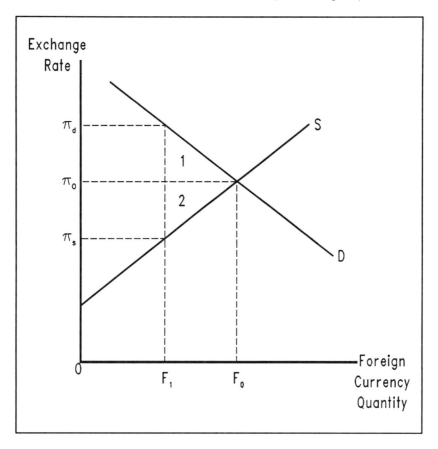

Figure 6.3. Foreign Exchange Supply and Demand for Country A.

its marginal worth to those who would import is π_d. The overvalued exchange rate can be maintained by exchange controls, import quotas or tariffs, or other means, causing a net social cost in foregone full national income of area $1+2$ in Figure 6.3. The gap between F_0 and F_1 is likely to be reduced by parallel (informal) market trading in foreign exchange but deadweight losses are raised by resources devoted to circumventing the distortions. Working backwards through the foregoing analysis, it is apparent that the overvalued currency reduces exports and increases imports, allowing consumers depending on imports to live better but disadvantaging agricultural sectors depending on export markets.

The international balance of payments BP as defined at the beginning of the chapter may be written as

$$BP = X - M = P_x x - \pi_D P_m m \qquad (6.7)$$

where X and M are values respectively of exports and imports, P_x and P_m are respectively domestic currency prices of exports and foreign currency prices of imports, and x and m are respectively quantities of exports and imports. At issue is how BP changes with a change in the exchange rate. If a large demand relative to supply of foreign exchange depreciates the dollar, that lower dollar must improve balance of payments for the economy to right itself.

The *terms of trade* P_x/P_m, defined as the ratio of prices received for exports to prices paid for imports, heavily influence the balance of payments.[2] To express exports and imports in the same currency units, it is necessary to correct either the export or import price for the exchange rate.

If the price of American export goods is $10, the price of imports is 20 marks, and the exchange rate is π_D in dollars per mark equals $.50, then the terms of trade T in dollars is

$$T = \frac{P_x}{P_m(\pi_D)} = \frac{10}{20(.5\,dollars)} = 1.0$$

or, alternatively, in marks is

$$T = \frac{P_x(\pi_F)}{P_m} = \frac{10(2\,marks)}{20} = 1.0.$$

Of special interest is terms of trade for a composite of goods and services over time. Terms of trade especially for third-world agricultural countries have fallen over time as farm products that they export have declined in price relative to industrial products and services that they import. Developing countries, voicing their concerns through UNCTAD and other outlets, have labeled declining terms of trade an injustice perpetrated by a conspiracy of multinational industrial cartels and governments of developed countries.

Declining terms of trade are not necessarily an indicator of low returns on resources, poverty, injustice, or market failure. The ratio of prices received to prices paid is only *commodity terms of trade*. A better measure of economic position is *factor terms of trade*, defined as real prices received for output per unit of input. It is commodity terms of trade multiplied by productivity. American farmers, for example, more than tripled (3.2 to be exact) productivity of resources from 1910-14 (a standard base period) and 1990. Hence the essentially unchanged constant dollar aggregate volume of farm production resources could earn as much as in 1910-14 with less than one-third the real price! In fact, commodity terms of trade fell only one-half so that factor terms of trade were 3.2(0.5) = 1.6 times or 60 percent higher in 1990 than in 1910-14. Countries which stagnate agricultural productivity by undue taxes and failure to invest in agricultural research and extension will find their economic position not static but worsening as other nations pass them by with productivity gains.

At issue is whether devaluation will improve or worsen the balance of payments. As noted earlier in Figure 6.1, devaluation lowers export prices expressed in foreign currency. If the quantity increase does not compensate, foreign exchange earnings from exports will fall. Effects can be different in the short and long run because the expansion in exports in response to exchange rates takes time. Furthermore, imports must be considered to gauge the full effect of devaluation on balance of payments. Some evidence exists for a so-called *J-curve response*, that is, the balance of payments at first worsens and later improves with devaluation.

The net impact of exchange rate adjustment on balance of payments is often expressed by the *Marshall-Lerner condition*

---

[2]Grennes (1990, p. 4) discusses an alternative measure of the terms of trade, the ratio of prices of traded goods to those of nontraded goods.

$$E_{x\pi} - E_{m\pi} > 1 \quad or \quad E_{x\pi} + |E_{m\pi}| > 1$$

where $E_{x\pi}$ is the elasticity of aggregate export quantity with respect to the exchange rate π_D, and $E_{m\pi}$ is the aggregate import quantity with respect to the exchange rate (see Annex for proof). Depreciation of currency will improve the trade balance if the export elasticity plus the import elasticity (absolute value) exceed 1.0. It is cautioned that the Marshall-Lerner condition requires fixed prices and initial equilibrium and other assumptions of partial equilibrium not met in the real world. Hence more complex models often are used to determine the response of foreign exchange to the exchange rate.

Empirical Estimates of Responsiveness to Total and Agricultural Exports to Foreign Exchange Rates

The elasticity of exports with respect to exchange rate depends not only on theoretical considerations such as outlined in Figure 6.1 and 6.2 but also on institutional considerations. From the Bretton Woods agreement of 1944 to the early 1970s, the world was on a de facto dollar standard. Because the dollar had a fixed ratio to gold of $35 per ounce, it was sometimes called a gold standard. However, the dollar provided liquidity and was the day-to-day operational standard.

The dollar, though in theory a fixed exchange rate, in fact was a flexible exchange rate because all other currencies could vary against the dollar to maintain balance of payments equilibrium worldwide. Although developing countries on the average overvalue currencies and tend toward trade deficits, many developed countries chose neomerchantilism (accumulation of hard currency) and trade surpluses that left the US with an untenable trade deficit. The dollar was devalued in 1971 and freely floated since 1973.

Three exchange rate regimes dominate the world (Henneberry, pp. 19, 20):

1. *Freely floating exchange rates* were found in only eight countries on June 30, 1984: United States, Australia, Canada, Japan, Lebanon, South Africa, the United Kingdom, and Uruguay.
2. *Managed floats* were found in several countries. With that system, governments intervene frequently to support the currency by using central bank reserves to buy or sell the currency to even out price fluctuations and avoid overvalued or undervalued currency. Examples were Ecuador, Greece, India, Mexico, New Zealand, Nigeria, the Philippines, and Spain -- as of June 30, 1984. In addition, the European Community had a special non-floating currency arrangement based on the European Currency Unit (ECU) with somewhat limited flexibility. Currencies of member countries were allowed to vary in value only within a limited range with respect to the ECU. The ECU, like the SDR, discussed below, was an accounting currency rather than an operational currency used as a medium of exchange in everyday transactions.
3. *Pegged exchange rates* as of June 30, 1984, were found in 90 of the 140 member countries of the International Monetary Fund (IMF). Of these, 33 were pegged to the US dollar, 13 to the French franc, 5 to other single currencies such as the British pound, 11 were pegged to the Special Drawing Rights (SDR) of the IMF, and 28 were pegged to other currency composites such as a weighted average of trading partners. (The SDR was a weighted average of the US dollar, French franc, British pound, German mark, and Japanese yen.)

Table 6.1 shows proportions of US agricultural exports by foreign exchange regime. In general, more agricultural exports than of nonagricultural exports were to countries with currencies pegged to or in other ways less than responsive to changes in the value of the dollar. A shift in the US exchange rate will not fully change the exchange rate with respect to countries pegged to the dollar, pegged to a composite containing the dollar, or managed with a float that accounts for the dollar. That diminishes effectiveness of devaluation by the US. Of course, a currency pegged to the dollar shifts its exchange rate with respect to the rest of the world as the dollar rises or falls.

A dilemma facing US agriculture is that the nations most fully realigning currencies when the dollar changes are Japan and Western European countries, which heavily protect their agriculture. Their currencies change value but low price elasticities limit the trade response. On the other hand, more open agricultural trade countries tend to have pegged currencies. They have high price elasticities but do not much change the real value of their currency, thus limiting the trade response. These considerations restrict responsiveness of US exports to price and exchange rate changes. The magnitude of responsiveness is an empirical issue examined below. Unfortunately, estimates differ widely among studies and are not highly reliable.

Despite these currency rigidities, American exports and imports appear to be sensitive enough to price and exchange rates to move balance of payments toward equilibrium. Long-run price elasticities of demand for US merchandise exports and imports

Table 6.1. Proportion of Agricultural and Nonagricultural Exports by Foreign Exchange Regime of the Destination Country, United States, 1983.

Foreign Exchange Regime As Of June 30, 1984	Proportion of Agricultural Exports	Proportion of Nonagricultural Exports
	(Percent)	
Pegged to US dollar	9.24	5.46
Pegged to French franc	0.17	0.18
Pegged to other currency	0.02	0.01
Pegged to SDR	0.36	0.41
Pegged to other composite	9.44	9.39
Flexibility limited: single	2.12	6.19
Flexibility limited: group	19.34	16.69
Adjusted by set indicators	5.83	3.23
Other managed floating	25.16	15.15
Independently floating	28.32	43.02
Total	100.00	100.00

Source: See Henneberry, p. 23.

provide a first approximate to exchange rate elasticities.[3] Twelve estimates averaged -1.1 for exports and, surprisingly, the same -1.1 for imports (Belongia and Stone, p. 18). The absolute sum of these estimates, 2.2, taken as rough measures of the sum of demand and supply elasticities of foreign exchange, more than satisfy the Marshall-Lerner condition for devaluation success in righting the balance of payments.

Price elasticities of demand for exports by commodity shown in Chapter 2 are expected to be higher (absolute value) than the exchange rate elasticities of demand because price has a large substitution effect. An offsetting factor is the larger income effect of exchange rates that influence all commodities and hence aggregate purchasing power of a country.

It is notable that if the Longmire-Morey estimates arbitrarily are taken as short-run elasticities of export demand with respect to exchange rates and the Chambers-Just estimates are taken as long-run elasticities, then the elasticities in Table 6.2 are roughly in line with the price elasticities of export demand shown in Chapter 2. The conclusion is that export demand, earnings, and foreign exchange are responsive to the exchange ratio but probably not very responsive in the short run.

No estimate is available of import supply elasticity with respect to exchange rate. However, if we arbitrarily assume equality of agricultural export and import response to the exchange rate as was found for total US exports and imports, then the elasticity of net agricultural exchange earnings to a 1 percent exchange rate devaluation is 0.7 + 0.7 = 1.4. That devaluation increases the net value of agricultural trade earnings and revaluation decreases net agricultural exchange earnings is consistent with past experience.

Pegged Exchange Rates and Inflation

The foregoing analysis emphasized the impact of fiscal policy on trade. Monetary policy also can be important. To avoid unstable flexible exchange rates set in "thin" markets, as noted earlier many developing countries peg their currencies to the US dollar, the United Kingdom pound sterling, the French franc, or the Standard Drawing Rights of the International Monetary Fund. The problem is that when inflation is more rapid in country A than in the country (or country group) to which its currency is pegged, the currency of A becomes overvalued. A moving peg exchange rate causes exchange rate distortions if the peg is not moved often enough in an inflationary economy.

Table 6.2. Estimated Impacts of a 1 Percent Appreciation in the Value of the US Dollar on US Agricultural Exports.

Commodity	Longmire-Morey	Chambers-Just	Batten-Belongia
Wheat	-0.19	-1.48	---
Corn	-0.25	-3.45	---
Soybeans	-0.31	-0.67	---
All Agricultural Exports	---	---	-0.71

Source: See Henneberry (p. 25) for original sources.

---

[3]Because $\pi_D = P_{US}/P_F$ where P_{US} is US price and P_F is foreign price, it follows that the elasticity of aggregate exports E_x and aggregate imports E_m with respect to price may be taken as crude measures of E_{xx} and E_{mx} respectively.

Suppose that country A's exchange rate is pegged at 20 shillings to the dollar and the general prices level in A doubles because of excessive expansion of money supply while the general price level remains stable in the US. A pound of coffee, formerly costing 20 shillings to produce and selling for $1 in world markets, brings 20 shillings under the old exchange rate. After domestic inflation, producers' costs are likely to be 40 shillings per pound of coffee. Producers paid only 20 shillings because the exchange rate does not adjust are likely to stop delivering coffee, causing a shortage of foreign exchange in A and reducing national income. Monetary policy mistakes are likely to be less costly with flexible than with pegged or fixed exchange rates.

Some nations with high inflation and pegged currencies periodically adjust their currency to maintain purchasing power parity. In the above case, the domestic price level went from an index of 100 to 200 while the US price level remained at an index of 100. Given an initial exchange rate of 20 shillings per dollar, the appropriate adjustment for purchasing power parity was to

$$sh20\,(200/100)\ =\ 40\ shillings\ per\ dollar.$$

This adjusted exchange rate would have kept A competitive and reduced trade distortions.

With flexible exchange rates set in international financial markets, exchange and interest rates are discounted for expected inflation so that real rates and incentives remain somewhat stable. For example, nation X with inflation expected to average 10 percentage points more than trading partners can expect to have market interest rates 10 percentage points higher than rates elsewhere and to have nominal exchange rates devaluing 10 percent annually.

Fixed Exchange Rates and the
Price-Specie-Flow Mechanism

David Hume long ago explained how macroeconomic and trade equilibrium occurs in a world on the gold standard. Suppose country A has a positive trade balance (exports exceed imports) due to sound macroeconomic policies, increase in productivity, or for other reasons. Gold reserves build in A as other nations settle trade deficits with payment of gold. This raises the supply of foreign exchange and the overall supply of money in A. Prices rise, making A's products less attractive to foreign buyers while foreign goods prices are more attractive to importers in A. Country A exports less and imports more, causing its foreign reserves, money supply, and general price level to fall. The supply of foreign exchange will fall and demand will rise to restore the foreign exchange supply-demand equilibrium at a fixed exchange rate.

A country persisting in expansionary macroeconomic policy with a fixed foreign exchange rate will incur foreign debt and exhaust foreign exchange, forcing monetary-fiscal restraint of aggregate demand and import demand. The general price level will fall relative to other countries, encouraging exports and discouraging imports. Thus fixed exchange rates under a gold standard force domestic monetary-fiscal restraint rather than world exchange rate adjustments to maintain exchange rate balances.

Modern economies are also influenced by exchange flows but such economies have tools to compensate. Foreign exchange inflow in the absence of the gold standard expands money supply but such inflow can be *sterilized* by appropriate domestic monetary contraction to avoid inflation and attendant de facto revaluation.

Many countries feel fixed exchange rates unduly restrict their macroeconomic policy options, forcing the "tail" of foreign exchange to "wag the dog" of domestic monetary-fiscal policy. National income and employment are held hostage and are unduly disciplined by trade balances, they contend. Flexible exchange rates allow countries to pursue independent domestic macroeconomic policies for long periods before the discipline of world capital and merchandise trade markets bring restraint. Flexible exchange rates create much short-term instability in trade profitability and seemingly fickle adjustments in terms of trade. Flexible exchange rates allow misguided macroeconomic policies to persist until egregious imbalances arise. Operating in a global economy with flexible exchange rates and efficient capital markets can be a boon to countries making wise use of capital and can be a curse to countries improperly using capital.

Some have advocated a return to the gold standard to bring stability to exchange and trade markets. The resulting fixed exchange rate with given money supply (gold) would restrain inflation and actually require a reduction in the general price level because output would expand more rapidly than the gold supply in the long run. With exceptions such as agriculture, prices and wages are notoriously inflexible downward in industrial economies because firms cut output and employment rather than wages and prices. Hence the gold standard and a falling general price level would contribute to recession. The world is unlikely to return to the gold standard.

BALANCE OF PAYMENTS

The balance of payments is a comprehensive statement of a nation's domestic and international receipts and expenditures. The balance of payments BP defined earlier in equation 6.7 is disaggregated as follows (see US Department of Commerce, *Survey of Current Business*, for complete accounts):

$$BP = (X_g - M_g) + (X_s - M_s) + T - K - \Delta R = 0$$

where X_g and M_g are respectively the value of merchandise (goods) exports and imports, X_s and M_s are respectively the value of service exports and imports, T is unrequited transfers such as net private and public donations between residents and foreigners, K is net capital outflow, and ΔR is the change in monetary reserves of the central bank. Inflow of capital must exactly offset trade deficits if T and ΔR are zero.

The BP is of interest because it provides insights into the macroeconomic state of a country and points to sources of possible economic imbalances. The information easily misleads, however, and must be interpreted with care.

X_g - M_g is called the *balance of trade* or balance of merchandise trade. X_s - M_s is the *balance of services*. The *current account balance* includes the balance of merchandise trade plus the balance of services trade.

Although a merchandise deficit is often viewed as undesirable, it merely means that more goods are being imported than are being exported. Drawing on the Heckscher-Ohlin synthesis, it is possible to predict a more or less normal progression of nations from underdeveloped to developed status in four presumed stages as shown below(see Halevi). The stages recognize that all countries do not develop evenly but that the merchandise account must approximately balance over all countries (two pluses, two minuses). The balance of services and the balance of capital account must do the same.

As capital accumulates, the income elasticity of demand and human capital formation favor a shift from goods to services exports. Also, accumulation of human, technological, and material capital shifts a country from a capital importer (+) to finance goods-services

Stage	Balance of Merchandise	Balance of Services	Balance of Capital Account
1	-	-	+
2	+	-	0
3	+	+	-
4	-	+	0

trade deficits in an early stage to a capital exporter (-) in a later stage. Accumulation of capital relative to labor with economic growth reduces capital costs relative to labor costs and encourages export of capital investments. Finally, however, capital investments abroad build to a point where a creditor country can purchase desired imports from investment earnings (positive service balance of payments) without exporting additional capital to build further earnings from investments abroad.

The US has for the most part conformed to the stages listed above. Prior to the 1890s, it was a net importer of goods and services financed by borrowing from abroad (stage 1). The young, growing nation was long on resources and investment opportunities but short on capital. Foreigners earned more investing in the US than at home. Low labor costs and accumulation of capital following the industrial revolution in the mid-1800s resulted in the nation being a net goods exporter each year in the 1890s to 1970 (stage 2). For Americans, stage 3 was short with merchandise surpluses some years and services surpluses every year in the 1970s.

A nation with abundance of capital relative to labor would be expected to have a relatively low price of capital relative to labor and hence would export capital for a positive balance in the capital account in stage 3 and perhaps in stage 4. That did not happen, however, for the US in the 1980s. Large infusions of capital from abroad in response to high real interest rates engendered by the low supply of savings (after adjustment for negative savings of federal budget deficits) in the 1980s made the US the world's largest net debtor. The balance of merchandise and the balance of services became negative. In the case of services, foreigners earn more from the US than the US earns abroad when foreigners have more capital invested in the US than vice versa but rates of return are similar.

In the future, the situation of the 1980s is expected to reverse to a net outflow of capital and a positive balance of services. As a high-tech, capital intensive industry with comparative advantages in world markets, American agriculture is expected to benefit from a turnaround that will be required to service world debt accumulated in the 1980s and eventually reverse the US capital account to a net outflow. In the long term, the US balance of service account is likely to be positive as earnings rise from exports of intellectual and cultural services such as books, music, and movies attending an advanced post-industrial economy. The lesson is that macroeconomic policy can distort the progression of stages listed above on a transitory but perhaps not on a permanent basis.

Stage of Development, the Savings Ethic, and Trade Protectionism

Sometimes trade deficits arising from normal workings of an efficient market are incorrectly interpreted as protectionism. Japan has a high propensity to save and invest and places a high value on current employment resulting from a relatively undervalued yen. It forgoes some of the higher standard of living attainable with a revalued yen. The United

States in contrast places a relatively higher value on current consumption than on savings for future consumption. Thus Japan ships goods to the US, creating a merchandise balance surplus, which in turn is returned to the US as a capital inflow. The trade surplus with the US blamed on trade barriers against American agricultural and other exports to Japan is more the result of culture, preferences, and American federal budget deficits than of Japanese trade barriers or an irrational market system. Unless such structural sources of deficits are understood, trade threats and counter-threats can develop into a trade war damaging to all as the US imposes trade sanctions against Japan and Japan retaliates.

A positive *current account balance* (merchandise and services exports in excess of imports) seems as widely sought by world nations as self-sufficiency in farm and food production. Drawing from Adam Smith's advice of over two centuries earlier, holders of the neomercantilist philosophy need to be reminded that the wealth of nations rests on goods and services consumed rather than accumulation of foreign exchange. There are serious drawbacks to a world divided into one set of nations with chronic trade deficits and characterized by the economic degradation process alongside another set of neomercantilist nations with chronic trade surpluses and accumulation of foreign exchange (see Tweeten, December 1989). A better balance can benefit all.

Dutch Disease:
A Deviation from Normal Exchange Rates

Macroeconomic policies and types of development interact in other ways to influence trade balances among stages. One of the best known is so-called *Dutch disease*. Export earnings from newly developed oil reserves or other major new source of foreign currency can equate supply with demand for foreign exchange at an appreciated exchange rate. At that rate a traditional export industry such as agriculture may find it no longer possible to compete in foreign markets -- it loses its comparative advantage.

Countries such as South Korea, Taiwan, and Japan experiencing sharp gains in productivity, exports, and foreign exchange earnings from nonfarm domestic industry also feel the influence of Dutch disease on their agriculture. The loss of agricultural comparative advantage from relatively slow productivity growth invites protectionist trade policies in an affluent country with a rising real exchange rate due to nonfarm productivity growth.

Options to deal with the situation include agricultural export subsidies or import taxes, farm input subsidies, or direct payments to producers. Such measures may be justified to maintain the farming industry until its exports are needed if oil reserves and appreciated exchange rates are transitory. If oil revenues are expected to continue for many years, the most satisfactory option may be to provide job relocation assistance, early retirement benefits, or other adjustment help to ease farmers' burden of transformation to less agricultural exports, more imports, and a downsized industry. In general, adjustment of domestic resources to changing trade realities is preferred to trade distortions erected to protect domestic industry.

MACROECONOMIC LINKAGES

Because of low and falling income elasticities of demand for farm output, T.W. Schultz's statement that "Instability in farm income has its origins chiefly in business fluctuations" is much less valid today than in 1945 when it was published. Macroeconomic conditions currently influence agriculture primarily through input markets and international trade.

Equipped with the above background on foreign exchange markets, we now examine in greater detail how import and export markets and the demand and supply of foreign exchange are influenced by macroeconomic policies. Major linkages to export, import, and foreign exchange markets come from government monetary and fiscal policies operating through the aggregate demand and supply and investment and savings markets subject to institutional constraints and expectations. The analysis in this section shows that efficient international capital markets and flexible exchange rates -- institutional innovations of relatively recent vintage -- considerably broaden the macroeconomic policy options of an open economy. That freedom magnifies the possibilities for economic success or for economic degradation. Of interest are the effects of domestic macroeconomic policies in a closed compared to an open economy. An unresolved issue is whether (1) monetary policy overshoot from the 1970s or (2) fiscal policy referred to as Reaganomics caused high real interest and exchange rates along with depressed farm exports and income in the mid-1980s.

Fiscal Policy and Reaganomics

Mainstream economics hold that a government deficit is appropriate to move toward full employment in a depressed economy. The Keynesian deficit is negative savings, which offsets high planned savings relative to investment to maintain aggregate demand and full employment. The deficit is financed from the excess of private savings over investment so that the trade balance, capital flows, interest, and exchange values need not be disturbed, as is apparent from earlier equation 6.3.

A government deficit in a full employment economy is justified under the capital account where the deficit finances high payoff investments that provide a future income stream that will return interest and principal plus a dividend to improve quality of life. *Reaganomics* is a term describing a policy of deficit spending mostly for consumption in a full employment economy accompanied by monetary policy restraint. Impacts are traced in the following pages using a conceptual framework of aggregate demand and supply, savings and investment, and foreign exchange markets.

Aggregate Supply and Demand

Aggregate supply of real national income in Figure 6.4 is a function of technology and resources, especially labor and human and material capital. Aggregate demand (AG) includes consumption, investment, and government expenditures. Aggregate supply (AS) includes all output of goods and services.

In the short run in a *closed* economy, supply intersects demand at national real income (output) Y_0 and general price level P_0. With full employment and industrial capacity utilized, the short-run aggregate supply curve slopes sharply upward to the right. Suppose expansionary macroeconomic policies move AD_0 to $AD_0 + \Delta G$ to induce additional output. This generates mostly inflation from P_0 to P_0' as real national income expands only from Y_0 to Y_0' with an accommodative money supply. Input suppliers soon recognize that additional earning rates are mostly inflation, and hence withdraw input supply to return output to Y_0. The general price level will remain at P_0' and output at Y_0 if the money stimulus is maintained but price level will return to P_0 if the money stimulus is withdrawn.

The price level in Figure 6.4 can be predicted from the quantity equation of money, that is

$$MV = PQ$$

where M is money supply, V is velocity of money, P is the general price level, and Q is aggregate output. If V is constant, then rearranging terms,

$$P = M/Q$$

and an expansion of money supply increases the general price level but does not generate significant additional output Q when a country is at full employment. In subsequent analysis of fiscal policy, M is presumed to rise at the same rate as Q so the general price level does not change. Variables are in real terms to abstract from monetary policy.

When aggregate demand is shifted from AD_0 to $AD_0 + \Delta G$ by a large government deficit in a full-employment closed economy with controlled money supply, aggregate demand remains at AD_0 and output at Y_0 because the increase in government spending by ΔG replaces or "crowds out" private investment. If the additional government spending is for consumption, the impact is to transfer consumption to the present generation from future generations.

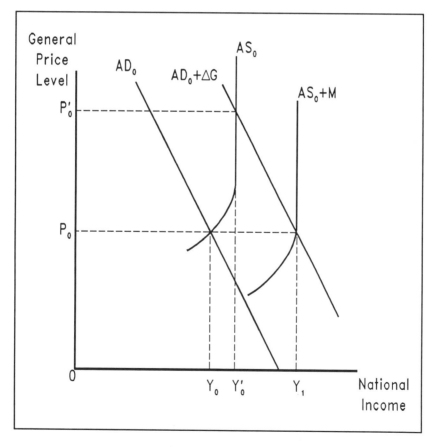

Figure 6.4. Aggregate Demand and Supply of Real National Income with a Closed and Open Economy.

In an *open* economy, however, the government deficit increment ΔG shifts aggregate demand and real income to the right. If aggregate supply increases from AS_0 to $AS_0 + M$ where M is net imports, the new equilibrium real income is at Y_1. With money supply increasing only to accommodate output, the general price level remains at P_0. As noted below, other markets also are changing in an open economy.

Savings-Investment

The savings function S in Figure 6.5 ordinarily slopes upward to the right, indicating that individuals and firms forego additional consumption with a rise in the interest rate -- the compensation for deferring gratification.[4] The investment function I slopes downward to the right, indicating the diminishing marginal efficiency of investment. Capital investments display diminishing returns as successively lower payoff investments are exploited. Closed-economy equilibrium with a given money supply is at investment i_0 and interest rate r_0 in Figure 6.5.

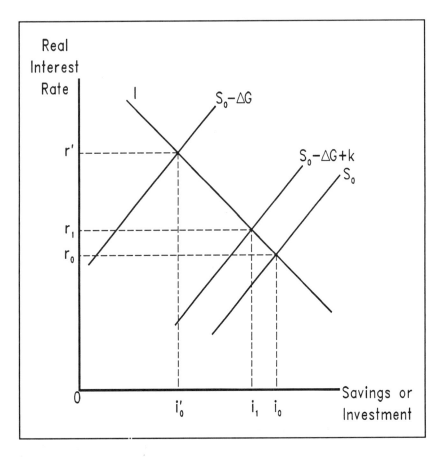

Figure 6.5. Savings and Investment in a Closed and Open Economy.

---

[4]A more comprehensive Hicksian analysis would include along with the investment-savings or I-S curve derived from Figure 6.5 the liquidity demand-money supply or L-M curve to show joint equilibrium in the I-S and L-M markets. Equilibrium in the L-M market is assumed herein.

A government deficit spent for consumption is negative savings because it shifts or absorbs savings so that the savings curve moves to $S_0 - \Delta G$. This raises the interest rate to r' and reduces investment to i_0' -- the *crowding-out* phenomenon discussed with regard to aggregate demand.

In the well-functioning, efficient financial capital market of today's developed world of open economies, inflow k from abroad of funds raises the savings curve to $S_0 - \Delta G + k$. The new equilibrium at interest rate r_1 and investment i_1 will be near r_0 and i_0 respectively because the foreign financial capital supply is highly elastic.

Foreign Exchange Demand and Supply in ROW

High real interest rates (see Figure 6.5) caused by a low supply of savings relative to demand for investment in a full-employment economy provide incentive for worldwide financial capital movement. Efficient world financial markets respond to higher interest rates in the US versus ROW by shifting the demand for dollars of foreign exchange in ROW from D_0 to $D_1 = D_0 + k$ (Figure 6.6). The impact is to depreciate the currency of ROW and appreciate the value of the dollar in ROW as shown by the rise of the exchange rate from π_0 to π_1. The rise in the exchange rate reduces US exports (see Figure 6.1) and increases imports (see Figure 6.2). Dollars are shifted from US to ROW. F_2 dollars are required to purchase goods and service imports from the US, leaving $F_1 - F_2 = k$ dollars of surplus from dollar earnings to return to the US where it supplements savings as noted in Figure 6.5.

The foregoing analysis helps to explain the accounting relationship between savings-investment and government net revenue on the one hand and export-import numbers on the other hand as presented at the beginning of this chapter. An open economy in a world of efficient capital markets and flexible exchange rates allows the US to enjoy a higher income (Y_1) than would have been possible (Y_0) in a closed economy (Figure 6.4). However, it is important to note that if the financial capital from abroad is used for consumption and not for capital investments generating low-cost future income streams, the open economy becomes a burden to the US in the long run as discussed below.

THE ECONOMIC DEGRADATION PROCESS

If aggregate real income expanded from Y_0 to Y_1 from macroeconomic policy in an open economy as shown in Figure 6.4, why condemn full-employment government deficits? Such deficits are appropriate if invested in high-return human and material capital. A problem is that the deficits were used mainly for consumption rather than for high-payoff investments in the 1980s. Full-employment government and attendant trade deficits mean that a country is consuming more than it produces. It is living beyond its means.

The sequence of events that attend unsound macroeconomic policies has been labeled the *economic degradation process* or EDP (Tweeten, December 1989). The process has major implications for trade and characterizes some developed and centrally planned countries but is especially prevalent in developing countries. Steps are as follows:

1. *Trade and government deficits.* The EDP begins when a nation attempts to live beyond its means by consuming more than it produces. Government budget deficits stimulate aggregate demand relative to aggregate supply. A country is able to consume more than it produces by running a trade deficit. If politics or

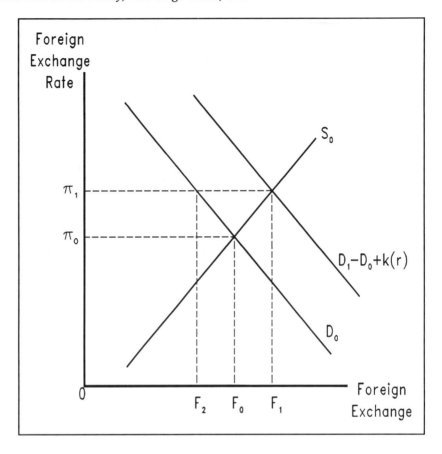

Figure 6.6. Foreign Exchange Demand and Supply in ROW.

other factors preclude reducing government expenses to restore fiscal responsibility, an alternative is to raise taxes. In developing countries, the result often is heavy deadweight losses from taxes on imports and/or exports because taxes less damaging to the economy (e.g., property, value-added, sales, or income taxes) are not politically or administratively feasible.

2. *Debt accumulation.* To finance attempts to live beyond their means, many countries accumulate debt until debt service becomes burdensome. Debt service may take such a high proportion of national savings and export earnings that domestic investment is below capital replacement (depreciation) levels. Capital stock falls, productivity declines, and per capita real income drops. The nation is bankrupt and requires debt relief.

   Debt financing of high-payoff capital investments is entirely appropriate; the problem is debt-financing of consumption and low-payoff investments. The latter do not produce output to service debt.

3. *Inflation.* As debt limits are reached, the alternative is to finance deficits by "printing money." As money supply growth exceeds real income growth, the general price level rises. Agricultural producers are often losers because they have no way to ensure that their prices and earnings will keep pace with inflation.

4. *Overvalued currency.* With a pegged or fixed exchange rate and inflation in excess of that of trading partners, currency appreciates. The result is less exports and more imports as noted earlier in Figures 6.1 and 6.2. Fixed-value export taxes become a high proportion of domestic price as the local currency becomes more overvalued. For example, Tanzania coffee producers received as little as 24 percent of the world price after taxes and Argentina wool producers as little as 12 percent (Tweeten, December 1989). An overvalued currency "taxed" Egyptian cotton producers 24 percent even after adjusting for government subsidies on irrigation water, fertilizer, pesticides, and credit. An overvalued currency often reduces exports and exchange earnings at a time when they are most needed.

5. *Foreign exchange shortage.* Unless the exchange rate is lowered, foreign exchange reserves run low. In extreme cases, insufficient reserves exist to finance spare parts and fuels. The commercial economy can come to a halt. An alternative is to ration foreign exchange. Exchange controls usually create problems of inefficient resource use, waste, and corruption.

The EDP has two general phases. In the first phase described above, a nation can indeed live beyond its means -- until credit and seigniorage run out. The second or austerity phase features hardship, sacrifice, and sometimes social unrest. Consumers do relatively well and producers of traded goods do poorly in the first phase; the roles reverse in the second phase. On the average over both phases, the economy grows slower than if it practiced sound macroeconomic policies of money growth approximately equal to real output growth and a balanced government current account.

The EDP is a macroeconomic phenomenon and is not necessarily associated with corruption, waste, central planning, market distortions, or parastatals. But these conditions often attend and contribute to the EDP. The EDP illustrates the close connection between macroeconomic policies and trade. Rarely does the EDP progress to the point where the commercial economy stalls. Rather, it slowly erodes the economic vitality of a nation. The EDP is most frequent in developing countries but the *relatively* modest EDP of Reaganomics in the US is instructive.

Figure 6.7 summarizes implications of Reaganomics for agriculture. Full employment deficits raising real interest rates induced capital inflow and an overvalued dollar, reducing US farm exports. The lower exports constituted a "tax" reducing farm prices and earnings, induced excess capacity removed by government programs, and raised government costs to remove production or to provide direct payments for maintaining farm income.

The direct effect was to raise interest expenses to producers and thereby lower residual earnings to land. Lower receipts caused by lower commodity prices and export earnings also reduced land earnings. The combination of lower current and future expected land earnings and higher real interest rate generated a lower present value of farmland, resulting in loss of net worth. The result in the mid-1980s was a farm financial crisis of proportions unprecedented since the Great Depression despite government commodity programs costing over $20 billion annually to alleviate farm distress.

Monetary Policy and the Overshoot Hypothesis

Monetary policy and theory provide an alternative explanation for depressed US exports in the 1980s. American agriculture prospered with soaring exports and loose monetary policy in the 1970s and suffered with depressed exports and tight monetary policy

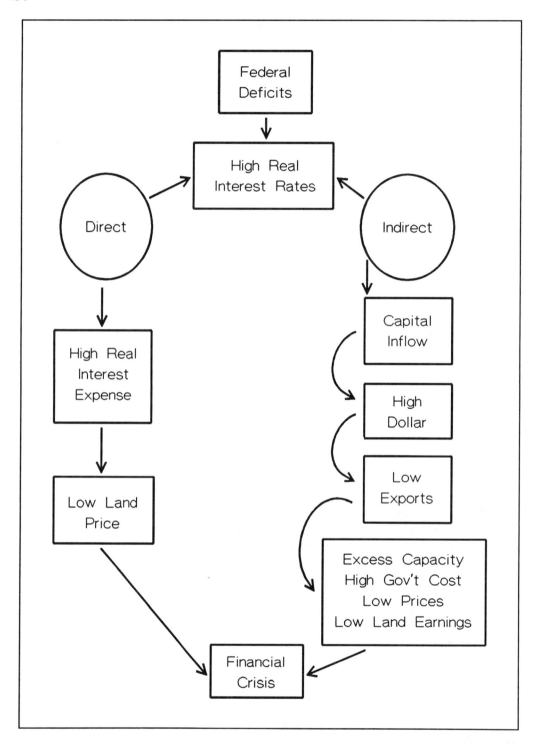

Figure 6.7. Flow Chart Showing Impact of Reaganomics on the Farming Economy.

in the 1980s. The *overshoot hypothesis* attempts to link monetary policy to the farming economy through interest and exchange rates and exports.

Impacts of monetary policy on agriculture are multifaceted but here our primary concern is through trade. Key variables are the interest rate and the exchange rate. Four critical developments underlying the overshoot hypothesis are:

1. Emergence of highly efficient financial capital markets throughout the developed world. Many buyers and sellers electronically transfer millions of dollars each day with inconsequential frictions of time, transport, or transaction costs. Transfers are sometimes thousands of miles. International interest rates thus quickly adjust to competitive equilibrium, differing among countries only by such factors as expectations of risk and inflation.
2. Flexible exchange rates. Exchange rates of the US and other major trading nations are now determined by supply and demand. Banks and other international currency traders bid for currencies until markets clear in this flex-price financial sector.
3. Increasing international dependence on trade. Countries are becoming less self-sufficient and more reliant on food and other goods and services from abroad.
4. Although commodity markets have become more efficient, the frictions of time, space, transport costs, crop forecast errors, and other factors cause commodity prices to respond slowly to changing circumstances. Reaching long-term equilibrium takes time in this sticky-price commodity sector.

The classical monetarist view is that prices are perfectly flexible. Unanticipated expansion of money supply only momentarily reduces nominal and real interest rates. The normal pattern is for the nominal interest rate to include a constant real rate plus an inflation premium. Because international exchange market participants anticipate future inflation rates among countries, rational expectations theory predicts these differences will be bid into nominal exchange rates to preserve purchasing power parity. Thus monetary policy does not change real rates among countries and financial capital does not move among countries in response to monetary policy. Nominal exchange rates reflect inflation premiums but real rates, and hence trade in goods and services, do not change.

In contrast, the Keynesian view (see Frankel, p. 610) is that commodity prices are sticky, at least in the short run, whereas financial markets for capital and foreign exchange are highly efficient and reach equilibrium quickly. Merchandise markets adjust slowly. Because the fixed or sticky price sector adjusts slowly, the flexible or flex price sector must overadjust or overshoot long-term equilibrium to reach short-term equilibrium. In response to an increase in the money supply, real interest and exchange rates presumably fall below long-term equilibrium because they are flex-price markets. Because farm commodity supply requires much time to adjust, the exchange rate can be low for several years as for the US in the 1970s. An increase in the money supply causes real US interest rates to fall more than foreign interest rates, causing financial capital to move abroad and the US exchange rate to fall as the supply stock of dollars outruns demand abroad. The lower exchange rate expands US farm and other exports, bringing prosperity and overexpansion to US farmers. Eventually, the process reverses so the net impact on exports is small.

In the 1980s, tight money raised real US rates relative to foreign interest rates, causing dollar appreciation and declining US farm exports according to the overshoot hypothesis. To the extent that tight money supply in the 1980s was forced to counter loose money in the 1970s, the depressed farm economy in the 1980s was part of the cycle featuring loose money and a prosperous farming economy in the 1970s. The process creates instability, adjustment problems for farmers, and calls for commodity programs to alleviate low farm prices in the second stage of the inflation cycle.

Dornbusch, credited with originating the overshoot hypothesis, and Frankel published papers providing at least mild support for the hypothesis.[5] A difficulty is that empirical analysis has been troubled by confounding influences such as petroleum price increases in the 1970s, changing fiscal policy and velocity of money, and international income growth. For example, Batten and Belongia found that US export changes were accounted for more by foreign income than by exchange rates. The low value of the dollar in the 1970s could have been caused by lack of confidence internationally in the future economic performance of the US economy; the high value of the dollar in the 1980s could have been caused by expansionary fiscal policy. It is not possible accurately to partition changes in US agricultural trade in the 1970s and 1980s into portions due to energy prices, overshoot, and Reaganomics. Barclay and Tweeten found strong empirical support for the process depicted in Figure 6.7, however.

Rausser (p. 131) found overshooting to be a direct implication of the fixed/flex price framework in the US feed grain and food grain markets. An expansionary monetary policy such as pursued in the 1970s was found to decrease the real interest rate and exchange rate and to increase long-run equilibrium feed grain and wheat commodity prices. A restrictive monetary policy had opposite effects in the 1980s. Seale and Moss found no evidence of overshoot, concluding that "no significant effects from macroeconomic variables were found to growth in either agricultural or nonagricultural exports."

In summary, theory and empirical studies provide no consistent evidence that agriculture averages higher or lower real net income from an expansionary monetary policy acting through the international trade and capital markets. Gains in one phase are offset by losses in the other phase. But unsound monetary policy creates instability for agriculture. Agriculture appears to have much to gain from a monetary policy that emphasizes general price stability. A crude rule of thumb is that the money supply needs to be expanded at the same rate as full-employment real national output.

CONCLUSIONS

Trade deficits blamed on foreign protectionism are frequently the result of domestic macroeconomic policies. The advent of flexible exchange rates and efficient financial capital

---

[5]Tweeten and Griffin (p. 8) earlier disputed the money neutrality assumption, using results from empirical analysis to answer "yes" to their question "Does national inflation have a real price effect on the farming industry, lowering the parity ratio?" They theorized that the farm input supply industry was an imperfectly competitive administered or negotiated wage-price sector able to pass rising costs quickly to the atomistic, competitive farming sector. The competitive farming sector meanwhile had no immediate means to pass higher costs to consumers in higher prices received by farmers. Also, the low income elasticity of demand for farm output meant that greater cash balances created by an expanding money supply mostly did not translate into greater farmland demand. Thus an expansion in money supply and inflation lowered the parity ratio, i.e., the ratio of prices received to prices paid by farmers. Later refinements (Tweeten, 1983) indicated that the parity price ratio decreased the first year, increased the second year, increased the third, etc. in a dampening harmonic that left the parity ratio essentially unchanged from the initial level five years after an unanticipated inflationary shock. Money neutrality holds for agriculture in the long run but the short run produces an erratic pattern in part because interest rates rise quickly to raise input prices paid while higher commodity prices received by farmers come later from expanding exports. An important distinction is that Tweeten and Griffin viewed the "fixed" administered or negotiated prices of the input supply sector of agriculture as more flexible at least upwardly than the "flex" prices of the competitive commodity marketing sector.

markets has given nations greater scope to pursue independent macroeconomic policies. Sometimes the result only delays needed corrections to unsound monetary or fiscal policy. Large full-employment US federal deficits of the 1980s would have been unsustainable in a closed economy because of resulting high real interest rates, inflation, and crowding out of private investment. In an open economy, Reaganomics sustained a record peacetime duration of growth stretching from 1982 to mid-1990.

Shortcomings are apparent, nonetheless, from energizing the Economic Degradation Process. One is that domestic and foreign debt is accumulated, burdening future generations. Another is that stimulative fiscal policy is not an option in a nation already holding excessive debt when recession arrives. Fiscal distortions cause misunderstanding: Other nations are blamed for unfair trade practices when they are only doing the market's bidding for capital sent to the US. That is, trade surpluses of ROW supplied the US with savings essential to maintain higher consumption than would have been possible in a full-employment closed economy. US trade deficits blamed on Tokyo more correctly should be blamed on Washington -- on government fiscal policy. Patterns of trade predicted by comparative advantage can be disrupted for long periods by trade-distorting macroeconomic policies, creating deadweight losses.

American farmers as net debtors, heavier users of capital per worker than other industries, and as major net exporters were economically injured in the 1980s by macroeconomic policies that raised real interest rates and appreciated the dollar. Government costs were high for commodity programs to cushion farmers from exports reduced (and competing imports expanded) by an appreciated dollar. Farmers sought border protection measures to further reduce unfavorable impacts of macroeconomic policies. Thus border, commodity program, and macroeconomic policies interact to influence trade and the well-being of farmers. The cycle of good times and bad times may even out *on average* but the instability is traumatic to agriculture.

Agriculture and the entire economy have a major stake in sound macroeconomic policy. That means a monetary policy of increasing the money supply at approximately the rate of real income growth in a full employment economy. And it means a fiscal policy of a balanced or surplus current account in a full employment economy and a deficit only in a depressed economy.

REFERENCES

Barclay, Tom and Luther Tweeten. 1988. Macroeconomic policy impacts on United States Agriculture. *Agricultural Economics* 1:291-307.

Batten, Dallas and Michael Belongia. October 1984. The recent decline in agricultural exports: Is the exchange rate the culprit? *Review* 66:5-14. Federal Reserve Bank of St. Louis.

Belongia, Michael and Courtenay Stone. November 1985. Would lower deficits increase US farm exports? *Review* 67:5-19. Federal Reserve Bank of St. Louis.

Dornbusch, Rudiger. December 1976. Expectations and exchange rate dynamics. *Journal of Political Economy* 84:1161-1176.

Frankel, Jeffrey. September 1979. On the mark: A theory of floating exchange rates based on real interest rate differentials. *American Economic Review* 69:610-622.

Gandolfo, Giancarlo. 1987. *International Economics II*. New York: Springer-Verlag.

Grennes, Thomas. 1984. *International Economics*. Englewood Cliffs, NJ: Prentice-Hall.

Grennes, Thomas. 1990. The link between financial markets and world agricultural trade. Ch. 1 in Thomas Grennes, ed., *International Financial Markets and Agricultural Trade*. Boulder, CO: Westview Press.

Halevi, Nadab. February 1971. An empirical test of the balance of payments stages hypothesis. *Journal of International Economics*.

Henneberry, David. 1985. Foreign exchange regimes and agricultural trade. AE 8584. Stillwater: Department of Agricultural Economics, Oklahoma State University.

Henneberry, David, Shida Henneberry, and Luther Tweeten. 1987. The strength of the dollar: An analysis of trade-weighted foreign exchange rate indices with implications for agricultural trade. *Agribusiness* 3:189-206.

Paarlberg, Philip, Alan Webb, Arthur Moray, and Jerry Sharples. 1984. Impacts of policy on US agricultural trade. Staff Report No. AGES840802. Washington, DC: Economic Research Service, US Department of Agriculture.

Rausser, Gordon. 1986. *Macroeconomic Environment for US Agricultural Policy*. Washington, DC: American Enterprise Institute.

Rivera-Batiz, Francisco and Luis Rivera-Batiz. 1985. *International Finance and Open Economy Macroeconomics*. New York: Macmillan.

Schultz, T.W. 1945. *Agriculture in an Unstable Economy*. New York: McGraw-Hill.

Seale, James and Charles Moss. 1989. The overshoot hypothesis: Are agricultural exports more sensitive? Paper presented at *American Agricultural Economics Association* annual meeting in Baton Rouge, LA. Gainesville: Food and Resource Economics Department, University of Florida.

Stern, Robert. 1973. *The Balance of Payments*. Chicago: Aldine.

Tweeten, Luther and Steve Griffin. March 1976. *General Inflation and the Farming Economy*. Report No. P-732. Stillwater: Oklahoma Agricultural Experiment Station.

Tweeten, Luther. July 1983. Impact of federal fiscal monetary policy on farm structure. *Southern Journal of Agricultural Economics* 15:61-71.

Tweeten, Luther. 1989a. *Farm Policy Analysis*. Boulder, CO: Westview Press.

Tweeten, Luther. 1989b. Macroeconomic linkages to agriculture. Ch. 13 in Luther Tweeten, ed., *Agricultural Policy Analysis Tools for Economic Development*. Boulder, CO: Westview Press.

Tweeten, Luther. December 1989. The economic degradation process. *American Journal of Agricultural Economics* 71:1102-1111.

US Department of Commerce. 1990. *Survey of Current Business*. Washington, DC: US Government Printing Office.

ANNEX TO CHAPTER 6

DERIVATION OF MARSHALL-LERNER CONDITION

The differential of the right hand side of text equation 6.7 is

$$dB = P_x dx - P_m(d\pi_D m + dm\pi_D)$$

where B is balance of payments. Because exports and imports are functions of the exchange rate π_D,

$$dx = \frac{\partial x}{\partial \pi_D} d\pi_D \quad and \quad dm = \frac{\partial m}{\partial \pi_D} d\pi_D,$$

dB can be written

$$dB = P_x x \left(\frac{\partial x}{\partial \pi_D} \frac{\pi_D}{x}\right) \frac{d\pi_D}{\pi_D} - \pi_D P_m m \left(\frac{d\pi_D}{\pi_D} + \left(\frac{\partial m}{\partial \pi_D} \frac{\pi_D}{m}\right) \frac{d\pi_D}{\pi_D}\right).$$

We define export demand and import supply elasticities with respect to exchange rates as

$$E_{x\pi} = \frac{\partial x}{\partial \pi_D} \frac{\pi_D}{x} \quad and \quad E_{m\pi} = \frac{\partial m}{\partial \pi_D} \frac{\pi_D}{m}.$$

For devaluation to improve the balance of payments, dB must be greater than zero. Factoring out $d\pi_D/\pi_D$ and rearranging terms, the expression for dB becomes

$$\frac{P_x x}{\pi_D P_m m} E_{x\pi} - E_{m\pi} > 1.$$

In considering deviations from equilibrium in the balance of payments, we may assume $P_x x \approx \pi_D P_m m$ so that devaluation will improve the balance of payments if

$$E_{x\pi} - E_{m\pi} > 1$$

or assuming that $E_{m\pi}$ is negative, we can write

$$E_{x\pi} + |E_{m\pi}| > 1.$$

CHAPTER 7

Introduction to
Strategic Trade Theory

Noting a man searching for something beneath a streetlight, a passerby asks "What are you looking for?"
"My car keys," the man replies.
"Did you lose them here?" the passerby queries.
"No, I lost them over there in the dark."
"Then why are you searching here?"
"Because there's no light over there."

1960s parable

Strategic trade theory provides a conceptual framework for firm or government policy in a world of imperfect competition, barriers to entry, economies of size, differentiated products, predatory practices, and reactions of competitors to one another's actions. It refers to conflict in trade rather than in arms but draws on the distinction between military *strategy* as opposed to *tactics*. Strategic trade theory has been applied mostly to firms but also is applicable to governments. Strategic trade theory holds that the government can play a critical role either directly (e.g., a wheat marketing board) or indirectly to give domestic industries a decisive advantage in trade to benefit the industries and the home country as a whole.

GENESIS

Strategic trade theory as employed herein is not one concept but instead is many streams of thought that do not necessarily converge. First, there is mercantilism, which in modern form, neomercantilism, holds that the government can manipulate exchange rates, subsidies, tariffs, quotas, and other measures to generate trade account surpluses. Thus, a nation can accumulate foreign exchange to achieve international prestige and economic power while promoting domestic full employment through exports. Because such gains may come at the expense of other countries, ethical questions arise.

Second, there is the countervailing power school which holds that foreign monopoly must be confronted with domestic monopoly (see Galbraith). A proponent of this view has contended that the US government should form a wheat export cartel to confront the optimal tariffs imposed by nations buying US farm products (see Carter and Schmitz). A problem with this approach, as illustrated earlier in Figure 2.7 and later in Chapter 8, is that deadweight losses are likely to be large -- the issue is who will bear them. Although the purpose of the cartel initially might be to force other countries to remove trade barriers, that lofty goal likely would be lost to greed.

Then there is the market conduct, structure, performance (CSP) approach originating with Mason (1939, 1949) and developed more fully by Bain (1951, 1956). That so-called industrial organization school rejects neoclassical models of perfect competition and monopoly in favor of a more pragmatic approach emphasizing oligopoly theory. In empirical studies, the school relates measures of market performance (e.g., profit, price markups over cost, export propensity, etc.) to firm concentration, size, and other structural explanatory variables.

Reviewers of numerous CSP studies generally conclude that seller concentration is associated with higher prices (see Handy and Henderson for sources). However, results have not been robust. For example, a massive US study by Marion found a statistically positive relationship between firm concentration ratio and retail food price levels whereas Kaufman and Handy in later analysis found no statistical association between these variables. The structure of the agricultural export industry will be addressed in the next chapter.

Then there is the "new" strategic trade theory initiated by Spencer and Brander (see also Brander and Spencer), noting that governments can intervene strategically with taxes, subsidies, or other measures to give domestic firms operating in imperfectly competitive markets a decisive and perhaps long-term advantage over foreign firms at potentially high domestic benefit-cost ratios. This chapter introduces such theory, which rationalizes an activist role for governments in foreign trade.

Next there is the more structural *new empirical industrial organization* (NEIO) approach to analyze imperfect competition in world markets (see Perloff). It has roots in the CSP school but recognizes that structural variables such as research and development expenditures, innovation, advertizing, firm size, and concentration must be viewed interdependently with market performance. Conjectural variations and other variables are used to measure the degree of competition and competitor reactions expressed in the market.

Finally, modern neoclassical economics takes a different view of the strategic role of government in international trade. It holds that the role of government is to supply public goods, including a competitive environment and absence of trade distortions. In contrast to other philosophic orientations, neoclassical competitive theory emphasizes policies giving favorable world benefit-cost ratios and low deadweight losses. That position, the foundation for Chapter 11, draws on neoclassical competitive theory but is eclectic in using empirical results from other schools. For example, the linkage is apparent from a CSP study by Henderson and Frank (p. 14), which concluded that "the most export-oriented US food manufacturing industries are those in which firms operate large and efficient plants, face relatively low entry barriers, and where there are only *modest concentrations of market power*" (emphasis mine). An in-depth study by Porter of 10 industrial countries accounting for 50 percent of world trade concluded that the strongest international trade performance was by firms that first had built competitiveness by fiercely competing with robust firms in the home market.

Much of strategic trade theory outlined in the following sections of this chapter is a rich source of hypotheses but remains in a formative stage. It applies more to industrial goods than to relatively homogeneous products of farms widely traded on world markets. It has been applied more to private firms or state trading companies in concentrated industries than to governments in open economies relying on competitive trading firms.

This chapter reviews two cornerstones of strategic trade theory: the theory of games and the theory of duopoly. The relevance of duopoly theory to agricultural trade remains in doubt (see 1960s parable above). To date, empirical applications to agriculture have been few and disappointing (see Thursby and Thursby). Despite its shortcomings, we must learn about strategic trade theory because it is part of the language of modern trade theory and may begin to yield useful empirical results. We emphasize basic concepts and terminology in this chapter. Chapter 8 will extend the analysis to alternative forms of competition and political economy.

THE THEORY OF GAMES

Game theory provides strategies to maximize utility or attain other goals for an individual, firm, or government with various courses of action facing a rival also with various courses of action. The rivals may choose courses of action independently (games against nature) or in a consciously competitive, even predatory, strategy (see Rasmusen).

The Prisoners' Dilemma

The Prisoners' Dilemma is a simple, basic illustration of a 2x2 noncooperative game. It is symmetric in Figure 7.1 but need not be. The game is not unlike many circumstances faced by firms and governments in the world of trade. It is a *2x2* game because each player, Mr. Row and Mr. Column in Figure 7.1, can choose from two actions: confess the crime they jointly committed or remain silent. The payoff is the same to each prisoner in a like situation. This symmetry also means that the payoff matrix is unchanged if Mr. Row and Mr. Column exchange places. All players in a game are assumed to be rational, maximizing their gains or minimizing their losses. The Prisoners' Dilemma is a *noncooperative game* because each prisoner is questioned separately. Players cannot communicate and conspire to achieve the most favorable joint outcome. If both remain silent, each spends a year in jail [Payoff (-1, -1)]. If Mr. Row confesses but Mr. Column does not, Mr. Row gets no jail time but Mr. Column gets 15 years (0, -15). If both confess, each prisoner gets 10 years (-10, -10). The game is played only once, simultaneously, and without collusion.

	Mr. Column	
	Silent	Confess
	Payoff (*Row*, *Column*)	
Silent	-1, -1	-15, 0
Mr. Row		
Confess	0, -15	**-10, -10**

Figure 7.1. Prisoners' Dilemma Game.

Unlike the early theory of games, which emphasized games against nature where "nature's" actions were taken as unknown or random and were uninfluenced by actions of a player, the modern theory of games recognizes that the action of one player can influence the action of another player. To determine the optimal or equilibrium play in Table 7.1, we examine what is rational for one prisoner responding to each action of the other prisoner.

If Mr. Row remains silent, Mr. Column will get one year in prison if he remains silent [Payoff (-1, -1)] but will get no years in prison if he confesses (-15, 0), so Mr. Column will confess. If Mr. Row confesses, Mr. Column will get 15 years in prison if he remains silent (0, -15) but will get only 10 years in prison (-10, -10) if he confesses, so Mr. Column will confess. Mr. Row will chose his best option knowing that, whatever his action, it is in Mr. Column's best interests to confess. Given that Mr. Column will confess, Mr. Row will get 15 years in prison if he is silent (-15, 0) but only 10 years in prison if he confesses (-10, -10) so he chooses the latter action.

The game is symmetric so *confess* is also the best action for Mr. Column. The overall dominant equilibrium strategy entails the best strategy for each player when all other players are in their best strategies. In the case of the Prisoners' Dilemma, the dominant strategy is *(confess, confess)* and its payoff is in bold face. In this example, the strategy entailed one course of action for each player.

In more realistic cases, a strategy could entail a combination of actions in a game repeated over many time periods and under prescribed rules. For example, the Prisoners' Dilemma game actually has been played (simulated) by a group of persons individually making decisions without collusion (Axelrod). The game was repeated many times. The winner was the player spending the least total time in prison. The winner in the simulated game over time followed a mixed strategy of *silent* as long as the other player chose *silent* but switched to *confess* for one period if another player used action *confess*.

Returning to the case of a one-time play in Figure 7.1, a conspiracy of silence would be the optimal joint strategy for the two players because it would bring only 2 years in jail for the prisoners (-1, -1) versus 15 [(-15, 0) or (0, -15)] to 20 years (-10, -10) for any other strategy. In a noncooperative game played only once, collusion to attain this outcome is impossible. But one player can learn behavior of others by observing outcomes over time. In a repeated game, player Mr. Row can signal to others willingness to cooperate by the action *silent* in Figure 7.1. Others observe this and switch to action *silent* to see if Mr. Row persists in this behavior. Mr. Row does and the prisoners continue in the (-1, -1) mode. Along the way, Mr. Column may realize that switching to *confess* will remove jail time (-15, 0) but Mr. Row then punishes that indiscretion by playing action *confess* for one period.

A *Nash equilibrium* refers to the optimal strategy for a player given the strategies of all other players. A Nash equilibrium is not necessarily unique; there may be numerous Nash equilibria. A *dominant strategy* for a player is the one best strategy for that player whatever the strategy of the other players, including, of course, their dominant strategies. Noncredible threats are ruled out. The *dominant strategy equilibrium* is that combination of strategies consisting of each player's dominant strategy. That dominant strategy equilibrium will be a Nash equilibrium but not necessarily the only Nash equilibrium. And the dominant strategy with collusion [e.g., (-1, -1)] is not necessarily the dominant strategy of a noncooperative game (-10, -10).

The tit-for-tat strategy by the player who won the repeated Prisoners' Dilemma game was a Nash equilibrium but it was not a dominant strategy equilibrium applicable to all players. To illustrate, suppose Mr. Row and Mr. Column in Figure 7.1 each play the tit-for-tat strategy in a repeated game. Suppose Mr. Row begins with the strategy of signaling Mr. Column that he is willing to remain silent if Mr. Column also pursues action *silent*. Mr.

Column begins with *confess*. The outcome is fifteen years of jail for Mr. Row (-15, 0). Because Mr. Column rewards Mr. Row for his silence by playing *silent* the next period and Mr. Row punishes Mr. Column by playing *confess* the next period, the outcome is 15 years of prison for Mr. Column (0, -15). This sequence is repeated, alternating each period between (-15, 0) and (0, -15). This is hardly "socially optimal" for the two prisoners viewed jointly or individually. It is not a *Pareto optimum*, defined as a policy position from which it is impossible to make one player better off without making the other worse off. By switching to a *silent* strategy given Column's tit-for-tat strategy, Mr. Row as well as Mr. Column are made better off because the payoff to each shifts to a year in jail (-1, -1) from the average outcome of 7.5 years in jail from pursuing simultaneous tit-for-tat strategies (-15, 0) and (0, -15) in a repeated game.

It may be noted that the (*silent, silent*) strategy resulting in outcome (-1, -1) is *not* a *Pareto better* position compared to the diagonal outcomes if the Prisoners' Dilemma is only a one period game. Compared to the diagonal outcomes in Figure 7.1, a move to (-1, -1) makes either Mr. Row or Mr. Column worse off while making the other better off.

Although the theory of games ordinarily assumes that players are rational in maximizing utility, in practice that assumption is interpreted in the real world as meaning players are rational in maximizing whatever is in the payoff matrix -- such as net income or gains from trade. Referring to Figure 7.1 again, if Mr. Row enjoys prison while Mr. Column detests it, the Nash and dominant strategy equilibrium will be (*silent, confess*) with outcome (-15, 0). We ordinarily do not add and compare elements of the payoff matrix. If we strictly avoid interpreting utility interpersonally or interpreting nonutility payoffs (e.g., years in jail) as utility payoffs, then we cannot say that strategy (*silent, silent*) is preferred to strategy (*confess, confess*) just because the former (-1, -1), giving 2 combined years in prison is more intuitively appealing than the latter (-10, -10), giving 20 combined years in prison.

The Prisoners' Dilemma is supposed to explain why nations choose inferior protectionist trade strategies when a little "collusion" (multilateral trade negotiations) could bring superior joint payoffs. We shall observe in Chapter 11 that the explanation for continuing market interventions is more complicated than that.

A Market Entry Game

Figure 7.2 shows outcomes for multinational firm A and firm B contemplating entry into a new foreign market. The game is symmetric.

The game has two Nash equilibria. If firm B does nothing (*sits*), the optimal action for firm A is to enter and the payoff is (4, 0). If firm B enters, firm A would lose 6 if it enters so it stays out (*sits*). There is neither a dominant strategy nor a dominant strategy equilibrium. With two Nash equilibria, (*enter, sit*) and (*sit, enter*), what is the outcome? Several suggestions give clues to behavior of firms in international trade facing such circumstances.

1. If the game can only be played once and firm A cannot afford a loss as large as 6, then A sits to be safe. By doing nothing, A will break even at worst. If firm B behaves the same way, the strategy is (*sit, sit*) for a payoff of (2, 2). If firm B knows A's precarious predicament that dictates caution and therefore anticipates that A will sit, then B will enter. The outcome is (*sit, enter*) for a payoff of (0, 4).

2. Usually, but not always, first entry is an advantage. Assume the game is played sequentially with (say) firm A going first. Firm A enters the market because it knows that if it sits B will enter for a gain of zero for A and 4 for B. After firm

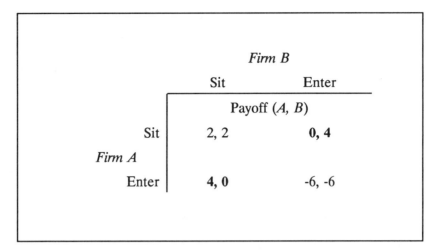

Figure 7.2. Market Entry Game.

A enters, firm B will lose nothing if it sits back but will lose 6 if it enters the new market to compete. Hence the strategy (*enter, sit*) will prevail with A gaining 4 units and B gaining nothing.

3. Other considerations such as access to financial reserves to take losses may be decisive even if firm A has located and appears to have the upper hand, forcing B to sit. If firm B has larger reserves, it can enter after A has entered. Both firms will be losing 6 units per period. This payoff will continue until firm A withdraws for lack of financial reserves to cover further losses. Thus payoff (0, 4) results as firm B exploits monopoly benefits.

4. The firms might collude in a cooperative game if it can be repeated enough to signal a strategy by past plays. That is, firm A can take the first new market, firm B the next, and so forth. Another option is to merge firms to realize the best overall payoff.

5. If the game is repeated without collusion or first-entry privilege, an alternative is to play *sit* and *enter* at random with probability θ for *sit* and $1-\theta$ for *enter*. Firms A and B will each play the game so they are indifferent between playing *sit* or *enter*, i.e. the expected payoff $\Pi(sit) = \Pi(enter)$. That requires for A that B's probability of sit θ be such that

$$\begin{aligned}\Pi\,(sit\,for\,A) &= \theta(2) + (1-\theta)(0) \\ &= \theta(4) + (1-\theta)(-6) \\ &= \Pi\,(enter\,for\,A).\end{aligned}$$

Solving this equation for $\theta = .75$, the expected average payoff of the game in the long run for both A and B is 1.5. Because the game is symmetric, the optimal strategy for each is at random to sit 75 out of 100 times and to enter new markets 25 times out of 100. For the game to work as predicted in the long run, each firm must be able to survive negative (-6, -6) payoffs. Suppose the firms go broke if payoff (-6, -6) occurs. The probability of that outcome is $(1-\theta)(1-\theta)$ or $(.25)(.25) = .0625$. Thus with each play of the game the probability of survival is $1 - .0625 = .9375$.

One can question why the firms should settle for a payoff of only 1.5 with the mixed strategy when a payoff of 2 could be assured for each with strategy (*sit, sit*). The answer is that if they cannot collude they presumably cannot help themselves. If firm A consistently plays *sit*, B will play *enter* so firm A's average payoff is 0. The same payoff of 0 occurs if Firm B consistently and naively plays *sit* so the strategy is (*enter, sit*). A problem with the real world may be that neither repeated play nor collusion is possible.

Sometimes the payoff, such as indicated above, of 1.5 is possible in a single period game by using a *mixed strategy* as opposed to the pure strategy of only *enter* or *sit* in any one period. The mixed strategy might be possible if enough new markets open each year to randomize entry among them per the above probabilities.

An example of a mixed strategy is a small tropical country with potential to produce fruits and vegetables for export or staples of maize and beans for home consumption. Suppose that on average far more maize and beans can be purchased abroad from fruit and vegetable exports than can be produced at home. Hence export cropping and trade maximize welfare in a certain world. The export market may be highly uncertain compared to relying on subsistence crops of corn and beans produced at home to supply local needs. One answer is to diversify to reduce risk. Some corn and beans are produced for security and some fruits and vegetables are produced to raise income and living standards through trade. Another alternative is to build foreign exchange reserves to buy corn and beans abroad when production or markets of export crops fail.

Concluding Comments

Game theory has become part of the popular vocabulary and thought process. For example, most everyone has heard of the *zero sum game* (gains and losses exactly offset for players). The conceptual framework of the game disciplines our thinking. A challenge is to insert realistic numbers in the payoff matrix. Most of this book directly or indirectly addresses that challenge. The payoffs often are continuous rather than discrete.

THEORY OF DUOPOLY

In the competitive models used widely in this book, a firm considers neither the impact of its actions on the market price nor the reactions of its rivals. If we are concerned with the behavior of markets in imperfect competition, monopoly (one seller) or monopsony (one buyer) is not very interesting because rival firms are absent.

Considerable international trade is carried out by firms in markets characterized by oligopoly. We know that such markets often are characterized by product differentiation, advertising, jockeying for market share, and theory-of-game-like behavior such as described in the last section. No neat models predict the behavior of oligopolistic markets, however, so we resort to highly simplified models. The simplest of all models accounting for actions of rivals is *duopoly*, defined as a market with two firms. In fact, a two-firm market is one variant of the two-person game just presented. To understand how and to relate rivalry to international trade, it is useful to review the theory of duopoly recognizing that such theory generalizes to some types of oligopoly.

We begin with competitive and monopoly equilibrium to observe how duopoly pricing and output differ. Assume that the total market inverse demand function is

$$P = a + bq \qquad (7.1)$$

where P is market price, q is quantity, and a and b (negative) are market parameters. For simplicity, assume that total variable cost is

$$C = cq \qquad (7.2)$$

so marginal cost is a constant c. In competitive equilibria, market price equals marginal cost so that supply (marginal cost) is equal to demand, i.e., at competitive market quantity q_c:

$$a + bq_c = c$$
$$or$$
$$q_c = (c-a)/b$$

and price is P_c.

If the market is characterized by one firm maximizing profit, equilibrium is where marginal cost c is equal to marginal revenue. Total revenue (TR) is q times (7.1) or

$$TR = aq + bq^2$$

so marginal revenue is the derivative

$$a + 2bq.$$

In equilibrium, monopolistic output q_m is where marginal revenue equals marginal cost c

$$a + 2bq_m = c$$
$$q_m = (c-a)/2b = q_c/2$$

or one-half of competitive output q_c under the assumption of linearity.

Reaction Functions and Conjectures

The reaction function traditionally is used to predict duopoly market behavior. That function expresses one firm's output or pricing depending on the behavior of the other firm. The term "reaction" is a misnomer, however, because moves are simultaneous -- there is no time to react. Expectations of anticipated actions of the other firm are called *conjectures*. In the simplest case, conjectures relate to price or quantity. Under the *Cournot conjecture*, each firm bases its action on the assumption that the other firm establishes an output. That is, duopolist 1 assumes that duopolist 2 sets an output q_2, which does not change when firm 1 sets output q_1.

Because consumers do not distinguish between the homogeneous outputs of duopolists, q_1 of 1 and q_2 of 2, the demand equation (7.1) can be written

$$P = a + b(q_1 + q_2) = P(q_1, q_2).$$

Each firm is assumed to have identical total variable cost C and marginal cost c or

$$C = C_1(q_1) = C_2(q_2).$$

Thus firm 1's profit Π_1 is price times quantity less its total variable cost or

$$\Pi_1 = P(q_1, q_2)q_1 - C_1(q_1)$$
$$= [a + b(q_1 + q_2)]q_1 - cq_1.$$

The first-order condition for profit maximization (derivative of Π_1 with respect to q_1) is

$$a + 2bq_1 + bq_2 - c = 0.$$

Rearranging terms the reaction function for duopolist 1 is

$$q_1 = \frac{c - a}{2b} - \frac{q_2}{2} = q_m - \frac{q_2}{2}. \qquad (7.3)$$

It is apparent that if duopolist 2 produces nothing so $q_2 = 0$, then duopolist 1 becomes essentially a monopolist, maximizing profit at $q_1 = q_m$ output. Similarly, the reaction function for duopolist 2 is

$$q_2 = \frac{c - a}{2b} - \frac{q_1}{2} = q_m - \frac{q_1}{2}. \qquad (7.4)$$

In a perfectly competitive industry, other firms will be viewed by any one firm as inconsequential so q_2 will approach zero in (7.3) and q_1 will approach zero in (7.4), giving in each case output q_m. The sum of these outputs gives competitive equilibrium output

$$q_c = q_m + q_m.$$

Nash equilibrium occurs when duopolists 1 and 2 are maximizing profit at conjectures for each other's output that are mutually consistent in the two reaction functions. Equilibrium can be found either by substituting reaction function (7.4) for q_2 in (7.3) and solving for q_1 or by substituting reaction function (7.3) for q_1 in (7.4) and solving for q_2. In the symmetric case

$$q_1 = q_2 = \frac{c - a}{3b} = \frac{q_c}{3}.$$

The sum of the two firms' outputs is *(2/3)q_c*, or two-thirds of competitive output. Thus duopoly is less distorting than monopoly, which gives one-half the competitive output.

Generalizing the Cournot Solution

The market solution operating under Cournot conjectures can be generalized to an oligopoly market consisting of n producers. Total industry output q is the sum of outputs of each firm i

$$q = \sum_{i=1}^{n} q_i = \frac{n}{n + 1} q_c.$$

As explained in the footnote below, industry output q is a function of the number of firms so that as n becomes large q approaches perfectly competitive output q_c.[1]

Of interest is the deadweight loss (national income sacrificed) as a proportion of industry receipts from various degrees of imperfect competition.[2] Table 7.1 illustrates a critical point: *Inefficiencies from imperfect competition initially decline sharply as the number of firms increases in a concentrated market.* Deviations from competitive market output and receipts decline at a geometric rate while firm numbers rise at an arithmetic rate. Empirical analysis supports the conclusion that not many firms are required in a market to approach competitive outcomes (Miller).

---

[1]Remembering that P = f(q) for firm i with Cournot conjectures

$$\Pi_i = Pq_i - cq_i. \qquad (i = 1,2,...n)$$

To maximize profit, the first-order condition is

$$\frac{\partial \Pi_i}{\partial q_i} = P + \frac{\partial P}{\partial q_i}q_i - c = 0.$$

Summed over n firms in the market, the result is

$$nP + q\sum_{i=1}^{n}\frac{\partial P}{\partial q_i} - nc = 0.$$

Given that

$$P = a + bq \qquad and \qquad \sum\frac{\partial P}{\partial q_i} = b,$$

the expression becomes

$$n(a + bq) + bq - nc = 0$$
$$or \quad q = \frac{n}{n+1}\frac{c-a}{b} = \frac{n}{n+1}q_c$$
$$so \quad \lim_{n\to\infty}q = q_c.$$

[2]Net social cost (deadweight loss or national income loss) C defined as a proportion of industry receipts sacrificed by imperfect competition is (Tweeten, p. 351):

$$C = 50\left(\frac{1}{\alpha} - \frac{1}{\beta}\right)\left(\frac{\Delta q}{q}\right)^2$$

where α is the elasticity of supply, β is the elasticity of demand for output, and $\Delta q/q$ is the proportional distortion of output. Arbitrarily assuming $\alpha = 1.0$ and $\beta = -1$ to represent long-run elasticities for farm output, social cost C may be written as

$$C = 100\left(\frac{\Delta q}{q}\right)^2.$$

We observed in earlier chapters that these elasticities are quite representative of long-term supply and demand elasticities estimated empirically for commodities in US export markets.

Table 7.1. Impact of Imperfect Competition on Economic Efficiency.

Number of Firms in Industry[a]	Output as Proportion of Competitive Output q_c $100q/q_c$	Social Cost (Deadweight Loss) as Proportion of Industry Receipts $100(1 - q/q_c)^2$
	(%)	(%)
1 (monopoly)	50	25
2 (duopoly)	67	11
3	75	6
4	80	4
10	91	1
20	95	Small
Large (perfect competition)	100	0

Source: See footnotes 1 and 2.

[a]Firms are assumed to exercise market power. As noted in the text, monopoly or duopoly firms can behave as perfectly competitive firms.

Stackelberg Leadership and Collusion

Thus far we have assumed that duopolists adjust simultaneously to conjectures regarding their rival's output. Now we consider so-called *Stackelberg* outcomes where one duopolist acts first (Stackelberg leader) and the other reacts (follower). Also we examine implications of conjectures based on price as well as those based on quantity.

1. *Stackelberg Leadership with Cournot Conjectures.* Duopolist 1, who takes the lead by acting first in the market based on full knowledge of duopolist 2's reaction function, is able to increase profit over those of simultaneous moves depicted previously in this chapter. Assuming duopolist 1 is able to act first, his reaction function can be found by maximizing the profit function derived by substituting duopolist 2's reaction function into the demand equation $P = a + b(q_1 + q_2)$ and hence

$$\Pi_1 = \left[a + bq_1 + b \left(\frac{c-a}{2b} - \frac{q_1}{2} \right) \right] q_1 - cq_1. \tag{7.5}$$

The first-order equation to maximize profit solved for q_1 is

$$q_1 = \frac{c-a}{2b} = \frac{q_c}{2}$$

and from (7.4) the output of the follower is

$$q_2 = \frac{c-a}{4b} = \frac{q_c}{4}.$$

Therefore

$$q = q_1 + q_2 = \frac{3q_c}{4}.$$

Because this Stackelberg equilibrium output exceeds the monopoly output $q_c/2$ by one-fourth, the industry price P is lower. Hence income of Stackelberg duopolist 1 is less than under monopoly despite the same quantity ($q_c/2$) produced in each case.

Figure 7.3 summarizes graphically the reaction functions for duopolists 1 and 2. Output of firm 1 is recorded on the horizontal axis and of firm 2 on the vertical axis. If firm 2 produces nothing, firm 1 acts as a monopolist with output q_m. If firm 2 supplies the competitive output q_c, price is driven to marginal cost so it will not pay firm 1 to supply any output. Hence for duopolist 1 the vertical intercept is $q_2 = q_c$ with $q_1 = 0$.

When each of the two firms in a duopoly market simultaneously makes decisions (without a leader), the equilibrium outcome is output (c-a)/3b for each firm as noted earlier. Because the equilibrium output at N in Figure 7.3 is from simultaneous moves, the equilibrium can be viewed as the result of numerous random moves until conjectures of each duopolist expressed by reaction curves are satisfied. Strictly speaking, the Nash equilibrium is instantaneous, but an intuitive explanation based on sequencing helps to see why N is an equilibrium. Suppose that the firms find themselves at point x rather than at

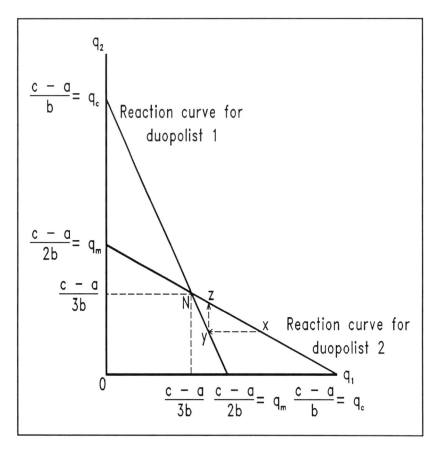

Figure 7.3. Reaction Curves and Equilibrium Output Under Cournot Conjectures of Duopoly.

point N in Figure 7.3. Firm 1 can increase profit by reducing output -- moving left to reach point y. (Readers wanting to see the position of profit curves can look ahead to Figure 7.4.) Point y is a lower profit point for firm 2 than is point z, hence it increases output to reach point z. This process is continued to the Nash equilibrium at N. In reality, and unlike the case in Figure 7.3, cost functions could be quite different for each firm so that the reaction curves would not be mirror images and the equilibrium would not fall on a 45° line from the origin.

Isoprofit curves in Figure 7.4 are formed by substituting $q_1 + q_2$ for q in the profit function and plotting various combinations of q_1 and q_2 for any given profit level Π_k. Π_{11} for example is the highest isoprofit curve attainable by firm 1 and Π_{21} the highest attainable by firm 2 when output of the other firm is $q_c/3$. The reaction curve for duopolist 1 is the locus of the highest isoprofit lines attainable by the firm for any given output of duopolist 2. The lowest isoprofit curve or point for duopolist 1 is at q_c on the vertical axis. Isoprofit curves *shown* for duopolist 1 range from a low level Π_{10} to the highest possible isoprofit curve Π_{13} which actually is only a point at q_m in Figure 7.4. Similarly, isoprofit curves *shown* for firm 2 range from a low of Π_{20} to the highest possible curve Π_{23}.

The instantaneous process of arriving at an equilibrium can be further illustrated in "slow motion" with Figure 7.4. If firm 1 initially is producing at q, an output that firm 2 conjectures would not be changed; firm 2 would produce q_d. If firm 1 viewed that output of firm 2 as permanent, firm 1 would move to a higher isoprofit line by shifting to an output

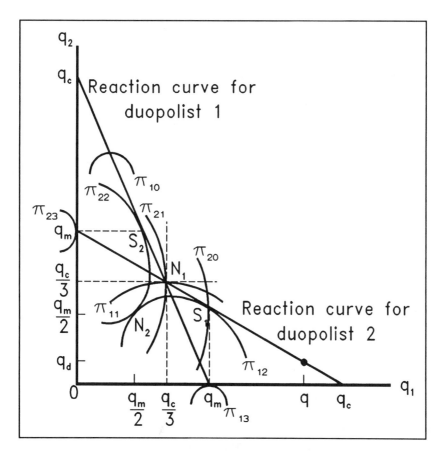

Figure 7.4. Reaction and Isoprofit Curves Under Cournot Conjectures of Duopoly.

just to the left of q_m (horizontal axis) along the reaction curve for firm 1. This process would continue until the firms would arrive at Nash equilibrium N_1. The Nash equilibrium N_2 at the tangency of Π_{12} and Π_{22} maximizes combined profit (each firm produces $q_m/2$) but is unattainable without collusion. It is called a Nash equilibrium because it maximizes profit only under certain conditions. Another Nash equilibrium might maximize welfare of consumers or of society. We recall that a Nash equilibrium is a maximizing position for one firm given the position of the other firm -- the equilibrium need not maximize welfare for the firms jointly or for society.

If simultaneity is replaced by the assumption that duopolist 1 is a Stackelberg leader, firm 1 will produce q_m of q_1. Firm 1 could have gone for an even higher profit by producing and selling less than quantity q_m of q_1, hoping that firm 2 would produce less than $q_m/2$. But if firm 1 produces less than q_m, the reaction curve for firm 2 indicates it will produce more than $q_m/2$ so that firm 1's profit will be less than Π_{12}. And firm 1 producing more than q_m of q_1 would be on a lower isoprofit curve. Hence point S_1 is the Stackelberg equilibrium in that it represents the maximum profit for quantity leader firm 1 subject to firm 2's reaction curve. A second Stackelberg equilibrium is at S_2 where firm 2 is the leader. It reaches its highest isoprofit curve Π_{22} subject to the reaction curve of firm 1.

2. Market Leadership with Bertrand Conjectures. Two firms have *Bertrand conjectures* if each firm acts as if the other firm will not change its price. In contrast to Cournot conjectures, which take the quantity of the rival as given, the Bertrand conjecture takes the price of the rival as given.

Bertrand equilibrium is elusive. If products of duopolists 1 and 2 are perfect substitutes (perhaps the same good), firm 1 can undercut firm 2's price slightly and capture all the market and profit. Firm 2 sees this, so it undercuts firm 1's price to capture the entire market and profit. The process continues until price equals marginal cost assumed to be equal for the two firms. If either firm raises price, it will lose its market and be out of business; if it lowers price it will lose profit and financial viability.

It may be reassuring to note such behavior in the real world reduces pure profit to zero and brings competitive pricing and output in an imperfectly competitive market. But the "equilibrium" of this so called *Bertrand Paradox* is likely to be unstable for several reasons. One is that no obvious formula establishes market share. The jockeying for market share causes market instability.

Second, the "other things equal" assumption is rarely met. If one firm has more limited production capacity, higher marginal costs, or less financial reserve to sustain losses than the other, the weaker firm will exit. The resulting monopoly and attendant pure profit of the remaining firm will invite entry. With entry the process of reaching a new equilibrium repeats itself.

The indeterminateness of Bertrand conjectures can be removed conceptually by assuming duopolists 1 and 2 sell slightly differentiated products. If the demand curve is linear and if duopolists 1 and 2 use Bertrand conjectures, reaction curves are as shown in Figure 7.5. Demand will be positive for output of firm 2 even if firm 1 sets price at zero, hence firm 2's reaction function intersects the vertical axis at a positive price in Figure 7.5. Goods are assumed to be substitutes. Thus an increase in price by firm 1 (horizontal axis) raises demand and profit-maximizing price for the product of duopolist 2 (firm 2's price is on the vertical axis). It follows that firm 2's reaction curve slopes upward to the right.

If firms react independently and simultaneously with Bertrand conjectures, the Nash equilibrium is at N. Given the position of the other firm, neither firm can improve its position. Profit of firm 1 is Π_{10} and of firm 2 is Π_{20}.

If duopolist 1 is the leader with Bertrand conjectures and knows duopolist 2's reaction function, equilibrium is at S_1 and profit Π_{11} which is on the highest isoprofit curve

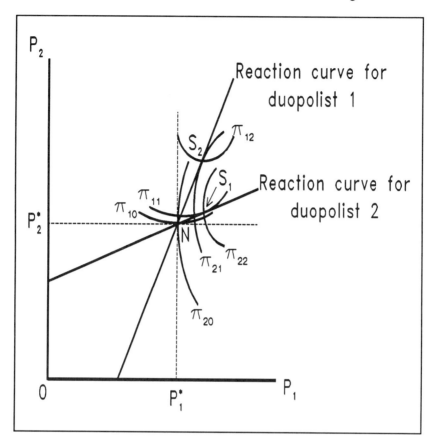

Figure 7.5. Reaction and Isoprofit Curves Under Bertrand Conjectures: Stackelberg Disequilibrium.

for 1 compatible with 2's reaction function.   The profit is above that (Π_{10}) at the simultaneous Nash equilibrium N. At the Stackelberg equilibrium S_1 firm 2's profit is Π_{22}, also an expansion over simultaneous equilibrium profit Π_{20}. If duopolist 2 is the leader, equilibrium is at S_2 and profit of duopolist 2 is Π_{21} and of duopolist 1 is Π_{12}.

Figure 7.5 makes an important point. Profit for 1 is higher when it is a follower (Π_{12}) than when it is a leader (Π_{11}). Profit for 2 is higher when it is a follower (Π_{22}) than when it is a leader (Π_{21}). Each duopolist would prefer to be the *follower* to maximize profit.

Both firms cannot be followers, hence Figure 7.5 illustrates *Stackelberg disequilibrium*. It would be easy to rearrange Figure 7.5 to illustrate a situation when both firms would be better off as leaders than as followers. Both cannot be leaders so that equilibrium also cannot be maintained. It is another Stackelberg disequilibrium.

Figure 7.6 illustrates a Stackelberg price leader equilibrium in a duopoly characterized by Bertrand conjectures. Profit is higher for firm 1 when it is the Stackelberg leader with equilibrium at S_1 and with profit Π_{11} than when it is a follower with profit Π_{10}. Profit is higher for firm 2 when it is a follower at equilibrium S_1 and with profit Π_{21} than when it is the leader with Stackelberg equilibrium at S_2 with profit Π_{20}. Hence S_1 is a *Stackelberg equilibrium*.

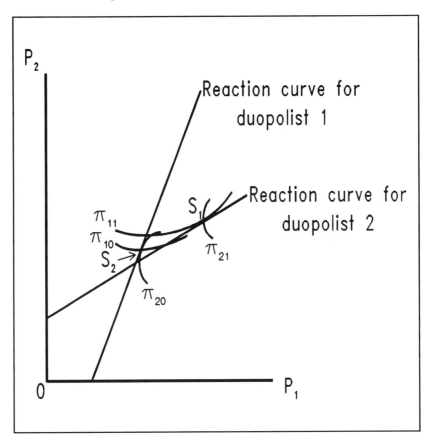

Figure 7.6. Reaction and Isoprofit Curves Under Bertrand Conjectures: Stackelberg Equilibrium.

An Application of Conjectures to Taxes and Subsidies

Strategic trade theory emphasizes opportunities for government interventions to improve outcomes. The potential as well as the pitfalls of this strategic intervention is illustrated below with conjectures.

1. *Subsidies and Cournot Conjectures.* Assume a duopoly of a local firm and a foreign firm, both selling solely in a third-country market under Cournot conjectures. The conceptual framework is shown in Figure 7.7 and is similar to that depicted earlier in Figure 7.4. Given the home firm's reaction function R_h and foreign firm's reaction function R_f, the simultaneous Nash equilibrium under Cournot conjectures is at N with q_{hn} produced by the home firm and q_{fn} by the foreign firm (Figure 7.7A). Neither firm initially is presumed to be credible as a Cournot Stackelberg leader. However, suppose that the home government intervenes strategically in this leadership vacuum with an export subsidy to bring the home firm's reaction function from R_h to R_h' and to raise output from q_{hn} to q_{hs}, the latter at Stackelberg leader equilibrium S. The home firm's higher isoprofit curve $\Pi_{h2} > \Pi_{h1}$ is consistent with the foreign firm's reaction function R_f. In short, the contest becomes a two-stage game when the government credibly precommits to a subsidy, bringing forth a perfect equilibrium.

173

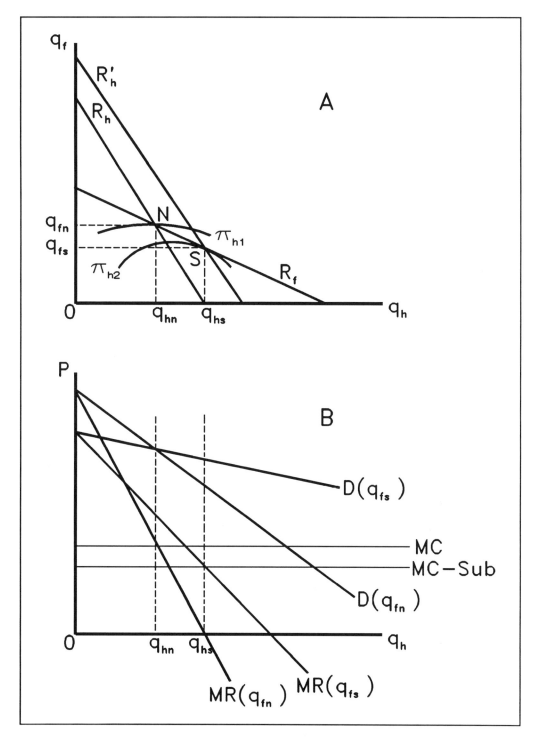

Figure 7.7. Impact of Government Export Subsidy on Duopoly with Cournot Conjectures.

Figure 7.7B illustrates what is happening to the home firm's marginal cost and demand curves. With demand for local output $D(q_{fn})$, when the foreign firm is producing q_{fn}, Nash equilibrium occurs at local output q_{hn} where $MR(q_{fn})$ is equal to MC. If the export subsidy is provided per unit of output and exports, it may be viewed as reducing marginal cost from MC to MC - Sub in Figure 7.7B.

The home firm's initial conjectures of demand were $D(q_{fn})$ with Nash equilibrium at q_{fn} for its foreign competition. With the foreign competitor's output given at q_{fn} by the home firm, marginal revenue for the home firm is $MR(q_{fn})$. With government intervention, output of the competitor is reduced to q_{fs}, causing the home firm's demand curve to shift to $D(q_{fs})$ and marginal revenue to shift to $MR(q_{fs})$. Optimal output of the home firm is raised from q_{hn} to q_{hs}, consistent respectively with the Nash and Stackelberg equilibria.

In essence, the government turned the home firm into a Stackelberg leader because it was profitable and the home firm lacked initiative. The home country benefits from a government export subsidy under assumptions in Figure 7.7 but not under a different set of assumptions as apparent below.

Figure 7.8 illustrates what happens to profits when the government in the country of the foreign firm uses a subsidy to try to be a Stackelberg leader when the government in the home country is also attempting that role. Before any subsidies, Nash equilibrium is at N_1 with home firm profit Π_{h2} and foreign firm profit Π_{f2}. In their competition for leadership

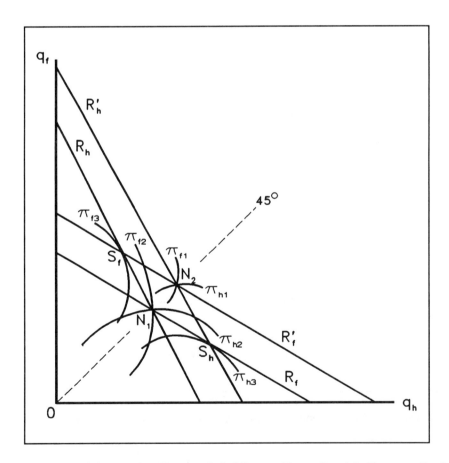

Figure 7.8. Impact of Competing Export Subsidies on Duopoly with Cournot Conjectures.

through subsidies, the new Nash equilibrium is at N_2 with lower profits Π_{h1} to the home firm and Π_{f1} to the foreign firm. Profit is reduced for both the home and foreign firms.

If only one government had subsidized exports as in Figure 7.7, the profit situation in Figure 7.8 could have been quite different. Stackelberg equilibrium at S_h maximizes home duopoly profit Π_{h3} with the home government export subsidy moving the reaction curve from R_h to R_h'. Stackelberg equilibrium at S_f maximizes foreign firm profit Π_{f3} with solely a foreign country export subsidy moving the reaction function from R_f to R_f'. In short, the case for an export subsidy breaks down with retaliation allowed by the competing firm or country.

It is notable that the Figure 7.8 has completed the circle by returning to the Prisoners' Dilemma game. Profit (Π_{h1} and Π_{f1}) is lowest for the duopolists if both governments subsidize, is highest (Π_{h3} and Π_{f3}) for the firms if only one government subsidizes, and is intermediate for each firm if neither government subsidizes. Left to their own devices, the Nash equilibrium is for each to subsidize to protect against a loss accruing if the other government subsidizes. But a better solution is to cooperate through multilateral trade talks and arrangements. Both countries can gain, although the consensus does not ensure a socially optimal equilibrium.

2. *Taxes and Bertrand Conjectures.* In contrast to a subsidy raising profits under Cournot conjectures in Figure 7.7, an export tax (tariff) raises profits under Bertrand conjectures as shown in Figure 7.9. Given reaction functions R_h for the home duopolist and R_f for the foreign duopolist competing for a third-country market with identical cost structures, the initial Nash equilibrium is at N_1 with simultaneous moves by the duopolists. Profit is Π_{h0} for the home firm and Π_{f0} for the foreign firm.

Equilibrium is at S_h if the home firm behaves as a Stackelberg leader, making the first price move and convincing the foreign firm that it will hold to this price. Equilibrium is at S_f if the foreign firm is the leader, attaining its highest isoprofit curve possible subject to the constraint of the home firm's reaction function.

If equilibrium is at N_1 but neither firm is able to exercise price leadership, the home country government can intervene strategically. It can raise the effective price from P_{h0} to P_{h1} with an export tariff, shifting the reaction function from R_h to R_h' to bring Stackelberg equilibrium S_h. If the government of the foreign country rather than of the home country taxes exports to raise price, the Stackelberg equilibrium is at S_f. If both countries impose equal tariffs shifting reaction functions to R_h' and R_f', Nash equilibrium is at N_2. Prices are P_{h2} for the home firm and P_{f2} for the foreign firm. Profits are highest, π_{h2} and π_{f2}, for both firms with tariffs imposed by the two exporters. Hence the choices are not a Prisoners' Dilemma game. Issues of how the profits from the tariff and higher price are divided between the government and the firm would need to be resolved.

In summary, if Cournot conjectures prevail, an export subsidy is optimal with a Stackelberg equilibrium; if Bertrand conjectures prevail, an export tariff is optimal. The dilemma is that market participants are unlikely to know which conjectures prevail. It is easy to make too much of this dilemma, however: Neither model may represent reality.

CONJECTURAL VARIATIONS

Difficulties in formulating empirically testable hypotheses have constrained application of strategic trade theory to international agricultural trade. A promising approach is *conjectural variations* quantifying the degree of cooperation among players. The

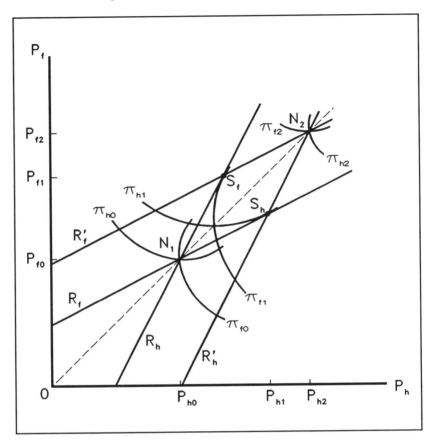

Figure 7.9. Impact of Single and Competing Export Taxes on Duopoly with Bertrand Conjectures.

approach was designed to measure cooperation among players in an oligopoly at equilibrium with Cournot conjectures, but is more widely applicable.

A firm (or country) i's conjectural variation refers to the change expected by i in the output q_j of another firm (or country) j if its output q_i changes by one unit, or

$$CV = \frac{\Delta q_j}{\Delta q_i}.$$

Examples of magnitudes of conjectural variations are as follows:

CV = 0   A Cournot-Nash equilibrium. Duopolist i does not believe output of j will change with a change in q_i.

CV = -1   Firm i believes that a change in its output will bring a compensatory change in its rival's output. The implication in duopoly is that firm i can change its output without changing industry output and hence price. This Bertrand-like conjecture is comparable to the situation in atomistic competition (many firms) but for a different reason. In a competitive market where firm i is a small part of the industry, a change in its output has no perceptible impact on industry output. Other firms are not reducing output in the competitive case as in the duopoly case, but the result is the same: Firm i can expand output without perceptibly influencing industry output or price.

CV = 1   Firm i expects its rival to match its expansion of output to maintain share or for other reasons. It can be shown that the profit maximizing behavior for firm j is to match a quantity increase or decrease by firm i if the two firms are operating at a monopoly output (see Rasmusen, p. 263).

Because conjectural variations can be estimated empirically and appear to be associated with market structure as noted above, it would seem feasible to quantify conjectural variations to give insights into the degree of competition in an industry. The approach has shortcomings. First, it is suited for measuring Cournot but not Bertrand conjectures. Second, as noted above, it is easy to confuse Bertrand conjectures (e.g., CV = -1) with a competitive market of many firms.

Third, conjectural variations may be confused with normal responses to price in competitive markets. For example, in a rapidly emerging new and price-elastic international market the United States and other countries may simultaneously expand exports of a food product. Or when the United States expands output other countries may reduce exports if demand is static and inelastic. Market structure may be identical but in the first case CV = 1 and in the second case CV = -1.

Empirical applications of conjectural variations to agricultural trade have been few (see Bresnahan; Thursby and Thursby). The focus has often been narrow (ignoring competing products, exporters, and importers), limiting generalizability and robustness of results. Applications have been troubled by problems other than those noted above. In wheat, for example, price leadership appears to have shifted unpredictably between the US, Canada, and the European Community, and sometimes a combination of countries (see McCalla; Alaouze *et al.*). New farm bills in the US in 1981, 1985, and 1990 significantly changed the competitive framework.

APPROPRIATENESS OF STRATEGIC TRADE THEORY

At issue is the appropriateness of strategic trade policy interventions to complement an industrial policy advocated by many. Under such policy, selected industry products and technologies would be promoted by government subsidies through research, tariff preferences, price supports, and other means. Collusion among firms in research, technology, and sales would be allowed in favored industries to realize economies of size and promote competitiveness with foreign firms and countries.

Critics note several shortcomings of such policies:

1. Governments in the past have subsidized politically well-placed and outspoken losers rather than dynamic winners. Losers such as cotton have received more subsidies than winners such as soybeans.
2. Even if the government succeeds in creating low-cost, highly competitive export industries, will these industries remain competitive? Public choice theory notes that subsidies creating economic rents draw a following of political rent-seekers to maintain those rents.
3. Strategic trade theory, which has attracted some of the first-rate minds in the economics profession, can give intellectual respectability to virtually any tax or

subsidy, depending on the assumptions used and who pays for the consulting. Predictions are highly sensitive to assumptions. The theory has no empirical tradition to establish which assumptions predict well and hence are realistic.

4. The "new" theory of trade has not demonstrated ability to predict or to prescribe a useful trade policy. Prescriptions from it can reverse with small changes in assumptions. In contrast, the traditional neoclassical theory of trade outlined earlier in this book is robust in prescriptions despite failure to meet assumptions of perfect knowledge, perfect mobility, large numbers of buyers and sellers, and the like.

5. Veeman (p. 109) notes that "Finally, it is clear that effective lobbying by commodity groups and other special interest groups, rather than abstract trade and welfare theory, shape the political economy of most trade policy for agriculture." It is convenient to label a variable levy imposed by Japan or the EC on US wheat imports an ingenious application of an optimal tariff when in fact it was merely an expedient response to politically well-placed farm lobbies.

REFERENCES

Alaouze, C.M., A.S. Watson, and N.H. Sturgess. 1978. Oligopoly pricing in the world wheat market. *American Journal of Agricultural Economics* 60:173-185.

Axelrod, Robert. 1984. *The Evolution of Cooperation.* New York: Basic Books.

Bain, Joe S. 1951. Relation of profit rate to industry concentration: American manufacturing, 1936-1940. *Quarterly Journal of Economics* 65:293-324.

Bain, Joe S. 1956. *Barriers to New Competition.* Cambridge, MA: Harvard University Press.

Brander, James A. and Barbara J. Spencer. 1985. Export subsidies and international market share rivalry. *The Journal of International Economics* 18:83-100.

Bresnahan, Timothy F. 1989. Empirical studies of industries with market power. In Richard Schmalensee and Robert Willig, eds., *Handbook of Industrial Organization.* New York: Elsevier Science Publishing Co., Inc.

Carter, Colin and Andrew Schmitz. August 1979. Import tariffs and price formation in the world wheat market. *American Journal of Agricultural Economics* 61:517-522.

Carter, Colin, Alex McCalla, and Jerry Sharples, eds. 1990. *Imperfect Competition and Political Economy: The New Trade Theory in Agricultural Trade Research.* Boulder, CO: Westview Press.

Galbraith, John Kenneth. 1952. *American Capitalism.* Boston: Houghton-Mifflin.

Handy, Charles and Dennis Henderson. 1991. Industry organization and global competitiveness in food manufacturing. Occasional Paper Series OP-26. Columbus: NC-194, The Ohio State University.

Henderson, Dennis and Stuart Frank. Fall 1990. Export performance of US food manufacturers. *Ohio's Challenge* 3:11-14.

Just, R., A. Schmitz, and D. Zilberman. 1979. Price controls and optimal export policies under alternative market structures. *American Economic Review* 69:706-715.

Kaufman, Phillip and Charles Handy. 1989. Supermarket prices and price determinants. Technical Bulletin No. 1776. Washington, DC: ERS, US Department of Agriculture.

Krishna, Kala and Marie Thursby. 1990. Trade policy with imperfect competition. Ch. 2 in Carter *et al.*

Marion, Bruce W. 1986. *The Organization and Performance of the US Food System*. Lexington, MA: D.C. Heath and Company.

Mason, Edward S. 1939. Price and production policies of large-scale enterprise. *American Economic Review* 29 Supp:61-74.

Mason, Edward S. 1949. The current state of the monopoly problem in the United States. *Harvard Law Review* 62:1265-85.

McCalla, Alex. August 1966. A duopoly model of world wheat pricing. *Journal of Farm Economics* 48:711-727.

Miller, Stephen. December 1982. The structural stability of the concentration-performance relationship in food manufacturing. *Southern Journal of Agricultural Economics* 14:43-49.

Perloff, Jeffrey. 1991. Econometric analysis of imperfect competition and implications for trade research. Occasional Paper Series OP-23. Columbus: NC-194, The Ohio State University.

Porter, Michael. 1990. *The Competitive Advantage of Nations*. New York: The Free Press.

Rasmusen, Eric. 1989. *Games and Information: Introduction to the Theory of Games*. Cambridge, UK: Cambridge University Press.

Sheldon, Ian and Dennis Henderson. 1990. Motives for the international licensing of branded food and related products. Occasional Paper Series OP-15. Columbus: NC-194, The Ohio State University.

Spencer, Barbara J. and James A. Brander. 1983. International R and D rivalry and industrial strategy. *Review of Economic Studies* 50:707-22.

Thursby, Marie and Jerry Thursby. 1990. Strategic trade theory and agricultural markets: An application to Canadian and US wheat exports to Japan. Ch. 4 in Carter *et al*.

Tweeten, Luther. 1989. *Farm Policy Analysis*. Boulder, CO: Westview Press.

Veeman, Michele. 1990. Discussion: Strategic trade theory in agricultural markets. Pp. 107-111 in Carter *et al*.

CHAPTER 8

Strategic Trade Theory, Market Power, and the Political Economy of Trade

In Chapter 7 we examined some contributions of game theory and duopoly theory to strategic trade theory. This chapter goes beyond duopoly to examine contributions of other forms of imperfect competition and political economy to trade theory.

The following analysis first shows how exposure to trade and how border measures influence gains from trade under imperfect competition. The second section analyzes cartel theory. The chapter returns to actual measures of structure, conduct, and performance before concluding with issues of political economy under strategic trade policy.

RELATING STRATEGIC TRADE ANALYSIS TO TRADITIONAL ANALYSIS

Figure 8.1 illustrates how price and trade policy can influence economic efficiency under imperfect competition. Suppose the domestic product demand and marginal cost curves of a monopoly firm are D and MC, respectively. Differences in economic analysis from conventional analysis reported earlier in this book include:

1. Traditional econometric analysis presumes that the price-quantity relationships at the intersection of MC and D formed from varying positions of the demand curve trace out the supply curve. Because price-quantity relationships such as at p_m and q_m under monopoly do not lie on the supply curve, it follows that traditional time series econometric techniques will not identify and measure the true marginal cost (supply) curve. Welfare measures from the biased curves will also be biased.
2. Traditional economic analysis presumes that the supply curve will slope upward to the right because of diminishing factor returns under the law of variable factor proportions. However, a policy *reducing* the market price from P_m to the price ceiling P_c *raises* quantity supplied from q_m to q. The demand curve facing the monopolist becomes P_cbD, which intersects MC at output q. The policy "distortion" of setting a price ceiling at P_c reduces deadweight loss from former area 1 + 2 by area 1. Deadweight loss 2 remains, symbolic of the difficulty of administratively determining the deadweight-minimizing price.
3. A third issue apparent from Figure 8.1 is the value of trade in an economy characterized by imperfect competition. Especially in a small country, only one firm may be able to operate at the low marginal cost MC. Two or more firms operating in the market might have very high costs. The single firm in Figure 8.1 operating at low cost will forego net potential benefits 1 + 2 if it practices

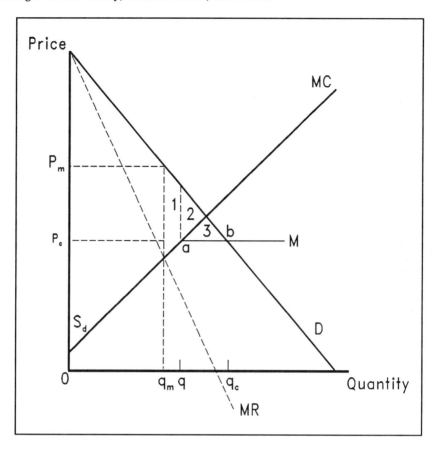

Figure 8.1. Impact of Imperfect Competition and Trade on Pricing and Output.

monopoly pricing and output. One option, as in (2) above, is to regulate price. An alternative is to open the industry to foreign competition. The import supply curve is M in this small-country case. Now the marginal cost of supplying output becomes S_daM. With competitive pricing and output the gain from trade is only area 3 but compared to monopoly pricing and output, the welfare gain from free trade is area 1 + 2 + 3. At the equilibrium price p_c the local firm supplies q, imports are q_c - q, and consumption is q_c. This outcome contrasts with the traditional assumption that opening to imports will reduce domestic production.

TARIFFS, QUOTAS, AND IMPERFECT COMPETITION

Figure 8.2 further illustrates how exposure to international markets restrains domestic monopoly power and how tariffs and quotas are not necessarily equivalent under imperfect competition (see Helpman and Krugman). As in Figure 8.1, domestic demand is D, marginal cost for domestic industry is MC, and import supply M is perfectly elastic at world price P_w.

In competitive equilibrium domestic production is q_m, imports are q_c-q_m, and consumption is q_c (Figure 8.2A). If the domestic market D is served by a monopolist with

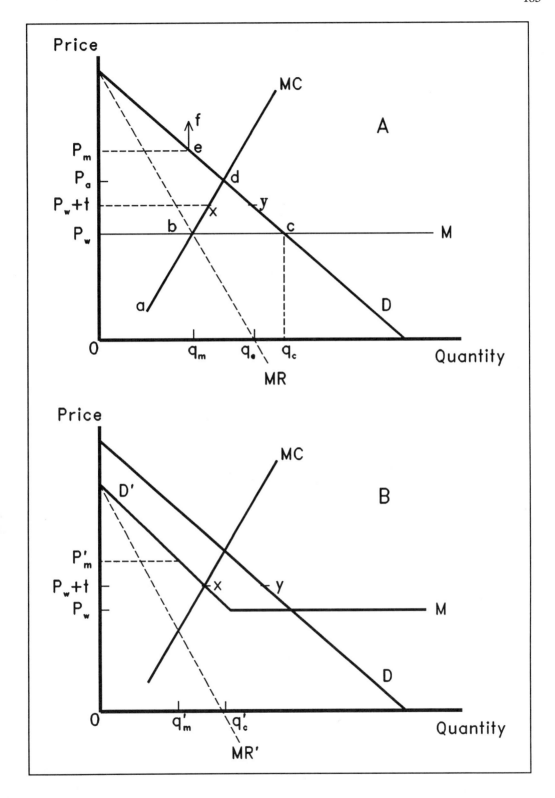

Figure 8.2. **Impact on Price and Quantity of Tariffs and Quotas Under Imperfect Competition.**

marginal cost MC, in the absence of an import market M the firm produces where marginal revenue MR = MC, price is P_m, and production and consumption are q_m. Opening the monopolistic domestic market to imports, the domestic monopolist's marginal revenue becomes M at world price P_w. Because MC is greater than MR = P_w to the right of q_m, the monopolist holds production to q_m, price is P_w, imports are q_c - q_m, and consumption is q_c. Exposure to world markets deprives the monopolist of market power so that the monopolistic and competitive outcomes are the same -- as noted earlier in Figure 8.1.

Imperfect Competition and Tariffs

Now assume that a specific tariff t is introduced on imports (Figure 8.2A). This raises domestic production to x because domestic marginal revenue P_w + t exceeds marginal cost to that point. Consumption is y and imports are y - x. The domestic monopoly would like to raise its price but cannot because it would be undersold by imports. So the firm continues to behave like a perfectly competitive enterprise, moving up supply curve MC from b to d as the tariff expands to raise domestic price protection from P_w to P_a, the latter the competitive price with autarky.

For tariffs that raise domestic price above autarky price P_a to P_m, the supply response for the domestic monopoly is the backward bending segment de. Imports are zero. For a high tariff P_w + t (not shown) above P_m, the monopolist is not restrained in price by the threat of imports. The monopoly firm is maximizing profit while price P_m is protected by the tariff from foreign imports. The supply response for the monopolist exposed to trade is bdef for P_w + t at ever higher values of t. This contrasts with the competitive supply curve bd (becoming vertical at d) for ever higher values of t. Thus the impact of a tariff can be quite different depending on whether the market is competitive or imperfectly competitive.

Non-Equivalence of Quotas and Tariffs Under
Imperfect Competition

Under competitive conditions, a quota and tariff are equivalent in that the price (quantity) effect of a given quantity (price) change is the same for each. Under imperfectly competitive markets, as illustrated in Figure 8.2B, a quota and a tariff are not equivalent. If the market is competitive in Figure 8.2B and the quota is y - x, corresponding with specific tariff t in Figure 8.2B, domestic production is x, consumption is y, imports are y - x, and price is P_w + t. A tariff t brings the same imports. Thus the quota y - x is equivalent to tariff t.

If the domestic firm is a monopoly, the situation is quite different. For domestic prices above P_w, the quota y - x lowers demand by that quantity at any price to level D´. The resulting marginal revenue curve is MR´, which intersects MC at q_m' < q_m. Domestic production is q_m', imports are q_c' - q_m' = y - x, and consumption is q_c'. Thus the quota and tariffs are not equivalent. The tariff t restricting imports to y - x brought price P_w + t, whereas a quota of the same quantity y - x brought domestic price P_m' > P_w + t, domestic production q_m' < x, and domestic consumption q_c' < y.

The analysis demonstrates that exposure to international competition weakens local firms' market power and that border protection can restore local firms' market power. Tariffs and quotas are not necessarily equivalent under imperfect competition; tariffs are preferred on welfare grounds over quotas.

GAINS FROM MARKET POWER

In Chapter 4 (see footnotes 2 and 3) we specified the optimal tariff as $t = p/|E_x|$. Thus the *optimal tariff rate* is

$$r = \frac{p-c}{p} = \frac{1}{|E_x|} \tag{8.1}$$

where p is product price, c is marginal cost, and E_x is the perceived elasticity of demand. The percentage markup over cost c is equal to the price flexibility of demand. While p-c is viewed as the optimal tariff in Chapter 3, it also may be viewed as the markup over cost of a profit-maximizing firm in either domestic or export markets. Alternatively, r is called the *Lerner Index* of market power, with higher values of r associated with high market power.

The perceived elasticity of demand E_x determines the firm's market power and hence the mark-up over cost. Given industry market demand quantity Q and the demand quantity q_i facing firm i in the industry, then

$$E_x = \sum_i E_{xi} s_i \tag{8.2}$$

where E_x is the global market elasticity of demand, E_{xi} is the elasticity of demand for firm or country i, and s_i is the share of that firm or country i in total demand. If each firm is of equal size and faces the same demand curve, then $s_i = 1/n$ so

$$E_{xi} = nE_x. \tag{8.3}$$

It follows that if n is very large (the perfect competition or small-country case), then E_{xi} is large, r approaches zero, and economic rent for firm i in equation 8.1 is zero. If n=1 (the monopoly or very-large-country case), $E_{xi} = E_x$. If market demand is highly inelastic, the Lerner Index is large and opportunity exists for sizable economic rents.

As a general approximation

$$E_{xi} = \frac{E_x}{s_i}. \tag{8.4}$$

Thus the larger the share of the world market the greater the value of r and the greater the opportunity for economic rent. The opportunity for economic rent for the US is greater for feed grains than in wheat because the US share of the world market is larger for feed grains. A wheat cartel encompassing Australia, Canada, Argentina, and the United States has a larger share s_i and hence greater market power r than does any of these countries acting alone but also has much greater problems of coordination. E_x is smaller (absolute value) and market power greater for commodities having few substitutes. Because wheat can be substituted for feed grains in production and consumption, it follows that E_x for an aggregate of *all* grains is lower than E_x for wheat alone in an international cartel. Although market power (the Lerner Index) is greater by including all grains, problems of coordination multiply as noted above.

Market share is a matter of firm or national pride as well as of market power. Trade skirmishes and some trade wars result from efforts to retain or gain market share. An important variable determining market share and hence market power is economies of firm size or, in the case of international trade, comparative and absolute cost advantage of countries in products. The greater the economies of size (cost reduction for larger firms) and the greater the size of firm or country necessary to realize such economies, the greater will be market shares, the lesser will be the number of sellers, and the greater will be market power and economic rent. Innovation also is critical. The strategic trade theory of Chapter 7 taught that credible threats discourage retaliation. A firm reducing costs by technological prowess gained from a strong research and development program is likely to be credible and hence able to raise market share without retaliation.

Government and Producer Cartel Theory

Numerous American legislators, individual farmers, and commodity groups have proposed formation of a cartel, especially in wheat, to provide bargaining power and to raise and perhaps stabilize farm prices and incomes. Those proposals are motivated in part by recognition of market imperfections in buyers' markets.

In the case of wheat, for example, government wheat boards in Canada and Australia give market power to competing exporters. Carter and Schmitz (p. 517) review previous papers which note "that price formation in the world wheat market is largely determined by the major exporters," but the two authors then conclude paradoxically that importing countries are using optimal tariffs to maximize social gains. In fact, the implicit tariff on Japanese wheat imports is not the product of strategic trade theory but a byproduct of the country's rice self-sufficiency policy.

Theoretical models are helpful to interpret implications of cartel arrangements and in particular to note the distinction between a government cartel (monopoly pricing designed to benefit consumers and producers in the cartel) compared to a producer cartel designed to benefit farmers in the cartel (see Schmitz *et al.*).

Figure 8.3 illustrates economic impacts of a government or producer cartel of a country or colluding group of countries acting in concert (here referred to simply as country A) exporting to the rest of the world (ROW). Country A has no domestic market so its domestic supply curve s and export excess supply curve ES are equivalent. With free trade, domestic and world price is P_w.

Tariff P_r-P_a is optimal for either a producer or government cartel in the absence of a domestic market in A. Quantity produced by A and exported (imported by ROW) is reduced from $q_p = q_e = Q_c$-Q_p with an unrestrained market to $q_p{'} = q_e{'} = Q_c{'}$-$Q_p{'}$ with an optimal tariff. Gains and losses as compared to a free market are depicted below. Welfare analysis of a government cartel and a producer cartel is as follows:

Gain to:	Country A		ROW
	Government Cartel	Producer Cartel	
Producers	-1-2	3-2	a
Consumers	---	---	-a-b-c-d
Government	1+3	---	---
Country		3-2	-b-c-d
World (3=c)		-2-b-d	

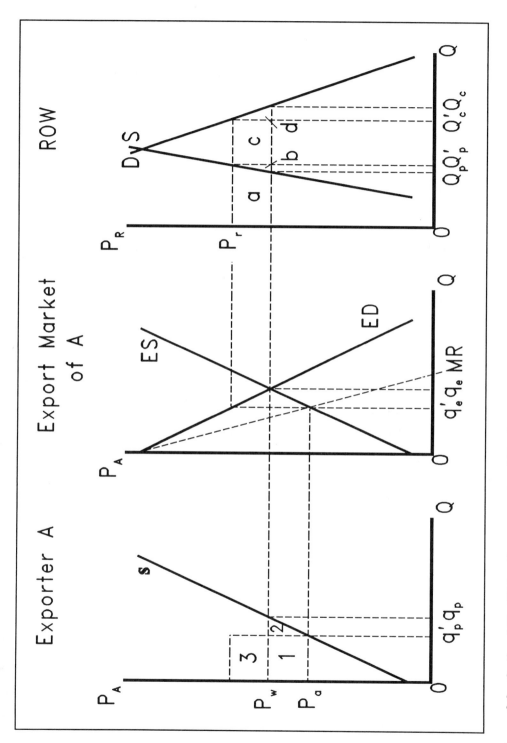

Figure 8.3. Optimal Tariff for Government and Producer Export Cartels with No Domestic Demand in Country A.

Several notable observations follow from Figure 8.3 and the associated welfare analysis.

1. ROW and the world are unequivocally worse off under the cartel of A.
2. In the small-country (cartel) case, ED is horizontal at P_w, hence area 3 is absent. Thus A unequivocally loses if a tariff is imposed while the welfare of ROW is not reduced. Success of a cartel depends on the elasticity of export demand ED. A cartel is not feasible in the small-country case; combining several exporters reduces the export elasticity. For revenue to increase from restricting supply, ED must be inelastic.
3. It is notable that producers are worse off by area 1+2 with a government cartel. The government can compensate producers from its cartel rent of area 1+3. However, transfers cannot be fully decoupled from incentives to producers because payments lessen capital constraints. Hence production controls may be necessary.
4. A cartel made up of several countries faces problems of coordination, sharing of rents, free riders, new entrants, and encroachment of substitute products. In the case of wheat, for example, a cartel of the US, Canada, Argentina, and Australia would encourage the rest of the world to produce wheat instead of feed grains. ROW would then purchase cheap feed grains from competitive markets in the cartel countries. An effective wheat cartel would need to include feed grains.
5. Retaliation by ROW can erode the gains from monopoly pricing. Actions and counteractions in a world trade war can raise instability and welfare costs.

Figure 8.4 illustrates cartel pricing, output, and welfare when the cartel country (countries) A faces both domestic and foreign demand for the product. As in Figure 8.3, the result of optimal tariff P_r-P_a is to reduce world trade in country A and ROW, to reduce price in A, and to raise price in ROW compared to free trade. Of interest is the impact on producers and consumers in A. Welfare analysis of a government cartel and a producer cartel compared to a free market is as follows:

Gain to:	Country A		ROW
	Government Cartel	Producer Cartel	
Producers	-a-b-c-d	-a-b-d+e	1
Consumers	a	a	-1-2-3-4
Government	c+e	---	---
Country	-b-d+e		-2-3-4
World (e=3)		-b-d-2-4	

Conclusions from welfare analysis in Figure 8.4 using a free market for comparison are that:

1. Consumers gain in A whether the cartel is operated by government or producers as long as a markup over cost is allowed only in the export market.
2. Producers lose in A if the government retains the revenue from an optimal tariff. Producers also will lose in a producer-run cartel if area e is less than area a+b+d -- a likely case if ED is not highly inelastic or if exports are a small

189

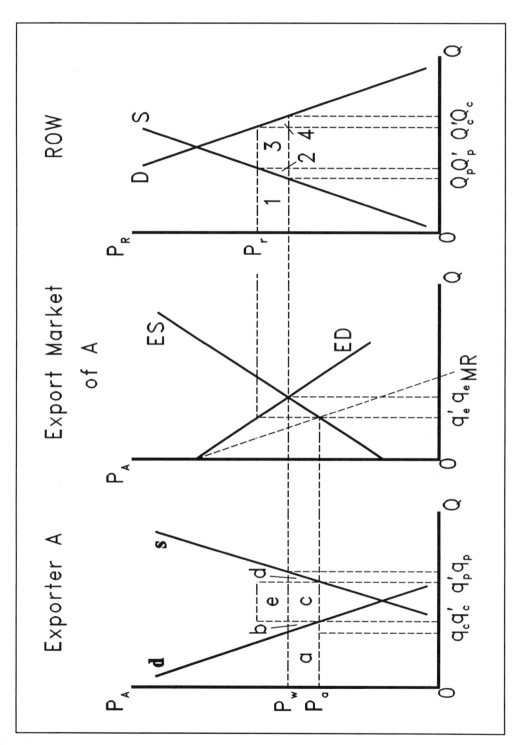

Figure 8.4. Optimal Tariff for Government and Producer Cartels with Domestic Demand d in Country A.

portion of the market of A. Redistribution by government of some of the tariff revenue c+e to producers might induce producers' support. But a cartel run by the government or producers could induce overproduction, requiring alleviation with production control or other measures.

3. Free riders, new entrants to wheat production and marketing, and substitutes can erode gains from the cartel.

Implications of a full producer cartel are depicted in Figure 8.5. The important difference from Figure 8.4 is that producers in Figure 8.5 maximize net revenue from the *export and domestic* markets. The cartel uses price discrimination among markets to raise profits.

Competitive equilibrium is where exports of A are $q_p - q_c = q_e = Q_c - Q_p$, the latter the imports of ROW. Compared to equilibrium free market price P_w, the price with the full cartel is higher both in ROW and in A. The profit maximizing solution for the cartel is found by horizontally summing marginal revenue MR_d in the domestic market and MR_f in the foreign market to form MR_{d+f}. Production q_p' is where marginal revenue equals marginal cost -- assumed to be represented by s. Of this production, q_c' is allocated to domestic consumption and $q_p' - q_c' = q_e'$ is allocated to exports. Exports are greater and the ROW price rise $P_r - P_w$ is less than with an export markup only, hence welfare losses to ROW are less than with a government cartel. To avoid charges of dumping, for administrative convenience, or for other reasons, the cartel might charge the same price in all markets. Production would be at q_p', but more output would go to the domestic market and less to the export market.

With a producer cartel, the welfare gains over competitive equilibrium at P_w are:

Gain to:	**Country A**		**ROW**
Producers	a+c+d-h		1
Consumers	-a-b-c		-1-2-3-4
Country	-b+d-h		-2-3-4
World (c+d=3)		-b-c-h-2-4	

Conclusions are as follows:

1. Unequivocal welfare losses accrue to ROW and the world.
2. Welfare gains to the producer cartel may be sizable but may not offset unequivocal welfare losses to consumers. Area d must exceed b+h for country A to gain.
3. Consumers in A can be expected to oppose the cartel unless they are bribed by producers to accept the cartel. If consumers must be fully compensated, the producer cartel would be better off to use monopoly pricing only in the export market as depicted in Figure 8.4.
4. The problems of supply management multiply with a full producer cartel because incentives would be great to cheat by producing in excess of q_p'. Procedures would need to be in place to keep traders from arbitrage between high- and low-priced markets. If the complications of coordinating between several countries in the cartel, substitutes, new entrants, free riders, and importers' retaliation are added, the destiny of a full producer cartel would be in doubt.

191

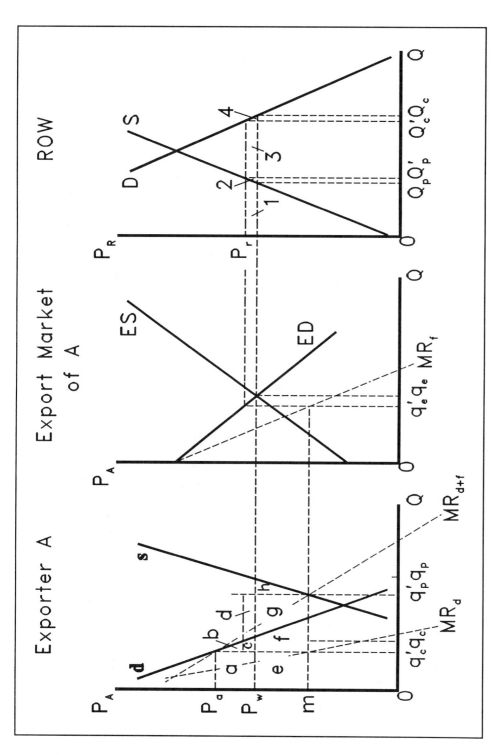

Figure 8.5. Optimal Pricing and Output for Producer Cartel in Country A Exploiting the Domestic and Export Markets.

Price Discrimination in Wheat Markets

Although the United States has no conscious policy of segmenting markets to maximize economic rents, its policies of export subsidies and food aid exhibit some such behavior. Figure 8.6 illustrates stylized behavior to maximize wheat revenue in a world wheat market with two characteristics needed for price discrimination to increase net revenue: Markets (1) can be separated and (2) exhibit different demand elasticities.

Three markets are identified in Figure 8.6 for wheat. D_c is the demand in commercial market economies, D_b is the demand in markets such as the Middle East and North Africa, heavily contested with the EC, which relies on export subsidies, and D_a which is the demand in low-income third-world countries with little buying power but where price is important.

Individual demand curves are shown to the left of the price axis with quantities increasing from right to left. Total demand to the right of the price axis is formed by adding horizontally the individual demand curves. Supply S, assumed to equal marginal cost, in competitive equilibrium intersects demand at quantity Q_T. Competitive equilibrium price (not shown) in all markets lies on the vertical axis precisely to the left of the intersection of S and D_T.

Optimal prices and quantities to maximize net revenue with market discrimination are determined in a two-step process in Figure 8.6. Marginal revenue MR_T, formed by the sum of marginal revenues in individual markets $MR_a + MR_b + MR_c$, intersects marginal cost S at quantity q_T, which is less than free market quantity Q_T. Then price and quantity in each market are determined by the intersection of marginal revenue in each market with marginal cost -- measured from the aggregate market discrimination curve MR_T and S to the right of the price axis in Figure 8.6. Price (not shown) in net-revenue-maximizing equilibrium without price discrimination can be read off the price axis precisely to the left of the intersection of D_T with a vertical line extending up from q_T. The same price prevails in all markets and is above the competitive equilibrium price.

With discrimination, the price differs among markets. Market A is developing country markets where effective demand is low for lack of buying power. Marginal revenue in that market is MR_a. Public Law 480 concessional food exports reduce the price to P_a and quantity is q_a. In reality, the effective price may be even lower partly for humanitarian reasons and partly as a long-term strategy to build markets by shifting tastes and preferences in developing countries to wheat from locally produced staples such as rice, corn, and cassava.

Market B, North Africa and the Middle East, where competition is keen from EC export subsidies, has marginal revenue MR_b given demand D_b. The Export Enhancement Program (export subsidies) and credit subsidies bring price to P_b and quantity to q_b in this market.

The highest, unsubsidized price P_c is charged for wheat in the developed commercial-country market depicted by the demand curve D_c. Japan illustrates a market where the aggregate demand for wheat appears to be highly inelastic. However, Japan has the option of purchasing wheat from other exporters. The European Community is a net exporter but continues to import some wheat for blending purposes. Because EC consumers and producers are insulated from world prices, the blended wheat demand would appear to be highly inelastic. While it seems that the US could discriminate to charge a high price and obtain greater revenue from the EC and Japan, a problem is that such markets are difficult to insulate from arbitrage of traders who would import US wheat in third-country markets

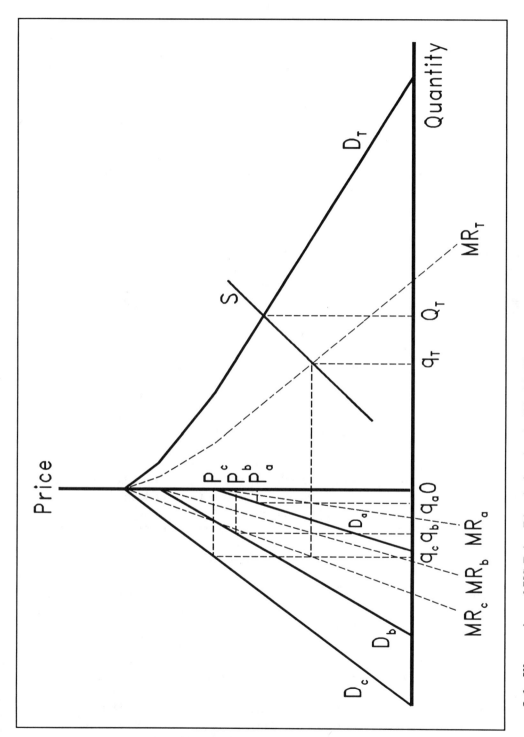

193

Figure 8.6. Illustration of US Price Discrimination in World Wheat Markets.

and sell it to the EC or Japan. Also, other wheat exporters such as Canada could undercut the US price.

GRAIN EXPORT INDUSTRY PERFORMANCE

Whether it makes sense for producers or governments to intervene to extract economic rents based on analysis depicted in this chapter depends on the behavior of markets. If markets are operating efficiently, the case for intervention is weak.

The classical analytical frameworks of pure competition, monopolistic competition, oligopoly, and monopoly here give way to the concept of *workable competition*, which is a more meaningful if less rigorous orientation. Market structure, conduct, and performance analysis operationalizes the concept of workable competition (see Tweeten, 1989, ch. 8). Market *structure* refers to characteristics of the market, including the supply and demand parameters, number and size of buyers and sellers, differentiation of products, barriers to entry, and extent of market integration. Market *conduct* is the behavior of enterprises, methods of determining price, sales promotion, efforts to vary products, and incidence of predatory or exclusionary practices. Market *performance* is the economic efficiency of the market. It is measured by efficiency in procurement, plant utilization, and distribution, by the amount and type of sales promotion, innovative activity, and quality of product, and by the level of profits.

A market need not have perfect information or perfect mobility to be efficient; it needs only to gather information or move resources if expected benefits exceed costs. A market that is characterized by a single large firm and high advertising costs may be viewed as efficient if economies of size are so large relative to the market that only one firm can produce at an efficient level and supply the market, if it is innovative, if it uses marginal cost pricing, and if its advertising is educational and its profits are in line with risk and capital costs. It may exercise price restraint to discourage competitors from entering the industry.

Many farm and food products in international markets are classified as oligopoly. Although economic theory provides no widely accepted models to predict behavior under oligopoly, firms in oligopolistic industries often display certain tendencies. Examples are innovation and heavy advertising to differentiate products and to enlarge demand and make it more inelastic, thereby enhancing ability to raise revenue and profit by raising price. Oligopolistic industries are often characterized by sizable barriers to entry because of: (1) economies of size growing out of real factors such as buying and selling in larger quantities, gathering information, or expensive apparatus; (2) because of mindsets created in consumers by advertising real or imagined properties of a commodity; and (3) in some instances because of predatory behavior. Established firms may sell below cost or use threats to drive out current competitors or to discourage potential entrants.

As noted in Chapter 1, grains constitute the largest category of US exports. Markets for oilseeds and many other bulk and high-value undifferentiated products sold in markets with numerous buyers and sellers have characteristics similar to grain markets. So studies of grain markets provide clues to performance of agricultural export markets. Some high-value products are traded in less competitive markets. These markets are becoming more important, but generalizations are difficult because high-value markets are highly diverse.

Numerous studies have examined international grain industry performance (for review, see Tweeten, 1989, pp. 244-246). Popular perceptions are that major grain companies constitute a cartel or shared monopoly in grain markets, that they manipulate price without restraint by government or any other institution, and that they cheat farmers and consumers through excessive profits and other costs creating unduly high marketing margins. These perceptions are myth.

Structure and Performance

The grain export industry is indeed concentrated as noted in Chapter 7. For several reasons, the concentration rates are not grounds for alarm.

1. The Foreign Agricultural Service of the USDA reported 395 firms actively exporting US farm products in 1982-83, up from 263 in 1978-79. Of these, 108 were active in grain (excluding rice) and soybean exports in 1982-83. Thursby and Thursby (p. 95) reported 30 to 60 US firms exporting wheat in the 1970s and 1980s. Many were small firms and a few were very large. Corrected to equal-size equivalents, the number of wheat exporting firms ranged from 9 to 14. Firms enter and leave the industry -- the rapid rise and demise of a once major exporter, Cook Industries, is an example.
2. Concentration ratios for export firms alone do not adequately reflect the degree of competition in the grain export industry. Grain exporters must compete with domestic merchandisers and processors for supplies of grain. The domestic grain industry is much less concentrated than the export industry.
3. Firms having Japanese ownership or affiliation and farmer-owned agricultural cooperatives increased their share of exports 5 percentage points between 1974-75 and 1980-81 at the expense of the five largest multinationals (GAO, p. 16). However, evidence (see Pakanati, Henneberry, and Warden, 1986, p. 67) indicates that in more recent years "...both the number and the export market share of agricultural cooperatives have declined." The decline appears to be the result of cost economies of larger, better managed private firms rather than the result of predatory practices.

The contribution of an industry to national goals such as equity and efficiency is measured not by market structure but by performance. Economies of size characterize the export industry, especially in *information* -- having a large enough staff to obtain extensive market intelligence and to seek out markets. The US grain export industry generally receives high marks for performance:

1. Profit margins have been small, averaging less than 2¢ per bushel above costs on grain, for example (see Tweeten, 1989, p. 245). Grain exporting firms are aggressive in holding down costs by securing the most favorable rates possible on storage, transportation, insurance, and the other expenses of doing business.
2. The grain export industry practices efficient pricing. The industry relies heavily on the futures market, which rates high in pricing efficiency as evident from use of all worthwhile public information to set market-clearing price. GAO (p. iii) found that the "...US grain export system translates information about grain sales into price changes with reasonable efficiency."
3. The federal government maintains over 50 programs affecting the US grain export trade. Some regulations such as export embargoes and a requirement that a specified percentage of PL 480 food aid shipments move in US bottoms reduce export performance. But other programs in the USDA ensure grade and weight standards, promote American products, and report grain sales and prices to improve market performance.

4. Wilson and Anderson (1980) analyzed the performance of the Canadian grain export system and concluded that it lagged behind the US system, although differences could not be attributed solely to the state marketing board used in Canada. Studies reviewed by Pakanati, Henneberry, and Warden (p. 4) comparing performance of export systems in the US and Canada were inconclusive. The Canadian system may be overrated, however; its performance would be less satisfactory without use of efficient US markets for price discovery. The Canadian state grain export system frequently uses private firms to transport grain once sale terms are worked out by the grain board.

Summary Comments

In-depth studies of the agricultural export industry produced conclusions such as

The popular conception of the export industry as one controlled by a cartel of major multinational corporations is not only an oversimplified view, but a misconception [Conklin, p. 137].

...[R]esearch has supported the [grain export] industry position that even though grain exports are dominated by a few large firms, the industry still remains competitive and efficient [Pakanati, Henneberry, and Warden, p. 2].

It is ironic that the critics who accuse the current system of exploiting producers seek to replace it with a single state marketing board or corporation (see the Weaver Bill, H.R. 4237, 96th Congress). Unlike the current system, a state board could indeed have great power and could indeed exercise control over price or quantity. The US could play a role in a grain cartel similar to the role played by Saudi Arabia in the OPEC oil cartel. A grain cartel might benefit US producers for a few years at the expense of consumers at home and abroad. After several years, however, US producers as well as consumers worldwide might be worse off based on conventional estimates of the long-term export demand elasticity reported in Table 2.1.

To be sure, the agricultural industry faces a large number of barriers to trade such as state trading, export subsidies, variable levies on imports, bilateral trade agreements, and high rigid price supports without production controls. The latter behavior characterizing the EC features dumping of surpluses on world markets at subsidized prices. Such practices distort comparative advantage, reduce world trade, raise world price instability, and reduce general economic well-being. The biggest losers from such policies are the nations that practice them -- as noted in Chapter 11 and elsewhere in this book.

REINTERPRETING ORTHODOXY IN THE CONTEXT OF MODERN TRADE THEORY

The theory of workable competition in a political setting helps to explain some seeming anomalies of conventional trade theory. Examples include intraindustry trade among countries, growing non-tariff barriers, the Leontief Paradox, and the poor showing of the US in high-value versus bulk commodities.

Growing Intraindustry Trade

Strategic trade theory makes much of intraindustry trade. Such trade is consistent with welfare maximization and neoclassical economic theory under competitive conditions where different types of (say) wheat are actually different products for which different nations have unique tastes and comparative advantage. Intraindustry trade is also consistent with economies of size in activities that add variety. Thus Americans export hamburgers (or more correctly the knowhow, image, and facilities through direct investment), the British export fish, the French export wine, and the Germans and Dutch export beer. Each of these countries also imports these products.

A narrow interpretation of orthodox trade theory would view intraindustry trade as irrational -- why ship the same types of food from Europe to North America and from North America to Europe? Or why ship cars from Japan to the US -- transport costs would be less by producing and consuming cars in one country.

A product is an arbitrary classification. Any given product as defined by a standard industrial classification code is in fact a bundle of goods and services possessing comfort, prestige, beauty, speed, reliability, safety, and other real and imagined attributes. Because no two automobile models possess the same attributes, then "a car is not a car is not a car." A differentiated product is a different product. Thus we should not be surprised to see Subarus shipped to the United States and Cadillacs shipped to Japan. Comparative advantage is apparent: the Japanese have enjoyed special qualities of workmanship and low-cost labor while the US has enjoyed special qualities of consumer preferences (remember in Chapter 2 we said consumer preferences also explain trade in the modern theory of comparative advantage) for large, comfortable cars. Japan does not have a sufficient domestic market to realize economies of size producing all kinds of cars without export; neither does the US. Each benefits by specializing in the products in which it has a comparative advantage gained in part through an early lead in economies of size in production. Many US and a few Japanese consumers want large, comfortable cars; many Japanese and some US consumers want small, economical cars. Trade makes all types of cars available in both countries.

In addition to varied tastes and economies of size, seasonal factors also account for intraindustry trade in agriculture. Canada imports fruits and vegetables from Florida, Texas, and California in winter months but ships fruits and vegetables to the US in the summer. Blending requirements for bread cause Europe to import hard red wheats while it exports soft wheats.

Alternative agriculture activists contend that intraindustry trade wastes petroleum energy and despoils the environment. The appropriate response is not to ban such trade but to properly charge for energy (including environmental costs) and allow the market free choice.

Bulk Versus High-Value Exports

Why does the US export a much higher ratio of bulk to high-value commodities than Europe? Such behavior has been viewed by some as irrational. However, rational explanations can be given for the seeming paradox:

1. The European Community heavily subsidizes high-value commodity exports.
2. The European Community has a comparative advantage in some high-value industries such as flowers in the Netherlands.

3. Some bulk commodity exports are more capital-intensive than are some high-value commodity exports. For example, labor is a higher proportion of the cost of some high-value fresh fruit, vegetable, and ornamental output than of lower-value grain or soybean output. High-value beef is exported profitably by labor-intensive Argentina.

4. Some high-value commodities are best supplied by direct investments. For example, it makes economic sense for American cold-cereal breakfast food manufacturers to invest directly in foreign processing plants. By supplying American technology and marketing and processing knowhow but using local raw materials, the finished processed product can reach the market quickly for higher quality and longer shelf-life. The following section on forms of trade elaborates on these issues.

The above explanations are not intended to foreclose past overlooked opportunities, lack of aggressiveness of US processor-exporters, or other factors influencing high-value exports. Continuing study is needed in this and other topics to discern trade opportunities.

FORMS OF TRADE

When most people think of agricultural trade, they think of bulk commodities moving from one country to another. Increasingly, however, trade in the food industry is in services as well as commodities from the farm. The most prized resources and their contribution abroad often are the brand name, patent, advertising strategy, processing technology, transport facilities, and management capability. Depending on which contributions earn high returns, the firm may elect to export farm commodities, a manufacturing process, or a service.

The firm's objective is to earn a favorable return to owned resources. The return to equity capital is enhanced by a management strategy encompassing one or more alternatives from an export portfolio of bulk commodities, high-value products, foreign direct investment, licensing, franchising, copacking, and contract production.

One explanation for the low share of high-value exports is that American food firms more than other American firms or foreign food firms have chosen to increase returns to equity by direct foreign investment and licensing or franchising (see Handy and MacDonald). A firm investing and operating in two or more countries is called a *multinational* or *transnational*. Factors that influence the decisions to invest in production facilities abroad rather than export from the home market include:

• Resource costs and availabilities
• Product differentiation, market support, and barriers to entry
• Perishability and sources of the product
• Government policies.

Resource Costs

Climate, soils, infrastructure, technology, and knowhow give American farmers comparative advantage in production of bulk commodities such as grain and soybeans. These American-source bulk commodities compete well in world markets.

Food is a highly complex combination of goods and services. Licensing makes sense where the bulk component is easy to add and is cheap locally (e.g., water) and the differentiated value-added component requires superior expertise that is fairly readily transportable (extract). In the case of colas, the US firm provides the extract, brand name, standards of quality, and broad market strategy. The local firm provides the plant, equipment, water, labor, and day-to-day management -- all at relatively low cost compared to the US.

In other instances, organizational management services are especially critical as in fast foods such as McDonalds or Kentucky Fried Chicken. In such instances franchising is frequent. The local firm provides labor, capital, and operational management, but under the careful supervision of the franchise to ensure high quality of the product, standardized services, and brand name identification. Licensing and franchising reduce capital requirements and risk, and can raise returns on equity capital to US firms.

Product Differentiation, Market Support, and Barriers to Entry

Handy and MacDonald found that highly differentiated and advertised food products with brand identification were especially likely to be involved in foreign direct investment, licensing, or franchising. Processing equipment may be complex and entail proprietary trade secrets that firms desire to protect by direct investment. US food production sometimes must be tailored to local tastes, customs, and advertising appeals. Entry into a foreign market can be difficult because of the high overhead of knowledge, access to retail outlets and shelf space, and general resistance by existing firms to foreign entrants. In such instances, direct investment in the form of buyout of an existing firm has advantages.

A local subsidiary can provide local expertise on regulations, culture, taste trends, and market support systems such as finance, technology, and marketing skills. Buying into a local firm may also broaden the product line and market share. A US-owned food firm in the European Community, for example, may have access to markets and freedom from border measures throughout the Community not available to farm and food products shipped from the United States.

Perishability and Sourcing

Bulk commodities such as grains and soybeans can be shipped long distances without much loss of quality but most foods are perishable. Highly differentiated and advertized foods with brand identification place a high value on consistently high quality. Many highly processed products such as breakfast cereals and snack foods lose quality with time and transport. Processing near the market where they are sold and using local or imported raw materials make sense.

Government Policies

Government macroeconomic policies and regulations influence choice of export strategies. Local content, health, sanitary, advertizing, and other regulations can be a minefield for the unwary. Access to local lawyers, accountants, and others with timely information on government regulations can avoid difficulties. A local food processing facility will be able to adapt to regulations more quickly than will a stream of products shipped thousands of miles from the US.

Shifting exchange, interest, and wage rates can influence the profitability of enterprises among countries. Diversified sourcing among countries frequently minimizes risks. Advantages of foreign sourcing when the dollar is high and US sourcing when it is low gives the multinational an edge over local competitors.

In short, the debate over export of high-value food products versus bulk commodities has been unduly narrow. The objective in international markets is to increase returns to US resources rather than to maximize farm product exports or multipliers. Sometimes the best strategy is to export food industry proprietary knowledge and technology rather than commodities. Conner has shown that rates of return have been high on foreign direct investment by US-based multinational food firms.

OTHER POLITICAL-ECONOMIC CONSIDERATIONS

A final contribution of strategic trade theory is to reemphasize the role of politics in protectionism. It recognizes that the trade strategy of a firm, industry, or country must consider the political options both within and without its influence. Several of the foregoing conclusions are from a review of the political economics of trade by Ray.

1. Protectionism is often found in an industry in which a country has a long-standing comparative advantage in trade but which is losing it because of rising wage rates at home and technological progress abroad. Protection is more likely to be associated with declining industries than with expanding industries in industrial countries. Examples for the US include consumer textiles, apparel, sugar, and dairy. Some processed agricultural commodities including frozen orange juice concentrate could be included.
2. Evidence that market structure affects the level of protection is mixed. Industries protected by relatively high tariffs are often those that concentrate production among a few firms geographically. Examples for US agriculture are potash, sugar beets, and sugarcane.
3. Macroeconomic variables play a key role influencing demand for protectionism. Protectionism in the steel industry in the early 1980s was more from a high dollar reducing employment in the steel industry than from unfair competition (dumping) with foreign steel.
4. Tariff cuts under GATT have been least for commodity groups in which developing countries have the greatest potential for exports to the industrialized countries. Examples from agriculture or related industries include sugar, textiles, apparel, and footwear. Ray states that "Efforts to provide developing countries with compensatory, duty-free access to industrialized country markets with programs like the GSP [Generalized System of Preferences in Trade] have not been successful."
5. Nontariff barriers (NTBs), the rising source of protection, tend to be largest for less concentrated industries. This suggests either (a) that less concentrated industries traditionally unable to form effective lobbies to gain tariff protection can gain protection in the form of NTBs, or (b) that less concentrated industries are late-comers in gaining protection and they have had to turn toward the only means available, NTBs.
6. NTBs influence bilateral trade flows but not overall trade balances for the industrialized countries. Nontariff barriers have been used to supplement tariff

barriers in the case of consumer goods, textiles, and processed agricultural commodities. NTBs in one country induce NTBs among trading partners. NTBs such as depreciation allowances, legal treatment of vertical restraints, cartels, and other market phenomena can influence bilateral trade flows, however.

7. Of interest is that self-interest rather than ideology determines protectionism votes. Voting on particular protectionist legislation reflects the economic interest of legislator's constituencies. Special interest campaign contributions, union strength within a state, and state unemployment all promote protectionist voting in the House and to a lesser extent in the Senate. The US dairy industry is especially noted for campaign contributions and for protection from foreign competition.

8. Growing opportunities for administrative protection (application of existing legislation by administrative decision) as opposed to specific legislated protection obtained from Congress have reduced the organizational costs of erecting barriers to trade. The current mix of tariffs and NTBs including quotas, VERs, countervailing duties, protection against dumping, escape clauses, and other arrangements provides a rich menu for industries seeking protection from foreign competition. Many of these measures can be imposed without new legislation. Even if demand for protectionism is constant, the supply price has decreased, increasing the level and types of protectionism. NTBs are the instrument of choice. Industries holding NTB protection recognize their vulnerability to reductions through GATT negotiation if converted to tariffs. After NTBs institutionalize, trade reform becomes more difficult. NTBs must be negotiated one by one (retail) whereas tariffs can be negotiated wholesale. Even if NTBs are converted to tariffs and phased out through wholesale negotiations, they reemerge because of continued pressure by firms for protection.

9. Studies of NTBs for automobiles, lumber, and steel indicate the supremacy of industry interests over consumer and national interests with costs to consumers many times the value of jobs saved in the industry. Protectionism in most instances is a triumph of political expediency over economics. In the United States, tariff concessions and reductions have not systematically altered the basic structure of protection among industries over the last 60 years. That could be expected with proportional reductions in tariffs, but the situation could be quite different if NTBs such as voluntary restraint agreements are allowed to expand in breadth and depth.

Congress has attempted to circumvent its inability to say no to protectionism by turning over more trade decisions to bureaucrats in the Executive Branch. The new process has not succeeded. In part this is because Congress has shifted trade restraint recommendations among the Office of Trade Representative and Departments of Commerce and Treasury to obtain the most receptive hearing for protectionism.

CONCLUSIONS

Despite the vast effort devoted by economists and other social scientists to analyze theoretically and empirically the behavior of firms and governments and the gains from trade in an environment of imperfect competition, surprisingly little can be said for certain. Tentative conclusions are that:

1.   Theoretical research is ambivalent on the relative benefits of trade under perfect versus imperfect competition but empirical research indicates "that as a rule, international trade [under imperfect competition] still leads to gains, and when they are there, they are two to three times larger than estimated under perfect competition" (Richardson).

2.   A corollary or reason for (1) above is that trade increases the "workability" of competition even if it does not create perfect competition. The American automobile industry is illustrative. The industry characterized by three major auto companies and one encompassing labor union was subjected to competition from abroad, especially the Japanese. The result was much higher quality and variety of automobiles at lower real cost to American consumers. The American food industry has been less analyzed by economists and less influenced by trade than the auto industry, but industry performance probably has been improved by trade.

3.   A third and much more tentative presumption as listed by Richardson is that "trade under imperfect competition *may* increase adjustment pressures on firms, workers, sectors, and nations precisely because competition is more workable." Efforts by Congress to create cartels and other forms of imperfect competition in world food markets would create more rather than less need for labor and other adjustments in agriculture.

4.   Concepts of workable competition, originating out of industrial organization theory, mostly reinforce neoclassical theory of competition. High performance does not require perfect knowledge assumed under perfect competition -- it only requires that decision makers gather information to the point where obtaining additional information is not worth the extra cost. High performance does not require perfect mobility -- it only requires mobility that pays at the margin. High performance does not require the atomistic competition of thousands of buyers and sellers -- economic efficiency is rather robust with respect to number of firms. A private sector with say two firms is likely to be more economically efficient than a public sector of one parastatal firm. And public or private firms will be more efficient if subjected to international competition.

REFERENCES

Carter, Colin, Alex McCalla, and Jerry Sharples, eds. 1990. *Imperfect Competition and Political Economy*. Boulder, CO: Westview Press.

Carter, Colin and Andrew Schmitz. August 1979. Import tariffs and price formation in the world wheat market. *American Journal of Agricultural Economics* 61:517-522.

Conklin, Neilson. June 1982. An economic analysis of the pricing efficiency and market organization of the US grain export system. GAO/CED-82-61S. Washington, DC: General Accounting Office.

Conner, John M. December 1989. Research puzzles arising from the internationalization of US food processors. *American Journal of Agricultural Economics* 71:1255-1258.

GAO. June 1982. Market structure and pricing efficiency of US grain export system. GAO/CED-815-61. Washington, DC: General Accounting Office, US Congress.

Handy, Charles and James M. MacDonald. December 1989. Multinational structures and strategies of US food firms. *American Journal of Agricultural Economics* 71:1246-1254.

Helpman, E. and P. Krugman. 1985. *Market Structure and Foreign Trade: Increasing Returns, Imperfect Competition, and the International Economy.* Cambridge, MA: MIT Press.

Henderson, James and Richard Quandt. 1971. *Microeconomic Theory, A Mathematical Approach.* New York: MacGraw-Hill.

MacLaren, Donald. 1990. Implications of new theory for modeling imperfect substitutes in agricultural trade. Ch. 5 in Carter *et al.*, eds.

Pakanati, Venugopal, David Henneberry, and Thomas Warden. May 1986. The US grain export industry: Survey responses and analysis. Stillwater: Department of Agricultural Economics, Oklahoma State University.

Ray, Edward. 1990. Empirical research on the political economy of trade. Ch. 7 in Carter *et al.*, eds.

Richardson, J. David. 1990. International trade, national welfare, and the workability of competition: A survey of empirical estimates. Ch. 3 in Carter *et al.*, eds.

Sarris, Alexander and Andrew Schmitz. December 1981. Toward a US agricultural export policy for the 1980s. *American Journal of Agricultural Economics* 63:832-839.

Schmitz, Andrew, Alex McCalla, D. Mitchell, and Colin Carter. 1980. *Grain Export Cartels.* Cambridge, MA: Ballinger Book.

Thursby, Marie and Jerry Thursby. 1990. Strategic trade theory and agricultural markets. Ch. 4 in Carter *et al.*, eds.

Tweeten, Luther. December 1983. Economic instability in agriculture: The contributions of prices, government programs, and exports. *American Journal of Agricultural Economics* 65:922-931.

Tweeten, Luther. 1989. *Farm Policy Analysis.* Boulder, CO: Westview Press.

Wilson, W.W. and D.E. Anderson. 1980. The Canadian grain marketing system. Paper presented at *American Agricultural Economics Association* annual meeting, Urbana, Illinois.

Wright, Bruce and Kenneth Krause. April 1976. Foreign direct investment in the US grain trade. *Report to the Congress: Foreign Direct Investment in the United States.* Volume 4, Appendix E. Washington, DC: US Department of Commerce.

Zwart, Anthony and David Blandford. May 1989. Market intervention and international price stability. *American Journal of Agricultural Economics* 71:379-388.

CHAPTER 9

Institutions and
Trade Policies

Laypersons could easily gain the impression that institutions rather than comparative advantage determine world trade. The popular press and trade fora rarely refer to comparative advantage but widely refer to regulations, laws, subsidies, councils, and other institutional dimensions of trade. Comparative advantage *is* important but it is also essential to examine the large role of institutions in trade -- the purpose of this and the next chapter.

This chapter lists the origins and roles of major international institutions most directly influencing trade, with emphasis on the General Agreement on Tariffs and Trade. Bilateral and bloc trade institutions also are addressed. The next chapter lists major actors in trade.

The abdication of world leadership by the United States after World War I was widely viewed as a source of the economic and political turmoil leading to World War II. After the latter, the US assumed an activist role in the world economic order.

The seminal event was the conference at Bretton Woods, New Hampshire, in 1944. That conference directly or indirectly created three premier institutions to support free multilateral trade and promote economic development: (1) the International Bank for Reconstruction and Development (IBRD or World Bank), which began operation in 1945, (2) the International Monetary Fund (IMF or the Fund), which opened in 1947, and (3) the General Agreement on Tariffs and Trade (GATT), which originated in 1947 indirectly out of a plan for an International Trade Organization that never materialized.

INTERNATIONAL MONETARY FUND

The International Monetary Fund was formed to maintain an orderly and stable international monetary system conducive to world trade and economic development. Eventually, nearly the entire non-communist world became members. The Fund originated out of recognition that the gold standard was no longer workable, that balance of payments disequilibrium of a *transitory* or *permanent* nature inevitably develops, and that each type of disequilibrium requires a different remedy. Minimizing economic trauma to world nations in a monetary system that was not inherently stable required cooperation, flexibility, expertise, and financial backing.

For transitory trade deficits, member nations are able to draw within limits from the pool of foreign currencies paid in as a requirement for membership. For long-term balance of payments disequilibrium, exchange rate adjustments are called for. Gold initially was the standard for the IMF monetary system. Each nation's currency was assigned a value in gold or gold-based currency -- which in essence was the US dollar. The dollar became the de facto currency standard around which other currencies could vary in value. Exchange rates were changed so seldom that the system functioned more as a fixed than as a flexible exchange rate regime.

Each member nation had to agree to open monetary movements among nations and to redeem its currency for foreign currency. However, allowances were made for a transitory period to convertibility. Because of the economic havoc of World War II, it was 1958 before most industrialized countries allowed currencies to be convertible. Meanwhile, most *less developed countries* (LDCs) continue to be in the "transition" period to convertible currencies. And many developed countries place arbitrary restrictions on convertibility between domestic and foreign currencies.

The IMF had relatively little to do before the widespread debt crises of developing countries in the 1980s. Then its compensatory financing provision, introduced in 1963 and expanded in 1975, along with other instruments became much in demand to provide loans to LDCs in the face of crisis in external debt, export earnings, and balance of payments. Numerous *economic stabilization* programs, mostly infusions of hard currency loans to alleviate acute foreign exchange shortages, have been initiated. A requirement that countries devalue currency in return for help has given way to more extensive conditionalities.

Structural Adjustments

Economic stabilization was like intensive care in the emergency room of an economic hospital, with transfusions of hard currency loans to continue import life. Increasingly, the Fund has continued with the patient into the recovery ward, demanding *structural adjustments* (SAs) in the form of policy reforms to be eligible for loans essential to maintain imports of fuel, spare parts, food, and other necessities. The reforms included privatization of state owned enterprises (SOEs or parastatals), devaluation of currency, decentralization of decision-making, reduction of government budget deficits, phase-out of subsidies and export taxes, an end to printing money to finance debt, and other changes (Tweeten, 1990).

In the 1980s, the World Bank also became much involved in providing structural adjustment loans and imposing conditionalities. SA programs of the World Bank and IMF have been the target of much criticism. Structural adjustments are faulted for being unjust to the poor. However, continuation of past policies intensifying the *economic degradation process* described in Chapter 6 are even more unjust to the poor. Most bankrupt third-world countries accepted SA because the alternative of defaulting on loans (and hence being ostracized by the world financial community) or of sharply reducing imports was even more objectionable than IMF terms. Valid criticisms are that SA lending (1) increased indebtedness of already over-extended bankrupt nations unable even to service current debt, (2) imposed conditionalities that were not enforced by IMF or World Bank because the measures were opposed by ruling elites, and (3) went to governments. Lending to governments encouraged a continued large public sector and state corporations when the countries really needed direct private investment, a larger private sector, and a diminished public sector supplying a few essential public goods well. SA sometimes perpetuated a suffocating bureaucracy. Numerous reforms in SA have been suggested (Tweeten, 1990).

Towards Flexible Exchange Rates

Use of the US dollar as the currency of world liquidity and the fixed exchange rate standard worked reasonably well from World War II to 1971 because the US was the predominant economic power, it exercised considerable macroeconomic discipline required for a stable currency standard, it was rewarded by purchasing power in real goods and services by other countries in return for supplying world dollar liquidity, and because only one currency was needed as numeraire around which all other currencies could be appreciated or depreciated to maintain an orderly world monetary system. A major disadvantage was that US trade balances, capital flows, and money management consistent with domestic policy objectives eventually became inconsistent with liquidity needs of a growing world economy.

To be sure, *Special Drawing Rights* (SDRs) were created by the IMF in the 1960s and expanded in later years to supplement the dollar and other currencies in creating international liquidity. But the measure was inadequate. One country could provide the world currency with a fixed exchange rate if all other countries adjusted their currency properly -- but they did not so the US experienced diminished control of its macroeconomic policy and balance of payments. Other nations such as Germany and Japan had not revalued their currencies as appropriate given their rising productivity and strong balance of payments positions. The dollar became overvalued, creating difficulties in selling US agricultural and other commodities.

The US closed its gold window by refusing to redeem foreign currencies for gold. The dollar was devalued 8 percent in 1971 and 10 percent in February 1973 (Ryan and Tontz, p. 13). Even this was inadequate so world monetary authorities later in 1973 allowed the dollar value to be determined by float in international financial markets.

As noted in Chapter 6, major world currencies are now allowed to float in currency markets, thereby permitting forces of supply and demand to determine exchange rates. Because flexible exchange rates are considered to be too unstable by most smaller countries, many peg their currencies to these major floating hard currencies or the SDR. Market forces are not given complete freedom because even nations with floating exchange rates sometimes intervene by buying or selling their currency to influence exchange rates deemed to be out of line with fundamentals. Intervening countries say currency markets do not function due to speculation or other forces judged not to reflect real supply and demand. In reality, some countries want their currencies to be undervalued to promote domestic employment and some countries want their currencies to be overvalued to reduce costs of consumption.

The Eurocurrency Market

The Eurodollar market, defined as dollars of financial assets held in foreign financial markets, originated from concern by the Soviet Union that the United States would freeze Soviet financial assets held in dollars. The market sharply expanded with sustained US balance of payments deficits in the 1960s and became a major source of readily convertible international liquidity facilitating international finance. The market eventually expanded to include other hard currencies and extended from traditional financial centers in London, Zurich, and Frankfort to Hong Kong, Singapore, Mexico City, Tokyo, and other world centers.

By mid-1987, the Eurocurrency deposits exceeded $4 trillion -- double the value of world trade in goods and services. International capital flows exceed $40 trillion annually, over 20 times the trade in goods and services. Flexible exchange rates "export" changes in domestic macroeconomic policies through changes in real interest rates and transfer of financial assets, increasing financial capital flows. Real interest rates influence real exchange rates, which in turn influence trade. Growth of transnational corporations also increases international capital flows. World financial markets are now highly efficient; billions of dollars or other currencies can be transferred electronically in seconds of time among banks all over the world. Thus changes in macroeconomic policies that influence real interest rates and capital flows are also quickly apparent in real exchange rates and trade volume among countries.

Other Considerations

The shift from the single US dollar exchange rate to a world system of flexible exchange rates means that America can unilaterally devalue the dollar but not necessarily in real terms against all other currency because other currencies can devalue along with the dollar. With no one currency to anchor the world financial system, the role of the IMF and international financial coordination becomes more important. Efforts such as the Plaza and Louvre accords of 1985 and 1986 to internationally coordinate macroeconomic policies and stabilize exchange rates among countries met with only modest success, however (see Shane and Stallings, p. 65).

The emergence of a strong central bank in the European Community coupled with strong systems in Japan and the US could enhance opportunities for international monetary policy coordination. If these central banks are patterned after the German Bundesbank -- relatively free from political interference and charged with one objective, price stabilization against inflation -- then the world will have a strong monetary anchor.

The IMF in 1981 established a *Cereals Compensatory Financing Facility* providing up to five-year loans with favorable terms to developing countries facing sharply increasing costs in grain imports because of production shortfalls or extreme economic shocks. In August 1981 this facility merged with other financial systems to form the *Compensatory and Contingency Financial Facility* providing economic adjustment programs in the event of adverse external shocks giving rise to a fall in export receipts, or to a rise in import prices or interest rates. Very limited use has been made of these facilities.

In summary, the world monetary system remains in disarray. The only thing worse than the current flexible exchange rate system buffeted by irresponsible domestic macroeconomic policies is to return to a fixed rate system or gold standard. A highly dynamic world economy comprised of several economic superpowers requires multilateral financial institutions able to grow and adjust. The IMF assists the current system by providing worldwide monitoring and statistical information along with help to mostly smaller nations experiencing balance of payments difficulties, but it is no substitute for sound macroeconomic policies of member nations. By removing the short-run discipline of foreign exchange over domestic macroeconomic policies, flexible exchange rates can allow unsound domestic policies for extended periods. If followed worldwide, the result can be economic instability and chronic imbalances of a magnitude that threatens the international financial community. IMF was created to provide relief for basically sound economies with temporary balance of payments problems resulting from "acts of god." It (along with the World Bank) increasingly must cope with third-world chronic balance of payments problems caused by the "moral hazard" of the economic degradation process. The IMF cannot be a substitute for domestic macroeconomic policy discipline in the Third World or in the First World.

WORLD BANK

The International Bank for Reconstruction and Development (IBRD or World Bank) has two affiliates: The International Finance Corporation (IFC) and the International Development Association (IDA). The IDA focuses on highly concessional loans to very poor nations; the IFC also emphasizes lending to LDCs but at more market-oriented interest rates and other lending terms.

World Bank lending has gone through three phases:

1. Post-World War II reconstruction, mostly to what are now developed countries.
2. Third-world economic development especially for investment projects to develop infrastructure, to improve production and marketing of exportable commodities, to finance imports of improved capital equipment and technology, and to train in-country technicians and other specialists.
3. Debt-restructuring in countries with unmanageable debt-export and debt-GNP ratios in the 1980s and 1990s.

Questions regarding World Bank lending are addressed below.

Should Loans be Provided to Improve Productivity of Foreign Competitition?

The United States is the largest contributor to World Bank lending authority (although it is now rivaled by Japan). As such, American interest groups have felt justified in questioning the thrust of World Bank lending. One example is loans for improving Argentina's agricultural export facilities or for farm-to-port roads in Brazil, or for agricultural crop production improvement in many less developed countries. These loans can increase competitiveness of third-world relative to US agriculture and hence reduce markets and income of US farmers. Some US commodity groups have opposed American aid for foreign agricultural development. In July 1986, farm state representatives pushed through Congress the so-called *Bumpers Amendment* (Section 209 of PL 99-349) stipulating that no US foreign aid funds shall be used in developing countries to assist production of agricultural commodities for export in competition with like commodities grown in the United States (Paarlberg, p. 125). A similar restriction, the Fair Agricultural Investment Reform Act (the FAIR Act) was promoted in Congress to limit agricultural development activities of multilateral assistance agencies, such as the World Bank.

Defenders of World Bank lending to improve agricultural productivity note that the largest gains in US agricultural exports have been to countries making the most rapid improvements in agriculture. This seeming paradox is explained by the fact that: (1) agriculture accounts for a major share of employment and income in developing countries; (2) improvements in agricultural productivity are synergistic with growth in other sectors and overall income growth in LDCs; (3) the income elasticity of demand especially for meat and poultry products is high (even above 1.0) in developing countries, hence an increase in income brings a more than proportional increase in demand for meat and the protein meal and feed grains imported from the US to feed livestock; and (4) local agricultural resources and productivity gains fall short of meeting the sharp increase in demand, especially in countries with high population growth. Agricultural research and extension infrastructure and services to improve productivity of crops and livestock often lag behind economic development. Hence, agricultural productivity gains lag demand, so imports rise. Even modest growth in domestic demand relative to supply can bring large *proportional* increases in agricultural imports of feed grains when the import base is small in LDCs. The US as a major exporter of grains and soybeans benefits from such developments.

Agricultural productivity gains in the economic development process help to provide lower-cost food and fiber while freeing labor and other resources for nonfarm industry. Meanwhile, nonfarm industry growth provides employment and income for farm workers and provides markets and improved inputs for the farm. The United States has nothing to gain economically from impoverished Haitis or Etheopias of this world. It has much to gain from having more LDCs become the likes of South Korea, Taiwan, and other such developing countries making rapid progress in agriculture and overall economic development and, coincidentally, increasing commercial food imports.

Should the World Bank Fund Structural Adjustment or High-Payoff Projects?

Another criticism is that World Bank funding increasingly is for bailout of bankrupt countries. As noted earlier, funds go to restructure bad debt incurred by third-world governments for consumption or investments with little or no payoff, or to replace debts owed to international private banks. Too little policy reform is obtained in return for the loans, and debt continues to mount in recipient countries. Rather, the argument goes, World Bank loans should be confined to high payoff public investment projects promoting economic development in third-world countries that practice sound economic policies. An example is roads and bridges that stimulate private investment and growth. First-world private and public banks that made bad loans should write down the loans or sell them to international investors at market-discounted rates. This would reduce third-world debt problems and burdens of adjustment financing by the World Bank. SA indirectly amounts to charging taxpayers of countries supporting the World Bank for past financial mismanagement by third-world borrowers.

The World Bank's ability to leverage policy reform in return for loans is compromised by pressures on the Bank to lend. In the post-communist world aware of the high opportunity and transaction costs of public lending and the discipline and efficiency benefits of private lending, the Bank's role needs to be redefined. Policy reform is needed before rather than after Bank help. And that help might best be guarantees of private loans to the private sector for public infrastructure rather than public loans to governments.

GENERAL AGREEMENT ON TARIFFS AND TRADE (GATT)

The Trade Expansion Act of 1934, sometimes called the reciprocal trade agreement act, represented a major redirection of policy away from protectionism. Under the act, the President was empowered to reduce Smoot-Hawley Tariff rates up to 50 percent in return for reciprocal tariff reductions from foreign countries. Negotiations were largely bilateral, but the benefits of agreements were more widely dispersed through frequent applications of the *Most Favored Nation* (MFN) principle. This treatment applied, as a rule, to all countries the lowest rate of duty or other import charge granted to any country. As noted in Table 9.1, negotiations in the 1934-47 period reduced duties by one-third. The emergence of the GATT continued that progress.

The *General Agreement on Tariffs and Trade* originated in 1947 by default on an ambitious plan for an International Trade Organization (ITO) to regulate trade relations and promote free trade among countries. The ITO was intended to rival IMF and World Bank as a strong and innovative institution to promote international commerce. GATT was intended to be a transitory arrangement to begin multilateral trade negotiations while the ITO charter was being ratified. Congress never ratified the ITO despite the support of President Harry Truman, but the GATT continued under Executive Agreement without official Congressional approval. Congress viewed the ITO as a potential threat to its

Table 9.1. Duty Reductions Since 1934 Under the US Trade Agreements Program.

GATT Conference	Proportion of Dutiable Imports Subjected to Reductions	Average Cut in Reduced Tariffs	Average Cut in All Duties	Remaining Duties as a Proportion of 1930 Tariffs
	(Percent)			
Pre-GATT, 1934-47	63.9	44.0	33.2	66.8
First Round, Geneva, 1947	53.6	35.0	21.2	52.7
Second Round, Annecy, 1949	5.6	35.1	1.9	51.7
Third Round, Torquay, 1950-51	11.7	26.9	3.0	50.1
Fourth Round, Geneva, 1955-56	16.0	15.9	3.5	48.9
Dillon Round, Geneva, 1960-62	20.0	12.0	2.4	47.7
Kennedy Round, Geneva, 1963-67	79.2	45.5	36.0	30.5
Tokyo Round, 1973-1979	n.a.	n.a.	29.6	21.2

Source: Lavergne.

authority over international trade, including protection of domestic farm commodity program supports from cheaper imports.

The GATT Secretariat, an administrative agency, began very small and weak but grew in influence and size to 300 employees by 1987 (Congressional Budget Office, p. 15). By 1990, 97 countries accounting for four-fifths of world trade were members of GATT and another 30 abided by its rules. Among significant world traders, only the Soviet Union, Taiwan, and the Peoples Republic of China were not members in 1987.

GATT Principles

The three guiding principles most important to the remarkable success of the GATT are *reciprocity*, *non-discrimination*, and *transparency*. These, along with other provisions as of 1990, are discussed below (see Annex to Chapter 9).

1. When country A lowers its import tariffs on country B's exports, country B is expected to similarly lower its import tariffs on country A's exports. This *reciprocity* principle seems naive but has been very useful. The principle ratchets only one way: Trade barriers can go down but they cannot go up. Tariffs can be lowered but they cannot be raised. Thus raising tariffs to force concessions from another country is inconsistent with GATT principles -- even if it works.
2. Countries are not to grant one or a group of countries preferential trade treatment. In a seemingly poor choice of terms, GATT calls this the *Most Favored Nation* (MFN) treatment; that is, tariffs must be applied equally to all members. This *non-discrimination* rule specifies that any concession offered to a nation must be extended to all other member nations. Unconditional MFN treatment precludes bilateral and preferential agreements that favor one or a group of countries. Variances have been generous for bilateral and multilateral trade agreements, including free trade regions such as common markets.
3. All laws and regulations regarding trade are to be applied in a *transparent* manner, which requires public disclosure and impartial administration of trade

laws. Tariffs are visible and hence are the trade barriers of choice, if a trade protection instrument is to be used at all. Tariffs can be bargained "wholesale" in international negotiations, hence are favored over "opaque" barriers such as quotas. An unwritten decision by an organization of middlemen to accept only domestically produced goods violates rules of GATT. Customs fee formalities or marks of origin that discriminate against foreign goods are prohibited. The provision is sometimes difficult to enforce. Japan, for example, inhibits trade through the custom and tradition of wholesaler guilds favoring domestically produced goods and services over imports. Many countries operating state trading agencies hide import taxes and export subsidies through opaque accounting practices.

4. The *national treatment* rule specifies that imports must receive the same treatment as domestic production. Taxes and regulations are to be applied at least as favorably to imported as to domestically produced goods. Dumping, selling abroad below cost or the price charged domestic consumers, must be proved and injury to domestic producers must be shown before antidumping duties can be imposed. Countervailing duties imposed to offset dumping or foreign government export subsidies are not to exceed the dumping margin or the export subsidy.

5. Any violation (rescission) of trade agreements causing harm to other countries must be compensated. Disagreements must be settled by consultation with affected parties.

6. Members are prohibited from circumventing tariff concessions by employing nontariff barriers to offset lower tariffs.

7. Article 11 requires that production be controlled if import quotas are employed to protect domestic agricultural price supports. The provision specifies that import restrictions

> shall not be such as will reduce the total of imports relative to the total of
> domestic production, as compared with the proportion which might reasonably
> be expected to rule between the two in the absence of restrictions.

GATT calls for removal of quantitative restrictions (QR) or quotas on trade. Voluntary restraint agreements (quotas) are overlooked because the exporter often is allowed to retain the economic rent and may lack bargaining power. The satisfaction from rents and the fear of retaliation discourage protests and remediation through GATT dispute settlement procedures.

Although Article 11 prohibits quantitative restrictions, Articles 12, 13, and 14 outline exceptions (see Annex). GATT has been especially lenient to developing countries, allowing them to use QRs to safeguard balance of payments and to temporarily relieve domestic industry suffering injury and adjustment problems from trade (see Article 18, Annex). Quantitative restrictions, if used, are to be applied on a nondiscriminatory basis.[1] Although longer-term balance of payment shortfalls need to be addressed by devaluation of currency, numerous countries use balance of payment arguments to justify trade barriers for extended periods of time.

---

[1]Australia filed a complaint and won a GATT ruling against the US in 1989 for sugar quotas which discriminated against countries viewed as political adversaries and rewarded friends.

Allowance for QRs to be imposed to restrain imports that "cause or threaten serious injury" to domestic producers raises questions of interpretation. The terms "threaten" and "serious" are subjective and easily abused to protect politically influential local industry threatened with no more than normal price competition from a more efficient producer abroad. Compensation is to be provided to the foreign country, and if not, the foreign country can retaliate by imposing exactly offsetting restraints under GATT sanction. This rule restrains imposition of QRs. Rules need to be strengthened to limit the duration of emergency restraints and restrict them to tariffs only. Also GATT rules could be adjusted to allow retaliations to focus narrowly on the offending country.

8. Export subsidies are discouraged and are to be eliminated on nonprimary products. Export subsidies for primary products are not to be used by a country to gain more than an equitable share of world market in the product. Section B, Paragraph 3 of Article 16, widely violated by the European Community, states

> Accordingly, contracting parties should seek to avoid the use of subsidies on the export of primary products. If, however, a contracting party grants directly or indirectly any form of subsidy which operates to increase the export of any primary product from its territory, such subsidy shall not be applied in a manner which results in that contracting party having more than an equitable share of world export trade in that product.

The meaning of "*primary* products" and "*equitable* share" of world trade especially need clarification. There is reason to believe that even concessional export credit widely used by exporters, including the US, could be restricted. The Tokyo Round introduced to the "equitable share" concept a clarifying phrase "in a previous period" -- hardly much help.

9. Sanitary and phytosanitary regulations are not to be used in trade to protect local industry but can be used if backed by scientific evidence of harm to health. Restrictions must be applied nondiscriminantly to all domestic and foreign products.

10. Trade barriers are permitted for national security purposes. Some countries interpret "national security" broadly and hence the provision is often abused.

11. GATT recognizes the right of a country to subsidize firms to help economically disadvantaged geographic areas, to facilitate economic restructuring, to maintain employment, and to promote other "important" objectives of social and economic policy.

Most of the above issues need clarification and more precise language if they are to be enforced. Many exceptions in addition to those noted above are allowed; variances are especially generous to developing countries as noted later.

A major limitation is that GATT has no police power and relies on passive enforcement of rules. If consultations between affected countries fail, disputes can be submitted to third parties for arbitration. A member may refuse investigation for violations and, if it allows an investigation by GATT, may reject the penalty prescribed. GATT Council rulings require a unanimous vote, hence can be vetoed by an offended party. Moral suasion and sanctioning of retaliation have had modest success in stopping improper behavior, including some such action by the United States. The most effective enforcement tool is GATT-sanctioned retaliation by countries damaged by trade barriers. Such retaliation tends to be ineffective against countries with strong bargaining positions. Small countries with weak bargaining positions are more vulnerable to GATT discipline.

Early negotiating rounds brought no substantive changes, but weaknesses of GATT were apparent. The articles of GATT were written to be weak on agriculture. Although nothing substantive was done to strengthen the GATT regarding agriculture in the 1950s, it was not for lack of study. The Habeler Report (GATT, 1958) is an example. The prescient report noted:

1. Domestic commodity programs as a source of distorted agricultural trade.
2. The need for reform of commodity programs and the border measures protecting them before efficient agricultural exporters would be able to reap the benefit of comparative advantage.
3. The long list of nontariff barriers to trade, and catalogued them.

The United States continued to be torn between the good sense behind liberalization apparent in that report and the effective politics of its domestic commodity groups.

Negotiating Rounds

The first GATT-sponsored multinational trade negotiation convened in 1947 (Table 9.1). Although much of the negotiation remained bilateral, the interplay among trading partners resulted in sizable tariff cuts. The seven GATT rounds and earlier negotiations brought tariff duties to about 5 percent of all imports by 1980, an almost negligible amount by standards of earlier decades.

Dillon Round. The Dillon Round of negotiations from 1960 to 1962 was notable for acquiescing to the variable import levy and export subsidy agricultural price support policy used by the European Community but for which there was no provision in the GATT. Zero binding (duty free access) was maintained on oilseeds and nongrain feeds imported by the EC. If the problems in world trade caused by these fateful decisions has been foreseen, undoubtedly other arrangements would have been made.

Kennedy Round. American authorities established early that a successful Kennedy Round (1963-1967) required a successful outcome in agriculture. The US was intent on constraining the Common Agricultural Policy (CAP) of the EC. The EC was just as intent on maintaining the CAP to justify a common market.

The initial US proposal was for EC variable levies to be converted to tariffs and halved, and for guaranteed continuation of at least current import levels for foreign products being crowded out by high CAP domestic price supports. The EC responded with a proposal to bind price supports *in all countries* at no higher than current ratios to world prices (*montant de soutien* proposal) or to guarantee access by binding self-sufficiency ratios at current levels (see Warley). The proposals were criticized and rejected by the US for not being real offers, for attempting to extend CAP to the world, for having only a three year duration, and for demonstrating the EC was unwilling to submit to external restraint. The highly touted new International Grains Arrangement attempting to fix wheat prices failed in about a year; only a Food Aid Convention committing wheat exporters to food aid survived. The Kennedy Round failed agriculture.

Tokyo Round. The Tokyo Round of GATT negotiations (1973-1979) was significant in taking place in a world trading system characterized by the breakdown of the fixed exchange rate system which had held since the Bretton Woods agreement (see Table 9.1). Oil prices had tripled in 1973 and protectionism was on the rise and was fed by instability and shifting trading patterns.

The US was determined to bring agriculture under GATT rules, treating agriculture no different than other commodities. The EC was determined to keep agriculture separate.

The EC won. To be sure, largely symbolic commodity arrangements were negotiated successfully for dairy products and beef. A weak export subsidies code was approved but that only gave legitimacy to a practice hitherto in violation of GATT rules.

The US had two high priorities in the Tokyo Round: agriculture and nontariff barriers. Success in the latter was about as dismal as in the former as noted below.

Nontariff Barriers. Nontariff barriers (NTBs) have replaced tariffs as the major barriers to trade (see Hillman). Table 9.2, even though not comprehensive, lists an impressive array indeed of nontariff barriers. It is impossible to deal with these one-by-one. A typical negotiating tactic is to condense as many as possible into a tariff (*tariffication*), then negotiate the tariff downward.

A most important contribution of the Tokyo Round was to hold back protectionism and make at least modest progress in dealing with nontariff barriers that had replaced tariffs as the principal form of protectionism. To be sure, the earlier Kennedy Round had for the first time addressed nontariff barriers, reaching agreements on an Antidumping Code and eliminating the US system of American Selling Prices. The latter applied a tariff rate for selected imports to a price set artificially high (to equal the price of a competing good produced domestically) instead of to the import's actual invoice price. The Tokyo Round established codes regarding antidumping rules, subsidies, countervailing measures, government procurement practices, customs valuation, technical standards, and import licensing.

Almost all governments subsidize domestic producers and products to some degree. Examples include education, research, concessional access to government-held natural resources, police protection, road construction and maintenance, and grades and standards. When a product is exported, at what point do such "subsidies" become unfair trading practices? Export subsidies on nonagricultural products were prohibited and a code was established to differentiate between a domestic subsidy acceptable under GATT for promotion of social and economic policy objectives and an export subsidy, which was not.

Protectionism not only in agriculture but in other industries grew in the 1980s. The share of trade that follows the rules of the GATT -- transparent and nondiscriminatory --has been shrinking. The movement has been to NTBs from tariffs, discriminatory from nondiscriminatory measures (tariffs to voluntary restraint agreements or VRAs), and from transparent to opaque measures such as domestic import substitution (e.g., in Europe through subsidies to oilseed production and through sanitary and phytosanitary regulations).

Uruguay Round. The eighth or Uruguay Round under GATT began in Uruguay in 1986. Negotiations were in Geneva with completion scheduled by the end of 1990. The completion date was extended two years. Negotiations were the most difficult ever attempted under GATT because many of the more easily settled issues such as tariffs on manufactured goods had already been largely resolved.

Many exceptions to GATT principles had been tolerated and needed to be addressed. Exceptions that violated the spirit if not the letter of GATT rules included (Congressional Budget Office, pp. xi, xii):

- The Multifiber Agreement governing trade in textiles and apparel, and placing limits on such imports into the US from developing countries.
- Voluntary export restraints (VERs) such as limits on automobile and steel imports into the US.
- Agricultural import quotas and export subsidies.
- Barriers to trade in services such as banking, insurance, domestic airline and water transportation, movies, and television programming.
- Failure to protect trade-related aspects of intellectual property rights (TRIPS) through copyrights, patents, and trademarks.

Table 9.2. Selected Nontariff Trade Barriers.

Explicit Trade Barriers	
1. Import quotas	Restrictions on quantity and/or value of imports of specific commodities for a given time period; administered globally, selectively, or bilaterally.
2. Voluntary export restraints	Restrictions imposed by importing country but administered by exporting country; administered multilaterally and bilaterally; requires system of licensing; essentially similar to an orderly marketing arrangement.
3. Domestic content and mixing requirements	Requires that an industry use a certain proportion of domestically produced components and/or materials in producing final products.
4. Antidumping duties	Imposition of a special import duty when the price of imports is alleged to lie below some measure of foreign costs of production; minimum prices may be established to "trigger" antidumping investigations and actions.
5. Countervailing duties	Imposition of a special import duty to counteract an alleged foreign government subsidy to exports; normally required that domestic injury be shown.

Implicit Trade Barriers	
1. Government procurement policies	Preferences given to domestic over foreign firms in bidding on public-procurement contracts, including informal procedures favoring procurement from domestic firms.
2. Macroeconomic policies	Monetary/fiscal, balance-of-payments, and exchange rate actions that have an impact on national output, foreign trade, and capital movements.
3. Competition policies	Antitrust and related policies designed to foster or restrict competition and that may have an impact on foreign trade and investment.
4. Government industrial policy and regional development measures	Government actions designed to aid particular firms, industry sectors, and regions to adjust to changes in market conditions.
5. Government financed research, development, and other technology policies	Government actions designed to correct market distortions and aid private firms; includes technological spillovers from government programs, such as defense and public health.
6. Health and sanitary regulations, quality standards, animal welfare, and environmental laws	Actions designed for domestic objectives but that may discriminate against imports.
7. Safety and industrial standards and regulations	Actions designed for domestic objectives but that may discriminate against imports.

Source: Adapted from Deardorff and Stern.

- Free trade areas, such as the European Community and US-Canada, which do not extend most-favored-nation treatment to countries outside the area. (A free trade area or customs union protects itself from world competition by erecting import barriers while pursuing free trade among nations within the area.)

- Preferential treatment for developing countries, including favored treatment for some imports from the Third World while allowing trade restrictions imposed by the Third World against imports.
- Nontariff barriers to trade.
- Retaliatory trade actions, such as "super 301" used by the United States.
- Barriers to international investment capital flows, especially regulations effecting direct capital investments such as requirement for local participation in joint ventures or foreign branch banking.

Most economists interpret variable levies used by the European Community to be nontariff barrier because unlike tariffs they are not constant per unit of product over time either on a flat amount or ad valorem basis. The variable grain quota used extensively by Japan to maintain domestic prices behaves like the variable levy and is also a nontariff barrier inconsistent with the rules of GATT. Significant agricultural trade reform would strictly prohibit import quotas (Article 11) and export subsidies (Article 16).

With a comparative advantage in agricultural products, the US has vigorously promoted joint negotiation for farm and nonfarm products under GATT. The attempt to link more open access to foreign markets for US farm products to more open access of foreign industrial products into the US has not succeeded, however. Agricultural trade has largely escaped the discipline of GATT. Principal reasons are:

- Nations contend that self-sufficiency in agricultural products is a matter of national security and national sovereignty, hence non-negotiable.
- Most major agricultural trade participants but especially western Europe and Japan have well-placed, well-organized farm interests over-represented in the political process. Such groups are skilled at special pleading and manipulating public opinion to serve farm interests. These developed nations subsidize their farmers with domestic commodity programs maintained in the name of transferring income to farmers, preserving the family farm, and serving national food security.

The contention may appear to be compelling that agriculture and family farms are a prized part of a nation's heritage which must be preserved. Proposals placed before GATT negotiators would allow countries to honor that perception but with direct payments *decoupled* from economic incentives to produce. Taxpayers rather than consumers would support such subsidies. The argument for such control of subsidies is that what arrangements a nation makes between producers, consumers, and taxpayers within the sanctity of its own borders is its own private business. But when such behavior destroys markets for other countries, then the issues become global externalities. International condemnation and control of such trade-distorting domestic behavior is in order, the argument goes.

In the Uruguay Round, the Reagan Administration initially proposed that nations confine their farm subsidies to direct farm transfer payments unrelated to production, consumption, and trade incentives. Producers would not be rewarded by payments for additional production. Payments would not interfere with access of consumers to food at border prices. While such decoupling of payments would not provide pure transfers, they would be a major improvement over current policies. The initial US proposal in the Uruguay Round of multilateral trade negotiations (MTNs) was to phase out all trade distorting agricultural interventions over a period of 10 years and all export subsidies in 5 years. Nations would be allowed to continue to support their farmers but only with decoupled lump sum direct payments. (Agricultural research, extension, grades, standards, conservation, and rural development programs were acceptable.) The EC was outraged by the proposal. A December 1988 meeting of trade ministers in Montreal broke up among acrimonious charges and countercharges.

In April 1989, the Midterm Review brought negotiations back on track. There was "a broad measure of consensus that agricultural policies should be more responsive to international market signals" and that "support and protection should be progressively reduced and provided in a less trade-distorting manner." Of greatest significance was the statement that the primary long-term objective of the MTN is "to provide for *substantial progressive reductions* [emphasis mine] in agricultural support and protection sustained over an agreed period of time, resulting in correcting and preventing restrictions and distortions in world agricultural markets" (Kennedy, p. 52). The latter commitment was reaffirmed by heads of the seven major industrial nations at the summit meeting held in Houston in July of 1990.

A framework agreement reached in mid-term of the Uruguay Round specified that certain subsidies such as for agricultural research would be allowed (green light or box), some would be subject to countervailing duties (yellow light or box), and others would be prohibited (red light or box). There was much disagreement over how to classify subsidies. The United States wanted strict discipline over subsidies while the Europeans wanted little discipline.

In later stages of the Uruguay Round, the US pressed for tariffication -- converting all trade interventions to tariffs, which then presumably would be multilaterally bargained downward in subsequent negotiations. Demands to decouple were muted because the US, the EC, and Japan were not in a position to replace price supports with direct payments from the government.

In the Uruguay Round, considerable attention was addressed to the *functioning of the GATT system* (FOGS). This included closer surveillance of trade policies, especially of major nations, and closer coordination with the World Bank and IMF.

Stalemate and Overtime. In December 1990, negotiations broke off when Latin American delegates walked out over feeble EC offers to reduce farm trade distortions. The US was calling for reductions in aggregate measures of support (AMS) by 75 percent and in border measures by 90 percent; the EC offered approximately a 15 percent reduction in supports from 1990 levels.

In April 1991, Congress extended *fast-track authority* for another two years to revive Uruguay Round and North American Free Trade negotiations. So called "fast-track authority" requiring a single approval or disapproval vote by Congress on a treaty was essential because otherwise Congress would amend it perhaps beyond recognition. The issue is not just that this would send US negotiators back to the bargaining table; the principal objection is that foreign negotiators would not begin negotiations on an agreement they know would be mutilated by Congress.

In December 1991, GATT Director General Arthur Dunkel placed a 500-page "Draft, Final Act" on the negotiating table, designed to be a reasonable compromise on all contested issues. Internal price supports would be reduced 20 percent by 1999 from a 1986-88 base, and export subsidy outlays 36 percent by 1999 from a 1986-90 base. All agricultural barriers would be converted to tariffs -- presumably to be eventually eliminated. The proposal was viewed by the EC and EFTA as too radical.

Americans considered some parts of the proposal also to be radical. Beloved voluntary restraint agreements on steel, autos, and other trade would be eliminated. Shipping between American ports would be open to foreign-owned vessels. Several prominent environmental organizations sued to force the US Trade Representative to conduct an environmental impact statement before continuing GATT negotiations.

The American Farm Bureau Federation advocates free trade but its President, Dean Kleckner, stated that "no deal is better than a poor deal." With the Europeans willing to offer much less than the rest of the world was willing to accept, results of the Uruguay Round could only be disappointing.

International trade liberalization and its promise for a revitalized global economy are hostage to EC farm programs. The Uruguay Round finally offered very modest reform targets indeed compared to those initially advanced by US negotiators.

INTERNATIONAL COMMODITY AGREEMENTS

International commodity agreements (ICAs) are of four general types (see Robinson, p. 234):

1. Buffer stocks
2. Bilateral agreements
3. Multilateral contracts without supply controls
4. Export cartels.

State trading also is briefly discussed in this section.

Buffer Stocks

In theory, internationally coordinated buffer stocks require fewer overall tons to stabilize world market prices than do buffer stocks held and managed independently by each country. Commodities subject to buffer stock agreements must be storable. Because as much stock is released as is stored, the net impact on *average* price and income of producers is modest over time. The challenge is to reduce market price fluctuations.

A case can be made that because of capital requirements, risk aversion, and high discount rates associated with high risks, the private trade will not hold socially optimal buffer stocks of food. Although public holding and controlling of international grain stocks appear to be attractive because food instability is a worldwide problem, there are formidable obstacles:

1. The social cost of mismanaged public buffer stock program may be greater than the social cost of private market failure a public stock policy is trying to correct (Tweeten, 1989, ch. 5).
2. The United States, Canada, and the European Community frequently have accumulated considerable, even excessive, stocks and storage capacity through their farm price support policies. This has abrogated the need for internationally financed and controlled reserves. However, a policy designed to support farm prices in developed countries is a haphazard policy to meet legitimate international buffer stock needs in an unstable world.
3. The lowest-cost means to provide international food reserves is to store them where surpluses are produced. Food grains are most cheaply stored in the temperate zone countries ordinarily producing and exporting large quantities of grains at relatively low cost. It would be costly to ship commodities to countries

where shortages might occur, then find they must be moved elsewhere. Furthermore, donors might be unwilling to replenish buffer stocks released prematurely by local decision makers in developing countries.

4. Developing countries most dependent on emergency world food reserves have not had funds to finance the reserve.   Commodity agreements to link international price fixing schemes with buffer stocks have been attempted without success.

An attempt to establish an internationally coordinated system of world food reserves collapsed in 1979 when participants could not agree on the overall size, distribution, and financing of the reserve as part of a proposed new International Wheat Agreement (Kennedy and Nightengale). The United States announced in 1981 that it was opposed to any international control or coordination of grain reserves. It did this in response to pressures by other nations to use the reserve to manage prices and world market shares.

The Food Aid Convention of the International Wheat Agreement in 1971 pledged member nations to supply 4.23 million tons of cereals annually, a number raised to 7.59 million tons in 1980. The US pledged 4.46 million tons. The US share of world food aid has averaged about 60 percent of world aid in the 1980s with the remainder mostly supplied by the EC, Canada, Australia, and Japan. The US also maintained a 4 million ton emergency wheat stock reserve in the 1980s. The reserve was drawn down by 1.5 million tons to meet 1988/89 Public Law 480 needs following the 1988 drought.

Bilateral Agreements

Competing exporters such as Argentina and Canada have been more aggressive than the US in establishing bilateral commodity trade agreements (Table 9.3). Agreements are prominent in grains and have been most numerous and provisions most influential when supplies are short.

Crop production shortfalls in the 1970s and concern by grain importers for having reliable suppliers led to a number of bilateral export agreements. The agreements typically guaranteed access of the buyer to at least a minimum quantity and assured the seller of at least a minimum sale. Prices were usually those of the market at the time of sale. In the case of the US-Soviet agreement, the Soviets were allowed to purchase more than the minimum by mutual consent.

The first US-Soviet long-term grain agreement was signed in 1976 as a means to restrain annual variation in Soviet purchases of US grain. On June 1, 1990, the US and Soviet Union signed a new five-year Long-Term Grain Trade Agreement or LTA. The Soviets agreed to buy a minimum of 20 million metric tons each of corn and wheat over the five-year contract. The Soviets agreed to purchase an additional 1 million metric tons of soybeans (or meal) or 2 million metric tons of grain each year. In contrast to the previous agreement, which called for yearly minimums of 4 million tons of corn and 4 million tons of wheat per year, the 1990 agreement allowed the Soviets to vary purchases as long as the five-year totals were met by the end of the agreement. The minimum purchase was waived if prices were not competitive. This provision allowed the Soviets to purchase less than the minimum under the agreement in the mid-1980s because the US initially refused to provide subsidies to compete with heavily subsidized wheat offered by the European Community.

Bilateral agreements have tied up a considerable portion of wheat supplies for export in short years but have been less used when supplies are plentiful. The problem with widespread use of bilateral agreements is that fewer free supplies are left to set prices, subjecting residual world markets to greater price instability than would be the case in their

Table 9.3. Long-Term Bilateral Grain Agreements, July 1987.

Exporter	Importer(s)	Term	Quantity
			(1,000 Tons per Year)
Argentina	Czechoslovakia	1986-88	200 - corn, soybeans
	Peru	1986-89	700 - wheat
	Mexico	1985-88	500 - corn; 240 - sorghum
	USSR	1986-90	4,000 - corn, sorghum
Australia	Egypt	1985-89	2,000 - wheat
	Iraq	1986-90	1,200 - wheat
Canada	Brazil	1986-88	1,500 - wheat
	Egypt	1985-89	500 - wheat
	Iraq	1986-90	800 - wheat, barley
	USSR	1986-91	5,000 - wheat, feed grains
China	USSR	1985-89	1,500 - corn
Turkey	USSR	1986-90	1,500 - grains
United States	USSR	1983-88	4,000 - wheat; 4,000 - corn; 500 - soybeans
Uruguay	Mexico	1985-88	100 - corn; 100 - soybeans; 100 - sunflowers
	Taiwan	1985-90	250 - corn; 150 - sorghum; 250 - soybeans

Source: International Wheat Council.

absence. The agreements particularly disadvantage developing countries using export markets as a buffer stock. Such countries cannot afford to commit themselves to bilateral agreements but find world import market quantities restrained and prices inflated by bilateral agreements between other countries when world supplies are short.

Multilateral Contracts

Commodity agreements can be between two nations as discussed above or can be *multilateral contracts* among many nations. Multilateral contracts can be a *market gain* arrangement whereby both buyers and sellers benefit or a *market pain* arrangement imposed by some countries on other countries for an overall welfare loss. Multilateral market gain contracts discussed in this subsection do not feature stringent supply controls but may use quota arrangements to provide a more orderly market. Under the agreement, buyers and sellers typically agree on a forward price band and quantities to be delivered within that band. Sellers are assured of a market within the prescribed price band. If weather fails, buyers gain because sellers are to supply the minimum quota at no higher than the top price -- requiring a buffer stock. If supplies are excessive, sellers gain from the agreement compared to a free market because buyers are to purchase the quota at the agreed price.

Since at least 1933 when the Monetary and Economic Conference was held in London, groups of nations have expressed an interest in commodity agreements. In the interwar period, stabilization schemes were formulated for copper, nitrates, potash, rubber, silver, sugar, tea, tin, and wheat. Coffee agreements have been attempted intermittently since 1902. Negotiations on a cocoa agreement began in the mid-1950s and were concluded in 1972. The history and principal features of five international commodity agreements are documented by Hillman *et al.* (p. 68).

An international wheat cartel was attempted by the United States, Canada, Australia, and Argentina in 1933. The cartel members agreed to cut acreage 15 percent in 1934 to raise prices. Only Australia honored the acreage cut. Argentina exceeded its export quota in 1934. The cartel collapsed that year.

Under later International Wheat Agreements, countries attempted to voluntarily hold wheat prices above a minimum designated level. The agreements worked as long as the United States, the principal exporter, was willing to restrain exports by domestic production controls or buffer stocks to maintain world price. Under the International Grains Arrangement concluded in 1967 as part of the Kennedy Round of GATT negotiations, major wheat exporters agreed to hold at least a minimum price. Signatories other than the US sold below that price in a wheat-surplus market. The US was no longer willing to perform its residual supplier role. The agreement collapsed in 1968 and has not been revived as a price setting device.

The International Coffee Agreement, administered by the International Coffee Organization (ICO), combined country quotas (but not production controls) with efforts to hold prices within a price band agreed upon by buyers and sellers signatory to the agreement. The International Coffee Association -- a group of 50 coffee-exporting countries and 25 coffee-importing countries -- accounted for approximately 85 percent of world coffee consumption and for 90 percent of world coffee production in 1989. Producing countries were issued stamps for their quota and consuming countries were required to admit only ICO certificate coffee with attached stamps.

The agreement, the most successful of all agricultural commodity agreements, helped to stabilize prices at levels slightly above those of a well-functioning market. It worked only because (1) price and other objectives were modest, (2) developed-country importers generously backed the agreement even when coffee could be procured at lower prices elsewhere, and (3) Brazil as the dominant supplier actively supported the agreement by restraining sales. However, when supplies were short, suppliers of coffee did not hold to the ceiling price. The agreement reduced the ability of efficient producers to obtain quotas and of buyers to obtain the types of coffee favored by consumers. It encouraged overproduction. Excess production was sold to Eastern European and Middle East markets not part of the ICO. The de facto two-tiered pricing system resulted in prices discounted as much as 50 percent in non-quota markets.

In July 1989 the agreement collapsed mainly over the issue of how coffee-export quotas were to be distributed among member nations. Brazil refused to support the Agreement because some of its coffee quota would be shifted to other producers. In addition, the United States and several European countries wanted flexibility in quotas to respond to changing consumer demand. By early 1990, prices fell to half the level prevailing before the agreement collapsed. Stocks depleted rapidly, however, and prices rose above those prevailing in early 1990.

Market gain commodity agreements have mostly failed. Attempts at price fixing without production controls either founder on prices initially set so high they bring excessive production, surpluses, and eventually low prices or set so low they bring shortages and eventually high prices. Lack of funds to hold buffer stocks to support pricing bands, lack of trust among signatories, and unanticipated market and technological developments work against commodity agreements. Success of international commodity agreements depends heavily on discipline of sellers (mostly developing countries) and generosity of buyers (mostly developed countries). Discipline and generosity are in short supply, however.

Export Cartels

Export cartels employ the *market pain* approach of bargaining power and supply control to achieve price objectives. An example is the Organization of Petroleum Exporting Countries (OPEC), with suppliers unilaterally withholding petroleum supplies and raising prices to unprecedented levels in the 1970s. Many LDCs look to OPEC and the riches it created for oil suppliers as a model for agricultural agreements. As with multilateral contracts, export cartels have numerous disadvantages.

1. Export cartels require export and production controls. Either members must exercise discipline among themselves or depend on self-sacrifice of a major supplier to control exports. Not only are discipline and self-sacrifice rare, as noted above, but the free-rider problem is not easily overcome.
2. No cartel, including OPEC, has been effective for long -- and with reason. Opportunities for substitution in consumption erode demand and for substitution in production augment supply. Entry of new producers becomes highly attractive. The result is excess supply. Benefits are capitalized into control instruments. Incentives to cheat are great and monitoring of compliance is difficult.
3. Relatively few commodities lend themselves to international commodity agreements of sizable benefit to third-world "South" countries (see Hillman *et al.*, p. 62). Gains are modest in transfers from the North to the South because: (a) few commodities are produced mainly in the South and consumed mainly in the North; (b) among those which are, value in many cases is very modest in relationship to foreign exchange needs of the South; and (c) benefits can easily be eroded by increased production of the same or related products in the North. Large South gains are possible for sugar, for example, but additional high-fructose sugar can be produced from corn in the North if price incentives dictate.
4. A food cartel is indefensible on ethical grounds because of large deadweight losses and hardships imposed on the poor. OPEC caused massive economic upheaval in the 1970s. Non-oil exporting third-world countries were major losers; the debt crisis of the 1980s is only one legacy of the excesses. An effective food cartel potentially could cause even greater havoc because food is more immediately essential to life than oil. A food cartel of the South would be especially damaging to poor consumers in the South.

State Trading

Among major world wheat exporters, only the United States and Argentina do not make extensive use of state trading, defined as publicly owned national corporations performing exporting and/or importing activities. Usually there is one corporation per commodity. Up to 95 percent of all wheat trading features a state trader as buyer, seller, or both.[2] In the Organization for Economic Cooperation and Development (OECD) countries in 1976, state trading accounted for an estimated 28 percent of exports and 27 percent of imports of 34 agricultural products (Kostecki, pp. 286-288). In 1974-75, the four largest firms (all private) accounted for 58 percent of US food grains exports, for 44 percent

---

[2]State traders such as the Canadian Wheat Marketing Board frequently use private traders such as Cargill to move grain after the terms of the sale are settled.

of feed grains exports, and 42 percent of oilseed and oilseed product exports (Wright and Krause, p. E-13). These statistics have alarmed American farmers because of possible opportunities for collusion and bargaining advantages.

High concentration rates of sales among sellers are not necessarily grounds for alarm, however, if firm entry is not difficult. As noted in Chapter 8, nearly 400 firms export US agricultural products. Large firms dominate, however. Large companies appear to maintain their position because of economies in information and trading systems that are passed to customers. Competitive terms of sale rather than predatory behavior deter competitors from entering the trade or expanding share.

Bargaining power issues are discussed elsewhere and are touched only briefly in this chapter. State trading by other nations does not necessarily imply exploitation of Americans who rely on private (including cooperative) export firms. Studies of export performance summarized by Tweeten (1989, p. 245) did not indicate that state traders have performed better than private traders.

BLOC OR REGIONAL INTEGRATION INSTITUTIONS

The subject of regional blocs addressed in this closing section constitutes a transition between the trade institutions of this chapter and trade actors in the next. Regionalism and unilateralism are reinvigorated as multilateralism recedes following the Uruguay Round.

Following a disappointing Uruguay Round of multilateral liberalization, attention is being directed to economic integration on a regional basis. The Canada-US Free Trade Area may be expanded to include Mexico in a North American Free Trade Area (NAFTA). A Western Hemisphere FTA also has been proposed for the more distant future. The European Community eventually may expand to include countries of EFTA and former East Bloc countries. Western Hemisphere and European trading blocs could motivate formation of one or more Asian trade blocs. Current and proposed trading blocs are listed in the next chapter.

Types of Regionalism

There are at least four types of economic integration (see Lindert):

1. A *free trade area* (FTA), defined as an area in which member nations remove trade barriers among themselves but trade barriers to the rest of the world differ among FTA members and are determined by each nation's policymakers. An example is the European Free Trade Association (EFTA) as noted in Chapter 10.
2. A *common market*, defined as an area in which there is free trade and full freedom of factor flows such as capital and labor among member nations. An example is the European Community.
3. A *customs union*, defined as an area with free trade among member nations and common trade barriers for non-member nations. In trade, the EC is considered to be a customs union.
4. An *economic union*, defined as an area in which member nations unify public economic policies such as monetary, fiscal, welfare, and environmental policies as well as trade and factor migrations. Although a common defense and foreign policy may be forthcoming, each nation maintains its own government that is

sovereign in most internal matters. An economic union is similar economically to one nation and is viewed by many as the EC's ultimate goal. An example of an economic union is that formed by Belgium and Luxembourg in 1921.

Regionalization of the world into integrated blocs can be a force for more or less trade liberalization. Blocs can free trade within but raise prospects for protectionism and trade wars among blocs. Or free trade blocs can form and then merge or expand to foster multilateral liberalization. The gains from specialization and internal and external economies of size can be enhanced.

Trade-Creating and Trade-Diverting Blocs

A critical issue in regionalization is whether blocs are *trade-creating* or *trade-diverting* for the rest of the world. Viner first defined trade creation or diversion among members of a customs union. The example below follows El-Agraa and Jones who define trade impacts of a FTA member replacing an outside member. The impact is illustrated in Figure 9.1 using as an example Canada, assumed to be a small-country case in a free trade area (Coughlin, pp. 48, 49).

Assumptions of Figure 9.1 are as follows:

S_c = Domestic supply in Canada
D_c = Domestic demand in Canada
M_{US} = Supply of US imports
M_A = Supply of imports from country A not part of the FTA
t = Specific tariff imposed by Canada on imports
M_{USt} = Supply of US imports in Canada with tariff
M_{At} = Supply of imports in Canada from country A with tariff.

In the trade-creating FTA case of Figure 9.1A, the US is assumed to be the low-cost supplier of imports. Canadian domestic consumption is q_c, production is q_p, imports are q_c-q_p, and domestic price is $P_{US}+t$ with the tariff. The FTA removes the tariff, bringing domestic price P_{US}, consumption q_c', production q_p', and imports q_c'-$q_p' > q_c$-q_p.

Welfare impacts of the trade-creating FTA are as follows for Canada:

Gain to consumers	a+b+c+d
Gain to producers	-a
Gain to government	-c
Gain to nation	b+d

Gains from the FTA are large if t is large and S_c and D_c become less inelastic. Welfare gains raising Canadian and FTA income are likely to create trade with countries outside the FTA.

In the trade-diverting case of Figure 9.1B, country A is assumed to be the lowest cost global exporter, presenting Canada with an import supply curve M_A lower than the US import supply M_{US}. With tariff t added, country A is the source of choice because P_A+t is less than $P_{US}+t$. Thus, without a FTA, domestic price is P_A+t, domestic consumption is q_c, production is q_p, and imports are q_c-q_p from A.

Next, Canada is presumed to enter a free trade agreement with the US, removing the tariff t on imports from the US but not from country A. The US is now a competitive

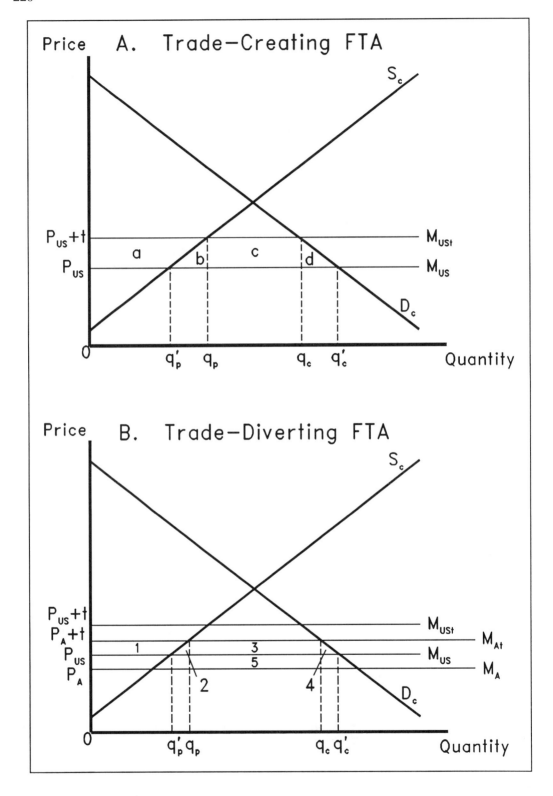

Figure 9.1. Illustration of a Trade-Diverting and a Trade-Creating Free Trade Area.

supplier with a Canadian price of P_{US} which is less than the price of A's imports, $P_A + t$. Domestic consumption is q_c', production q_p', and imports $q_c' - q_p'$. The FTA displaced trade $q_c - q_p$ from nonmember country A.

Welfare impacts of the trade-diverting FTA for Canada are as follows:

Gain to consumers	1+2+3+4
Gain to producers	-1
<u>Gain to government</u>	<u>-3-5</u>
Gain to nation	2+4-5

With this trade-diverting FTA, Canadian producers and the government lose as in the previous case. However, Canada as a nation gains only if area 2+4 exceeds area 5. Country A loses and the US gains. Because areas 2 and 4 are less than areas b+d and because Canada forsakes a lower cost source of imports from A, the chance of loss from a FTA are greater where there is a low cost outside supplier A as in Figure 9.1B than when there is none as in Figure 9.1A.

It is not possible to say whether the world is better or worse off from an FTA in the trade-diverting case of Figure 9.1B. However, important principles apparent from the illustration are that welfare gains are largest from an FTA that (1) contains countries with widely differing rather than with similar comparative advantage among commodities, and (2) contains countries with lowest cost global sources of goods and services consumed in the FTA.

CONCLUSIONS

The thrust of trade liberalization under GATT has been confined mostly to trade in manufactured goods, excluding textiles and apparel, to developed nations without severe balance-of-payments problems, and to tariff reduction. Nontariff barriers, which have replaced tariff barriers as the principal restraint to trade, pose new problems for GATT. To deal with NTBs, techniques need to be developed to quantify and report NTBs, perhaps on a tariff-equivalent basis. Appropriate rules will need to be developed to delineate what is "fair trade" in this context and sanctions devised to deal with violations. Much effort must go into making nontariff trade barriers more transparent, tarrification, developing rules that gradually reduce such barriers on a multilateral MFN basis, and streamlining and strengthening enforcement procedures.

To make progress in trade negotiations, the "request and offer" process in which each country brings what it is willing to offer in concessions to the bargaining table, must be replaced with a "wholesale" aggregate measure of protection. The producer subsidy equivalent (PSE) will not do because it does not distinguish between trade distorting and nondistorting policies.

Flaws of GATT are many: failure to encompass service, intellectual property, investment, and agricultural markets; failure to have a mutually-acceptable, impartial, and binding dispute settlement process; and failure to address nontariff barriers in trade negotiations. Some issues are not easily decided and may never be resolved. Examples are whether a country can ban imports of commodities produced using chemicals banned in the home country on the grounds of very real political but no scientific merit, and whether a country can protect strategic industries such as staple food production considered essential for its national security. Also at issue is whether a country can erect trade barriers to protect its domestic agriculture facing high production costs because of especially stringent animal welfare and environmental regulations.   Unlike traditional trade distortions established by special interests, the environmental- and animal-welfare motivated trade distortions may enjoy widespread popular if not scientific support.

It may be argued that any individual country is entitled to some latitude in its domestic agricultural policies as long as its actions do not adversely affect other countries. The challenge is to keep countries from exporting their agricultural problems through trade.

In summary, the situation is aptly described by T.K. Warley, who stated in 1988 that agriculture is "... the most highly protected sector in national economies, the most undisciplined area of international commerce, and the cause of the most dangerous frictions in international economic relations." Improving that situation remains a challenge to GATT.

REFERENCES

Congressional Budget Office. June 1987. *The GATT Negotiations and US Trade Policy.* Washington, DC: US Government Printing Office.

Coughlin, Cletus. September/October 1990. What do economic models tell us about the effects of the US-Canada Free Trade Agreement? *Review* 72(5):40-58. Federal Reserve Bank of St. Louis.

Deardorff, Alan and Robert Stern. 1985. Methods of measurement of nontariff barriers. United Nations Conference on Trade and Development. Geneva: United Nations.

El-Agraa and A.J. Jones. 1981. *Theory of Customs Unions.* London: Philip Allan Publishers Limited.

GATT. 1958. *Trends in International Trade: A Report by a Panel of Experts* (The Habeler Report). Geneva: General Agreement on Tariffs and Trade.

GATT. 1989. General Agreement on Tariffs and Trade: What it is, What it does. Geneva: Information and Media Relations Division, GATT.

Hillman, Jimmye. 1978. *Nontariff Agricultural Trade Barriers.* Lincoln: University of Nebraska Press.

Hillman, Jimmye, Anne Peck, and Andrew Schmitz. 1978. International trade arrangements. Ch. 4 in *Speaking of Trade.* Special Report No. 72. St. Paul: Agricultural Extension Service, University of Minnesota.

International Wheat Council. July 1987. *International Wheat Council Report.* London: IWC.

Kennedy, Richard. 1990. Exports and the farm sector. Pp. 51-56 in *The US Farming Sector Entering the 1990s.* Agricultural Information Bulletin No. 587. Washington, DC: ERS, USDA.

Kennedy, Richard and Ray Nightengale. June 1989. Short-term world food security. Pp. 68-76 in *World Agriculture.* RS-89-2. Washington, DC: ERS, USDA.

Kostecki, M. 1982. State trading in agricultural products by the advanced countries. In M. Kostecki, ed., *State Trading in International Markets.* New York: St. Martin's Press.

Lavergne, Phillipe Real. 1981. The political economy of US tariffs. Ph.D. Dissertation. Toronto: University of Toronto.

Lindert, Peter. 1986. *International Economics.* Homewood, IL: Richard Irwin.

Paarlberg, Robert. 1988. US agriculture and the developing world. Ch. 3 in Valeriana Kallab and Richard Feinberg, eds., *Growth, Exports, and Jobs in a Changing World Economy.* US-Third World Policy Perspective No. 9. New Brunswick: Transaction Books.

Ryan, Mary and Robert Tontz. 1978. A historical review of world trade policies and institutions. Ch. 1 in *Speaking of Trade*. Special Report No. 72. St. Paul: Agricultural Extension Service, University of Minnesota.

Robinson, Kenneth. 1989. *Farm and Food Policies*. Englewood Cliffs, NJ: Prentice-Hall.

Shane, Mathew and David Stallings. June 1989. The global trade environment and agriculture. Pp. 59-67 in *World Agriculture*. WAS-55. Washington, DC: ERS, USDA.

Tweeten, Luther. 1989. *Farm Policy Analysis*. Boulder, CO: Westview Press.

Tweeten, Luther. 1990. Current status of policy reform and structural adjustment in the Third World. Proceedings of *Association for International Agriculture and Rural Development* meeting in Washington, DC, June 12, 1990. Columbus: Department of Agricultural Economics and Rural Sociology, The Ohio State University.

Viner, J. 1950. *The Customs Union Issue*. New York: Carnegie Endowment for International Peace.

Warley, T.K. 1988. Agriculture in the GATT: A historical perspective. Proceedings of *20th Conference on the International Association of Agricultural Economists* meeting in Buenos Aires, Argentina. Guelph: Department of Agricultural Economics, University of Guelph.

Wright, Bruce and Kenneth Krause. April 1986. Foreign direct investment in the US grain trade. *Report to the Congress: Foreign Direct Investment in the United States*. Vol. 4, Appendix E. Washington, DC: US Department of Commerce.

ANNEX TO CHAPTER 9

THE GENERAL AGREEMENT ARTICLES AS OF 1989

The General Agreement has thirty-eight Articles. They are briefly described below.

Article	Description
1	Is the key article guaranteeing most-favored-nation treatment among all members. Trade must be conducted on the basis of non-discrimination. All contracting parties are bound to grant, to each other, treatment as favorable as they give to any country in the application and administration of import and export duties and charges. Thus no country is to give special trading advantages to another or to discriminate against it: all are on an equal basis and all share the benefits of any moves towards lower trade barriers. Exceptions to this basic rule are allowed only in certain special circumstances for regional trading arrangements and developing countries. In another context, trade without discrimination requires that once they have entered a market, imported goods be treated no less favorably than equivalent domestically-produced products. This is referred to as "national treatment."
2	Provides for the actual tariff reductions agreed to under GATT.
3	Prohibits internal taxes and other internal measures that discriminate against imports.
4	Concerns cinematograph films.
5	Concerns freedom of transit.
6	Concerns anti-dumping and countervailing duties. Revised GATT Anti-Dumping Code covers "dumped" goods, which are broadly defined as imports sold at prices below those charged by the producer in his domestic market. Participants in the Tokyo Round agreed on a revision of the earlier GATT Anti-Dumping Code.
7	Concerns customs valuation. Customs valuation sets a fair, uniform, and neutral system for the valuation of goods for customs purposes: a system that conforms to commercial realities, and which outlaws the use of arbitrary or fictitious customs values. Developing countries may delay applying the agreement for five years, and are given greater powers to counter potentially unfair valuation practices.
8	Concerns fees and formalities.
9	Concerns marks of origin.
10	Concerns trade regulations. Articles 4 to 10 are the "technical articles" designed to prevent or control possible substitutes for tariffs.
11 to 14	Articles 11 to 14 deal with quantitative restrictions. Article 11 is the general prohibition of them. Article 12 specifies how they may be used for balance-of-payments reasons. Article 13 requires that they be used without discrimination, apart from exceptions specified in 14 (see also Article 18).
15	Concerns GATT's cooperation with the International Monetary Fund.
16	Calls for the elimination of export subsidies.
17	Requires State-trading enterprises not to discriminate in their foreign trade.

GATT Articles cont.

Article	Description
18	Recognizes that developing countries may need tariff flexibility, and to be able to apply some quantitative restrictions to conserve foreign exchange. The main exception to the general GATT rule against quantitative restrictions allows their use in balance-of-payments difficulties (Article 12). Even then, restrictions must not be applied beyond the extent necessary to protect the balance of payments and must be progressively reduced and eliminated as soon as they are no longer required. This exception is broadened, for developing countries, by the recognition (in Article 18 of GATT) that they may need quantitative restrictions to prevent an excessive drain on their foreign exchange reserves caused by the demand for imports generated by development, or because they are establishing or extending domestic production.
19	Prescribes when emergency action can be taken against imports injuring domestic producers. Under "waiver" procedures, a country may, when its economic or trade circumstances so warrant, seek a derogation from particular GATT obligations. Among others, the United States has a waiver relating to the implementation of certain agricultural policies that would otherwise be contrary to GATT.
	It is also recognized that, on occasion, governments feel they have no choice but to offer domestic industries temporary protection from imports. The "safeguards" rule of GATT (Article 19) permits, in carefully defined circumstances, a member country to impose import restrictions or suspend tariff concessions on products that are being imported in such increased quantities and under such conditions that they cause or are likely to cause serious injury to competing domestic producers. In recent years, GATT members have become concerned at the resort by some governments to discriminatory bilateral arrangements -- often called "voluntary" export restraints -- which have avoided the disciplines of Article 19.
20 & 21	Specify, respectively, general and security exceptions to the Agreement (e.g., to protect public health).
22 & 23	Deals with consultations and with the settlement of disputes, respectively. These Articles lay heavy emphasis on bilateral consultations as the first step in settling disputes. In fact, most disputes never need go further than the stage of bilateral consultation. But when they cannot be resolved bilaterally, the GATT panel system can be employed.
	A panel usually consists of three experts from countries without an interest in the matter in question. They meet as a kind of court, hearing the case on both sides and the views of interested parties. They form a judgment based upon an interpretation of the General Agreement itself and upon previous cases.
	The report, which is submitted to the Council, contains conclusions on the rights and wrongs of the case, and in its final paragraphs, a recommendation. If the Council adopts the report of the panel -- which it does by consensus -- then there is a duty on the part of the contracting parties concerned to act in accordance with its finding.
	If the "violating" party does not implement the recommendation, the injured party may seek authority from the other members of GATT to take retaliatory action. Pressure stemming from the need of GATT members for negotiating credibility within the multilateral system has proved to be the most effective means of bringing about settlements.
	Some ten or twelve disputes are now handled by GATT panels every year.
24	Regulates how customs unions and free-trade areas may constitute exceptions to the most-favored-nation rule. Duties or other regulations affecting trade of members of the group with non-members are required to be no more restrictive than those that were applied before the group was set up.
25	Provides for action by the member governments. It is under this Article that waivers are granted. See Article 19.

GATT Articles cont.

Article	Description
26 to 35	These Articles are rules about the operation of GATT itself. They deal with its acceptance and entry into force (26), withdrawal of tariff concessions from former members (27), rules for tariff negotiations and changes in tariff schedules (28), the relationship between GATT and the still-born Havana Charter (29), amendment of the Agreement (30), withdrawal from GATT (31), the definition of "contracting parties" (members) (32), accession of GATT (33), the annexes to the Agreement (34), and non-application of the GATT rules between particular members (35).
36 to 38	These Articles, added in 1965, concern the special needs of the developing countries. Article 36 sets out GATT's principles and objectives in meeting these needs. Article 37 states commitments that members undertake to this end, and Article 38 provides for joint action by them. In 1965, a new chapter (Part IV) on trade and development was added to the General Agreement, committing developed countries to assist the developing countries. Developed countries would not expect developing countries, in the course of trade negotiations, to make contributions inconsistent with their individual development, financial, and trade needs. Developed countries also agreed that, except when compelling reasons made it impossible, they would refrain from increasing barriers to exports of primary and other products of special interest to developing countries, and would give high priority to reducing existing barriers, including fiscal taxes.

Source: GATT, 1989.

CHAPTER 10

Major Players in World Trade

The cast of characters on the world trade stage is colorful. The critical roles are played by developed countries but efforts are being made to bring into trade fora the less developed countries (LDCs) now represented more in form than substance. Trade barriers utilized by various countries were defined in Chapter 2 and other earlier chapters; here trade postures are emphasized. The final section summarizes and critiques the reasons given for trade barriers.

The East or Second World of centrally planned economies has disintegrated out of weakness while the West or First World of democratic-capitalist countries out of strength is forming into three superpowers that will dominate the international economy. While the three superpowers will vie for economic supremacy, the Third World of hard-core developing countries will struggle to keep from falling further behind. These "worlds" and their policies are discussed in this chapter.

THREE ECONOMIC SUPERPOWERS

The three economic superpowers are the United States (and Canada in the FTA), the European Community, and Japan. These economies account for over half of the world's trade.

The United States and Canada

As the world's most efficient large producer of agricultural products, the United States has a stake in open world markets. Its agricultural markets are fairly open with notable exceptions for sugar, dairy products, peanuts, wool, and tobacco. The US has led the world trade liberalization movement since the early 1930s except in agriculture. That position appears to have changed in agriculture, as noted in Chapter 9, by calls for decoupling and tariffication in the Uruguay Round.

A major change has occurred since World War II in the US trade negotiating position. In the 1930s Congress gave power to the President to make binding decisions on mostly bilateral trade barrier reductions. Under current legislation, Congress must approve changes negotiated under the General Agreement on Tariffs and Trade (GATT). A problem with decoupling and tariffication is that Congress is unlikely to accept for US agriculture the proposals made by US negotiators for other countries. Because Congress is more inclined than the Administration to serve special interests, the scope for trade liberalization by the United States is circumscribed. Chapter 11 treats US trade policy in much greater detail.

The folly of protectionism is seldom more clear than in the case of duties imposed in the 1980s on the 85 percent of US potash coming from Canada to protect the 5 percent of US potash consumption supplied from US mines. The result was to drive the US potash price up $50 per ton at significant cost to farmers. Depletion of strategic domestic reserves of minerals is speeded by such triumphs of political expediency over common sense.

The *Canada-US Free Trade Agreement* (FTA), which went into effect in 1989, will phase out all tariffs on US and Canadian goods by 1999. That compares with 35 percent of US exports subject to Canadian tariffs and 20 percent of Canadian exports subjected to US tariffs in 1988. Trade will not be completely free, especially in agricultural products. For example, for 20 years, either country may impose temporary duties on imports of fresh fruits and vegetables to protect domestic producers. Nontariff (mainly quota) barriers will remain in the case of peanuts, tobacco, and dairy products to protect domestic price supports. Canada agreed to eliminate import licenses for US small grains (if support levels are equal in the two countries) and also to eliminate its "Crow's Pass" rail subsidies of approximately 50 cents per bushel of grain.

European Community (EC-12)

The European Community vies with the US for being the world's largest agricultural exporter. It is approximately equal to the US in GNP and is one-fourth larger in population. The EC has relatively fewer trade commodity policy distortions than does Japan but rivals Japan for the world's largest deadweight losses due to sheer size of the Community of 12 nations. The (somewhat) Common Agricultural Policy, while helping to hold the EC-12 together, ironically also has created internal conflicts because the CAP has absorbed the major share of the EC budget (see reference to Harris *et al.* in Chapter 5). That high cost has been the principal impetus for CAP reform.

The European Economic Community organized under the *Treaty of Rome* in 1957 included six countries: Belgium, France, West Germany, Italy, Luxembourg, and the Netherlands. By 1990 it had expanded to six more countries: Denmark, UK, and Ireland joined in 1973; Greece in 1981; and Portugal and Spain in 1986. A complex governing system is evolving for the EC. In 1990 it contained the following components (Kelch, p. 38):

EC Parliament. The EC's only directly elected body, it has 518 members elected every 5 years. It does not legislate but has final budget approval authority. It can question and dialogue with the Commission and Council described below but has little power.

EC Commission. The Commission proposes legislation, implements EC policy, and enforces EC treaties. Commissioners are appointed from member states by unanimous agreement among member states, serve for four years, and can have consecutive terms. Each of the five largest countries in the EC (France, Germany, Italy, Spain, and the UK) has two members each; the other countries have one commissioner each for a total of 17 commissioners. The EC Commission President has traditionally exercised major leadership within the EC. The Commission derives considerable power by virtue of the administrative responsibilities carried out by its staff -- numbering 11,000 in 1990.

EC Agricultural Council. The Agricultural Council, one of several EC councils, is composed of the 12 ministers of agriculture from the member states. As the final EC decision making body on agriculture, the Council "disposes" the proposals made by the Commission. Presidency of the Council rotates among member states every six months. Provisions for majority approval in certain areas (replacing previously required unanimous approval) would heighten the influence of the Council.

EC Court of Justice. As the ECs "Supreme Court," the Court of Justice rules on interpretation of EC laws and treaties. Its 13 judges, appointed for six-year terms by mutual consent of member states, have consistently ruled in favor of EC law over national laws.

The hegemony of EC rule over national sovereignty will remain a major point of controversy for the foreseeable future. The UK for the most part has championed the vision of the EC as solely a common market while Germany and France have championed the vision of a "United States of Europe."

The movement toward an EC without internal borders was initiated by EC Commission Chairman Jacques Delor's blueprint which in turn was given shape and form in the Cockfield White Paper of 1985. The *Single European Act*, which legislated *Europe 1992* and amended the Treaty of Rome, was ratified by all member states in 1987. Barriers are too great for the EC to achieve a community without internal economic borders by the end of 1992, however. The European Community not only proposes to end all internal border restrictions on trade, labor, and capital movement by 1992 but also intends to work toward a central bank and common currency that extends well beyond the European Currency Unit (ECU), now used as an accounting medium of exchange. The *ecu* will become the day-to-day circulating currency.

The EC is regarded as the major villain in world agricultural trade because it uses export *restitutions* (subsidies equal to the difference between its high domestic support price and the world price) to export its agricultural surpluses to the rest of the world while insulating its producers from world prices, imports, and a buffering role through *variable* levies. The variable levy is not technically a tariff but taxes imports by the difference between the high domestic support price and the lower world price, thus supporting a stable domestic price. Because EC producers and consumers are insulated from world price signals of shortage or surplus, the EC does not buffer weather or other shocks to the world food system. Rather, it exports its instability to the rest of the world. The EC has accumulated considerable buffer stocks in recent years, however.

In the Uruguay Round of GATT, the EC initially proposed a market sharing arrangement and hence managed world trade in farm products. Later, it supported "substantial sustained reductions" in commodity trade distortions worldwide in the Uruguay Round. It was unwilling to end export subsidies, to institute comprehensive effective supply controls, or lower support prices enough to end major distortions in world markets.

The EC position stems from (1) the presence of many small, inefficient producers in several countries unable to compete in open world markets, (2) the power of agricultural groups in its political system, (3) the nonfarm wealth to afford farm subsidies, and (4) problems of reaching consensus on change among 12 countries on any issue. The EC has made some accommodations to reduce internal costs of the CAP and to reduce criticisms of the world trading community from which it has become increasingly isolated in trade negotiations. It has imposed quotas on dairy and sugar output, removed a small amount of cropland from production, and established economic stabilizers triggering lower price supports on grains when production exceeds a prescribed level.

The EC is not united in its opposition to agricultural trade liberalization. In general, the UK and Netherlands most favor free trade and Germany and France most favor protection. In the final negotiations, France led opposition to a compromise toward freer world trade in agricultural products and hence in all goods and services.

The US and EC have been and may remain principal adversaries in international trade negotiations. Conflicts have been frequent. A few examples illustrate.

1.   The entrance of Spain and Portugal into the EC threatened the previously large market for US grains to the two countries. The US threatened major retaliation

if not compensated for the loss of these markets. A compromise was reached after a period of intense confrontation including threats of retaliation and counter-retaliation.

2. A year-long controversy in 1988 arose over refusal of the EC to permit imports of beef from the US, which allowed use of growth hormone implants in cattle feeding. Backed by public opinion and a need to restrain beef output, the EC had imposed a ban on use of such hormones by its own feeders despite lack of scientific evidence that such hormones used in beef production posed a threat to the health of humans. The US was forced to accommodate to the ban despite inability on scientific grounds of the EC to justify regulation of such imports.

3. The EC refused to negotiate on agricultural products during the 1965-67 Kennedy Round of GATT. The US wanted the EC to guarantee that at least 13 percent of EC grain requirements would be reserved for foreign suppliers. The EC would offer only 10 percent. In frustration with only one month left to complete negotiations, the US dropped its demand -- another opportunity was missed to restrain relentless expansion of EC output generated by high price supports and vented by export subsidies.

4. In December 1987 the American Soybean Association filed a section 301 Unfair Trade Petition against the EC. The petition alleged that the EC oilseed subsidies constituted unfair discrimination against imports. During the 1962 Dillon Round of multilateral trade negotiations, the EC committed itself to no import restrictions on soybeans and soybean meal. But during the 1980s, subsidies paid to crushers for processing domestic oilseeds rose dramatically. By 1986 the subsidy had increased European producer prices $216 per metric ton. The oilseed subsidies more than doubled the internal price over world price, and European producers responded by doubling their production over the period. A Dispute Settlement Panel of the GATT ruled in December 1989 that the European oilseed subsidies violated GATT trading rules and discriminated against oilseed imports. EC officials agreed in principle to abide by the ruling and bring their programs into compliance. But they reserved action until completion of the Uruguay Round, awaiting an opportunity to "rebalance" oilseed protection at the same level as grain with variable levies.

Meeting in Maastricht, the Netherlands, December 12 and 13, 1991, the leaders of the 12-nation EC created a treaty rivaling the original Treaty of Rome in long-term impact. The treaty establishing new directions for the EC had two parts. One covered an economic and monetary union (EMU) notable for establishing a central bank and a common currency, the *ecu*. The bank will be patterned after the German Bundesbank characterized by political independence and singular focus on price stability.

The EMU was one of three pillars comprising the so called *European Union*. The treaty made provision, if only in embryonic form, for a common foreign and defense policy, the second pillar. The third pillar provided for cooperation on immigration and asylum. Progress was also made on a common social and employment policy, and a strengthened parliament. Many of the treaty provisions will require years to implement. Britain opted out of the EMU and social and employment provisions, but reserved the right to join later.

Concepts of *subsidiarity* and *cohesion* were contained in the treaty. *Subsidiary* calls for the EC to act only on matters best achieved by the Community and that cannot be achieved by members acting individually. *Cohesion* means that rich countries are committed to help poor countries in the EC. The northern members (except Ireland) will help Greece, Portugal, and Spain pay for environmental and transport projects.

The implications of Maastricht are clear: The EC will be a more cohesive and hence formidable force in future trade policy.

An EC without internal borders will require considerable discipline over external immigration, national industrial policies, environmental and health regulations, and social policies. This discipline plus desire for greater power in international economic and political matters will push the EC toward greater political union in a European parliamentary system. Federation is likely to be slowed, however, not only by opposition from current members such as the UK but also by the prospect of enlarging the EC to include disparate countries from the European Free Trade Association (discussed later) and formerly East Bloc central European countries such as Czechoslovakia, Hungary, and Poland. A common EC military seems remote given widely different objectives of countries (including several officially neutral members) within an enlarged EC.

Japan

Along with the EC and the US (with Canada in the free trade agreement), Japan is the third economic superpower. Japan protects its agriculture more than any other major country, has a powerful agribusiness lobby, is committed with religious fervor to rice self-sufficiency, and can afford to subsidize agriculture. In early Uruguay Round GATT negotiations, Japan favored a phase-out of export subsidies after an initial freeze and modest reductions in trade distorting policies but not driven by PSE or a related aggregate measure of support. It deemed that GATT should have a rule allowing a nation to protect domestic staple food production from international competition.

Japan has played a passive and, some would say, cynical role in world trade negotiations. Perhaps no country has benefitted more from open world markets, yet it maintains some of the most restrictive import markets for food among all major nations and does not assume leadership in multilateral trade negotiations for more open markets. Large welfare gains are possible for Japan if it allows its consumers to buy at world rice and other food prices even if it uses subsidies to maintain rice producers' income and output at current levels (Gleckler and Tweeten).

Japan imports over half its food and the US generally has been patient with the rice self-sufficiency policy of its single largest farm export market. However, in September 1986 and November 1988, actions were brought by US rice millers to open Japanese rice markets. Partly because rice is the staple of Japan and partly because in 1988, for example, Japan was only 32 percent self-sufficient in grains, opposition there to opening rice markets was intense. Removal of all food trade barriers might increase US exports only $2 billion because other countries such as Thailand and Australia would gain a share of markets (Kada). The $2 billion gain is worthwhile but a small share of the $40 billion US trade deficit with Japan in 1991. In GATT negotiations in 1992, Japan offered to open its market to foreign rice. Because of powerful internal opposition, only a modest opening was offered -- not more than 5 percent of its market.

In 1984 America strongly pressured Japan to open beef and citrus markets. In an agreement signed in Tokyo on June 20, 1988 by the US and Japan, the latter agreed to end all quotas on imports of beef and fresh oranges in three years, and on fresh orange juice in four years. Tariffs, called for in the agreement to replace quotas, would also be reduced over time.

OTHER PLAYERS

The following players in world trade except the Cairns Group and the Nordic countries are *preferential trading associations* (PTAs). The Cairns Group and Nordic countries are not PTAs but are discussed briefly because each put forth initial negotiating positions in the Uruguay Round and frequently coordinated activities within their group.

Cairns Group

The Cairns Group of 14 exporters of farm commodities (several developing countries but including the major US agricultural commodity export competitors outside of Europe such as Australia and Canada) was especially disadvantaged by export subsidies in the US and EC. In the Uruguay Round, the Group favored an initial freeze on subsidies and other trade distorting measures to be followed by lowering trade distortions over time. In preliminary GATT discussions, it favored a phase-down of supports and trade interventions based on a PSE-type measure attended by strengthening of GATT rules to preclude reemergence of protectionism. The Cairns Group was an important ally for the US in Uruguay Round trade negotiations.

Many of the members such as Thailand, Argentina, Brazil, New Zealand, and Australia protect their agriculture very little. Their producers, unlike those of Japan and the EC, would gain from less world commodity program distortions in markets. The result would be higher world and domestic commodity prices for them.

European Free Trade Association (EFTA)

The six-member EFTA includes Iceland and other Nordic countries (except Denmark) along with Austria and Switzerland. The Association was formed in 1960 upon the urging of the United Kingdom, a founding member. The UK saw EFTA as a counterweight to the EC, but ironically dropped out to join the European Community. The EFTA countries, like the EC countries, have many small, high-cost farms that could not withstand exposure to world-class competition. These countries oppose significant movement toward free trade if it means compromising domestic support programs for agriculture.

Sweden took action to move toward a market-oriented agriculture in the 1990s. Finland and Norway, other Nordic countries, heavily protect agriculture and have many small inefficient farms that could not survive in a world of open markets. (Denmark is also a Nordic country, has an efficient agriculture, and is in the EC.) In the Uruguay Round, the Nordic countries favored measures to avoid buildup of excess world supplies and to reduce export subsidies. They opposed PSE-type measures for reducing protectionism.

Plans to combine EFTA and the EC in a *European Economic Area* (EEA), initiated in 1991, took more concrete form in 1992. The EEA would create a border-free trading zone for Western Europe. Several members of EFTA continued to seek membership in the EC, partly because EFTA would be subordinated to the EC in making the rules of the EEA.

Eastern Europe and the Soviet Union

The *Council for Mutual Economic Assistance* (CMEA or COMECON) was organized by centrally planned countries of eastern Europe and the Soviet Union in 1949. It later was joined by several countries outside the region including Mongolia and Cuba. Realignment of central European countries towards democratic-capitalism led to termination of CMEA in 1991. However, many troublesome issues for world trade confront present and former "Second World" centrally planned countries.

Because CMEA countries did not have convertible currencies and were not active in GATT negotiations, they had little influence on trading rules. However, centrally planned countries, especially the former Soviet Union and to a lesser extent China, have been major sources of world trade and price instability since the early 1970s. China has progressed but many current and former Marxist countries are struggling to shed unworkable communal farming and become more efficient in agriculture to save foreign exchange and improve living standards. The former Second World will continue to be a destabilizing force in international trade for some time because reforms will not quickly end central planning and revive the work ethic, entrepreneurial and managerial skills, private property, and market and financial institutions required for major economic progress. Former CMEA members in Europe are striving to have convertible currencies and become responsible members of the world trading community including GATT, IMF, and World Bank.

Former republics in the USSR (excluding Georgia and the Baltic republics) formed the *Commonwealth of Independent States* simultaneously with the collapse of the former Soviet Union on December 8, 1991. The Commonwealth, a free trade area of potential economic significance, will share some elements of an economic union. The Commonwealth will be dominated by Russia and to a much lesser extent Ukraine.

With a market-oriented growth strategy, the Commonwealth (if it survives) eventually could rival the three economic superpowers listed earlier. In the meantime, however, the former East Bloc countries are likely to require considerable food aid and other assistance in restructuring to market economies.

Other Preferential Trading Arrangements (PTAs)

In addition to the first- and second-world PTAs listed above, Table 10.1 lists a number of preferential trade arrangements formed over the years by third-world and other countries to obtain gains from specialization and economies of size in a larger market. Examples include the *Latin America Integration Association* (LAIA), the *Caribbean Common Market* (CARICOM), and *Central America Common Market* (CACM). LAIA (formerly LAFTA) was created in 1960 by Argentina, Bolivia, Brazil, Chile, Columbia, Ecuador, Mexico, Paraguay, Peru, Uruguay, and Venezuela (Ryan and Tontz, p. 16). CACM included Costa Rica, El Salvador, Guatemala, Honduras, and Nicaragua. ASEAN includes Brunei, Indonesia, Malaysia, the Philippines, Singapore, and Thailand. Third-world efforts to develop free trade areas have not succeeded for the most part (Goodloe and Normile, p. 18).

Developing countries have had difficulty forming cohesive free trade areas in part because they tend to have comparative advantage in similar tropical agricultural commodities, have little intra-bloc trade, pursue import-substitution policies, are disrupted by competition among each other for world markets, and have unstable economies and governments. Third-world countries have protected inefficient industries, raising costs of inputs to agricultural and food and fiber processing industries that could become competitive

Table 10.1. Regional Trade Agreements.

Association[a]	Year Formed	1988 Combined Population (Millions)	1986 Combined GNP	Exports, 1987 (Billion US Dollars)		Regional Exports as Share of Total Exports, 1987 (Percent)	
				Total	Agricultural	Total	Agricultural
Andean Common Market (ANCOM)	1969	88	126	7.1[b]	3.0[b]	4	[c]
Association of Southeast Asian Nations (ASEAN)	1967	321	214	40.2	6.6	14	14
Australia-New Zealand Closer Economic Relations (CER)	1983	20	212	31.1	13.4	7	3
Caribbean Common Market (CARICOM)[d]	1973	7	10	NA	NA	NA	NA
Central American Common Market (CACM)	1961	26	22	3.5[b]	2.6[b]	[c]	[c]
Council for Mutual Economic Assistance (CMEA)	1949	477	1,858[e]	NA	NA	NA	NA
East African Community (EAC)	1967	64	16	NA	NA	NA	NA
European Community (EC)	1957	325	2,902	950.8	109.1	59	72
European Free Trade Association (EFTA)	1960	32	430	150.7	5.0	15	19
Latin American Integration Association (LAIA)[f]	1960	374	632	69.6[b]	21.5[b]	3	2
Canada-US Free Trade Agreement (CUSTA)	1989	272	4,589	336.6	39.3	38	15

Source: see Goodloe and Normile, p. 15.
[a]Data on population and GNP are the latest available, and include the countries currently in the association.
[b]Data are from 1985.
[c]Less than one percent.
[d]Data not available for St. Kitts and Montserrat.
[e]Data are for 1988 in real 1980 terms and do not include Cuba, Vietnam, and Mongolia.
[f]Formally the Latin American Free Trade Association.
NA = Not available.

in world markets. *The most notable feature of successful third-world economies is their openness to world trade and avoidance of overvalued currencies.* Many third-world countries would benefit significantly from reducing trade barriers as part of the multilateral trade negotiations (MTNs). The fear is that division of the world into trading blocs could intensify trade wars between blocs and disadvantage third-world countries most likely to be excluded from FTAs.

Prospective Free Trade Arrangements

Perhaps motivated by poor prospects for multilateral trade liberalization, several free trade area proposals are in various stages of realization.

North American Free Trade Area (NAFTA): Canada, Mexico, and the United States. Prospects for combining the low-cost labor of Mexico with the capital and technology of Canada and the US make NAFTA attractive. Fruits and vegetables would flow north from Mexico and grains and soybeans would flow south to Mexico. The proposal is opposed by environmentalists and labor unions but could become a reality in the 1990s.

Mercosur. Originated in 1988 as a free trade pact between Brazil and Argentina, it expanded to include Uruguay and Paraguay in March 1991. The intent is for free trade in goods, services, and labor by 1994.

Central America. Central America is attempting to revive a common market (CACM) established in 1961 and lost in 1969 with war between Honduras and El Salvador. A common market, to be established by 1994, would include El Salvador, Honduras, Guatemala, Nicaragua, and Costa Rica.

Caribbean Community (CARICOM). Attempts at a CARICOM customs union under auspices of the Caribbean Community have been attempted since 1973. English-speaking countries of the Caribbean are included.

Western Hemisphere FTA. President George Bush proposed the Enterprise for the Americas Initiative (EAI), an FTA to include countries of North and South America. The area could be formed by merging NAFTA with free trade associations in South and Central America.

East Asian Economic Group (EAEG). In April 1991, Malaysia proposed the EAEG to include ASEAN countries of southeast Asia as well as China, Japan, Hong Kong, Taiwan, and South Korea. The original proposal was floated after the December 1990 meeting of world trade ministers under GATT in Brussels. The intent was for EAEG to formulate a common trade position for GATT negotiations. Differences between Japan and selected other proposed members run too deep for early reconciliation. But if European and Western Hemisphere free trade associations succeed, the principle of countervailing power will create strong incentives to form an Asian bloc along lines of the proposed EAEG.

A Western Hemisphere FTA would be unattractive for American agriculture because it would include countries such as Argentina and Brazil that compete effectively with American farm products. Welfare gains to American agriculture are much greater from a free trade agreement with the land-poor countries of East Asia. On the other hand, American nonfarm industry lacks enthusiasm for free trade with Japan, Taiwan, South Korea, and China.

THIRD-WORLD DEVELOPMENTS

The Third World includes oil-rich Middle East countries, newly industrialized countries in East Asia, debt-burdened countries of Latin America, and poverty-stricken countries in sub-Saharan Africa. The extreme heterogeneity defies generalizations, so the following discussion refers mostly to very low-income countries.

Developing countries cannot buy our farm and industrial products because trade barriers will not allow us to buy labor-intensive industrial and service industry output, which they produce with comparative advantage. Negotiations to end this socially and economically disastrous situation for less developed countries are complicated because GATT is dominated by developed countries. Opening of their markets to LDC raw, manufactured, and processed exports could be the single greatest contribution of first-world countries to third-world development.

Structural adjustment policies mandated by the International Monetary Fund and the World Bank in return for loans to developing countries experiencing serious debt problems usually call for trade liberalization. Major bilateral as well as multilateral lenders insist upon domestic and trade policy liberalization by developing countries. Protection rates shown in Chapter 3 indicate that third-world countries typically tax rather than subsidize their farm exports. Thus open trade and less distortion would bring higher returns to their producers.

Article 18 of GATT, allowing developing countries to use trade barriers to protect their balance of payments, is paternalism at its worst: giving developing countries license to mismanage their economies and hold second-class membership in GATT. Drives for import substitution, food self-sufficiency, and protection of local industry have immiserated millions.

The International Agricultural Trade Research Consortium in 1988 stated that "... the GATT has almost no control over trade restrictions in developing countries." The developing countries have sought and obtained special and differential treatment in the GATT. They are exempt from making reciprocal tariff cuts. GATT has allowed developing countries to restrict imports to protect infant industries or remedy balance of payments problems. Since 1971, developed countries have been permitted to reduce barriers to developing country imports below levels applied to other developed countries and to select developing countries for preferential quota and other treatment.

As their trade volume has grown, LDCs have more to gain by becoming active participants in GATT. Developed countries will be more willing to reduce trade barriers to imports from third-world countries if these developing countries offer concessions in return. But large gains could come from more open trade among developing countries themselves.

Import barriers of developing countries remain considerably higher than those of developed countries (World Bank, p. 138). Developing countries' exports gained less from tariff reductions in GATT rounds than did exports from industrial nations mainly because developed countries export many commodities not included in mandated tariff cuts. Most countries levy higher tariffs on manufactured products than on the raw materials used to produce them. This discriminates against processing in developing countries. The restrictions by developed countries against exports of developing countries are especially notable for steel, automobiles, electronics, footwear, sugar, and textiles (see World Bank, p. 140).

The trade restrictions most affecting developing countries are nontariff barriers (NTBs). The most damaging to developing countries of all NTBs, the *Multifiber Agreement* (MFA), was preceded by the Short-Term Cotton Textile Arrangement negotiated in 1961 under GATT auspices at the request of the United States. Subsequent agreements (the first MFA was in 1974) grew ever more comprehensive in scope, covering more products and countries. NTBs increased significantly between 1981 and 1986 particularly in Canada, the EC, and the United States. Some $230 billion of imports were covered by NTBs in 1981.

Barriers of developed countries against third-world nonfarm exports need to be of concern to American agriculture for several reasons.

1. Third-world development normally begins with agricultural productivity gains. These provide a surplus to build human, material, and technological capital enabling developing countries to move into light industry such as textiles, eventually into heavier industries, and, finally, into service industries. Internal markets in many developing countries are too small alone to support efficient domestic industry -- they must export to realize advantages of economies of size and specialization. Even countries such as India, China, and Brazil with sizable internal markets have been unable to develop efficient local industry through protectionism. Protection thwarts innovation and reduces incentives for efficiency. High income elasticities of demand for food, high population growth, and rapid income growth with successful development all combine to create food demands that are met by increasing imports from efficient agricultural producers such as the United States. Trade distortions by developed and developing countries thwart this entire development process, making both sets of countries worse off.

2. If developing countries are to import American grains, soybeans, meat, and processed foods, they must have buying power. Countries unable to export are also unable to import.

3. The cost to developed countries of protectionism from nonfarm imports is sizable in lost jobs and national income. For example, each job preserved in the US by protection of the automobile industry was estimated to cost customers between $40,000 and $108,500 per year (World Bank, p. 152). Voluntary export restraints in the specialty steel industry cost US consumers an estimated $340,000 per job saved in 1988 (Council of Economic Advisors, p. 199). Protection of the textile industry cost the US $25 billion or $238 per family -- a figure expected to rise to $85 billion by year 2000 if current policies are maintained (estimates by William Cline in Truell, p. A20). Such injury to the national economy and lost job creation in other sectors from foregone trade reduce demand for the output of American agriculture. The link between agricultural exports and US manufacturing trade also was apparent in 1983-84 when China retaliated against unilateral US textile import restraints by canceling an anticipated $500 million purchase of US wheat.

Generalized System of Preferences (GSP)

The US Trade Act of 1974 provided for unilateral tariff preferences for developing countries. Thus the nation joined virtually all other developed countries in providing trade preferences to developing nations. In 1971, GATT had adopted a waiver authorizing developed countries to give tariff preferences to developing countries for 10 years without violating the Most-Favored-Nation principle upon which GATT is anchored (Porter and

Bowers, p. 15). By 1973, 98 countries had been designated, and sugar was the most important agricultural commodity covered. Under the *Generalized System of Preferences*, the US has been an active participant in granting tariff preferences, but nontariff barriers remain a larger impediment to third-world exports.

Within a year after passage of the Trade Act of 1974, the US had eliminated duties under GSP on over 2,700 items imported from developing countries. Some of these were agricultural products including citrus fruits, melons, certain nuts, and fresh cucumbers, which carry duties of over 25 percent when imported from non-GSP countries.

Lomé Convention

The Lomé convention signed in 1975 and renewed in 1979 and 1984 gives 66 low-income African, Caribbean, and Pacific countries preferential access to EC markets. The Lomé accord goes beyond only tariff reductions as encompassed in the Generalized System of Preferences to include relaxation of nontariff barriers, exemption from certain multilateral agreements such as the Multifiber Agreement, and less stringent enforcement of other trade barriers.

The Lomé accord has benefitted low-income signatories but the extent of benefits has been less than anticipated. For example, the EC share of Lomé country exports fell from 46 percent before Lomé to 37 percent in 1979-84 (World Bank, p. 159).

United Nations Conference on Trade and Development (UNCTAD)

Developing nations noting domination of IMF and GATT by developed nations felt their needs were not being met. They also sensed market conspiracy because prices for agricultural products exported by developing countries had fallen relative to prices of industrial and other products imported by developing nations. Holding a majority of votes in the United Nations, the LDCs were successful in establishing the *United Nations Conference on Trade and Development* in 1964. The organization has held periodic conferences resulting in calls for *growth with equity* and a *new international economic order* to redistribute income and resources from the North (developed countries) to the South (developing countries). The mechanisms for stabilization included commodity stocks, food aid, disaster relief, international commodity agreements, and marketing quotas.

Attempts at price fixing schemes to assure markets at no less than specified minimum prices have failed as noted below. Income transfer proposals of UNCTAD have been unworkable because they have been poorly conceived and because developing countries lack bargaining power to impose demands on other countries.

Reciprocal trade barrier reductions accomplish much; commodity agreements on the other hand offer little hope for sustained betterment in the terms of trade. Declining terms of trade in agricultural products in which developing countries have comparative advantage is not the result of a conspiracy against them and will not be solved by price fixing. Instead, developing countries increasingly must recognize that development proceeds as nations increase productivity through human, material, and technological capital formation. Diversification into new industries is vital. That process is cut off by trade barriers.

JUSTIFICATIONS FOR TRADE BARRIERS
IN TODAY'S WORLD

Despite compelling economic reasons for free trade, protectionism abounds. Numerous reasons are used to justify trade distortions. This final section reviews a few. It evaluates their validity in our shrinking, interdependent world based on what has been learned from strategic and other theory and experience (see Tweeten, ch. 7).

National Security and Self-Sufficiency

Protection is said to be required for some items to maintain necessary domestic production when foreign supplies are cut off by drought, by political decree in peacetime, or by enemy attacks in wartime. Rather than depend on cheaper foreign sources, the reasoning goes, it is better to maintain domestic production as security, even at high cost.

One weakness of this conclusion is that the pattern of wars has changed. Brush-fire wars of the Korean, Vietnam, and Persian Gulf types do not cut off foreign supplies, and a major war using nuclear weapons would probably not last long. In peacetime, diversification of supply sources and opportunities for substitution of one commodity for another limit serious supply shortages. Livestock provide a major food buffer stock in developed countries. On the average 5 pounds of feedgrain and soybean meal or equivalent are required to produce a pound of meat. By consuming first the animals *and* then the grain directly, the food supply is increased up to sixfold.

Food production often requires imported commercial fertilizers, fuel, and pesticides, which are vulnerable to intervention in wartime. Food self-sufficiency that depends on imported inputs is not food security.

Developing countries that impoverish themselves and exhaust foreign exchange to become self-sufficient are highly vulnerable to hunger when domestic harvests fail as they often do. Without income or foreign exchange to purchase in the export market, they are at the mercy of charitable food donors. A policy of *food security* emphasizing broad-based, sustainable economic growth and ability to access world food markets makes more sense than import substitution and food self-sufficiency. Recognition that economic progress, imports, and stocks are lowest-cost sources of food security can free developing countries to pursue a policy of comparative advantage rather than an ill-advised policy of food self-sufficiency.

Nonetheless, difficult issues remain for international negotiations. For example, Japan imports more than half of its food. How low must self-sufficiency fall before a country has a legitimate case to protect what production remains?

Commodity Programs

The single greatest source of protectionism in developed countries is to shield domestic farm commodity programs from foreign import competition. As noted in Chapters 3 and 11, these programs have brought large deadweight losses to countries that practice them. However, it may be argued that a country has the right to transfer income to any group and to promote national security.

One compromise proposal is that any country be allowed by GATT rules to be self-sufficient in one main staple. It would be allowed to make payments to producers to become self-sufficient but consumers would be allowed to purchase the staple (and other goods and services) at world prices. No border protection would be allowed: Producers of the staple would receive only coupled government payments while producers of other commodities would receive only decoupled payments or no assistance. The politics of maintaining large government outlays to producers from taxpayers would constrain programs to modest levels minimally interfering with world commerce. A country electing to follow the policy might be bound against subsidizing production beyond that in a base period or beyond self-sufficiency. Thus the United States would not be allowed to couple price supports to wheat -- a crop for which it is more than self-sufficient.

Infant Industry

The protect-infant-industry argument has validity where a domestic industry needs to grow to achieve external and internal economies of scale. Initially, the industry is not competitive in world markets. With time, economies of scale and maturity of knowhow reduce costs to competitive levels, eliminating the need for protection. This argument has particular appeal in developing nations, but it lacks validity for protected dairy, beef, sugar, textile, steel, auto, and chemical industries in the United States.

Balance of Payments

Apologists have justified trade barriers to improve balance of payments. This argument would have greater validity if exports were independent of imports, but efforts to curtail imports, such as the notorious Smoot-Hawley Tariff of 1930, lead to countermeasures by foreign countries to protect their trading position. Unless there is a real need, well recognized by other nations, to protect a balance-of-payments situation (and then only after domestic policies such as currency devaluation, budget deficit reduction, and money supply restraint have been pursued), increasing trade barriers are not likely to be tolerated without reciprocal action on the part of foreign nations. Flexible exchange rates set by market forces remove the case for trade restrictions to end trade deficits.

Countervailing Power

Proponents of trade barriers have reasoned that unilateral reduction of trade barriers may not be in the interests of the United States and that countervailing trade barriers may be necessary. Out of such thinking has grown a theory of the second best, i.e., what kind and level of trade barriers are optimal for country A facing a world of existing and mounting institutional barriers to free trade? A strategic trade policy of subsidizing exports of potential winning industries also lacks appeal because the record of governments on this has been unfavorable. The classic case used by proponents of strategic government intervention, Boeing versus the European Airbus, is an example of the advantages of reliance on private industry rather than chronic strategic subsidies from government to Airbus. This issue of a trade and negotiating strategy for the US agriculture is addressed in Chapter 11.

Major support for trade barriers comes from domestic commodity industry and labor lobbies that want their price and income position protected from foreign competition. The fight for trade barriers is seldom waged in the name of maintaining or increasing income of the protected industry. Though this is the real reason, "good" reasons are officially stated such as protection against dumping (goods sold here below the market price or production cost in the exporting country), contributions to national defense, and maintaining jobs and family farms.

Employment

The presumption of trade barriers to protect jobs is that workers are incapable of adjusting to alternative employment. The massive and largely successful readjustment of workers among industries in the past belies that presumption. To honor the presumption would be to cut off virtually all economic change and progress. Programs of counseling, training, job search, and other mobility assistance can ease labor adjustment pains.

Countries reduce imports when they cannot export. Cutting back on imports to save jobs is often counter-productive; jobs lost in export industries exceed those saved in import industries. Maintaining high food and farm prices all the time in the European Community and Japan to avoid occasional food shortfalls and high prices some of the time does not maximize national well-being.

If trade cost jobs, we would expect to see extensive joblessness in free-trading nations and full employment in self-sufficient nations. In fact, trade-dependent countries tend to have the least unemployment and underemployment. Trade does not markedly influence employment in the long run but it raises productivity and hence living standards.

National Health, Safety, Environment, and Animal Welfare

A nation is justified in protecting the health and safety of its citizens and resources by keeping out threatening imports. Chapter 11 notes such measures used by the United States. A problem emerges, however, when nations use sanitary and phytosanitary regulations not to protect the physical health of the general population but the economic health of well-placed special interests. In addition, activists are sometimes successful in erecting trade barriers to protect against imagined rather than real health and safety risks.

The answer is an informed public and extensive use of multinational institutions such as GATT to foster trade rules justified by real but not by bogus health, safety, environmental, and animal welfare concerns.

Raising Revenue and Terms of Trade

Countries sometimes use tariffs to raise revenues or improve terms of trade. Developing countries especially use export tariffs to raise revenue for government. Such countries might well be encouraged to seek other revenue sources such as property taxes that entail less deadweight loss and would especially benefit local areas providing basic schooling and roads. Tariffs account for less than 1 percent of US government revenue. Prospects are not great for raising that share.

In theory, a large country can improve terms of trade (ratio of prices received for exports relative to prices for imports) by taxing imports and thereby reducing their price. GATT rules, market conditions, and retaliation have diminished success of that option. Rather, the tendency of developed countries is to reduce terms of trade by subsidizing exports, also a questionable policy.

CONCLUSIONS

The US sees its once predominant position in the international economy contested by economic superpower competitors -- Japan and the European Community. It has not been easy to accommodate to that reality, especially because the EC has pursued a Common Agricultural Policy with unusual disregard for the spirit and often the letter of GATT principles.   Trading blocs and economic superpowers are likely to dominate trade negotiations in coming decades.   The blocs can be a force for confrontation or cooperation to achieve multilateral trade liberalization.

The peripheral role of developing countries in the GATT has not been constructive. The exemption from trade discipline awarded developing countries by GATT Article 18 has become a license for market distortion.   Resulting trade restrictions and price interventions imposed by developing countries frequently damage developing countries, including the perpetrator, more than developed countries.   The GATT negotiations exclude many tropical products.   The Multifiber Agreement and developed-country-imposed sugar quotas, subsidies, and tariffs work against developing countries that would be better off if these products were brought under GATT discipline.   While some studies indicate that developing countries would lose on the whole from worldwide free trade in agricultural products, the studies do not account fully for overvalued currency and export taxes that discriminate against agriculture and would be alleviated under a broader definition of unrestricted markets.   Trade liberalization would benefit developing countries.

This chapter has addressed world trade actors, their negotiating positions, and reasons for trade barriers.   The next chapter addresses US trade policy.

REFERENCES

Congressional Budget Office.   June 1987.   *The GATT Negotiations and US Trade Policy*. Washington, DC: US Government Printing Office.

Council of Economic Advisors.   1992.   *Economic Report of the President*.   Washington, DC: US Government Printing Office.

Gleckler, James and Luther Tweeten.   1990.   The economic impact of a US-Japan free trade agreement.   Pp. 87-104 in Luther Tweeten, ed., *The Asian Market for Agricultural Products*.   ESO 1704.   Columbus: Department of Agricultural Economics and Rural Sociology, The Ohio State University.

Goodloe, Carol and Mary Normile.   June 1990.   Preferential trade arrangements and agriculture.   Pp. 14-23 in Arthur Dommen, ed., *World Agriculture*.   WAS-59. Washington, DC: ERS, USDA.

International Agricultural Trade Research Consortium.   1988.   Negotiating a framework for action.   Summary report of *Bringing Agriculture Into the GATT*.   Ithaca, NY: IATRC, Cornell University.

International Wheat Council.   July 1987.   *International Wheat Council Report*.   London: IWC.

Kada, Ryohei.   January 1988.   The future of US-Japan agricultural trade relations. *Economic Issues*.   No. 108.   Madison: Department of Agricultural Economics, University of Wisconsin.

Kelch, David.   July 1989.   Europe 1992: Implications for agriculture.   Pp. 36-46 in *Western Europe Agriculture and Trade Report*.   RS-89-2.   Washington, DC: ERS, USDA.

Nichols, John.   1990.   Export promotion effectiveness for agricultural products.   Pp. 67-76 in Luther Tweeten, ed., *The Asian Market for Agricultural Products*.   ESO 1704. Columbus: Department of Agricultural Economics and Rural Sociology, The Ohio State University.

Porter, Jane and Douglas Bowers.   1989.   *A Short History of US Agricultural Trade Negotiations*.   Staff Report AGES 89-23.   Washington, DC: ERS, USDA.

Ryan, Mary and Robert Tontz.   1978.   A historical review of world trade policies and institutions.   Ch. 1 in *Speaking of Trade*.   Special Report No. 72.   St. Paul: Agricultural Extension Service, University of Minnesota.

Truell, Peter.   May 16, 1990.   Textile makers demanding more protection.   *The Wall Street Journal*, A20.

Tweeten, Luther.   1989.   *Farm Policy Analysis*.   Boulder, CO: Westview Press.

World Bank.   1987.   *World Development Report 1987*.   New York: Oxford University Press.

CHAPTER 11

American Agricultural Trade Policy

A comprehensive strategic trade policy must have numerous components, several of which are addressed in this chapter. These components include the institutional framework for trade; domestic monetary, fiscal, and commodity program policies; and research and environmental measures that influence competitiveness.

The Bush Administration's (Yeutter, p. 2) strategy for US agricultural trade stated succinctly in 1988 is reasonably representative of that in the 1980s and 1990s:

1. Change economic policies worldwide that discourage US exports.
2. Use US farm commodity programs to restore our international competitiveness.
3. Move aggressively against unfair foreign trade practices.
4. Improve international rules governing trade in agriculture.

The above outline contains clues but does not constitute an overall trade policy. This chapter attempts to complete the outline of current trade institutions and policies. The first section reviews current policies and institutions. The second section reviews new directions for selected trade institutions. The third section suggests a trade negotiating action and reaction strategy. Some aspects of past US trade policy especially relating to the US negotiating position in the GATT were discussed in previous chapters.

US TRADE INSTITUTIONS FOR
FORMULATING AND ADMINISTERING TRADE POLICY

Congress and the President enact trade legislation. The day-to-day activities of formulating and administering trade policy are carried out by several agencies and offices, most in the Executive Branch. Notable specialized trade institutions are the Office of the United States Trade Representative (USTR), US International Trade Commission, and agencies administering agricultural export programs.

Under the constitution, the US Congress has power over tariffs and treaties. However, Congress in its wisdom recognizes that it cannot handle day-to-day trade policy matters and the pressures for protectionism from constituents. Consequently, operational trade policy matters rest with the Executive Branch. In 1979, Congress conditioned approval of the Tokyo Round GATT agreement on elevation of trade priorities in the Administration. Consequently, by Executive Order, the President removed the trade negotiation position from the Department of State and created the Office of the USTR.

Trade Policy Within the Executive Branch

Office of the United States Trade Representative (USTR)

The government's principal trade policy agency is the Office of the United States Trade Representative, a cabinet level agency headed by the US Trade Representative who reports to the President. The USTR and five deputies hold ambassador rank (World Perspectives). In 1990, one Assistant Trade Representative was for agriculture and was aided by a deputy along with a staff of advisors and staff economists.

The Office of the USTR is the focal point for a number of trade advisory committees from outside government as well as for administrative activities within the Executive Branch. The USTR leads bilateral and multilateral trade negotiations. The *Office* receives advice and complaints from businesses, individuals, and members of Congress regarding matters of trade.

Other Agencies Within the Executive Branch

Although the Office of USTR is the President's chief agency on trade policy, nearly every Department and many cabinet level agencies are involved in some issues of trade. Hence, interagency coordination is critical. The *Economic Policy Council* (EPC), comprised mostly of cabinet heads, is the chief Executive Branch unit coordinating trade policy. The President is officially the chairman but the Secretary of Treasury ordinarily presides as President *Pro Tempore*.[1] This council seeks common ground after the various cabinet units involved in trade fail to agree on appropriate action. Recommendations from the EPC are forwarded through the US Trade Representative to the President for action.

The *Trade Policy Review Group* (TPRG) operates below the EPC at the Undersecretary cabinet level to reach agreement among government agencies on matters of trade policy that cut across cabinet lines. This reduces the burden on the EPC, which resolves those issues that cannot be resolved by the TPRG. In addition to the deputy USTR who serves as chair, the TPRG included representatives from 14 Executive Branch departments and agencies during the Bush Administration.

The *Trade Policy Staff Committee* (TPSC) operates below the TPRG and does most of its work through 40 subcommittees and additional technical task forces. Members are government career experts and technicians in numerous fields including agricultural trade. The TPSC prepares staff working papers for use by other groups, agencies, and top administrators and officials who make trade policy decisions.

Committees Advisory to the Executive Branch

The Executive Branch draws heavily on expertise from outside the government through several advisory groups. The following listing sheds light on who influences trade policy.

The *President's Export Council* is the top national committee advising the President on international trade. Five members presumably represent agricultural interests, but private sector exporters predominated during the Bush Administration. Farm, consumer, importer, and taxpayer interests had little visibility on the Council.

---

[1]In addition to those listed above, the EPC includes Secretaries of Commerce, Agriculture, Defense, Labor, Transportation, State, the Director of the Office of Management and Budget, and the Chairman of the Council of Economic Advisors.

The *Advisory Committee for Trade Policy Negotiations* is the lead committee advising the Administration on overall trade policy negotiations. The committee represents private interests. The *Agricultural Policy Advisory Committee* more directly counsels the government on trade issues of agriculture. In 1991 its 25 members were drawn from producer, processor, cooperative, trade, and other groups. The *Agricultural Technical Advisory Committee* worked mainly through 10 commodity committees. Committee members were chosen for technical expertise to advise government officials mostly on technical and administrative matters regarding agricultural trade.

US International Trade Commission (ITC)

The *US International Trade Commission* is especially known for its investigative powers and recommendations regarding agricultural programs and industries harmed by imports in violation of US trade laws. It is an independent agency of the government consisting of six commissioners and a support staff of experts in trade and law. The President appoints commissioners for nine-year terms with no more than three from the same political party.

ITC investigations regarding agriculture frequently deal with alleged violation of three laws (World Perspectives):

- *Section 22* of the *Agricultural Adjustment Act of 1933* as amended in 1935. The President is authorized by this law to impose duties or quotas on imports that interfere with farm commodity support programs or with products processed from such supported commodities.
- *Sections 201* and *301* of the *Trade Act of 1974*. The President is authorized to impose duties, quotas, or other orderly marketing arrangements to domestic industries unduly hurt by imports of products that are the same as or similar to those produced by the affected industries.
- *Tariff Act of 1930*. This law provides for investigation in cases where imports are subsidized by governments or "dumped" at less than fair value on US markets.

The ITC also is responsible for other types of investigations, particularly where agriculture or other American industries are or potentially might be harmed by actions of other countries, including as a result of trade agreements.

It is apparent that the ITC is positioned to be a force for protectionism. For the most part, the Commission has exercised restraint in the cases accepted by it and in the remedies recommended by it after investigation.

The Office of the USTR may initiate an investigation of unfair practices but most investigations begin with petitions to the USTR from private industry. The allegations may be investigated by (1) the ITC, or (2) a special *Interagency 301 Committee*, including public hearings. Congress may also hold hearings. For a trade practice judged to be unfair and damaging, the next step is for the USTR to negotiate a settlement with the offending party or submit the matter to the dispute settlement procedures of the GATT. The US may retaliate if relief is not forthcoming.

US TRADE RESTRICTIONS

American restrictions on international trade are numerous and long-standing. Tariffs date to the nation's founding. Early tariffs were solely to raise revenue; the first to protect industry was the *Tariff Act of 1816*. The first US antidumping legislation was the *Antidumping Act of 1921*. It was designed to protect against foreign exporters selling goods in US markets at less than "fair value." An international antidumping code was negotiated during the Kennedy Round of GATT.

Agricultural Trade Restrictions

Several other US provisions affect imports of farm commodities. Quotas were used to restrict meat imports in 1976. The *Meat Import Act* of 1979 may be used to restrict meat imports. The law has been little used; voluntary restraint agreements have been the instrument of choice to restrict imports of meat from Australia, New Zealand, and Canada. US health and sanitary regulations forbid imports of uncooked meat from areas with selected animal diseases, most notably foot-and-mouth disease. Fresh fruits cannot be imported from areas with Mediterranean fruit flies except under prescribed conditions of shipment.

The US has often been at the forefront in obtaining special trade exemptions for agriculture under the GATT. A notable example is the breaching of the prohibition against import quotas. Provisions introduced in the US to protect domestic price support programs include Section 22 and Section 32. Established under 1935 amendments to the Agricultural Adjustment Act of 1933, Section 22 allows for import quotas and Section 32 allows for export subsidies to aid domestic price support programs (Ryan and Tontz, p. 9).

Section 22 requires the Administration to impose qualitative restrictions or special fees whenever imports are likely to interfere with any US farm program. The existence of that section made it necessary in 1955 to request a waiver from GATT from the provisions of GATT Article 11. In 1964, legislation was passed allowing import quotas on beef, veal, and lard under no pretense of abiding by Article 11 because no stipulation was made to restrict production. Similar violation occurred for sugar and dairy output. The 1964 beef quota was never implemented; instead, voluntary restraint agreements were made with other countries to restrict imports. This met the letter of GATT but violated the spirit. Johnson, Kenzo, and Lardinois (p. 53) contend that "the critical first step is for the United States to give up the waiver of Article 11 obligations it obtained in 1955 and has maintained ever since."

Section 8e of the Agricultural Marketing Agreements Act, known as the "golden rule" added to marketing orders in 1954, specifies that size, grade, quality, and maturity regulations established under US fruit, vegetable, and nut marketing orders shall apply equally to imported products. The problem is that arbitrary regulations enacted by marketing orders to enhance income and restrain competition can be used against foreign competitors. An example is tomato minimum size limitations, which American tomato producers tried to use to keep out small fresh tomatoes imported from Mexico. The Secretary of Agriculture refused to countenance this trade barrier, and the provision became inoperative.

The US has restricted imports of subsidized pork and lumber from Canada, inviting retaliation by Canada to subsidized US grain exports. This chapter later lists various US low-interest or guaranteed loan credit arrangements and payment-in-kind subsidies. (Humanitarian food assistance is permitted under GATT.) Quotas restrict US imports of sugar, dairy products, beef, footwear, textiles, and apparel.

The Multifiber Arrangement permits a multilateral system of import quotas on textiles and apparel trade. The self-interest protectionist tendencies of Congress in contrast with the trade liberalization stance of the White House is seldom more apparent than in textiles. In July 1990, for example, the US Senate voted 68-32 to effectively scrap 38 bilateral textile, footwear, and apparel accords the US Administration had negotiated to restrict trading partners. Congress would replace the accords with a more restrictive arrangement. Only Canada and Israel, both of which have free trade agreements with the US, were exempted from the allowable annual increase of 1 percent in imports, which contrasts with an average 3.5 percent annual increase from all sources in recent years. Similar protectionist legislation was passed by a 60-39 Senate majority in 1985 and by 59-36 in 1988. Each of the bills was vetoed.

Trade Act of 1974 and Super 301

Congress continued interventions with a number of provisions allowing protection against imports in the Trade Act of 1974: Sections 201-203 allowed protection against an increase in imports judged to be a "substantial cause of injury" to US producers. Section 331 allowed protection against foreign government payments of a "bounty or grant" to assist exports. Section 321 provided protection against dumping at less than "fair value", defined as less than the home market price. Section 341 was used to stop violations of US patent laws.

Section 301 of the Trade Act of 1974 is the chief policy mechanism for confronting unfair trading practices. It authorizes the President to take appropriate action, including retaliation, to end those practices.

Section 301 was designed to address issues not addressed by other sections including the EC's flour export subsidies to third-world countries, Canada's quotas on egg imports, and the like. Section 301 cases are administered by the US Trade Representative.

The "super 301" provision of the *Omnibus Trade and Competitiveness Act* of 1988 took Section 301 of the Trade Act of 1974 further by requiring the USTR to name countries using unfair trade methods. If 12 to 18 months of negotiations failed to reach agreement with the offending country, retaliation was called for by law. The President could postpone retaliation if the offending country was making a good faith effort to negotiate a solution. Super 301 expired in 1991.

In May 1989, President Bush designated Japan, Brazil, and India for barriers to US exports. It is notable that two of the three offenders were less developed countries. Such unilateral action to correct world trade distortions is highly applauded by many Americans but has shortcomings:

1. Unilateral action to reduce foreign trade barriers ignores the delicately balanced formal trade arrangements established under previous multilateral negotiations.
2. Retaliation often hurts the US more than the intended target country and has innocent victims. In 1988, the US placed a 35 percent tariff on Canadian red cedar shingles; Canada retaliated with a 30 percent tariff on oatmeal, Christmas trees, and other items. In 1985, the US imposed duties on imports of European pasta in retaliation for discriminatory duties on US citrus. The European Community responded by raising duties on US walnuts and other commodities.

3. Whèn the US runs a large federal budget deficit in a full-employment economy, the Japanese do us a favor by financing the deficit with dollars acquired through a trade surplus. American macroeconomic policy was a larger source of US-Japan trade imbalance in the 1980s than were Japanese trade barriers. Countries with trade surpluses became scapegoats for US macroeconomic policy failures too painful to confront.
4. Trade deficits arise from normal workings of well-functioning markets. Even if each country has no overall net trade balance deficit, when trade is multilateral any one country is likely to have surpluses with some countries and deficits with others. Countries with profitable internal investment opportunities are likely to run trade deficits when external investments are being made in the country and surpluses when investments are being repaid.
5. The US has major trade distortions of its own -- it well might place these on the table to trade for concessions from other nations with trade barriers.

AGRICULTURAL EXPORT ASSISTANCE, PREFERENCES, AND PROMOTION

Whereas much of the legislation discussed above was designed to reduce imports, other legislation has encouraged imports. The *Generalized System of Preferences* (GSP) was authorized by the Trade Act of 1974 and amended by the *Trade and Tariff Act* of 1984. GSP provides duty-free access to developing countries. Imports under GSP have totalled approximately $1 billion annually in recent years. Sugar-producing countries in South and Central America have been major beneficiaries.

The *Caribbean Basin Economic Recovery Act*, known as the *Caribbean Basin Initiative* (CBI), removed import duties from products of a number of countries in the Caribbean. The *Customs and Trade Act* of 1990 included the *Caribbean Basin Economic Recovery Expansion Act* of 1990 and removed the 1995 termination data of the original CBI. A number of products of the countries are not eligible for duty exemption; some that are eligible such as sugar, beef, and veal are subject to quotas or assurances by the exporting countries that they will maintain current domestic food production for their citizens.

The United States maintains a host of programs to provide financial assistance, information, and market promotion to exports. Financial assistance in 1990 covered nearly one-fifth of all exports at a cost in credit, subsidies, or aid of approximately $8 billion (World Perspectives). Many of these programs originated directly or indirectly from farm commodity price and income support programs at home and abroad. Many of the programs were authorized by the *Food, Agriculture, Conservation, and Trade Act* (farm bill) of 1990. Major programs are discussed below and outlays for FYs 1987 and 1988 are shown in Table 11.1.

Export Cartel Guarantee Under GSM Programs

Agricultural export commodities furthering the government's long-term market development objectives may be eligible for credit guarantees under the short-term GSM-102 (six months to three years) and intermediate-term GSM-103 (3-10 years) programs. Credit for export sales is extended by private banks at "commercial" interest rates. The private interest rate would be higher without the guarantee.

Table 11.1. Value of US Agricultural Exports Assisted Under Government Programs, Fiscal Years 1987-1988.

Program Grouping/Program	FY87	FY88
	($ Million)	
Export Guarantee/Credit Programs		
Short-Term Export Credit Guarantees (GSM-102)	2,119.6	2,626.2
Intermediate-Term Export Credit Guarantees (GSM-103)	44.6	134.1
Export-Import Bank Insurance (FCIA)	211.0	NA
Export Subsidy Programs		
Export Enhancement (EEP)	1,116.8	2,323.9
EEP/GSM-102 Credit Guarantees	471.3	786.0
EEP/GSM-103 Credit Guarantees	109.2	160.3
Dairy Export Incentive (DEIP)	0.3	11.3
Subtotal: Commercial Export Programs	**4,072.8**	**6,041.8**
As Percent of Total Government-Assisted Farm Exports	*72.2%*	*79.5%*
OTHER PROGRAMS		
Direct Sales of Commodity Credit Corporation (CCC) Commodity Stocks	187.9	97.4
As Percent of Total Government-Assisted Farm Exports	*3.3%*	*1.3%*
FOOD AID PROGRAMS		
P.L. 480 - Title I/III Concessional Sales Program	788.0	716.0
P.L. 480 - Title II Food Donations	371.0	458.3
Section 416 Overseas Donations plus Food for Progress	159.2	194.0
Commodity Import Programs (CIPs)	59.6	94.5
Subtotal: Food Aid Programs	**1,377.8**	**1,462.8**
As Percent of Total Government-Assisted Farm Exports	*24.4%*	*19.2%*
TOTAL FARM EXPORTS ASSISTED UNDER US GOVERNMENT PROGRAMS	**5,638.5**	**7,602.0**
Total US Agricultural Exports	27,876.0	35,334.3
Government-Assisted Farm Exports as Percent of Total US Agricultural Exports	20.2%	21.5%

Source: Jurenas and Vogt (p. 4). See original for footnotes.
NA = Not available.

The Commodity Credit Corporation (CCC) administers the program through the Office of the Assistant General Sales Manager of the Foreign Agriculture Service (FAS), all components of the US Department of Agriculture. The credit guarantees have largely replaced direct interest subsidies or financing by the CCC. In the case of default by importers, the US Department of Agriculture covers the loss to the lender. In recent years, losses have been sizable to Poland and some other countries. The program promotes exports to countries too wealthy to be eligible for food aid but too poor to be unsubsidized commercial importers. GSM guarantees are for countries that need credit but are capable of paying principal and interest.   For countries for which credit worthiness is more questionable but yet not eligible for food aid, Eximbank remains a credit option.

GSM-102, in operation since 1980, is to provide $5 billion of agricultural export credit guarantees for each year from 1991 to 1995. GSM-103 operating from the Food Security Act of 1985, is to provide at least $500 million in guarantees each year from 1991 to 1995 (see Table 11.1 for FYs 1987 and 1988).

In 1991, GSM-102 extended $2.5 billion of credit guarantees, half of the overall available allocation, to the Soviet Union to purchase mostly grains. Purchases were under the *Long Term Agreement* (LTA), committing the USSR for up to 4 million metric tons of food and feed imports in 1991.

Export-Import Bank of the United States

This bank, frequently called the Eximbank, was established in 1934. It is an independent federal agency chartered by Congress to provide loans, guarantees, grants, and insurance on US exports. The Eximbank is governed by a five-member board of directors appointed for four-year terms by the President of the United States with approval by Congress. The Secretary of Commerce and USTR are nonvoting members. The board appoints Eximbank officers and prescribes policies.

Loan guarantees have been made for exports of timber and cattle but most agricultural commodities are eligible only for export credit insurance administered by the *Foreign Credit Insurance Association* (FCIA) for the Eximbank. Such insurance programs on agricultural exports totaled $211 million in FY1987 (Table 11.1).

Export Enhancement Program (EEP)

Export subsidies were used extensively in the 1960s but were terminated in 1972 when the "Great Grain Robbery" by the Soviet Union combined US export subsidies with market failure at a time of world grain shortage. The market failure was information failure -- the Soviets secretly purchased millions of bushels of wheat in total but in sufficiently small quantities from each exporting firm so that the price was not increased with each sale as it would have in an efficient market featuring full disclosure. The subsidy received so much public condemnation that it was not revived until 1985.

The *Export Enhancement Program* originated in 1985 largely to stop the loss of US international wheat and flour market share to heavily subsidized European Community exports. The export subsidy was justified as a means to maintain market share in the face of EC export subsidies, to provide a bargaining chip in GATT negotiations, to raise farm income, and to reduce burdensome stocks. The program is administered by the Foreign Agricultural Service. Private exporters submit bids to FAS to export commodities in return for a payment-in-kind subsidy bonus of commodities. FAS presumably accepts bids requiring the least bonus out of CCC stocks per unit of exports. As government stocks fell in 1991, payment in cash often replaced payment in kind to exporters.

EEP provides a bargaining chip in GATT negotiations. Willingness of the US to end the subsidy in return for like concessions from the EC tends to isolate the EC in negotiations and confront them with pressure for reform from competing exporters in addition to the US.

Market share is not useful if it is won at high cost relative to returns. The program is credited with expanding wheat exports from 10 percent to 30 percent in the 1980s but at an estimated cost of $4 per additional bushel of wheat exported (Paarlberg, p. 16). That was above the market price, the cost of production, or the cost of alternative means for the government to control excess capacity.

The program has subsidized mainly wheat and flour exports, especially to Middle East and North African markets contested with the EC. Because international markets are highly competitive and not easily separated, targeting wheat exports to selected countries has been only of limited success in combating EC export subsidies. The EEP program has had to be more widely used and has become very expensive (see Table 11.1). Criticisms are that (1) export subsidies merely transfer income from the US and EC to grain importers, (2) subsidies unfairly capture markets of smaller competing exporters such as Australia, (3) US consumers deserve the same low prices for products available to foreign buyers, (4) subsidies to US high-value exports would have a higher payoff, and (5) supply control, direct payments to producers, or other uses of EEP would be more cost-effective.

The *Dairy Export Incentive Program* (DEIP), which originated in 1987, operated much like EEP as a export bonus program to help US dairy products compete with subsidized EC sales in contested export markets. The program of dairy export assistance included assistance for meat exporters as a means to reduce surpluses accumulated under the whole-herd dairy cow buyout program of the 1980s.

Market Promotion Program (MPP)

The *Market Promotion Program* created by the 1990 farm bill replaces but is similar to the *Targeted Export Assistance* (TEA) program authorized by the 1985 farm bill. The 1990 farm bill authorized $200 million for MPP for each of the years 1991 through 1995.

MPP differs from the EEP in several respects: (1) EEP is limited to commodity exports suffering injury from unfair practices of competitors, whereas MPP is not so limited although priority is given to countering unfair trading practices; (2) EEP is an export subsidy that tends to reduce world export prices, whereas MPP is primarily for export product promotion designed to expand world markets without lowering price; (3) MPP focuses on high-value exports, whereas EEP emphasizes bulk commodities; and (4) MPP is administered by FAS mainly in joint efforts with Cooperators from trade organizations and private firms. Methods of promotion are wide-ranging and include brand identification, product demonstrations, liaison between domestic sellers and foreign buyers, and advertising through foreign media. In 1992, political backlash arose from large subsidies to fast-food chains.

Foreign Agriculture Service (FAS)

The FAS of the US Department of Agriculture conducts a wide-ranging set of activities to promote agricultural exports. These include the Cooperators program, overseas trade fairs and food exhibits, agricultural attaches and trade officers, and an extensive information system of foreign market statistics and analysis.

Many of these activities originated under the Agricultural Act of 1954 and were continued by the farm bills of 1981, 1985, and 1990, along with the Omnibus Trade and Development Act of 1988. The Cooperators program is a joint effort, which in 1989 included 44 nonprofit agricultural trade and producer associations, four domestic regional organizations or trade centers, and the National Association of State Departments of Agriculture. In FY 1989, FAS contributed $35 million and Cooperators contributed approximately $60 million to pay costs of the program.

Public Law 480

Public Law 480, originating with the Agricultural Trade and Assistance Act of 1954, has been the principal food aid program. This so-called Food for Peace program has been revised repeatedly.

Title I provides for the sale of US food to low-income countries for dollars at highly concessional payment terms -- 40 years at very low interest rates. The 1985 farm bill restored a feature to Title I removed in 1971 -- sales for payment in local currency. The local currency usually has little value outside the country, is subject to high inflation and hence decreasing value, and is not paid at all when waived under features of Title IV. One purpose of Title I is to expand commercial markets for US farm products.

Title II (food donations) and Title III are administered by the US Agency for International Development to achieve food security in recipient low-income countries. Under Title III, used to leverage policy reform and promote economic development, food aid usually is "monetized" by selling it through local markets at the going market price. Accumulated local currency (counterpart fund) is used to finance development projects such as agricultural research and extension in the recipient countries.

Projects must not expand foreign production of commodities in surplus in the US or compete with American commodities. PL 480 exports are not to compete with commercial exports of the United States or other friendly countries. Food aid must not discourage local production. It is impossible for food aid to avoid violating these provisions. Title I can require too much lead time and bureaucratic agreement over terms of sale to be of much use for emergency food aid. It can entail arbitrary repayment terms inequitably applied among countries and can reduce incentives for domestic producers. Title I also has been criticized for overemphasis on market development over foreign assistance.

Title II of PL 480 provides donations to meet emergency food needs. Food is donated to private voluntary organizations (PVOs), cooperatives, and non-US and multilateral relief agencies for distribution to the hungry. To avoid conflict of interest and corrupt practices, emergency food aid cannot be distributed through government or state-owned enterprises in the recipient country. The Agency for International Development is not allowed to distribute food under Title II.

Under Title III of PL 480, the 1990 farm bill provided a *Food for Development* grant program administered by AID. These grants were available to countries with per capita incomes of under $580 per year, with consumption less than 2300 calories of food per capita, and with child (under age 5) mortality rates of over 100 per 1,000 births.

Title II and III programs are of modest size (Table 11.1). Title I is the largest program of an overall PL 480 effort typically providing assistance of approximately $1.5 billion annually in recent years.

Other programs not part of PL 480 have functions similar to it. Section 416 of the Agricultural Act of 1949 provides authority for donation of surplus food from CCC stocks. AID is mainly responsible for administering the program.

The *Food for Progress* program, providing funds or surplus CCC commodity aid, originated under the 1985 farm bill and was continued by the 1990 farm bill. The program encourages free enterprise and policy reform in the agricultural sectors of developing countries, especially those with emerging democracies.

Commodity Import Programs (CIPs)

Countries judged important for US political and security interests receive assistance in the form of *commodity import programs*. A notable example is the *Economic Support Fund* (ESF) allocated among countries by the Department of State and administered at the local level by AID. CIPs, authorized by the *Foreign Assistance Act* of 1961 as amended, provided assistance of $95 million in FY1988, much of it corn and wheat (Table 11.1). Egypt and Pakistan have been major recipients.

ECONOMIC DEVELOPMENT ASSISTANCE

In the section on the World Bank in Chapter 9, a case was made that the United States has much to gain from promoting international economic development. US economic assistance encompasses more than food and influences third-world agricultural development and trade. Features of US foreign aid affect agricultural development abroad and demand for exports at home:

1. US foreign economic aid effort is *relatively* small. Japan is the world's largest single donor. The US contributes under 0.2 percent of its GNP to foreign economic assistance compared to nearly 1 percent by France, the Netherlands, and the Scandinavian countries. The US share of Organization for Economic Cooperation and Development (OECD) countries foreign economic assistance fell from 58 percent in 1965 to 29 percent in 1986 (Congressional Budget Office, p. 61). The US ranks last in effort (percent of GNP to economic assistance) among industrialized market economies.
2. Over half of US foreign aid has been military assistance. Of all US foreign aid outlays shown in Table 11.2, security assistance accounted for 51 percent in 1976-77 and for 62 percent in 1987. The Economic Support Fund can be used for a wide variety of purposes including agricultural development consistent with US security and political interests and totaled $3.5 billion in 1987. It was the largest single category of economic assistance.
3. US foreign aid is concentrated in a few relatively wealthy countries. Israel and Egypt alone accounted for about half of total US foreign aid in the mid-1980s. In the case of Israel, the aid allocation is not supervised by the US.
4. In recent decades, the share of all funds devoted to agriculture by the Agency for International Development has declined. Given the importance of agriculture to developing countries, that trend is of concern.

An increasing proportion of the aid budget was spent on international security assistance rather than development assistance in the 1976-1987 period (Table 11.2), but that trend is reversing with reduced East-West tensions. Needs in central and eastern Europe placed special demand on foreign aid funds in the early 1990s. Worldwide, US development assistance was spread thinly indeed.

Most bilateral development aid was through the Agency for International Development. Such aid helps to build the capacities of third-world countries' people and institutions through agriculture, nutrition, family planning, health, and education. Emphasis

Table 11.2. US Foreign Aid Outlays, 1976-77 and 1987.

Kind of Aid	1976-77 Average	1987
	(Million Dollars)	
Total Foreign Aid	5,609	11,614
Security Assistance	2,879	7,106
Military	1,998	3,640
Economic Support Fund	882	3,466
Development Assistance	2,730	4,508
Multilateral	1,085	1,306
Agency for International Development	989	2,012
Public Law 480	772	1,159
Other (Peace Corps, refugee assistance, etc.)	-116	31
	(As Percentage of Total Foreign Aid)	
Security Assistance	51	61
Development Assistance	49	39
	(As Percentage of Total Federal Outlays)	
Total Foreign Aid	1.44	1.14
Development Assistance	0.70	0.43

Source: Congressional Budget Office, p. 60.

in AID has varied over time from industrialization and modernization of infrastructure to basic needs (Carter Administration) to influencing national policies (Reagan Administration) through greater emphasis on the private sector and price incentives. In 1990, AID policy under the Bush Administration emphasized (1) policy dialogue with recipients, (2) private-sector initiatives, (3) technological transfer, and (4) institution building (higher education, research capabilities, etc.). Policy reform increasingly was a condition for aid.

The AID was established in 1961 to carry out the functions of the Foreign Assistance Act. The AID has responsibility for carrying out nonmilitary US foreign assistance programs and for continuous supervision and a general direction of all assistance programs under the Foreign Assistance Act. As noted earlier, it also helps to administer Titles II and III of PL 480. Multilateral development assistance is channeled with aid from other developed countries through the World Bank, Inter-American Bank, Asian Development Bank, African Development Bank, and other agencies such as the International Fund for Agricultural Development.

The following set of priorities are suggested for developed countries (DCs) to promote international trade and development in less developed countries (LDCs):

1. *Open markets to LDC exports.* If countries are not allowed to export, they can't import, and the world loses. Opening up DC markets would do more to promote development in LDCs than do current direct aid programs.

2. *Hold emergency food reserves.* Adequate food reserves are unlikely to be held by LDCs to meet emergency food needs. Nor is it economic for them to hold such reserves. Financial insurance to enable purchase of food in export markets when supplies are short is much cheaper for LDCs' food security than are food stocks held in the country or attempts at food self-sufficiency. LDCs must have a place to turn for food supplies in the world when nature and pestilence provide a short crop. Availability of international food reduces incentives for import-substitution and hence enhances demand for US farm exports. Food reserves can be held by food-exporting developed countries. To avoid disincentives to producers in recipient countries, food aid should be provided only for emergency purposes and for carefully supervised food-for-work programs.

3. *Basic research in DCs.* LDCs cannot afford basic research to improve agricultural productivity. It and lower birth rates are the brightest hopes for dispelling the Malthusian specter in the long run. Biotechnology offers vast promise, but LDCs cannot afford the luxury of investing in costly research with such uncertain payoffs and large spillover of benefits to other countries.

4. *Adaptive research in LDCs.* It is critical for the LDCs to have local research capacities to adapt research from elsewhere. Failure of LDCs to attract and hold the brightest and best scientists available to them and maintain operating support is a major oversight that needs to be corrected by the LDCs with sustained financial assistance from the DCs. Earnings from PL 480 imports can help pay for research and infrastructure investments. Technology for environmentally sound agriculture is being developed in the First World but it frequently must be modified to meet third-world needs.

5. *Improve infrastructure in LDCs.* The market alone will not provide adequate infrastructure in the form of roads, bridges, port facilities, and schools. Public sector involvement is essential. Adequate infrastructure assists the market to work better. Roads reduce hunger because food can be readily shipped from food surplus to shortage areas.

6. *Human resource development.* The major contribution of foreign aid is the development of skills and competence in human resources of the Third World. Higher education is only one part of that effort. DCs can help LDCs improve basic educational and vocational training facilities and services. Improved primary health care and family planning is possible in part from outside help in technology and funding from DCs.

7. *Macroeconomic, trade, and commodity program policies.* Unfavorable monetary-fiscal policies in the United States and high, rigid commodity price supports in the European Community and Japan have had unfavorable repercussions for LDCs in recent decades. One result is unstable world prices and markets as well as unfair competition in agricultural commodities. Ending or sharply revising such policies in developed countries would assist LDCs. Substantial efforts will be needed in the future to avoid rising levels of trade protection, especially as newly industrialized developing nations gain greater wealth to subsidize farmers.

NEW DIRECTIONS FOR TRADE POLICY

Americans do not agree on a strategic trade policy defined as a set of principles, laws, and institutions for increasing benefits from trade. Some critics say the United States has no agricultural trade policy. Others say no policy is the best policy.

Strategic trade policy recognizes that the US must act and react to policies of other nations to be competitive. Several issues and components of a coherent policy follow.

1. *US Department of International Trade.* A cabinet-level Department of International Trade has been proposed to consolidate the activities now performed by various government Departments and the Office of US Trade Representative. US agricultural trade policy is now formulated mostly by the US Department of Agriculture and the Office of US Trade Representative but policy is implemented by the US Department of Agriculture and to a lesser extent Commerce. Some have proposed that the Department of Commerce could be included in the Department of International Trade.

   Some contend that a unified Department of International Trade containing the former Department of Commerce would be unduly protectionist. However, if the behavior of the US Trade Representative is any guide, to date it has been free-trade oriented. Clayton Yeutter, formerly USTR, stated that "the attitudes of the Commerce Department, which have from time to time seemed protectionist in nature, would overwhelm the open trade philosophy that has traditionally been attributed to the Office of US Trade Representative" (see Henneberry *et al.*, p. 2). In addition, some people believe that agricultural issues would be subordinated to industrial concerns in a department consolidating government trade policy and implementation.

   A full cabinet-level comprehensive international trade office would organize the policy-making and implementing process for international trade. Although the Reagan Administration proposed such a department, Congress showed little interest. Between 1951 and 1975 more than 14 studies addressed the reorganization of trade and policy activities.

   Advocates of a department note that international trade policy decisions made by one government agency, such as the US Department of Agriculture, sometimes conflict with decisions made in other government agencies. For example, attempts to increase US agricultural exports to Japan are blunted by lobbying to place quotas or tariffs on industrial imports from Japan. A single Department of International Trade could make US trade policy more coherent and forceful. The Department would give trade policy greater visibility and increased importance. Also, this department would be in a position to obtain compromises from individual groups whose interests must be reconciled in a comprehensive trade policy and negotiations.

2. *US Commodity Marketing Boards.* Would American farmers and consumers be served better if exports were handled by government boards rather than by several private exporting firms?

   Presently, private (including cooperative) exporting firms handle US grain exports. A wheat board would be a central government authority directing the marketing of wheat. Individual boards might be established also for coarse grains, oilseeds, cotton, and other commodities. With export decisions centralized, producers would give up title to their commodities at harvest. All storage and marketing functions would be managed by the government. All producers would receive the same price (pool price) adjusted for location and quality.

Advocates of an export board note that a government agency operates as buyer or seller in a large part of world agricultural trade. A government grain board would give the United States more bargaining power to realize a larger share of the potential gains from trade. A government grain board presumably could better implement trade policy decisions than could several private exporting firms making decisions independently. A single commodity board would be less susceptible to market segmentation and myopia which allowed the American market to be victimized in the Soviet grain purchases of the early 1970s.

Opponents of an export board note that a grain board would force producers to accept the board's marketing decisions and pooled prices. An export board might be viewed as an agent of government and be susceptible to manipulation by political forces not in producers' best interests. Individual firm marketing strategies would be sacrificed with no guarantee of price increases or reductions in price fluctuations. The aggressive marketing and extensive information systems maintained by private exporters would be lost. (However, some export boards such as the Canadian Wheat Board make decisions on sales but leave actual delivery to private firms.)

Grain boards of foreign countries have not performed better than private firms. Their performance would have been even worse in the absence of private US grain markets, such as Chicago futures on which to base prices. Boards might be tempted to control exports of high-value products, a market segment too complex for the public sector to run efficiently. Government central planning and industrial policies have failed globally. To manage trade under marketing boards would indicate we have learned nothing from history.

3. *A Grain Cartel.* Should the United States actively seek arrangements with other countries to control prices and stabilize markets? These arrangements might be joint with other exporting countries or with importing countries. Such agreements could take various forms.

   A cartel would raise the international price by restricting the quantity of exports. A cartel may raise total revenue by restricting supply if export demand quantity changes relatively little in response to a change in price. In this case the percentage decline in quantity is less than the percentage jump in price and, as a result, total revenues rise.

   An alternative is more international commodity agreements, multilateral agreements among normally competing countries to affect the terms of trade. The terms of trade affected by an international commodity agreement may include the price level, quantity sold, quantity produced, or quantity held in reserve. Legally, commodity agreements are treaties among nations.

   Another alternative is bilateral trade agreements -- a contract between two countries that specifies the quantity of a commodity to be traded over a certain period. Bilateral trade agreements typically run for a period of 3 to 5 years, although they may be simple 1-year agreements that are renewed annually. Normally, the agreements specify the minimum quantity an importer will purchase and the maximum the exporting country will supply.

Opponents contend that a grain cartel could unduly disrupt world food markets just as OPEC disrupted energy markets. Grain importers would turn to noncartel exporting countries and pursue self-sufficiency policies in an attempt to increase domestic production and reduce imports. Exporters not in the cartel would expand production and exports.

Although a need for price stability is used to justify multilateral and bilateral commodity agreements, their true objective from the exporter's standpoint is to raise prices. Multilateral agreements such as those for wheat and coffee have not worked. Bilateral trade agreements may commit so much production to contract markets that the few remaining open markets would experience great price volatility as they struggle to balance supply and demand.

For a grain cartel to raise farm revenues in exporting countries, the demand that exporters face must be unresponsive to price. Economists do not agree on the elasticity of demand for grain exports, but many contend that, after about 4 years of restricted exports and high prices under a cartel, cartel revenues would fall.

International agreements and cartels in the past have not worked to control price; they probably will not work in the future. Such agreements are now largely out of favor. Multilateral and regional (e.g., FTAs) arrangements, which attempt to open trade (at least among members) rather than extract monopoly profits, are preferred.

4. *Trade Embargoes.* The effects of trade embargoes are the same as export quotas. They reduce the quantity of exports, lower the domestic price, and raise the international price for the benefit of US competitors. Compensation to damaged US producers taxes other Americans.

Since 1973, several export embargoes have been imposed.

- A general restriction on exports of selected oilseeds and oilseed products applied in 1973.
- A moratorium on grain sales to the Soviet Union in 1974.
  Restrictions on grain sales to the Soviet Union and Poland in 1975.
- An embargo on agricultural commodity sales to the Soviet Union beginning January 4, 1980, and lasting until April 24, 1981.
- A restriction on agricultural and other exports to Iraq beginning in 1990.

The first three restrictions were to restrain and stabilize domestic prices in the face of short world supplies. The restrictions were short lived, were of modest scope, and had small impact on US exports. For example, by August 1, 1973, the order was given to honor 100 percent of soybean contracts following the embargo announcement June 27, 1973. Food supplies in Japan and other nations were not jeopardized. The fourth embargo differed from the first three in that it was designed to discipline the USSR after the invasion of Afghanistan. The fifth embargo, against Iraq, also was designed to achieve national security objectives.

Most past embargoes were economically counterproductive: they hurt America more than they hurt the intended victim. An exception is when other countries joined the embargo as in the case of the somewhat effective embargo against Iraq. Because US embargoes largely were ineffective, they never jeopardized world food supplies. Embargoes cannot be ruled out as long as food, national security, and politics are linked -- as they always will be.

A series of laws are designed to discourage future grain embargoes (for an excellent summary, see World Perspectives, pp. 114, 115). The *Export Administration Act* (EAA) no longer allows national security sanctions on farm products. "Foreign policy" and "short-supply" sanctions on farm exports remain a possibility but presumably only so long as they can be shown to be effective.

Opponents of embargoes note that farm production and trade are so decentralized that no one country can impose effectively a grain embargo against any other country. A unilateral embargo is counterproductive for the United States. Embargoes harm America's reputation as a reliable source of supply and traditional importers turn to more reliable sources. For these reasons, export embargoes are not effective political or economic weapons except with committed multilateral support as in the case of Iraq.

Trade embargoes are a political tool that will be used occasionally whether or not producers like them. An appropriate policy for producers is legislation to (a) ensure that embargoes will be imposed only in a national emergency and with appropriate compensation to producers, (b) require approval by Congress for continuation beyond 60 days, and (c) recognize the sanctity of existing contracts.

5. *Promoting Third-World Agriculture.* Should the United States help developing countries improve yields of cotton, grain, and other crops competing with American farm commodities?

The prosperity of developing countries is the key to their increased imports of our farm products. Their economic progress depends on agricultural progress. US exports can be expanded as a result of their accelerated economic growth. As income grows so does the demand for meat, other livestock products, and grains to feed livestock. US exports of soybeans and feed grains to these countries will increase, although US exports of rice, wheat, or cotton may decrease (see also Chapter 1).

6. *Removing Requirements for Use of US Ships.* The American government, in an effort to support the merchant marine industry, mandated that three-fourths of the bulk commodity shipments under PL 480 be transported on US flag vessels.

Proponents of US cargo preference contend that such legislation supports maritime workers and the merchant marine industry. Without this legislation, they contend, foreign flag vessels would replace the US maritime industry.

Opponents contend that excessive cost of shipping on US flag vessels has retarded US agricultural exports. The added expense of the cargo preference requirement can offset real aid benefits, rendering such assistance cost-ineffective. If national security is of concern, opponents contend that US ocean freight can be handled by foreign flag (but often American owned) vessels in national emergencies.

7. *Export Instability and Buffer Stocks.* Some (Tweeten, 1989, ch. 1) contend that economic instability is the major problem facing commercial US agriculture. Trade is a major source of that instability.

In the 1980s, the Soviet Union and China accounted for 63 percent of variation in US farm exports (Table 11.3). Major developed-country markets such as Japan, Canada, and the European Community were steady importers. They were responsible for very little variation in US exports. Some areas such as Africa in the 1980s actually reduced variation in our exports by importing countercyclically. Perhaps a reason is because food aid was greatest when commercial exports were down.

Table 11.3. Share of US Farm Export Variation by Source, 1970-1990.

Country or Region	1970s	1980s
	(Percent)	
China	8.3	34.3
Soviet Union	31.1	28.8
Latin America	17.8	14.4
West and South Asia	5.0	11.3
EC-12	3.0	5.1
Canada	7.4	3.9
Other Asia and Oceania	6.6	2.2
Japan	4.3	0.8
Africa and Others	16.5	-0.8
	100.0	100.0

Source: Unpublished worksheets from Michael Simms.

The main conclusion from Table 11.3 is that second-world countries and, to a lesser extent, third-world countries were the major sources of export variation in the 1970s and 1980s. Successful political and economic stabilization programs for such countries could reduce variation in American exports while maintaining or even expanding our total volume of exports.

The temptation to reduce export instability by export embargoes and other trade restrictions needs to be resisted because of large deadweight costs. Slaughter of livestock and release of land in conservation use are alternative responses. Buffer stock policies offer greatest promise, however.

The US holds much of the world's carryover stocks. From 1979 to 1983, for example, the US accounted for nearly 44 percent of the world's carryover stocks of wheat and over 80 percent of coarse grains. The US share has fallen as surpluses have accumulated in the European Community in recent years.

Proponents contend that US reserves of grain help the United States capture a larger share of world markets if world supplies are short and prices high. Reserves give the US the reputation of being a reliable supplier. As a wealthy nation with an abundance of agricultural products, the United States plays an important role in stabilizing world markets and meeting emergency food needs. The private storage trade may not provide sufficient reserves. Importing countries would probably adjust their domestic grain policies if they were to face more risk of shortages. These adjustments could include pursuing self-sufficiency policies, negotiating bilateral contracts with other exporters, and building their own stocks. These adjustments would eventually lead to fewer US exports.

Opponents of US reserves contend that holding of buffer stocks for the emergency needs of the rest of the world is too costly to US taxpayers. We have allowed ourselves to become the world's residual supplier of grains and oilseeds.

Our policies have allowed foreigners to transfer costs of storage to US taxpayers. Excessive buffer stocks unduly depress farm prices.

The US can provide food security without the massive, costly, market-depressing public buffer stocks held in the 1960s and 1980s. Others such as the EC can hold more stocks. By cutting exports and domestic livestock feeding, this country can meet domestic food needs even if the weather is unfavorable and production low. The private trade might hold sufficient stocks if the competition from governmental storage programs were removed (see Pai and Tweeten for comparisons).

8. *Nonrecourse Loan Rates.* Farm commodity support loan rates act as a price floor for US agricultural exports. In most years since 1950, the nonrecourse loan program has supported American farm grain prices and world grain prices. Under the 1981 farm bill, US loan rates exceeded world commodity prices. The result was a loss of exports and a price umbrella that encouraged competing exporters.

High loan rates price American farm products out of world markets, reduce much needed farm export earnings, require export subsidies to retain markets, and encourage idling and waste of productive resources. If farm income is to be supported, it is appropriate to use direct payments to small, poor producers rather than to use nonrecourse loans, supply controls, and export subsidies. Lower loan rates as under the 1985 and 1990 farm bills help to retain US competitiveness and reduce excess production capacity and stocks.

9. *Tightening Antidumping Laws.* The definition of foreign cost is so vague that virtually any import can be unilaterally restricted for violating US dumping laws. Such laws enacted in the name of "fair trade" are actually protectionist. The Institute for International Economics estimates that such laws and barriers cost the average American family $1,200 per year (Fair trade, p. 30).

Vague rules forbidding "dumping" of foreign products in the US are designed to protect American industries from foreign competition. In conjunction with the GATT, rules to restrict "dumping" need to be rewritten. Selling of foreign goods in the US below cost is a legitimate and US-welfare-enhancing policy in many if not most instances. US consumers benefit by more than producers and taxpayers lose. "Dumping" charges are an all too convenient means for domestic firms to escape foreign competition and to deny US consumers the welfare benefits of lower cost imports.

Of course, *predatory* practices need to be stopped. But predatory practices require "deep pockets" and a large share of the market to drive out competitors. Most "dumping" cases do not deal with such cases but rather with foreign firms with a small share of markets. Tighter requirements to prove guilt, and damage to the national economy (not just producers), and use of impartial international hearing panels would reduce the frequency of "dumping" charges and retaliation to protect local industry.

10. *Adjustment Assistance.* A job safety net is essential to make humane a market-oriented trade policy. Adjustment assistance helps workers displaced by foreign competition. The *Trade Adjustment Act* of 1962 attempted to do just that but was fatally flawed. It (a) provided mostly unemployment compensation rather than training and mobility assistance for new jobs, (b) could not sort out workers displaced by foreign competition versus other reasons, and (c) was bureaucratically lethargic so that assistance came too late -- workers had already made adjustments. An improved public policy would help any displaced workers

(not just by imports), would provide low interest loans for improving their skills, would provide knowledge of new jobs, and would obtain repayment of retraining loans out of future earnings.

11. *The New Protectionism.* Sanitary and phytosanitary safety and health regulations, environmental legislation, and animal welfare laws could be the foundation for a new *green protectionism.* As nations formulate such regulations for farmers based not on scientific evidence but public activism, their farmers justly contend that higher resulting costs of production require protection from lower priced foreign competition. The difficult challenge will be to work out in international fora the worldwide common standards that are non-trade-distorting, acceptable to rich and poor nations, and meet legitimate needs to protect people, animals, and the environment.

12. *Redirecting Aid.* With the end of the Cold War, American policy toward third-world nations can be based less on political consideration and more on need and demonstration of domestic economic reform essential for aid to stimulate growth. Economic assistance can replace much military assistance. Corrupt, despotic, and inefficient governments need no longer be supported just because they are anti-communist.

13. *Rejecting an Industrial Policy.* It is appropriate to reject an *industrial policy* that picks "winning" industries for subsidies and ignores "losers." But with the decline of the Cold War, considerable research can be redirected from military to civilian uses. *Sound domestic structural* (including infrastructure and education), *monetary, fiscal, science, and environmental policies are the key to international competitiveness.* Basic and applied civilian science, schools, and infrastructure have been neglected in America.

14. *Other Policies.* Tax policies that discourage savings and investment and encourage debt-financing erode economic growth, stability, and trade. Double-taxation of corporate profits hardly promotes investment. As noted in Chapter 8, an antitrust policy that avoids concentration of power promotes exports. An economy open to world trade is one of the best antitrust policies. An effective but modest-size public sector doing a few vital things well is a formula for international competitiveness. Full-employment federal budget deficits cause high real interest and exchange rates, reducing exports and weakening the nation's ability to compete. Public investment in science, education, and infrastructure enhances competitiveness.

TRADE NEGOTIATION STRATEGY

Negotiating strategy is a most important component of a trade policy. Based on analysis reported in this and previous chapters, a trade negotiating stance is proposed herein with four key concepts summarized as follows:

1. The first-best policy is worldwide free trade. Free trade is a worthy but elusive target for which we strive through bilateral and multilateral negotiations but will not attain.

2. In a world of trade distortions, the second-best trade policy is confrontation that reduces trade barriers. Political and economic pressures on other countries can

win concessions moving the United States and others toward free trade. That approach too has severe limitations.

3. The third-best policy is unilateral free trade by the US. The third-best policy by default becomes the preferred policy after (1) and (2) have been tried and have failed.
4. The fourth-best or worst policy is continuation of failed policies used to confront countries refusing to dismantle market distortions.

This strategy is from common sense, empirical results reported later, and the tit-for-tat game theory strategy found to be optimal in Chapter 7. Each of these components is discussed in more detail below. Past agricultural trade strategy has been preoccupied with a free trade strategy that is unattainable and a second-best strategy of confrontation. The continuing commitment to the second-best strategy has resulted in the fourth-best or worst strategy. A superior course of action is unilateral movement toward free trade by the US. Such strategy will encourage other countries to move toward free trade.

Free Trade -- The First-Best Policy

Trade principles and practice demonstrate that a first-best world would feature free trade with its advantages of specialization and comparative advantage. Empirical studies cited in Chapter 3 indicate that free agricultural trade would increase annual world income by $51 billion, would sharply diminish variability of world food prices, and would benefit the United States given its comparative advantage in grain, soybeans, and meat production.[2]

To be sure, some competitiveness studies indicate that parts of Argentina and Brazil can produce soybeans more cheaply than the US, parts of Argentina and Australia can produce wheat more cheaply than can parts of the US, and parts of Argentina and Thailand can produce corn more cheaply than can the US (see Barkema *et al.* and Barkema and Drabenstott for the list of sources; also OTA). But the natural resource intensive agricultures in these countries are unable to supply world food needs at the world prices that would be associated with open markets. The US share of world trade would rise in the absence of trade distortions.

Chapters 9 and 10 noted that the United States has taken leadership for over half a century to promote, with some success, free trade through multilateral negotiations and reciprocal, bilateral trade agreements. The tradition was continued in the Uruguay Round of the General Agreement on Tariffs and Trade (GATT) negotiations.

Negotiations under the GATT have had considerable success reducing nonagricultural industry trade barriers but little success reducing agricultural trade barriers. Regardless of the degree of US commitment to free trade of agricultural commodities, the likelihood of global free trade is zero. America must continue multilateral agricultural trade liberalization through GATT but only modest success can be expected.

---

[2]The $51 billion is estimated deadweight or national income losses for 1995 in 1985 dollars. The Anderson-Tyers model does not include interventions of centrally planned countries, and does not include oilseeds and tropical agricultural products. Deadweight losses also do not include costs of instability, foregone specialization, imperfect market behavior, rent-seeking lobbying, failure to gain internal and external economies of size, and other indirect effects. If these were included, the cost shown here and later of policies interfering with world trade would be far larger.

Confrontation to Reduce Trade Barriers --
The Second-Best Policy

Because of the limitations of multilateral trade negotiations under the GATT, the US has placed major emphasis on confrontation to reduce barriers to trade. This is apparent from former Secretary of Agriculture Yeutter's statement:

> Some have expressed concern that we might unilaterally phase out our EEP program, dairy quotas, beef quotas, and a lot of other items without obtaining similar commitments from our trading partners. This is ludicrous, of course. We will agree to changes in our programs only if there are reciprocal, multilateral actions by our trading partners.

The commitment of the United States to this policy is evident in numerous challenges to foreign impediments to trade as noted in Chapters 9 and 10. The threat of retaliation if negotiations failed sometimes helped our bargaining. The *Super 301* provision of The Omnibus Trade and Competitiveness Act of 1988 had brought some concessions from Japan and Brazil by 1990. India, the third country named to the list of countries with sizable barriers to trade, proved less tractable. Retaliation offers only modest trade liberalizing opportunities. Worldwide, distortions of agricultural trade worsened in the 1980s.

Despite highly publicized confrontations with Japan over access to beef and citrus markets, the principal instrument of confrontation has been the Export Enhancement Program (EEP) subsidizing primarily wheat exports in markets contested with the EC. Data cited earlier indicated that EEP is not cost-effective.

Although EEP is a small part of the $300 billion transferred worldwide from taxpayers and consumers to farmers each year, as of 1991 the cost of the program was continuing to rise. The US confrontation with the EC over contested grain markets was not getting results. The major beneficiaries of these transfers were consumers in these contested markets, which consist in large part of eastern bloc countries and third-world countries. Producers within these countries are unjustly hurt by price disincentives resulting from low cost imports.

The continued aggressive pursuit of a policy of confrontation has other drawbacks for the United States:

1. Export subsidies, quotas, commodity programs, and other devices instituted to confront competitors develop a clientele of supporters making such devices difficult to terminate. For example, it is naive to expect that a wheat export cartel to force free markets on buyers would be dismantled in the unlikely case that it succeeded. Vested interests earning economic rents continue distortions long after any need for them has passed. Billions are spent each year on lobbying to maintain distortions.
2. The budget costs of US confrontational policies places additional pressure on the federal budget already burdened by deficit spending and pressing alternative needs for funds. Additional spending requires additional borrowing from foreigners and greater foreign debt by the US.
3. Competing "friendly" exporters operating more nearly open markets often lack the resources to compete with subsidies and are disadvantaged. Examples are countries in the Cairns Group. Many third-world exporters desperately need foreign exchange for economic development. Developing countries whose producers are discouraged by short-run prices held below longer-term market

equilibrium by EC-US confrontation may be prone to food shortages when confrontation policies change.

4.   An atmosphere of confrontation invites needless trade wars. An example is the Gephardt Congressional proposal to impose a duty on imports from countries accounting for much of the trade deficit. But trade deficits are quite normal when the US runs large federal budget deficits in a full-employment economy -- as noted at the beginning of Chapter 6.

5.   The US is losing its capacity for confrontation and hence its bargaining advantage. Large federal budget deficits and associated large trade surpluses of (say) Taiwan and Japan with the United States seem to give the US a bargaining advantage. That is, countries with trade surpluses have the most to lose in a confrontation that could terminate trade. However, the United States has become dependent on foreigners to finance federal debt. Withdrawal of these funds would devastate the US economy.

In theory, the winner in the subsidy battle over world food markets is the party with the strongest will and the "deepest pockets." Much has been written about which of the two antagonists, the US or the EC, will triumph in this confrontation. In all likelihood, both will lose, as will competing exporters.

Unilateral Dismantling of Trade Barriers --
The Third-Best Policy

Unilateral trade liberalization has been rejected in the past. Refusal to drop trade barriers unless other countries dismantle theirs is essential bargaining rhetoric, but is not sound policy after negotiations are over.

An examination of who gains and loses from trade helps to understand why countries maintain protectionism despite potential gains from trade and why the Uruguay Round of trade negotiations was disappointing to many. Estimated gains to producers, consumers, taxpayers, and the public at large from agricultural trade and commodity program liberalization are shown for 1989 in Table 11.4. Drought in 1988 temporarily reduced excess capacity and raised world prices, reducing deadweight costs (national income losses) of protectionism to only $11 billion in 1989, much less than levels for earlier years shown in Chapter 3. (Totals would be much higher if lobbying, administrative, and third-world costs were fully included.)[3] Commodity supports as well as border distortions were assumed to be eliminated at considerable loss to producers and gain to governments (or taxpayers), but national benefits (NB) would remain as shown if governments compensated producers for losses with direct payments decoupled from incentives to produce, consume, and trade.

Several conclusions from Table 11.4 are notable:

1.   Each of the countries or regions benefits as a whole from liberalization. Net national social benefits are positive in every case.

2.   Taxpayers gain in every country or region. However, in some cases they would be worse off if direct payments were used to compensate producers for loses -- but not if the direct payments were from consumers as well.

----

[3]The model included third-world and other countries but results for third-world countries were not considered to be very reliable due to data deficiencies.

Table 11.4. Benefits from Trade Liberalization, 1989.

Country or Region	Unilateral Liberalization				Multilateral Liberalization			
	PS	CS	GS	NB	PS	CS	GS	NB
				($ Millions)				
Australia	-133	-3	150	14	581	-361	150	370
Canada	-1,533	75	1,812	354	-617	-703	1,812	492
EC	-15,280	15,808	4,069	4,597	-12,337	12,162	4,069	3,894
Japan	-14,080	16,418	2,263	4,601	-13,292	14,154	2,263	3,125
US	-11,434	763	13,392	2,721	-7,642	-3,167	13,392	2,583
W. Europe	-3,057	3,576	269	788	-2,567	2,881	269	583

PS = producer surplus; CS = consumer surplus; GS = government savings; and NB = net benefits.
Source: Makki *et al.*

3. Consumers in the EC and Japan receive massive gains of from $12 billion to $16 billion from liberalization. Consumers in Australia, Canada, and the US lose under multilateral liberalization as higher world prices are passed to their domestic markets.

4. Most importantly for this section, the table indicates that the United States and the EC, the two most influential participants in the Uruguay Round, would gain more from unilateral than from multilateral trade liberalization! This result is not a quirk of this trade model or year 1989. Similar conclusions have been reached by other researchers working independently with different models and with earlier years of data. For example, analysts estimated net welfare gains to the United States to range from $3.9 billion (Anderson and Tyers) to $4.2 billion (Roningen *et al.*) with *unilateral* liberalization compared to only $3.1 billion to $3.9 billion for the respective studies with *multilateral* liberalization. Hertel *et al.* and Johnson *et al.* also showed major gains to the US from unilateral liberalization.

If unilateral liberalization pays so handsomely, why hasn't it happened? Table 11.5, which presents impacts of trade liberalization in the "two-person" game framework illustrated earlier in Chapter 7 on strategic trade theory, provides some clues. To save space, results are shown only for the principal trade players (the US versus the EC or ROW), and for producers, consumers, and the public at large. Payoffs are liberalization gains compared to the status quo (interventions) in 1989.

Main results are summarized below first for national benefits, for consumer benefits, and finally for producer benefits.

National Benefits

If the US maintains the status quo of 1989 distortions, the rest of the world (ROW, all countries other than the US and including the EC) gains nothing if it too maintains distortions but gains $8,208 million if it liberalizes trade (see Net National Benefits panel 1, Table 11.5). If the US liberalizes agricultural trade, ROW loses $1,799 million if it maintains distortions but gains $5,758 million if it liberalizes agricultural trade. In principle, the US would expect unilateral liberalization from a rational ROW.

Table 11.5.   Payoffs Matrices, US vs. Rest of the World and EC, for Gains in 1989 Compared to Status Quo.

		Strategies	
		\$ Million (US , ROW or EC)	
Net National Benefits			
		Status Quo	Liberalize
		1. ROW	
United States	**Status Quo**	(0 , 0)	(145 , 8208)
	Liberalize	(2721 , -1799)	(2583 , 5758)
		2. EC	
United States	**Status Quo**	(0 , 0)	(171 , 4597)
	Liberalize	(2721 , 333)	(2608 , 4062)
Consumer Benefits			
		3. ROW	
United States	**Status Quo**	(0 , 0)	(-2965 , 9979)
	Liberalize	(763 , -11570)	(-3167 , -136)
		4. EC	
United States	**Status Quo**	(0 , 0)	(-3074 , 15808)
	Liberalize	(763 , 37)	(-2069 , 13450)
Producer Benefits			
		5. ROW	
United States	**Status Quo**	(0 , 0)	(3110 , -10334)
	Liberalize	(-11434 , 9979)	(-7642 , -2669)
		6. EC	
United States	**Status Quo**	(0 , 0)	(3245 , -15280)
	Liberalize	(-11434 , -14)	(-8715 , -13457)

Source: Makki *et al.*

If ROW liberalizes, the US gains only \$145 million if it maintains 1989 policies but gains \$2,583 million if it liberalizes trade. If ROW is irrational and does not liberalize, the US will have no gain if it maintains barriers but will gain \$2,721 million if it liberalizes unilaterally. When the US liberalizes, the choice confronting ROW, to lose $1,799 million if it retains distortions but to gain $5,788 million by liberalizing, would appear to make the latter strategy for ROW irresistible. Multilateral liberalization is a Nash equilibrium (see Chapter 7), a Pareto-better position (it makes both the US and ROW better off, compared to the status quo) and a social optimum for the world (the sum of payoffs is greatest).[4] Multilateral liberalization is not a Prisoners' Dilemma. That Dilemma depicted in Chapter 7 featured an equilibrium outcome less satisfactory to participants than the social optimum of a cooperative game.

ROW in fact is a conglomerate of many countries which, though net gainers, may include many losers from liberalization. Hence it is instructive to examine the optimal strategy for the key US opponent to free trade, the EC, in the second panel in Table 11.5. The payoff matrix indicates that if the US maintains the status quo the EC will gain nothing by maintaining the status quo but will gain $4,597 million by liberalizing trade. If the US liberalizes trade, the EC will gain only $333 million by retaining distortions but will gain $4,062 million by liberalizing trade. Thus the US would expect the EC to liberalize. The payoff to a liberalized EC would be greatest if the US maintains distortions but that strategy makes no sense for the US because the additional payoff is much greater, $2,608 million, by liberalizing trade when the EC liberalizes.

It pays the EC or the US to liberalize whatever its opponent does, hence the Nash equilibrium and socially optimal strategy from world perspective is again multilateral liberalization. However, it must be kept in mind that the best position for either the US or EC is unilateral liberalization. Each liberalizes with the hope that the other will be foolish enough to retain distortions. Thus the numbers in Table 11.5 and elsewhere reveal that the proper strategy in the Uruguay Round was for each main country to try to sabotage the agreement so it could go home and liberalize unilaterally. That would have brought multilateral liberalization when all countries acted. Presumably countries know this and would be expected to agree in multilateral negotiation to free trade, but with protocols to make adjustments less painful.

Clearly, the explanation for continuing trade distortions is not to be found in net national social welfare payoffs shown in the top two panels of Table 11.5. Neither can it be found in taxpayer payoffs noted earlier in Table 11.4. We must look to consumer and producer payoffs in the bottom four panels of Table 11.5.

Consumer Benefits

If the US liberalizes, ROW consumers lose $11,570 million if ROW maintains the status quo but only $136 million if it liberalizes. If the US maintains the status quo, consumers of ROW gain $9,979 million by liberalizing but gain nothing with the status quo. If ROW liberalizes trade, US consumers will lose $3,167 million if the US liberalizes but only $2,965 million if the US maintains trade and commodity program distortions. Thus the Nash equilibrium for consumers is for ROW to liberalize but for the US to retain distortions. However, keep in mind that, given no evidence that ROW in fact is liberalizing, the optimal strategy for US consumers is to liberalize trade because they gain $763 million annually under 1989 conditions.

The fourth panel for US versus EC consumers shows massive gains to the latter from liberalization. Given EC liberalization, the best strategy for US consumers is liberalization also. American consumers lose $3,074 million annually by maintaining the status quo compared to $2,069 million by liberalizing. Whatever the EC does, the best strategy for US

---

[4]The combined payoff is slightly greater when ROW liberalizes while the US maintains the status quo. That small difference is insignificant, however.

consumers is liberalization. And whether or not the US liberalizes, the best strategy for the EC is liberalization.

Although multilateral liberalization is a Nash equilibrium for consumers, American consumers are best off with US liberalization while the EC or ROW foolishly maintains the status quo. In short, Tables 11.3 and 11.4 make a strong case that US trade distortions cannot be justified for rational taxpayers, consumers, or the public at large.

Producer Benefits

We must look to payoffs of producers to explain continuation of distortions. As shown in the last two panels in Table 11.5, ROW producers are worse off by $10.3 billion and EC producers by $15.3 billion when the respective entities liberalize but the US does not. If the US liberalizes, producers of ROW gain $10.0 billion if they maintain distortions but lose $2.7 billion if they liberalize. If the US liberalizes, EC producers lose only $14 million if they retain distortions but lose $13.5 billion if they liberalize. Hence, rational EC and ROW producers unequivocally favor maintaining distortions. If US producers deem that the EC and ROW will maintain the status quo, the optimal strategy for American producers is also to maintain the status quo. They lose $11.4 billion by liberalizing.

For American producers the best outcome is retention of distortions while the EC or ROW liberalize. Such an outcome is improbable indeed in the real world. The second-best outcome for American producers and the Nash equilibrium for the world is worldwide retention of trade and commodity program distortions. The third-best outcome for American producers is multilateral liberalization. The worse outcome for American farmers is unilateral US liberalization. The important conclusion from the foregoing analysis is that creation and maintenance of agricultural market distortions makes sense only from the perspective of payoffs to agricultural producers, although price stability and food security objectives also play a role.

This outcome of continuing trade distortions to benefit producers could be quite rational and even welfare maximizing for the public at large under certain circumstances. One might be if producers are less wealthy and hence have higher marginal utility of income than others. That hypothesis cannot stand scrutiny for at least three reasons: (1) For benefits to farmers of $11.4 billion from maintaining distortions to outweigh benefits to consumers and taxpayers of $14.2 billion from unilateral liberalization in 1989 would require marginal utility of farm income to be $14.2/$11.4 billion = 1.25 times or 25 percent higher for farmers than nonfarmers, an income specific difference not supported by empirical findings (see Tweeten and Mlay). (2) Wealth of commercial farmers who receive the majority of rents from interventions averages about ten times that of nonfarmers (see Tweeten, 1989, ch. 1). Thus diminishing marginal utility of wealth hardly makes a case for transfers to producers. (3) Direct payments from governments can maintain farm income if necessary without the market distortions losing the world billions of dollars of output each year.

A second hypothesis is that the distortions are the result of a truly representative and informed political process that rewards producers based on their voting power. The small share, 2 percent, of the US population on the farm refutes this hypothesis.

The best explanation is that distortions continue because the well-organized, well-funded, producer political lobby is successful in imposing its interests on Congress without opposition from the indulgent, poorly informed, and disorganized consumers and taxpayers (Tweeten, 1989, ch. 3). In the political arena, a few big losers (producers) are more than a match for millions of small gainers (consumers and taxpayers) even though *total* benefits to the latter exceed losses to producers by billions of dollars each year. Similar explanations have been offered for continuing trade distortions in other countries. The conclusion is that failure to liberalize trade mainly rests with failure of the political process. *Producer sovereignty* reigns rather than *consumer sovereignty*, which would prevail in a well-functioning market.

The optimal strategic policy of unilateral liberalization does not eliminate the search for a "level playing field" in trade. But instead of consistently maintaining distortions to bargain them away, the proper stance is to use sporadic retaliation if other countries maintain barriers (see tit-for-tat game strategy in Chapter 7). In addition, removal of American commodity subsidies, price supports, and deficiency payments to move toward a freer market domestically provides a continuing competitive challenge to other countries. This generates a credible threat and opportunity cost likely to win more long-run changes in the Common Agricultural Policy than will confrontation.

With unilateral liberalization, producers can be compensated for losses with adjustment assistance and direct payments at much lower cost than the gain to consumers and taxpayers from freer trade. But it is useful to remember that adjustments required by American farmers would be less if all countries simultaneously reduced trade protection for agriculture. Multilateral trade talks to remove distortions is a continuing need even if the US unilaterally removes its trade distortions.

With trade liberalization, decoupled payments can help to maintain farm income for a while. Ultimately, decoupling is not direct payments but is phasing out price and income supports. Supports could be reduced over a ten-year period to minimize hardship. Land prices would fall as commodity programs diminish. Rather than continue current programs, it is much less costly for the nation to provide generous adjustment programs of early retirement, long-term cropland buyouts to protect the environment and preserve production capacity, vocational and technical training, counseling, mobility assistance, and job information. Studies indicate producers eventually feel they are better off for having made adjustments (see Perry *et al.*). Programs of environmental protection and economic stabilization with buffer stocks also could be continued.

If sound macroeconomic policies are followed, commercial farmers who account for most farm output are quite capable of competing in world markets at a profit without price and income supports. Many of them are livestock producers who would fare better without programs that have raised feed prices.

Small farms with under $40,000 in sales account for approximately three-fourths of all farm operators. A large proportion of small farmers are retirees or part-time operators who with their family receive substantial income from off-farm sources. They are almost independent of what happens to the farming economy but benefit mightily from improvements in the nonfarm economy with more open trade.

Confrontation Without Success -- The Fourth-Best Policy

The fourth-best or worst agricultural trade strategy is continuing unsuccessful trade interventions. That policy actually is a variant of the second-best policy where extended confrontation fails to win major concessions towards free trade from competitors. Any concessions made are unlikely to be sufficient to compensate for continuing this nation's losses from its interventions distorting domestic and foreign markets. It makes little sense to continue such US policies just because that practice is fashionable in other countries.[5]

---

[5]Critics may argue that we cannot know the social welfare function, hence cannot judge the value of self-sufficiency and preserving the family farm. However, the EC has moved well beyond self-sufficiency except in tropical products. In Japan the petroleum imports for pesticides and nitrogen fertilizer to increase farm production are more vulnerable to cutoff than food imports. Neither the EC nor Japan has saved its family

CONCLUSIONS

The major losers from market interventions are countries that practice them. Continuing past US trade policies and confrontations will bring large economic costs to the nation from market interventions of its own making. The major gainers from liberalization are the countries that terminate interventions. As such, the US gains from unilateral liberalization. Such policies also can be effective in reducing trade barriers in other countries because competitive US prices will make their intervention more costly and counterproductive. For example, the approximately 10 percent reduction in the level of market intervention in the European Community from 1986 to 1990 was not the result of negotiations, but was due to the high cost to the consumers and taxpayers in the EC of continuing these policies. If subsidies are no longer necessary to counter US policies, then EC policies become less appealing to consumers and taxpayers of the Community.

The lesson of this chapter is not that American free trade makes sense if the rest of the world practices free trade. *The lesson of this chapter is that American free trade is best for our economy even if the rest of the world distorts trade.* Buzz terms such as "fair trade," "managed trade," "industrial policy," and "level playing field" have become euphemisms for protectionism.

Along with containment of farm export market distortions of the European Community and Japan, the US needs to direct attention to the growing protectionism in the newly industrialized developing countries such as Taiwan and South Korea. As these and other developing countries become more wealthy, they will be prone to emulate the protectionist and self-sufficiency policies of the First World. These policies need to be contested before they emerge. It is much easier to stop these policies before rather than after they have become institutionalized.

Steady progress towards market liberalization, unilaterally if necessary, will require informed and involved consumers, compensation to producers, and perhaps political process reform. The latter would diminish the role of special interests and enhance the encompassing role of public interests in Washington (see Tweeten, 1989, ch. 3). Among many internal policy reforms needed by the US, none is more basic than to provide a safety net for workers displaced by trade adjustments. Counseling, loans for retraining and relocating, and job information are a few important features of the policy.

The appropriate US trade strategy is not to give up on GATT -- many tools are needed to confront protectionism and work toward multilateral reduction of trade barriers. Unilateral moves toward free trade can begin immediately. It is unwise to hold such moves hostage to GATT negotiations or any other agenda. However, it is essential to avoid *chronic* retaliation policies such as the EEP. If a western hemisphere free trade area is formed, the goal might be to merge it with other free trade areas.

Numerous other components of a strategic and comprehensive trade policy were addressed in this chapter. Debate has been especially intense on whether to place greater emphasis on high-value exports. The issue is best left to markets to resolve. Major export

---

farms -- rates of decline in farm numbers have been greater in the EC than in the US in recent decades. Japanese farmers are for the most part full-time factory or other off-farm workers who "moonlight" producing crops and livestock on a couple of acres, hence cannot accurately be labeled "farmers." Comprehensive analysis indicates that commodity programs have had little net impact on farm size and numbers in the United States (see Tweeten, 1990, pp. 123-154).

subsidies are unwarranted but some efforts at market promotion have high payoffs (see Nichols) and are worthy of continuation.

REFERENCES

Anderson, Kym and Rodney Tyers. 1987. *Global Effects of Liberalizing Trade in Agriculture*. London: Trade Policy Research Centre.

Barkema, Allan and Mark Drabenstott. 1988. Can US and Great Plains agriculture compete in the world market? *Economic Review* 73:3-17. Federal Reserve Bank of St. Louis.

Barkema, Allan, Mark Drabenstott, and Luther Tweeten. 1990. The competitiveness of US agriculture in the 1990s. Pp. 253-284 in Kristen Allen, ed., *Agricultural Policies in a New Decade*. Washington, DC: Resources for the Future and National Planning Association.

Congressional Budget Office. June 1987. *The GATT Negotiations and US Trade Policy*. Washington, DC: US Government Printing Office.

Fair trade. December 7, 1991. *The Economist*, p. 30.

Henneberry, Shida, Luther Tweeten, David Henneberry, and Mechel Paggi. 1985. A coherent agricultural trade policy. Ag Trade 3. College Park: Cooperative Extension Service, University of Maryland.

Hertel, W.H., R.L. Thompson, and M.E. Tsigas. 1989. Economywide effects of unilateral trade and policy liberalization in US agriculture. Pp. 200-221 in A.B. Stoeckel, D. Vincent, and S. Cuthbertson, eds., *Macroeconomic Consequences of Farm Support Policies*. Durham, NC: Duke University Press.

Johnson, D.Gale, Hemmi Kenzo, and Pierre Lardinois. 1985. *Agricultural Policy and Trade*. Triangle Paper 29. New York: New York University Press.

Johnson, Martin, Louis Mahe, and Terry Roe. 1990. Politically acceptable trade compromises between the EC and the US. IATRC Working Paper 90-5. St. Paul: Department of Agricultural and Applied Economics, University of Minnesota.

Jurenas, Remy and Donna Vogt. 1989. Agricultural exports: Federal assistance and promotion programs. 89-351 ENR. Washington, DC: Congressional Research Service, Library of Congress.

Makki, Shiva, Luther Tweeten, and James Gleckler. 1991. Agricultural trade negotiations as a strategic game. Columbus: Department of Agricultural Economics and Rural Sociology, The Ohio State University.

Nichols, John. 1990. Export promotion effectiveness for agricultural products. Pp. 67-76 in Luther Tweeten, ed., *The Asian Market for Agricultural Products*. ESO 1704. (Proceedings of Realizing Opportunities for Farm and Food Product Exports to the Pacific Rim.) Columbus: Department of Agricultural Economics and Rural Sociology, The Ohio State University.

Office of Technology Assessment (OTA). 1986. *A Review of US Competitiveness in Agricultural Trade*. Washington, DC: Congress of the United States.

Organization for Economic Cooperation and Development. 1987. *National Policies and Agricultural Trade*. Paris: OECD.

Pai, Dee-Yu and Luther Tweeten. 1991. Farm income enhancement versus stabilization in a wheat buffer stock policy. Proceedings of *Farm Income Enhancement Conference*. Columbus: Department of Agricultural Economics and Rural Sociology, The Ohio State University.

Perry, Janet, Dean Schreiner, and Luther Tweeten. January 1991. Analysis of the characteristics of farmers who have curtailed or ceased farming in Oklahoma. Research Report P-919. Stillwater: Agricultural Experiment Station, Oklahoma State University.

Roningen, Vernon, John Sullivan, and John Wainio. August 1987. The impact of removal of support to agriculture in developed countries. Paper presented at the American Agricultural Economics Association annual meeting, East Lansing, Michigan.

Ryan, Mary and Robert Tontz. 1978. A historical review of world trade policies and institutions. Ch. 1 in *Speaking of Trade*. Special Report No. 72. St. Paul: Agricultural Extension Service, University of Minnesota.

Tweeten, Luther. 1989. *Farm Policy Analysis*. Boulder, CO: Westview Press.

Tweeten, Luther. 1990. Government commodity program impacts on farm numbers. Pp. 123-154 in Arne Hallam, ed., *Determinants of Size and Structure of American Agriculture*. (Proceedings of NC-181 Committee on Farm Size and Structure.) Ames: Department of Economics, Iowa State University.

Tweeten, Luther and Gilead Mlay. 1986. Marginal utility of income estimated and applied to problems in agriculture. Agricultural Policy Analysis Background Paper B-21. Stillwater: Department of Agricultural Economics, Oklahoma State University.

Tyers, Rodney and Kym Anderson. 1988. Liberalizing OECD agricultural policies in the Uruguay round: Effects on trade and welfare. *Journal of Agricultural Economics* 30:197-215.

World Perspectives. 1991. *US Agricultural Policy Guide*. Washington, DC: World Perspectives Policy Guides.

Yeutter, Clayton. 1988. Challenge to world agricultural trade. *International Agriculture* 3:1-3.

CHAPTER 12

Agricultural Trade Models[1]

Agricultural economics research has been pragmatic, that is, problem-oriented. Modeling and analysis of trade in agricultural commodities have been no exceptions. Agricultural trade models have made extensive use of theory but their genius has been applied rather than theoretical economics.

Like other scientific endeavors, research in agricultural trade begins with a problem in need of explanation. Theory and experience are drawn on to catalog reasonable explanations. Models of trade are formulated during this deductive process. The next step in the research process often is *quantitative* specification and empirical testing. Using parameter estimates that have proven to be statistically significant, models are employed to predict future conditions, and to gauge market impacts of policy decisions.

This chapter will focus on the research process in agricultural trade. Special emphasis is on empirical models that are used to estimate impacts of the policies discussed in previous chapters.

THEORETICAL RESEARCH

The theories presented in Chapter 2 and other chapters attempt to explain trade between countries. The classical and neoclassical theories emphasize dissimilarities between factor endowments and technology among countries to explain trade. Research during the last 20 years has expanded in the directions of demand analysis and imperfect competition as illustrated in Chapters 7 and 8. Neoclassical theory and recent extensions will be the focus of this section of the chapter.

Neoclassical trade theory, as it developed early in this century, holds that each trading region has an excess supply or excess demand function for a commodity. Figure 12.1 illustrates a multiregion neoclassical trade model with the familiar price-quantity panels. Supply and demand functions for each region determine the excess functions in the world market. The world market clears (imports = exports = Q_T) at the world price of P_w. The absence of restrictions to trade allows the world price to determine quantities consumed and produced in each region.

The neoclassical theory of trade relies on the strong assumptions of one price, product homogeneity, and perfect competition. The law of one price and homogeneous products means that domestic production and imports are not discriminated in consumption. Products from all regions are perfect substitutes in consumption. Perfect competition assumes no exercise of power by trading regions in international markets. Gains from trade

---

[1]James Gleckler is co-author of this chapter.

284

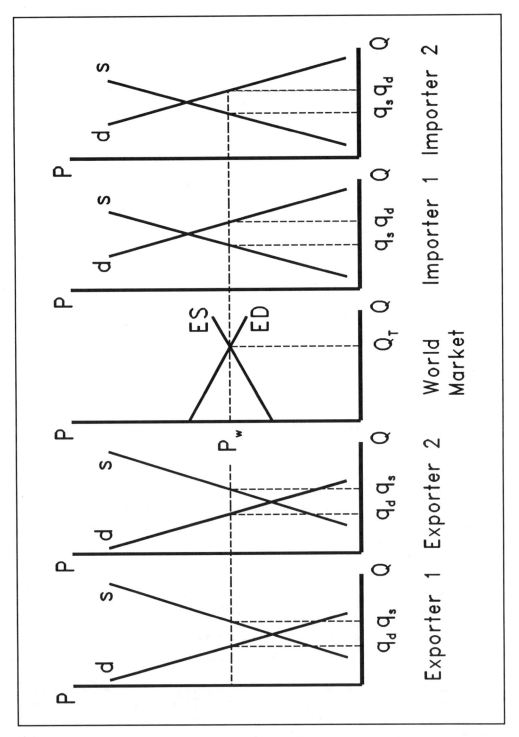

Figure 12.1. A Multiregion, Static Equilibrium, World Trade Model.

or incentives to trade are the net producer surplus gains over consumer surplus losses in exporting regions and the net consumer gains over producer losses in importing countries.

Trade theory is constantly evolving. Empirical models often imperfectly predict trade behavior. To improve the predictive power of empirical models, researchers attempt to extend and refine theory and techniques. Recent extensions of trade theory have attempted to differentiate products and describe and predict behavior in imperfectly competitive markets.

The law of one price does not always hold in world markets. Unlike classical and neoclassical theory, which emphasize trade incentives based on differences in factor endowments, product differentiation extensions of the theory emphasize unique market relationships. Three theoretical extensions relating to product differentiation have evolved in recent years. They are the market share or Armington theory, horizontal differentiation, and vertical differentiation of products. The Armington approach emphasizes differentiation of products on the basis of location of production. Horizontal differentiation refers to consumer preference based on increased variety in a product. Vertical differentiation allows preference for goods based on quality differences.

Imperfectly competitive trade behavior is the other major extension of neoclassical theory. State trading through national marketing boards and differentiated product sales through oligopolistic private firms have highlighted the importance of imperfect competition in theories of trade. Monopolistic and oligopolistic behavior between trading partners has been the theme in several recent investigations of international trade in agricultural and food products.

As noted in Chapters 7 and 8, a significant gap remains between theory and empirical testing of the product differentiation and imperfect competition extensions to trade theory. Serious problems have been encountered in empirical model specification. A theoretical model must be specified in a form that can make use of available data before statistical analysis is employed in testing the theory. Estimates of parameters such as elasticities of substitution between differentiated products have been difficult or impossible to obtain. Reaction functions and conjectural variations of interacting firms have been elusive to measure. Although empirical trade models incorporating recent extensions of trade theory generally have not been encouraging, one possible exception is the Armington market share specification, which differentiates products based on their place of origin. Some trade flow models have produced results as consistent as traditional neoclassical specifications. Even though some models do not predict trade better than the standard neoclassical specifications, theoretically they may be more appealing. Because much of the usefulness of trade theory is in its application to forecasting and estimating impacts of policies, empirical shortcomings are critical to modeling.

EMPIRICAL MODELS

Empirical models of agricultural trade, based on trade theory, often are used to estimate impacts on world and domestic markets of actual or potential policy decisions, demand shifts, and input alterations such as weather. These latter changes are referred to as shocks.

Empirical trade models require estimates of behavioral parameters, most based on neoclassical theory. A neoclassical model may be two-region or multiregion, single or multicommodity, spatial or nonspatial, partial or general equilibrium, stochastic or deterministic, static or dynamic. A common neoclassical specification is a nonspatial, static, partial equilibrium trade model. An example of a multiregion, multicommodity quantitative model is given in Annex A to this chapter. For some purposes, a simple model such as illustrated in Annex B provides useful results at relatively low research cost. A simple model may be small or large, the latter illustrated by simple excess supply and demand equations for many commodities and countries. A complex model also may be small or large, but is usually large. A useful rule is to keep models as small and simple as possible consistent with sufficient detail to answer questions put before the model.

Classification of Empirical Models

Trade models are based on the behavior of domestic markets. In fact, the simplest method of estimating trade is to begin with a trade relationship in a domestic market system. A rest-of-world excess demand or rest-of-world excess supply equation is added to a single domestic market supply and demand system of equations. In this way domestic price changes have an effect not only on production and consumption behavior, but on export or import quantities as well. When a domestic market model is "opened" to trade in this manner, it is classified by some economists as a two-region trade model. Parameters in the rest-of-world function may be estimated by econometric methods. All importing or exporting behavior by the rest-of-world is embodied in the one excess supply or excess demand equation. This limits the two-region model's ability to predict changes in the rest-of-world behavior that would occur in reaction to domestic market conditions and policies.

Multiregion trade models do not use the "domestic economy" and "rest of world" dichotomy. Individual countries and aggregated regions are specified as having markets that clear simultaneously with all other regions in the model. The graphical example in Figure 12.1 and the quantitative models in the Annexes illustrate such a multiregional empirical trade model. Most multiregion models specify each economy and each product with a supply and demand function. Since these models are based on neoclassical economic theory, exports (or imports) equal supply minus demand. Alternatively, a country may be modeled with excess supply or excess demand functions. Trade is calculated directly from these "excess" expressions, but domestic supply and demand functions still underlie the estimates. Simultaneous solution of a multiregion empirical model is accomplished by balancing exports with imports for all regions. World supply equaling world demand is the multiregion equilibrium condition.

Multiregion empirical models use solution techniques that search out a particular world price that will balance world trade (see examples in Annex). Generally speaking, the world price enters each country or region and determines the consumption and production, which in turn determine net trade from that economy. Domestic supply and demand parameters must be estimated and included in the equations for each region. The model is initialized with price and quantity data yielding an equilibrium in the base year. The base solution usually assumes that current policies exist in the individual countries. In other words, the price and quantity data are policy-laden.

Price wedges and/or world price transmission elasticities may be used to simulate policy shocks. Because agricultural and food policies usually modify consumption and production, the impacts of policy change can be simulated by changing the producer and/or consumer price in the countries. A price "wedge" is the difference between world and domestic prices in the model. Price transmission elasticities specify the degree to which the world price effects the domestic price. Other policy and weather or income related changes may be modeled by shifting supply and demand functions in the countries. All such shocks to the model modify the net trade of one or more economies and cause an imbalance in the world market. Changes in the world price entering each country through border measures and domestic policies included in the base solution determine a new demand and supply quantity in each country. When the search for a new world price is complete, changes in prices and quantities are the model's estimate of the impact of the shock on world and country markets. The new equilibrium world price balances trade once again.

Spatial refers to location, as reflected in transportation costs, being a behavioral part of the model. Spatial models use behavior, as it is related to transportation costs, to determine trade flows. Spatial models embody the neoclassical assumptions about competitive behavior in world markets and no differentiation among products. Source-destination trade flows are generated by a spatial model. Trade flow behavior is a function of spatial patterns of world prices, which differ in equilibrium due to transportation costs.

Virtually all empirical models must be classified as *partial equilibrium* because not all factors having a bearing on the solution are included. Excluded elements are assumed to remain constant during an adjustment process. Some models are more complete than others. A large, nearly *general equilibrium* model might include all factors of production, all agricultural commodities, and all non-farm sectors as well as macroeconomic relationships. These are termed *computable general equilibrium* (CGE) *models*. The simplest CGE models add input functions to typical partial equilibrium product markets of international trade. CGE models often consider macroeconomic as well as trade variables to be *endogenous*, that is, determined within the model. A model becomes more partial as it excludes consideration of other commodities and goods, or assumes that technology, macroeconomic variables, and factors of production are exogenous (determined outside the model) or remain constant throughout the adjustment process (see Robinson *et al.*, 1990 and Hertel and Tsigas, 1988).

This is not to say that general models are always better. The term "computable general equilibrium" is contradictory: A complete general equilibrium model is never computable, and a computable model is never a fully general equilibrium model! The very essence of a model is to abstract from reality, using only essential components of the political-economic system to predict that which is important within a manageable mathematical framework. A model should never be judged on how complete it is; rather it should be judged on its predictive power. General models can become a "black hole" swallowing an inordinate amount of resources in estimation, data collection, computation processes, and maintenance. Once developed, they may be too expensive to maintain and consequently are abandoned. On the other hand, a partial model may omit critical components of a larger system and hence may give biased predictions.

Static models estimate an equilibrium reached at some point in a process of adjustment. The solution price and quantity can be compared with the base price and quantity, but the adjustment path is not revealed by the model. The solution point may be the equilibrium attained after one month, one year, or one decade of adjustment. The length of adjustment from the base to the solution is determined by the behavioral parameters. Econometric estimations, which include lagged regressors, allow calculation of parameters that will solve for an equilibrium early or late in the adjustment process. Although such models are partially dynamic, all changes are attributed to the shocks administered to the model because everything else is assumed to remain unchanged during the adjustment process. The estimated impacts obtainable from a static equilibrium model are similar to those obtained when one of the domestic supply or demand functions in the graphical model of Figure 12.1 is shifted; then new quantities supplied and demanded in all countries result from the change in world price.

In contrast to static models, *dynamic models* reveal the path of adjustment that the market takes in response to policy changes. A dynamic model is estimated and parameterized on the basis of continuous or periodic (e.g., yearly) changes. Income and technology developments are usually a part of the adjustments made by the market. Impacts at any point in the process can be analyzed in a dynamic model. Dynamic models can be difficult to specify correctly and may add distortions which can make them less accurate than static versions. For most applications, predictions are not needed for every point in time but only for specific points such as 1, 3, or 10 years in the future. Such predictions are often easily obtained from static models designed to estimate the short, intermediate, and long run using supply and demand elasticities and other parameters appropriate to the length of run.

Deterministic models are widely used in analysis of trade. They ignore unexplained variation in markets and yield simple point estimates of policy impacts. *Stochastic models* on the other hand include random elements in markets and analyze variability under different policy scenarios. Econometrically derived stochastic models simulate the variability derived from the error terms estimated during statistical analysis. Estimated standard deviations, variances, coefficients of variation, or ranges in prices and trade quantities are compared before and after a policy changes.

Market share theory, an extension of neoclassical theory, has produced empirical models with considerable predictive ability and has gained popularity since the concept was first published in the early 1970s. Market share models allow for product differentiation based on location. *Armington models* are a type of market share model. Theory underlying Armington models holds that products are differentiated on the basis of country or origin. Consumption of traded commodities is assumed to be a two-stage process. First, total imports are decided; then, the allocation of purchases among suppliers is determined.

The market share model often includes estimates of the elasticity of substitution reflecting buying power among alternative sources of supply. The elasticity of substitution is difficult to estimate because of the high correlations among international prices of the same or similar commodities.

Buyers of traded commodities differentiate commodities on the basis of quality, political considerations, historical trading patterns, and an attempt to diversify supply sources. The problem in describing trade with the neoclassical framework may not be with the theory of one price, however. It may be that most models and the available data describe an aggregate commodity that in reality is made up of several individual and distinct component products that need to be treated as separate products in analysis. Wheat may be hard or soft, and it may be of US or Argentine origin. The United States, the largest "wheat" exporter in the world, actually imported 572,000 metric tons of wheat in 1986. The European Community was the largest exporter of beef in the world (1.18 million metric tons in 1986) while EC imports ranked second only to the United States in recent years. The problem with models of trade, which define such commodities as "wheat" and "beef," may be the aggregate nature of such definitions. Were these products treated separately in modeling, the neoclassical framework of one price might do a better job of describing trade flows. Thus the shortcoming of many neoclassical models is not with the theory but with the data. Disaggregation to rectify this problem brings new problems of multicollinearity, missing data series, and model complexity. Such issues plague application of any theory.

A distinction is sometimes made between *structural* and *predictive* models. If we are interested in predicting the exchange rate next month, we may not worry whether excellent predictor variables represent a real or spurious correlation. On the other hand, if we want to predict the impact of the interest rate on the exchange rate, we want a structurally valid equation. The ideal is to have a model that is structurally valid and predicts well.

Uses and Abuses of Empirical Trade Modeling

Multiregional models are superior to two-region models in capturing interactions among countries. No particular type of multiregion model is consistently superior to others in modeling this interaction, however. All model types have strong points and weak points. Spatial price equilibrium models often predict trade flows less well than do market share models. But the elasticity of substitution common to market share models is neither well understood nor easily estimated. Market share models fall short when an important objective is to determine impacts on price of alternative international trade policies.

Most of the trade models developed in recent years to analyze the impacts of multilateral trade liberalization have been static, nonspatial, multiregional partial equilibrium models. This includes the OECD MTM model, the USDA GOL model, the Newcastle model, and most of the models constructed using the USDA SWOPSIM framework. The Anderson-Tyers and the IIASA models are also nonspatial models, but both are dynamic rather than static.

Trade models frequently pose several problems worthy of note. By their very nature, multiregional models have the potential to become very large. This is especially true when they are multicommodity as well. First, models require reliable parameter estimates for high predictive ability. Second, data requirements (base year prices and quantities) can be enormous even after the model is parameterized.

Static models predict impacts of changes in policies or other variables from base year data. Because global market conditions are nearly always significantly different in the base year compared with the current year, the impacts estimated by the model are unlikely to predict what is happening currently. Data used to initialize the model in the base year are also assumed to reflect a full equilibrium with no latent adjustments from previous years. Actual data for any base year will embody many abnormal elements caused by unusual weather, domestic policies, the level of world stocks in the base year, and other sources of disequilibrium. Finally, models that use price wedges to simulate policy shocks need data on support measures which may be peculiar to a particular year. The support rendered by a government through border measures or commodity programs depends to a great degree on the world price in the base year.

Models which assume that behavioral parameters remain constant after a shock and during the process of adjustment to a new equilibrium have been criticized. To some degree this criticism can be addressed in trade models by endogenizing policy. Dynamic multiregion trade models can accommodate a policy reaction function which modifies domestic and/or border policies in response to changes in world price as the shocks to the model take effect.

The agricultural trade models most highly regarded by the profession are theoretically elegant and mathematically refined. Quality of parameter estimates and data are less emphasized. The elasticities and other parameter values are the core of the behavioral responses predicted by trade models. Inaccurate measures of behavioral reactions to changes in prices as embodied in biased price elasticities render unrealistic predictions even if models are theoretically sound, data are accurate, and the solution technique is mathematically sophisticated.

Because models and assumptions of necessity must be simplified abstractions of the real world, one might ask, "Why even attempt to model trade quantitatively?" The world may be better off with quickly reasoned answers to trade questions, or with the simpler results obtained from graphical analysis. Bruce Gardner (1988) addressed this issue when he observed (p. 8),

> what confidence can we have in the point estimates of estimated price effects and welfare consequences of agricultural trade and policy liberalization that the large-scale simulation studies have generated? The answer . . . appears to be zilch, based on some admittedly sketchy considerations. Nonetheless the studies are useful in showing the range of billions in gains and losses being fairly narrowly circumscribed.

Empirical trade models yield point estimates of changes due to shocks. Often they predict less accurately than we would like, but their indications of the direction and general magnitude of impacts are valuable nonetheless. Point results obtained from empirical models must always be treated as estimates. Sensitivity and validation analysis of a quantitative model can reveal weaknesses in its structure and parameters. Such analysis should be performed before estimating policy shocks. The world is hungry for empirical estimates and quantitative trade models can provide more detailed and refined estimates of impacts than any other method. In the final analysis, those estimates are most valuable to those who understand their limitations.

REFERENCES

Adelman, I. and S. Robinson. 1988. Macroeconomic shocks, foreign trade, and structural adjustment: A general equilibrium analysis of the US economy, 1982-1986. In C. Carter and W.H. Gardiner, eds., *Elasticities in International Agriculture Trade.* Boulder, CO: Westview Press.

Anderson, K. and R. Tyers. 1987. *Global Effects of Liberalizing Trade in Agriculture.* London: Trade Policy Research Centre.

Buckwell, A.E., D.R. Harvey, K.J. Thompson, and K.A. Parton. 1982. *The Costs of the Common Agricultural Policy.* London: Croom Helm.

Burniaux, J.M., F.Delorme, I. Lienert, and J.P. Martin. August 1990. WALRAS - A multi-sector, multi-country applied general equilibrium model for quantifying the economy-wide effects of agricultural policies: A technical manual. Working Paper No. 84. Paris: Growth Studies Division, Department of Economics and Statistics, OECD.

Gardner, Bruce. August 1988. Recent studies of agricultural trade liberalization: What the models say. (Paper presented at the American Agricultural Economics Association meetings.) College Park: Department of Agricultural Economics, University of Maryland.

Hertel, T.W. and M.E. Tsigas. May 1988. Tax policy and US agriculture: A general equilibrium analysis. *American Journal of Agricultural Economics* 70:289-302.

Kilkenny, Maureen. February 1991. Computable general equilibrium modeling of agricultural policies: Documentation of the 30 sector FPGE GAMS model of the United States. Staff Report forthcoming. Washington, DC: Agriculture and Rural Economy Division, ERS, USDA.

Organization for Economic Cooperation and Development (OECD). 1987. *National Policies and Agricultural Trade.* Paris: OECD.

Paarlberg, Philip L. and Jerry A. Sharples. August 1984. *Japanese and European Community Agricultural Trade Policies: Some US Strategies.* Foreign Agricultural Economic Report No. 204. Washington, DC: ERS, US Department of Agriculture.

Parikh, K.S., G. Fischer, K. Frohberg, and O. Gulbrandsen. 1986. *Towards Free Trade in Agriculture.* Laxemburg, Austria: International Institute for Applied Systems Analysis.

Robinson, Sherman, Maureen Kilkenny, and Kenneth Hanson. June 1990. The USDA/ERS computable general equilibrium (CGE) model of the United States. Staff Report No. AGES9049. Washington, DC: Agriculture and Rural Economy Division, ERS, USDA.

Roningen, V., J. Sullivan, and J. Wainio. August 1987. The impact of the removal of support to agriculture in developed countries. (Paper presented at the American

Agricultural Economics Association meetings.)   Washington, DC: ERS, US Department of Agriculture.

Thompson, Robert. September 1981. A survey of recent US developments in international agricultural trade models.   Bibliographies and Literature of Agriculture No. 21. Washington, DC: ERS, US Department of Agriculture.

ANNEX A TO CHAPTER 12

A MULTIREGION, MULTICOMMODITY, NONSPATIAL, PARTIAL EQUILIBRIUM, EMPIRICAL MODEL USING CONSTANT ELASTICITY BEHAVIORAL EQUATIONS

THE MODEL

Country 1

Prices

$$P_{pw1} = P_{W_{wt}} + M_{w1} + W_{pw1}$$ producer wheat price

$$P_{pc1} = P_{W_{ct}} + M_{c1} + W_{pc1}$$ producer corn price

$$P_{cw1} = P_{W_{wt}} + M_{w1} + W_{cw1}$$ consumer wheat price

$$P_{cc1} = P_{W_{ct}} + M_{c1} + W_{cc1}$$ consumer corn price

Supply

$$Q_{Sw1} = \alpha_{Sw1} \, P_{pw1}^{\beta_{w1}} \, P_{pc1}^{\beta_{cx1}}$$ wheat production

$$Q_{Sc1} = \alpha_{Sc1} \, P_{pc1}^{\beta_{c1}} \, P_{pw1}^{\beta_{wx1}}$$ corn production

Demand

$$Q_{Dw1} = \alpha_{Dw1} \, P_{cw1}^{\delta_{w1}} \, P_{cc1}^{\delta_{cx1}}$$ wheat consumption

$$Q_{Dc1} = \alpha_{Dc1} \, P_{cc1}^{\delta_{c1}} \, P_{cw1}^{\delta_{wx1}}$$ corn consumption

Net Trade

$$Q_{Sw1} - Q_{Dw1} = NTD_{w1}$$ wheat

$$Q_{Sc1} - Q_{Dc1} = NTD_{c1}$$

corn

Country 2

Prices

$$P_{pw2} = P_{W_{wt}} + M_{w2} + W_{pw2}$$

producer wheat price

$$P_{pc2} = P_{W_{ct}} + M_{c2} + W_{pc2}$$

producer corn price

$$P_{cw2} = P_{W_{wt}} + M_{w2} + W_{cw2}$$

consumer wheat price

$$P_{cc2} = P_{W_{ct}} + M_{c2} + W_{cc2}$$

consumer corn price

Supply

$$Q_{Sw2} = \alpha_{Sw2}\ P_{pw2}^{\beta_{w2}}\ P_{pc2}^{\beta_{cx2}}$$

wheat production

$$Q_{Sc2} = \alpha_{Sc2}\ P_{pc2}^{\beta_{c2}}\ P_{pw2}^{\beta_{wx2}}$$

corn production

Demand

$$Q_{Dw2} = \alpha_{Dw2}\ P_{cw2}^{\delta_{w2}}\ P_{cc2}^{\delta_{cx2}}$$

wheat consumption

$$Q_{Dc2} = \alpha_{Dc2}\ P_{cc2}^{\delta_{c2}}\ P_{cw2}^{\delta_{wx2}}$$

corn consumption

Net Trade

$$Q_{Sw2} - Q_{Dw2} = NTD_{w2}$$

wheat

$$Q_{Sc2} - Q_{Dc2} = NTD_{c2}$$

corn

Rest of World

Prices

$$P_{pwr} = P_{W_{wt}} + M_{wr} + W_{pwr}$$ producer wheat price

$$P_{pcr} = P_{W_{ct}} + M_{cr} + W_{pcr}$$ producer corn price

$$P_{cwr} = P_{W_{wt}} + M_{wr} + W_{cwr}$$ consumer wheat price

$$P_{ccr} = P_{W_{ct}} + M_{cr} + W_{ccr}$$ consumer corn price

Supply

$$Q_{Swr} = \alpha_{Swr} \, P_{pwr}^{\beta_{wr}} \, P_{pcr}^{\beta_{cxr}}$$ wheat production

$$Q_{Scr} = \alpha_{Scr} \, P_{pcr}^{\beta_{cr}} \, P_{pwr}^{\beta_{wxr}}$$ corn production

Demand

$$Q_{Dwr} = \alpha_{Dwr} \, P_{cwr}^{\delta_{wr}} \, P_{ccr}^{\delta_{cxr}}$$ wheat consumption

$$Q_{Dcr} = \alpha_{Dcr} \, P_{ccr}^{\delta_{cr}} \, P_{cwr}^{\delta_{wxr}}$$ corn consumption

Net Trade

$$Q_{Swr} - Q_{Dwr} = NTD_{wr}$$ wheat

$$Q_{Scr} - Q_{Dcr} = NTD_{cr}$$ corn

World

Prices

$$P_{wwt} = P_{wwt-1} \left[1 - \frac{\Sigma NTD_{wi}}{\Sigma Q_{swi}} \right] \qquad\qquad \text{wheat}$$

$$P_{wct} = P_{wct-1} \left[1 - \frac{\Sigma NTD_{ci}}{\Sigma Q_{sci}} \right] \qquad\qquad \text{corn}$$

Equilibrium Condition

$$\sum_{i=1}^{n} NTD_{wi} = \varnothing \qquad\qquad \text{wheat}$$

$$\sum_{i=1}^{n} NTD_{ci} = \varnothing \qquad\qquad \text{corn}$$

P_{pji} = Producer price for commodity j in country i.
P_{cji} = Consumer price for commodity j in country i.
P_{wjt} = World price for commodity j in current period (t).
M_{ji} = World price minus domestic price margin for commodity j in country i.
W_{pji} = Domestic producer policy wedge for commodity j in country i.
W_{cji} = Domestic consumer policy wedge for commodity j in country i.
Q_{Sji} = Quantity supplied for commodity j in country i.
Q_{Dji} = Quantity demanded for commodity j in country i.
α_{Sji} = Supply equation constant term for commodity j in country i.
α_{Dji} = Demand equation constant term for commodity j in country i.
β_{ji} = Own price supply elasticity for commodity j in country i.
β_{jxi} = Cross price supply elasticity for commodity j in country i.
δ_{ji} = Own price demand elasticity for commodity j in country i.
δ_{jxi} = Cross price demand elasticity for commodity j in country i.
NTD_{ji} = Net trade of commodity j in country i.
P_{wjt-1} = World price for commodity j in previous iteration (t-1).

Notes

The model behaves very similar to the graphical presentation in Figure 12.1. This example illustrates only three trading regions. The rest-of-world region aggregates data and behavior for all economies outside countries 1 and 2.

Each trading region has domestic supply and demand price equations for each commodity. These prices are linked to the world price by a fixed margin (M), which accounts for transportation costs. World price transmission elasticities are 1.0 whenever world price has unrestricted access to domestic markets. A world price transmission elasticity of less than 1.0 simulates border policies, which tend to isolate domestic producers and consumers from world markets. A domestic policy wedge (W) accounts for domestic distortions.

Prices are key elements of the supply and demand behavioral equations. Production and consumption behavior is simulated in the constant elasticity equations with prices and corresponding own and cross elasticities. The model is initialized with data from a base year. The data include domestic and world prices, supply and demand quantities that determine trade, and policy wedge information. The initializing quantity data must ensure the world market clearing condition holds initially. Constant terms in the equations are calculated based on the initializing data and behavioral parameters.

Impacts of policy changes or shocks can be estimated in the model by changing the wedge term in a price equation. The simulated domestic policy change results in an altered price, which changes the quantity supplied and/or consumed. Shifts in supply or demand due to factors such as weather, technology, or income changes can be simulated by modifying the constant term in the behavioral equations. Shocks change the net trade position and the world trade balance. Using an iterative process, the model searches an equilibrium with new prices and net trade positions (world price equations). The results of modeling a shock are obtained by comparing base prices and base quantities with solution prices and quantities.

ANNEX B TO CHAPTER 12

POLICY ANALYSIS WITH A
SIMPLE WHEAT TRADE MODEL

A five-region world wheat trade model provides a simple illustration (Paarlberg and Sharples). The trading regions are the United States, EC, Japan, other exporters (Canada, Australia, and Argentina), and other importers (all other countries). Although many simplifying assumptions are made to reduce a complex system of world trade into a small abstract model, these assumptions do not negate the model's conclusions.

The model represents the world wheat market during the 1980/81 and 1981/82 marketing years, referred to as the *base period*. During this period, world wheat trade is assumed to be in a long-run equilibrium. This model is a long-run static model, meaning that wheat production in all world price-responsive countries adjusts fully to any change in price. It also means that year-end stock levels may be ignored since stocks primarily adjust to short-run disequilibrium conditions; that is, they do not respond to long-run changes. All transportation costs are omitted. All currencies are converted to their dollar equivalents. Also, all wheat and flour are assumed homogeneous and sold as grain at one annual price worldwide. Finally, all price-quantity relationships are assumed to be linear. The following regional wheat supply and demand equations are used:

United States (U):
$$\text{Domestic Demand: } DU = 26.4 - 0.022P \tag{1}$$
$$\text{Domestic Supply: } SU = 53.6 + 0.067P \tag{2}$$
$$\text{Excess Supply: } XSU = SU - DU$$
$$= 27.2 + 0.089P \tag{3}$$

Other Exporters (X):
$$\text{Domestic Demand: } DX = 13.2 - 0.011P \tag{4}$$
$$\text{Domestic Supply: } SX = 34.4 + 0.043P \tag{5}$$
$$\text{Excess Supply: } XSX = SX - DX$$
$$= 21.2 + 0.054P \tag{6}$$

European Community (E):
$$\text{Excess Supply: } XSE = 9.0 \tag{7}$$

Japan (J):
$$\text{Excess Demand: } XDJ = 5.5 \tag{8}$$

Other Importers (M):
$$\text{Excess Demand: } XDM = 137.3 - 0.284P \tag{9}$$

World (W):
$$\text{Excess Supply: } XSW = XSU + XSX + XSE$$
$$= 57.4 + 0.143P \tag{10}$$
$$\text{Excess Demand: } XDW = XDJ + XDM$$
$$= 142.8 - 0.284P \tag{11}$$

Price, P, is an average cif price in dollars per metric ton. All quantities are in million metric tons. Japan and the EC are assumed not to adjust the quantities of wheat traded in response to changes in world price. At P = $200, this system reproduces the base period quantities produced, consumed, and traded by the United States, and the quantities traded by the other three regions.

Domestic demand equations (1 and 4) have price elasticities of -0.2 and domestic supply equations 2 and 5 have price elasticities of 0.2 at P = 200. Excess supply equations 3 and 6 are obtained by subtracting demand equations from the supply equations. The elasticity of demand for US wheat exports is assumed to be -1.5 in the long run when production has time to adjust to world wheat price changes. Given the elasticities of equations 6, 7, and 8, and the above assumption, the slope of equation 9 may be computed. The world excess supply equation is the sum of equations 3, 6, and 7. The world excess demand equation is the sum of equations 8 and 9.

The base period trade equilibrium is shown in Appendix B Table 1. In total, 86 million tons are traded at a world price of $200. Exports from the United States, the EC, and other exporters are 45, 9, and 32 million tons, respectively. This is called the base solution. All other solutions are modifications of this base solution.

Annex B Table 1. Annual Production, Use, and Trade of Wheat, Five Regions, Average of 1980/81 and 1981/82 Marketing Years.[a]

Region	Production	Use	Net Exports[b]
	(Million Metric Tons)		
United States	67.0	22.0	45.0
EC	54.0	45.0	9.0[c]
Other Exporters	43.0	11.0	32.0
Japan	0.6	6.1	-5.5
Other Importers	280.4	360.9	-80.5
World	445.0	445.0	0.0

[a] Adjusted to account for changes in stock levels.
[b] Excludes within-region trade.
[c] The EC exported 13.7 million tons and imported 4.7 million tons for a net export of 9 million tons.

Free Trade by the EC and Japan

The excess supply equation for the EC and the excess demand equation for Japan are replaced in the free trade problem.

EC (E):
$$\text{Domestic Demand: } DE = 53.91 - 0.033P \tag{12}$$
$$\text{Domestic Supply: } SE = 32.41 + 0.080P \tag{13}$$
$$\text{Excess Supply: } XSE = SE - DE = -21.50 + 0.113P \tag{14}$$

Japan (J):

Domestic Demand: $DJ = 7.32 - 0.0042P$ (15)

Domestic Supply: $SJ = 0.37 + 0.0083P$ (16)

Excess Demand: $XDJ = DJ - SJ = 6.95 - 0.0125P$ (17)

These equations assume supply and demand elasticities of 0.4 and -0.2 at base period internal price levels. Equation 14 yields the base period quantity exported at a domestic price of $270 ($200 world price plus an export subsidy of $70). Equation 17 yields the base period quantity imported at a domestic price of $288 ($200 world price plus an import tariff of $88). Because of these changes, world excess supply and demand equations also need revision.

World (W):

Excess Supply: $XSW = 26.89 + 0.256P$ (18)

Excess Demand: $XDW = 144.25 - 0.289P$ (19)

Equations 18 and 19 are solved with $XSW = XDW$ to yield an equilibrium price of $215 and 82 million tons of wheat traded among the five regions.

Results

If Japan and the EC had no barriers to wheat trade, they would produce less and consume more. The EC would still be a net exporter, but exports would be reduced by 6.2 million tons. Japan would increase imports only 0.4 million tons because of its inelastic demand. Free wheat markets in the EC and Japan would raise the world price and induce the United States and other exporters to expand production and exports, and cut consumption. The United States would increase wheat exports 1.4 million tons and increase the value of exports $1.0 billion. Other exporters would also benefit. Wheat importers would reduce wheat imports in response to the higher price. EC wheat producers' income would fall substantially, but EC consumers would pay less for wheat products, and the CAP treasury cost of the wheat export subsidy would be eliminated.

Glossary

Absolute advantage. When one country is more efficient in the production of a certain good than is another country. A country exports what it can produce more cheaply and imports what others can produce more cheaply.

Ad valorem **tariff.** Duties calculated proportional to the value of goods; e.g., 15 percent of the value (15 percent *ad valorem*).

Agricultural attache, counselor, or trade officer. An agricultural expert on the staff of his or her country's embassy, consulate, or trade office.

Antidumping measures (also see **dumping**). Retaliation taken against a country selling abroad below its cost of production or below its domestic price.

Autarky. Without trade. Implies self-sufficiency.

Balance of payments. Receipts from foreign countries less payments to them including all transactions, private and governmental. The difference between the two, the balance of payments, is zero. The plus side (export sales; money spent by foreign tourists; payments to the US for insurance, transportation, and similar services; payments of dividends and interests on investments abroad; returns of capital invested abroad; new foreign investments in the US; and foreign government payments to the US) is just offset by the minus side (cost of goods imported, spending by tourists overseas, new overseas investments, and the cost of foreign military and economic aid). Capital flow offsets net goods, services, and transfer flows to make total inflow equal outflow.

Balance of payments deficit. When international payments are greater than receipts. Difference is filled by capital inflow.

Balance of trade. The relationship between merchandise (goods) imports and exports. A country's balance of trade is only one aspect of its balance of payments. A country's *balance of current account* includes imports and exports of *goods and services*.

Barter. A system of exchange in which goods and services are traded without the use of money as a medium of exchange.

"Beggar-thy-neighbor" policy. A trade policy designed to exploit trading partners. An example is an optimal tariff or competitive exchange rate depreciation. During the 1930s many countries depreciated their currencies beyond the equilibrium rate of exchange in an attempt to stimulate exports, thereby creating a surplus in their balance of payments. This policy required a deficit disequilibrium in the balance of payments of other countries also faced with depression, hence it amounted to exporting unemployment.

Bilateral. Two-party or two-country, such as a bilateral trade agreement between the US and one other country.

Bound. Trade term meaning to not change. A *bound* tariff is not allowed to increase. A duty-free *binding* forbids the EC from imposing a border tax on soybean imports.

Border price. World market price adjusted to specific location by port price less cif for exports and plus cif for imports. Market price at specific location if markets function well and in the absence of distortions.

Buffer stocks. Stocks stored to reduce year-to-year fluctuations in supply and prices. Supplies of a product set aside and used to moderate extreme price fluctuations by assuring a more stable supply between years. *Seasonal stocks* are released as the marketing year progresses to reduce seasonal (within year) price fluctuations. *Pipeline stocks* are *minimum* requirements to keep transport, mills, and shelves going, especially notable at the end of the marketing season before the new crop is brought in.

Cargo preference. A legal requirement that export cargoes of government-owned commodities or products shipped under government-financed arrangements must be carried on US-flag vessels.

Caribbean Basin Initiative (CBI). Formally the Caribbean Basin Economic Recovery Act, an initiative designed to increase private sector involvement in investment and trade in Caribbean countries; permits duty-free entry of certain products from these countries for twelve years beginning in 1983.

Carnet. A customs document permitting the holder to carry or send merchandise temporarily into certain countries (for display, demonstration, or similar purposes) without paying duties or posting bonds.

Cartel. A formal arrangement embodying written or explicit verbal agreements among producers to regulate price or output or to divide markets geographically. The most recent and most successful example is OPEC.

Chaebol. South Korean business conglomerate. An example is Hyundai.

cif. Cost, insurance, freight. All costs of transporting goods and services.

Commodity. An article of trade or commerce that can be transported, especially an unprocessed agricultural or mining bulk product. A *product* may be a high-value item changed or differentiated by processing, advertising, or sorting.

Commodity terms of trade. A ratio consisting of the price of one product expressed in terms of another. "Product" can be aggregate, such as ratio of export prices to import prices.

Common market. For example, the European Community (EC). Member countries attempt to reduce trade barriers and harmonize price and other selected policies over a geographical area where common interests exist. Free flow of capital and perhaps other resources and commodities among member countries.

Common Agricultural Policy or CAP. Policy of agricultural price supports, export subsidies, and variable levies used by the EC.

Comparative advantage. Commodities or products that can be exported at greatest net return per unit of fixed (nontraded) input cost compared to other commodities or products in the absence of trade distortions. Refers to the theory that it is best for a country to devote its energies not to all lines of production in which it may have superiority but to those in which its superiority is relatively greatest.

Competitive advantage. Same as comparative advantage but presuming undistorted markets only at home. Markets abroad are as they exist -- with imperfections.

Complementary goods. Goods that "go together" such as gasoline and autos. When the price of one good rises, the demand for the other falls.

Complementary imports. Commodities imported that are not competitive with locally produced commodities. For the US, examples are coffee, tea, bananas, and natural-rubber.

Cohesion. The EC principle that rich member countries should subsidize poor member countries.

Concessional sale. The buyer is allowed payment terms more favorable than those obtainable on the open market. Under Public Law 480 the concession may be the type of currency accepted as payment, the length of credit and grace period, or the interest rate charged.

Contract sanctity. The concept that when the US government imposes an embargo on agricultural exports to a country or area, the ban should not affect export contracts that were already in existence when the embargo was declared.

Cooperator Program. An agricultural export promotion program operated by the Foreign Agricultural Service (FAS) of the USDA jointly with producer/agribusiness organizations.

Countertrade. The sale of goods or services that are paid for in whole or in part by the transfer of goods or services from a foreign country.

Countervailing duty (CVD). A charge levied on an imported article to offset the unfair price advantage resulting from a subsidy paid by the exporting country on its production or export.

Current account. See *balance of payments.*

Currency exchange rate. Number of units of one currency that can be exchanged for one unit of another currency at a given time.

Customs. The authorities designated to collect duties levied by a country on imports and exports. The term also applies to the procedures or collections.

Customs union. Free trade area without internal border restrictions on trade. Common barriers to trade with non-members. An example is the EC. As opposed to *monetary union*, which uses common currency, *economic union*, which has common economic policies, or *political union*, which has federal government.

Decoupled payment. Direct transfer payments (to producers) that do not influence incentives for production, consumption, or trade.

Deficiency payment. Direct payment by government supporting farm income. Usually reflects the difference between the actual domestic market price (or loan rate; see *non-recourse loans*) for a commodity and a higher guaranteed or *target price*. This payment is paid on some prescribed program yield times program area.

Deflation. A reduction in the general price level, brought on by a decrease in the money supply or decrease in velocity of money.

Demand conditions. Factors that shift the demand curve for a product including tastes and preferences of consumers, income of consumers, prices of related goods, and consumer expectations of future prices and income.

Developing country. A low-income nation beginning to utilize available resources to bring about a sustained increase in per capita production of goods and services. Also called *less developed country* (LDC) or *third-world country*.

dirigiste. French term refering to policies of central planning or a strong role of government in controlling industry.

Disinflation. A slowing of the inflation rate.

Dumping. Selling in a foreign market at a price below the cost of production or the price received for the same product in the home market.

Duty. Special tax applied to imported goods, based on tariff rates and schedules.

EC (European Community). Established by the Treaty of Rome in 1957 and originally called the EEC (European Economic Community). It originally included six countries -- France, West Germany, Italy, Belgium, the Netherlands, and Luxembourg -- to unify and integrate their economies by establishing a customs union, common economic policies, and common agricultural policies. The UK, Ireland, and Denmark became members in 1973. Greece, Spain, and Portugal were added later. Popularly called the *Common Market* and in 1992 included 12 countries.

Elastic and inelastic demand. Responsiveness of consumers to price changes in a product. If a price increase results in a proportionally greater reduction in demand quantity, the demand is elastic; if a price increase results in a proportionally smaller reduction in demand quantity, the demand is inelastic.

Elastic and inelastic supply. If producers are responsive to price changes, supply is elastic; if producers are relatively insensitive to price changes, the supply is inelastic.

Eurodollars. Dollar deposits maintained in banks outside the US, mainly in Europe. *Eurocurrency* refers generally to deposits of a nation's currency held in another country.

Exchange controls. Direct government control of the demand and supply of foreign exchange to regulate balance of payments movements and maintain existing exchange rates.

Exchange rate. See *currency exchange rate.*

Exports. Products shipped to foreign countries.

Export Enhancement Program (EEP). A US government farm export subsidy program. Paid in the form of certificates redeemable only for USDA-owned surplus commodities.

Export license. A government document that permits the "holder" to engage in the export of designated goods to certain destinations.

Export subsidy. A government grant made to lower the price of a product for the purpose of facilitating exports.

Fast track consideration. Congressional approval or rejection of legislation, within strict time limits, through an up or down vote; no amendments.

fob. Free on board. Does not include transportation cost. (See *cif.*)

Food and Agricultural Organization (FAO). Component of United Nations. Headquarters in Rome. Its primary goal is to assist the developing world in producing more food by technical assistance, better information, and other means.

Foreign Agricultural Service (FAS). An agency of USDA. Its responsibilities include promoting export trade in agricultural products and administering USDA's export assistance programs.

Foreign exchange. Involves converting money of one country into that of another and the transfer of money values from one country to another. A country's holdings of foreign currency; foreign currency reserves.

Free port. An area such as a port city into which merchandise may legally be moved without payment of duties.

Free trade. Exchange of goods without trade barriers or restrictions such as tariffs or import quotas.

Free Trade Area (FTA). Free trade among members but each member sets own trade policies with non-members. Examples are EFTA and Canada-US Free Trade Agreement.

Free trade zone. A port designated by the government of a country for duty-free entry for any nonprohibited goods. Merchandise may be stored, displayed, used for manufacturing, etc., within the zone, subject to the country's customs authority.

GATT (General Agreement on Tariffs and Trade). Multilateral agreement originally negotiated at Geneva in 1947 among 23 countries (including the US) for the substantial reduction of tariffs and other trade barriers. Numbered approximately 100 countries in 1992. Provides a forum for inter-governmental tariff negotiations.

Generalized System of Preferences in Trade (GSP). Special low tariff rates are permitted on selected products from developing nations. GSP is part of the United States Trade Act of 1974.

Gold standard. Values of national currencies defined in terms of gold. A modified form of this system was in effect until 1971, when the US suspended the dollar's convertibility into gold.

Green rates. Calculations of European Community agricultural prices and values made in units of accounts are converted into a special set of administratively determined exchange rates referred to as green rates. Exchange rates uniquely established for farm commodities.

Gross domestic product. Total market value of goods and services produced in the domestic economy. Omits a country's factor earnings abroad.

Gross national product. Total market value of all final goods and services produced by a nation's economy before deducting depreciation charges and other allowances for consumption of durable capital goods. Includes country's factor earnings abroad.

GSM-102, 103. See *guaranteed export credit.*

Guaranteed export credit. A federal export promotion program (designated GSM-102 and GSM 103) under which the Commodity Credit Corporation guarantees loans made by commercial lenders at market interest rates to foreign buyers of agricultural commodities.

Hard currency. A national currency that is freely convertible into gold or into the currencies of other countries.

IBRD (International Bank for Reconstruction and Development, or World Bank). Makes or guarantees loans for development of infrastructure and services in developing countries with funds borrowed in private capital markets with base capitalization from developed country sponsors. Headquartered in Washington, DC.

IMF (International Monetary Fund, or the Fund). An international regulatory institution formed to: (1) promote international monetary cooperation by providing machinery for consultation and collaboration on international monetary problems, (2) facilitate growth of international trade, (3) promote exchange stability, (4) assist in the establishment of a multilateral system of payments for current transactions between members, and (5) give economic stabilization to members by making the Fund's resources available to alleviate balance of payments shortfalls under safeguards (conditionalities). Headquartered in Washington, DC.

International Wheat Agreement (IWA). IWA consists of significant exporters and importers of food grains. The IWA attempted to regulate surplus and prevent wide swings in world prices but since 1967 has confined its role mainly to consultation and to reporting of information.

Import quota. Government measure that limits total volume or total value of particular goods imported into a country during a specified period. Frequently, import quotas are implemented by "import licenses" issued by a government to individual importers to permit them to import a specified quantity or value of a restricted product. (See *VRA*.)

Imports. Products brought into a country from abroad.

Infant industry argument. The doctrine that tariff duties are needed for the protection of new industries.

Inflation. An increase in the general price level. Caused by expanding money supply faster than real output of goods and services.

Keiretsu. Powerful Japanese industrial and bank groupings characterized by interlocking directorates and finance.

Less developed countries (LDCs). Also referred to as "developing" or "third-world," or "South" countries. These generally are countries in which the gross national product is below $500 to $600 per capita.

Letter of credit. A letter issued by a bank, instructing a correspondent bank to advance a specified sum of money to a third person.

Levy. An import charge not in accordance with a definite tariff schedule.

Liberal trade. Refers broadly to trade that is relatively free of controls or restrictions, in contrast to "restricted trade." "Liberalism" in trade is the opposite of "protectionism."

Line of credit. An arrangement by which a firm agrees to provide funds up to a certain limit for a business firm.

Market Promotion Program (MPP). A program established by the Food, Agriculture, Conservation, and Trade Act of 1990 to share with the private sector the cost of developing export markets for US agricultural products. Its predecessor was the Targeted Export Assistance Program (TEA).

Market share. The ratio of a company's (nation's) sales to total industry (world) sales on either an actual basis or a potential basis for a specific time period.

Mercantilism. The theory and system of political economy prevailing in Europe after the decline of feudalism (approximately 1500 to 1750), based on national policies of accumulating gold bullion, establishing colonies and a merchant marine, and developing industry and mining to attain a favorable balance of trade. *Neomercantilism* is a modern concept defined as the tendency of a country to accumulate large amounts of hard foreign exchange.

Most-favored-nation. Refers to agreements between countries to extend the same favorable trading privileges to each other (including tariff concessions) that they extend to any one country.

Multilateral. Refers to many countries, as opposed to two countries (bilateral). GATT is an example of a multilateral agreement or agency.

Multiple exchange rates. May be used by a government to control foreign exchange by limiting the import of certain types of goods. With such a system, the country sets different rates of exchange between its own currency and foreign currencies for various classes of imports.

Nonrecourse loan. A price-support mechanism of the US Commodity Credit Corporation (CCC). Farmers put up their crops as collateral for a loan from the CCC. If the market price is below the government loan rate at maturity of the loan, farmers may choose to pay back the loan with their crops, thereby transferring crop ownership to the government.

Nontariff trade barriers (NTB). NTB's are protectionist policies practiced by nearly all countries and include regulatory policies, grades and standards, health and inspection laws, quotas, etc.

Nontraded good. A good or resource ordinarily not traded by the home country in international markets. Its price lies between the export and import prices.

North-south dialogue. Informal negotiations between industrialized countries of the world, generally located in the northern hemisphere, and developing countries, many located south of them.

Oligopolistic market. A market dominated by a relatively small number of sellers of a good or service.

OPEC (Organization of Petroleum Exporting Countries). International organization formed to control the export price of petroleum.

Organization for Economic Cooperation and Development (OECD). OECD is composed of the old Marshall Plan countries of western Europe plus the United States, Japan, and Canada. It is a forum for developed countries and is headquartered in Paris.

Overvalued currency. Exchange rate at which demand quantity exceeds supply quantity of foreign currency. When a country holds its exchange rate at too high a level, its costs are not competitive, and it chronically runs a balance of payments deficit.

Payment-In-Kind (PIK). PIK most commonly refers to acreage diversion programs in which diversion payments are made in kind. May also refer to the use of in-kind commodity payments for other purposes as in "export PIK."

Perfect competition. Assumes the presence of a large number of independent buyers and sellers in the market with no individual firm exerting significant control over price.

Phytosanitary inspection certificate. A certificate issued by the US Department of Agriculture to satisfy import regulations for foreign countries, indicating that a US shipment has been inspected and is free from harmful pests, diseases, and toxins.

Policy laden. Economic relationships (e.g., price or quantity in supply-demand relationships) are influenced by policies.

Preferential trade. Often used interchangeably with "tariff preferences." Refers to favorable tariff or other trade treatment accorded by one country or group of countries to all exports of certain other countries.

Primary commodities. Usually commodities in the raw, bulk, or unprocessed state. For example, wheat is a primary commodity, flour is a semi-processed product, and bread is a processed or manufactured product.

Protectionism. Measures taken by a country to protect industry from foreign competition. A common type of protectionism is a protective tariff designed to shield domestic producers.

Quotas. Quantitative limits applied to exports or imports.

Reciprocal trade agreements. Agreements concluded with one or more foreign countries under which tariffs or other trade barriers in country A are reduced in return for like reductions by other countries.

Retaliation. Action taken by one country against another because of the imposition of tariffs or other trade barriers.

Specific, flat rate, or fixed tariff. A duty levied on imports or exports on the basis of some physical unit; e.g., 20 cents per pound or per gallon.

Subsidiary. This EC principle retains all powers in national authorities except powers requiring collective decisions -- the latter to be vested in EC institutions.

Supplementary imports. Similar to commodities produced in the importing nation. Also referred to as *competitive* imports. Examples in the US are beef, wheat, and cotton.

Tariff. Schedule, system, or scheme of duties imposed by a government on goods imported (usually) or exported. Tariffs may be protective (designed to protect domestic production against the economic effects of imported goods) as contrasted with revenue-raising (established to bring revenue to the government). (See *specific* and *ad valorem* tariffs.)

Terms of trade. The ratio of export to import prices of a country or region. If export prices received are higher or rising relative to import prices, the terms of trade are said to be "favorable." When the reverse is true, the terms of trade are "unfavorable." Sometimes terms of trade refer to the ratio of prices of traded to nontraded goods (or services).

Third-world countries. Term applied to low-income developing or less developed countries as a whole. The other two "worlds" include the *first-world* industrialized countries of the West, and the *second-world* communist countries or centrally planned economies.

Traded good. A good or resource actually or potentially traded in international markets.

Undervalued currency. When a country holds its exchange rate low so that foreign exchange supply quantity exceeds demand quantity and hence runs a chronic balance of payments surplus. With a floating exchange rate determined by forces of supply and demand, markets clear so that supply equals demand for foreign currency.

Unilateral. Refers to one country, as in *unilateralism*, wherein each country makes it own trade rules.

United Nations Conference on Trade and Development (UNCTAD). UNCTAD, whose member countries are primarily the developing world, has attempted to promote economic development through a *new international economic order* of trade restrictions to favor those countries' own domestic industrial sectors.

Voluntary Restraint Agreement (VRA). A promise by government A to government B to limit exports from country A to country B of a certain commodity (e.g., meat or cotton textiles) to a specific annual level. The effect is that of an import quota. Similar to Voluntary Export Restraint (VER).

Wedge. In trade it refers to tariff or other instrument causing a difference (wedge) between the domestic and border prices.

World Bank. See *IBRD*.

Index

About the Book and Author

This timely volume answers a need for a comprehensive, user-friendly analysis of trade principles, institutions, and policies necessary to understand international agricultural trade. The book provides the most complete coverage available of strategic trade theory and application, imperfect competition, market power, and the political economy of agricultural trade. Designed as a core text for students with a background in micro- and macroeconomics, *Agricultural Trade* also provides government and industry professionals with a basic understanding of the issues and methods as well as the tools to carry out their own in-depth analyses.

Agricultural Trade will also serve as a convenient reference for trade and economic development practitioners. The book describes how to measure trade distortions, the gains from trade, and competitive advantage. Further, it demonstrates why the big losers from trade distortions are the nations that practice them. Its reference features include an extensive listing of trade laws, institutions, and policies; a detailed listing of elements in a sound American trade policy; and a glossary that defines trade terms.

Luther Tweeten is Anderson Professor of Agricultural Marketing, Policy, and Trade in the Department of Agricultural Economics and Rural Sociology at The Ohio State University.